Changing Is Not Vanishin

EDITED BY Robert Dale Parker

Changing Is Not Vanishing

A Collection of Early American Indian Poetry to 1930

PENN

University of Pennsylvania Press

Philadelphia

Published by
University of Pennsylvania Press
Philadelphia, Pennsylvania 19104-4112

Printed in the United States of America on acid-free paper
10 9 8 7 6 5 4 3 2 1

Library of Congress Cataloging-in-Publication Data
Changing is not vanishing : a collection of early American Indian poetry to 1930 / edited by Robert Dale Parker.
p. cm.
Includes bibliographical references and index.
ISBN 978-0-8122-4262-1 (hardcover : alk. paper)
1. American poetry—Indian authors. 2. Indians of North America—Poetry. 3. Indian poetry—Translations into English. I. Parker, Robert Dale, 1953–
PS591.I55C47 2010
811'.0080897—dc22

2009049139

Contents

The Garden of the Mind:
An Introduction to Early American Indian Poetry

In 1854, a young Cherokee at the Cherokee nation's Female Seminary wrote a poem to introduce a newspaper of student writings in Cherokee (written in the Cherokee writing system recently invented by Sequoyah) and in English, signing herself as "Corrinne." Corrinne's invitation to what she calls "the garden of the mind" can also introduce this book:

I.

We offer you a wreath of flowers
Culled in recreation hours,
Which will not wither, droop, or die,
Even when days and months pass by.

II.

Ask you where these flowers are found?
Not on sunny slope, or mound;
Not on prairies bright and fair
Growing without thought or care.

III.

No, our simple wreath is twined
From the garden of the mind;
Where bright thoughts like rivers flow
And ideas like roses grow.

IV.

The tiny buds which here you see
Ask your kindly sympathy;
View them with a lenient eye,
Pass each fault, each blemish by.

V.

Warmed by the sunshine of your eyes,
Perhaps you'll find to your surprise,
Their petals fair will soon unclose,
And every bud become—a Rose.

("Our Wreath of Rose Buds")

CHEROKEE ROSE BUDS.

VOL. I. Devoted to "The Good, the Beautiful and the True." NO. 2

FEMALE SEMINARY, CHEROKEE NATION, WEDNESDAY, AUGUST 2, 1854.

THE
CHEROKEE ROSE BUDS
Is published at stated periods
BY THE
CO-EDITRESSES,
CATHARINE GUNTER,
NANCY E. HICKS

TERMS.

The terms of subscription, as regulated by the committee, are 10 cents per copy.

ORIGINAL POETRY.

Our Wreath of Rose Buds.

I.

We offer you a wreath of flowers
Culled in recreation hours,
Which will not wither, droop, or die,
Even when days and months pass by.

II.

Ask you where these flowers are found?
Not on sunny slope, or mound;
Not on prairies bright and fair
Growing without thought or care.

III.

No, our simple wreath is twined
From the garden of the mind;
Where bright thoughts like rivers flow
And ideas like roses grow.

IV.

The tiny buds which here you see
Ask your kindly sympathy;
View them with a lenient eye,
Pass each fault, each blemish by.

V.

Warmed by the sunshine of your eyes,
Perhaps you'll find to your surprise,
Their petals fair will soon unclose,
And every bud become—a Rose.

VI.

Then take our wreath, and let it stand
An emblem of our happy band;
The *Seminary*, our *garden* fair,
And *we*, the *flowers* planted there.

VII.

Like roses bright we hope to grow,
And o'er our home such beauty throw
In future years—that all may see
Loveliest of lands,—the Cherokee.

CORRINNE.

Report of the Secretary.

It having been proposed to elect new Editresses for our paper, a meeting was convened for the purpose; it, however, proved ineffectual, and a second meeting was called, at which, after being called to order,

Miss Catharine Gunter and Nancy E. Hicks were chosen as Editresses of the Paper.

The meeting then adjourned.

Figure 1. Corrinne's "Our Wreath of Rose Buds" as it appeared in the Cherokee Female Seminary *Cherokee Rose Buds*, 2 August 1854.

Popular culture has no place for an American Indian in 1854 writing at all, let alone writing words like these. This book sets out to help change that way of thinking about American Indians. It sets out to make visible the mostly unknown landscape of early American Indian poetry, offering a wide selection of poems written by American Indians up to 1930 and, in the process, providing a dramatically changed picture of early American poetry at large. Indian writers did not have access to the networks of publication, publicity, and readers that might lead to a wide audience for their writing, and they rarely sought a wide audience. As a result, most of these poems remained unknown to readers of American poetry in general and even to readers of American Indian literature. A legacy was almost lost, and this book sets out to recover that legacy.

In the garden of the mind that these poems offer, readers will find an exciting variety of styles, forms, ideas, regions, cultures, and purposes. These poems invite us to enlarge our historical sense of American Indian literacy, aesthetics, and imagination. They were written in a time when the United States government and many non-Indian Americans focused on driving Indian people away from their lands and traditions, expecting that Indian people would mostly die off or assimilate. It didn't work out that way, but the myth of the vanishing Indian and the last of the Mohicans achieved such dominance that many Americans still suppose that most Indians long ago rode their horses over the horizon and into the sunset, and that Indians who haven't vanished yet will surely vanish soon. On the contrary, millions of Indian people live in the United States, more than lived in the same area at the time of Columbus, and most of the people in the American hemisphere are Indians or descended from Indians. The history of Indian literacy and art is not, therefore, an obscure curiosity. It is, instead, central to the cultural and literary history of the United States and the American hemisphere.

The last few decades have seen rapid growth in the reading and study of American Indian literature, but the bulk of Indian literature that teachers bring to the classroom and that scholars and critics write about comes from the outpouring of writing that began with N. Scott Momaday's Pulitzer Prize-winning *House Made of Dawn* in 1968. This pattern of concentrating on more or less recent writing fits the general impression, often unwitting, that American Indians are marginally literate and that such literacy as Indian peoples have is recent. Realizing that Native American literacy, broadly defined, goes back far before Columbus, and that, defined narrowly as alphabetic literacy, it has a far longer and wider history than people usually realize or take into account, I decided to research early American Indian poetry, a previously almost unrecognized and unwritten about field of literature. My hunch was that I would find a good deal of early Indian poetry, undermining the stereotype of unlettered Indians and expanding the history of American Indian writing.

And that is what I found. This introduction frames early Indian poetry for a variety of different audiences, including people interested in American Indian literature or history, in nineteenth- or early twentieth-century American literature, and in American poetry and its history. I have tried to keep in mind the varying knowledges of different groups of readers. Some readers will already know the outlines of Indian history, and some will need more historical explanation. Some readers will be accustomed to reading poetry, and some will not be, and some will be accustomed to reading premodernist poetry, while others will have their expectations shaped by the poetry of recent times. The issues and stereotypes that weigh heavily on Indian poets may need explaining for some readers, while others will come already primed with curiosity about how the poets respond to those issues and stereotypes. I hope that this introduction can serve as an invitation to all these varying readers and perhaps help put the differing and overlapping questions of different readers in conversation with each other.

Contexts

American literary history ordinarily assumes that only Euro-Americans wrote early American poetry, but in the lands now known as the United States, American Indians have written poetry in English or Latin for about as long as Euro-Americans. In the seventeenth century, soon after English colonists, relying on the hospitality of Indians, established the first lasting British colonies in the future United States, Harvard College was founded with a special interest in educating Indian students. In those early years, the Harvard curriculum concentrated on writing poetry—in Latin and ancient Greek. It was no easy matter for English students to prepare for the college. It was still harder for Indian students raised first in Indian languages and with a Native rather than an English set of cultural expectations. Indian students had to learn not only Latin and Greek but English as well. Nevertheless, a fair number of Indian students prepared for Harvard, and a smaller number entered the school (though no one recorded exactly how many). Only one graduated, Caleb Cheeshahteaumuck, in 1665. Cheeshahteaumuck's friend and classmate Joel Hiacoomes, son of a prominent Christian Indian on Martha's Vineyard, was killed by other Indians just before graduating. The other Indian students either left school or died amid the often unfamiliar and unwelcoming surroundings (W. T. Meserve, Szasz 121–27). Indian students surely wrote a great many poems in Latin and Greek as school exercises, and perhaps sometimes for their own pleasure. Perhaps some of them also tried their hand at writing poetry in English or in Massachusett or other Algonquin languages. According to John Leverett, a president of Harvard College, an Indian student named Benjamin Larnell, who died as a junior in 1714, was "An Acute Grammarian, an Extraordinary Latin Poet, and a good Greek one" (Sibley 203). Cotton Mather reports that Larnell wrote poetry "in the three learned languages," meaning Latin, Greek, and Hebrew (Mather, *Selected Letters* 151). Larnell's writing has not survived, but Mather saved one poem from a Harvard Indian student whose name we know only as Eleazar. It appears in this volume in Eleazar's Latin and Greek and in an English translation. No other record of Eleazar has survived. He wrote his poem in 1678, the same year as the second edition of Anne Bradstreet's poems and just sixteen years after the first published volume of poetry in what would later become the United States, Michael Wigglesworth's hugely popular *The Day of Doom*. Historians of American literature usually think of American poetry as beginning with Bradstreet and Wigglesworth, but it also began with school poets, and among those school poets were American Indians. Thus American Indians were already writing poetry when American poetry was born, more than a century before the American Revolution.

Most of the earliest Indian poetry is probably lost. I hope that this volume will provoke readers to find some of that lost poetry. Some of it might have survived, perhaps in manuscript and eventually, from the eighteenth century on, in newspapers. I have found poems by nearly 150 different Indian writers from before 1930, about a third of them from before 1900. While I cannot include poems by all of them in this volume, I have included poems by eighty-two different Indian writers, and readers will find a full bibliography of known poems by American Indians through 1930 at the back of the book.

Though I chose to focus on poetry from before 1930, I might almost as well have extended the volume to 1960 or 1975, that is, to the great flowering of American Indian literature sometimes known as the American Indian Renaissance. I decided on the earlier date because, if the volume extended another three or four decades, there would be little room left for the earlier writing and its neglected record of literacy and literary imagination. I hope that someone else will gather the poetry of the next several decades. The later poems in this book often move away from rhyme or meter or both. Around 1930, a good deal of change in the poetry world seemed to reach its threshold. Modernism came to the fore, but so did the poetry of the proletarian left that the celebration of Modernism led later readers to forget. And so did the poetry of the Harlem Renaissance and African American poetry more generally, with its many ways of leading, joining, or resisting what might otherwise seem like competing Modernist and proletarian styles. Meanwhile, federal Indian policy changed dramatically in the early 1930s, with mixed consequences for Indian people, consequences that often varied from one community to another. How much these changes affected Indian poetry probably varied a great deal as well from one poet to another. I hope that scholars will go on to uncover that story.

In choosing which poems to include, I have tried to balance breadth with depth, covering a wide range and large number of different poets, and representing some poets generously. All but one of the few poets who already have attracted notice (at least among scholars of Indian literature or history) are amply represented, including (in chronological order) Jane Johnston Schoolcraft, John Rollin Ridge, Alex Posey, D'Arcy McNickle, and Lynn Riggs, but even these better known writers are known mainly for their prose, not their poetry. The research for this book uncovered so much writing by Jane Johnston Schoolcraft (whose earliest dated poem, which is not among those chosen for this volume, comes from 1815), that I edited a separate volume of her writing: *The Sound the Stars Make Rushing Through the Sky: The Writings of Jane Johnston Schoolcraft*. That volume includes prose and translations as well as poetry, most of it published for the first time. Schoolcraft usually wrote in English, but she is the only writer I have found before 1930 who wrote poetry in a Native language, in her case Anishinaabemowin (the Anishinaabe language, also called Ojibwe or Chippewa). Ridge is known mainly for his sensationalist novel, *The Life and Adventures of Joaquín Murieta, the Celebrated California Bandit* (1854). Only a few specialists have paid attention—and even then, not much attention—to his posthumous 1868 collection of poems, but some of the best of his poems included here are new even to specialists, not having returned to print since their appearance in an obscure Arkansas newspaper in the late 1840s. Riggs is known for drama, not poetry. Posey is known for his brilliant prose, but readers of his prose will turn to the poetry with accelerated interest. As it happens, for much of his short adult life Posey identified more as a poet than as a prose writer, and his poems, which finally appeared in a reliable collected edition as this book was reaching completion, represent a major accomplishment that deserves far more attention than it has received. Some specialists have also seen the poetry of Zitkala-Sa/Gertrude Simmons Bonnin, who is well known for her prose, but poetry, it turns out, was not one of Bonnin's many talents. For that reason her poems do not appear in this volume, though they are in the bibliography and are easily available in an excellent modern edition of her writings. McNickle is widely acknowledged in Indian literary studies as a major writer, but his poetry has not been noticed before either in criticism or bibliographies, and it is reprinted in this volume for the first time. I have also included a good number of poems by writers who today are barely or not known at all: Olivia Ward Bush-Banks, Alfred C. Gillis, James Roane Gregory, Mary Cornelia Hartshorne, Hen-toh/Bertrand N. O. Walker, Ruth Margaret Muskrat, Molly Spotted Elk (Molly Alice Nelson—known as a dancer but barely known as a writer and not at all as a poet), Too-qua-stee/DeWitt Clinton Duncan, and Julia Carter Welch, as well as a good number of poems by Carlos Montezuma, who is known mainly for his political work and interesting life but not for his poetry (which is here reprinted or sometimes even published for the first time).

In deciding which poems to include, I have favored earlier poems, because readers often care about the early history and care about the way that early poems shatter the stereotype of illiterate Indians. I have also tried to select poems by their topic and by their aesthetic interest. There is a tradition of reading those two categories as if they were contradictory, that is, of supposing that interesting topics do not necessarily make for interesting art and that interesting art does not go together with interesting topics, especially if the poems explicitly address politics. But I join with those who do not see art and topicality as at odds with each other. I join with those who see an art to imagining a topic and who see topicality in all art. Thus, for example, a poem that carries political interest and a poem with exciting language do not necessarily belong to two opposed worlds. Readers can find provocative dialogues between the poetic art and the subject matter in many of the poems in this anthology. Politics has its aesthetics, and art has its politics.

The audiences for these poems differ from the audiences for early Native American fiction as described by Bernd C. Peyer in his pathbreaking anthology of early Indian short stories. Peyer has argued that early Native American fiction was mostly written for a white audience and often for an audience of children. It also tended, he says, to take an ethnographic approach. That is, it focused on explaining Indian culture to non-Indians (Peyer xii). The focus on children shared in and contributed to the colonialist sense of Indian people as childlike and Indian life as a realm of play for white people. By contrast, Indian people wrote poetry much more for an Indian or a mixed Indian and non-Indian audience. Early Indian poetry rarely worries about ethnography. It rarely sets out to explain or analyze Indian people and culture as if they were alien and exotic, though—as the title of this volume indicates—many of the poems try to record Indian ways and histories that the poets fear are disappearing or changing. Nor do these poems infantilize Native people by imagining an audience of children. Before 1930, the audience for poetry differed greatly from the audience for poetry later in the twentieth century or today. It was more of a general audience and less of an elite audience. Most newspapers published poetry, in contrast to newspapers of later years. Poets tended to identify with large numbers of readers, whereas in later years poets have tended to see themselves as part of an elite separated from and perhaps more sophisticated than typical readers.

Most of the poems in this collection come from newspapers and magazines, not from books of poetry. Just as newspapers and early Indian magazines often published poems by Indians, so they also published stories by Indians. Indeed, the research for this book made visible a vast quantity of forgotten early American Indian fiction. While the stories might not be so wide-ranging or political, and surely not so overtly political, as the poetry, they do not dwell as much in the ethnographic and infantilizing direction as the stories in Peyer's anthology. I mention the vast archive of still unstudied early American Indian short fiction as a way of contextualizing the recovery of early Indian poetry and planting a seed that might lead other readers and scholars to exciting research.

Poets' sense of the audience for newspapers and magazines influenced their poetry's style and form. Most of the poetry in this book is accessible to typical readers in a way that later poetry might not be. Usually, it does not aim at erudite subtlety. Instead, it seeks an art in metrical directness. Such poetry has grown out of fashion with modern poetry readers, but in the years represented in this book it commanded large audiences, far larger than poetry attracts today (when not larger in raw numbers, then still larger in proportion to the overall audience of readers). In some ways, therefore, readers of this book interested in seeing early Indian poetry but who may not typically read poetry from our own age will find this poetry easier to read than much modern and contemporary poetry. Other readers more accustomed to the poetic styles of our own times may want to ask questions about how we read that differ from the questions they bring to poetry of later times. It can help to think respectfully about poetry that identifies with its audience more than it tries to distinguish itself from its audience. Some readers may even find that the tendency to identify with the aesthetic expectations of a poem's audience, as opposed to the modern desire to surprise or shock, might better fit their understanding of Native aesthetic traditions, which often ground themselves in an address to Native people's own communities.

While early Indian poetry has received little attention, a great deal of writing from before 1930 has been published and discussed as Indian poetry, even though—strangely—it is not poetry or was not written by Indians. The oral portions of many Indian rituals and songs were transcribed and translated (not always well transcribed or translated) for anthropological purposes. Later, a bevy of white poets retranslated these texts without knowing the original languages, arranging them in "lines" and often rewriting them extensively. Poets and editors then published the anthropological texts, or the revised, retranslated versions of them, as "Indian" "poetry," even though Indians did not write them and the Indians who in some sense produced the texts, at least at the time of the texts' oral inception, did not think of them as poetry. Such works, along with the verse of white poets trying to imagine how Indians think and trying to take on an Indian voice, provide the material for early anthologies of Indian poetry. Meanwhile, the anthropological poems, labeled as Indian poetry, often continue to appear in contemporary anthologies, although in recent decades a lively debate over their cultural status and role has discouraged the continued production and (less so) the continued reproduction of these curious texts. As I argue in *The Invention of Native American Literature* (2003), the routine representation of this sometimes highly interesting body of work as Indian poetry, when it was not written by Indians or, in the case of the anthropological poems, was not originally conceived of as poetry, had the effect, for many years, of pushing out actual poetry by actual Indians (82–84). Without thinking about it, scholars and other readers supposed that since Native American poetry did not reach publication in national forums, it did not exist before the explosion, since around 1975, of actual poetry published for a national audience by contemporary Indians. Meanwhile, precontemporary Indian literacy and self-conscious, written aesthetic practice, together with the long history of Indian poetry, including written poetry in dialogue with Euro-American poetic traditions, have remained almost invisible, even to specialists in Indian literary studies. This book sets out to change that.

Readers have typically identified poetry, more than any other genre of writing, with high literacy and refined art. And the capacity for high literacy and refined art serves as a marker for elite culture. Actually, I believe that even dedicated readers of poetry should question the privileged, elite status of poetry over other forms of writing. Nevertheless, the absence of American Indian poetry from literary and historical memory, along with the popularity of phony Indian poetry, props up the myth of Indian people as illiterate or marginally literate. In this context, I have set out to join a number of other recent scholars in bringing more attention to precontemporary Indian writing, and here I expand that effort beyond the recovery of fiction and of nonfiction prose to poetry, where it has barely gone before.

Some of the poems in this book would hold their own in any anthology. But given the nearly complete invisibility of early American Indian poetry and the minimal visibility of early Indian literacy, those poems, and many of the others, take on special resonance. Often, they already attracted interest in their own time, as indicated by reprints in newspapers and magazines, as the bibliography at the back of the book shows. As most of the reprinting publications had Indian editors or served heavily Indian communities, the reprints suggest that Indian readers often took pride and pleasure in many of the poems in this book.

At the same time, and despite the wide range of poets and poems in this book, in many ways these poems cannot offer a representative sampling. By definition, poets are not representative. And in several ways the cultural and geographical distribution of these poems, though wide, tilts according to gender, schooling, and region. It tilts especially to Indian Territory (present-day eastern Oklahoma), Oklahoma, and Cherokees. A majority of the poets, and a majority of those who wrote many poems, were men. Yet over a third of the early Indian poets in this book were women, a larger number and proportion than we might expect from previous accounts of early Indian writing (apart from those that include only women's writing, notably the anthology of *Native American Women's Writing* edited by Karen Kilcup).

Many poems come from school newspapers and magazines. The Cherokee boarding schools were centers of Cherokee pride, especially for the Cherokee elite. The poems from Cherokee schools, and the one poem from the Cornwall Foreign Mission School in Connecticut, come from students genuinely proud of their schools and their position as students. The later boarding school poems are trickier to read. They appeared in newspapers and magazines that the schools—most famously the Carlisle Indian School—published for publicity and for vocational training in printing. Not all school newspapers and magazines survived, so probably a good number of school poems have been lost. While I approach the later school poems with an interest in the position of students taken from their families, peoples, and regions, often against their will, and pressured or forced, often violently, to submit to a condescending and assimilationist colonialism, I must admit that, at least to my taste, the school poems typically carry less interest than the other poems. The school poems chosen for this volume stand above the rest. As a group, the larger set of school poems lean toward bland clichés about how wonderful school is, along with the usual trite pieties about classmates and graduation. And yet the poignant position of the students, and a recognition that they wrote and published under the watchful eyes of sometimes dedicated but still colonialist overlords, cannot help lending even the school-bound platitudes an extra interest. And so, while I have selected only the best school poems, a small proportion of those available, I have also grouped them together in a separate section, placed in the overall sequence at roughly the time the federal boarding schools most flourished. Reading the boarding school poems as a group can help them shed light on each other and on the common experience that they represent. Though many schools had literary clubs, none of the federal boarding school poets seems to have kept on writing poetry for very long after graduation, at least not poetry that I have found. It appears that their literary ambitions were soon snuffed out, probably by the labor of earning a living and raising children, and sometimes perhaps by isolation from the many other Indians, including former schoolmates, who shared their literary interests, as well as by little sense that the surrounding Euro-American world offered hope for wider publication or a respectful and welcoming audience.

Over half the poets in the collection come from Indian Territory and Oklahoma, and two-thirds of those are Cherokees, though many of the poets from elsewhere are represented by a good number of poems. The preponderance of Cherokee and Oklahoma poets is not surprising. It is not unusual for a cultural practice to chance to catch on more for one people or region than for another people or region. But more than chance comes in here, for the Indian nations forcibly "removed" from the southeastern United States to Indian Territory, which became part of the new state of Oklahoma in 1907, and especially the Cherokees, are famous for their commitment to schools and newspapers. A good school education—and the Cherokee schools, especially, surpassed the federal boarding schools on that count—can lead to more readers and writers of poetry. Good schools and active newspapers reinforced each other, and during these years, unlike today, newspapers were the principal venue for publishing poetry.[1]

Some readers may wonder why, apart from a few poems by Schoolcraft (two of them included in this volume), no poems survived in Indian languages. While I would suggest that these poets and the peoples they come from made English an Indian language, that observation still dodges the question. Perhaps poems written in Indian languages (other than English) were less likely to survive. Regardless, they were less likely to be written. Few poets in the American Indian Renaissance of recent years spoke their Indian languages or spoke them well, let alone wrote in them. Simon Ortiz (Acoma), Luci Tapahonso (Navajo), and Ray Young Bear (Meskwaki) stand out as exceptions. Since the Renaissance, more Indian poets have emerged who speak their own languages, and many as adults have worked to learn their languages. But in the earlier years represented in this volume, many of the poets spoke their languages, often fluently, and some of them use words or phrases from those languages in predominantly English-language poems. That they nevertheless concentrated their writing of poetry in English tells us that the Indians who wrote poetry and who had the most access to the concept of writing poetry and to the conditions that foster writing poetry came from those who were fluent in English. Those who had the kind of education that provided such access were less likely to be fluent in Indian languages (even though many of them were). They also associated poetry with English rather than with Indian languages. And they wrote for readers of English, even when they mostly wrote for Indian readers. Moreover, apart from those who published in *The Cherokee Advocate*, they relied on English-speaking and usually on non-Indian publishers.

Though mainly in English, the poems speak to a wide range of topics. They include idiosyncratic works that do not fit into a pattern shared by other Indian poems, such as Tso-le-oh-woh's breathtaking half-Romantic and half-Miltonic poem about a comet, a poem about a Cherokee election for Principal Chief (by the pseudonymous "Hors de Combat"), Mary Cornelia Hartshorne's poem about hills on the Irish coast, Lynn Riggs's poem about a creaky weathervane, Francis L. Verigan's poem about a cat named Funny Face who dies after getting caught between the ceiling and the attic, a poem about Texas chorus "girls" by Molly Spotted Elk, herself a chorus girl ("We are the famous Aztec girls . . . "), and many others.

Still, despite the variety, patterns stand out, both in what the poems talk about and in what they do not talk about. They rarely talk about the nonpublic features of Indian life, about ritual or religion, apart from Christianity. They sometimes describe customs, almost anthropologically, but such poems, as noted earlier, are not typical. The school poems do not criticize the schools—at least not openly. Surprisingly, the school poets sometimes criticize their fellow students, and not always as playfully as we might expect. As we will review below, the issues and ways of thinking that characterize these poems include colonialism and the federal government, land, the condition of the world in general, nature, Christianity, and other Indian peoples. Often, as well, sadly but understandably, the poets imagine Indian people through internalized racism, and sometimes (though not often) they imagine other people of color through what we might call externalized racism.

Poems About Colonialism and the Federal Government

Outside the school poems, many of the poems are fervently critical, even scornful, of white colonialism and the federal government. Such scorn drives many of the most powerful poems in this book. Mabel Washbourne Anderson tells the tale of a white teacher at the Cherokee Male Seminary who trifles with the gullible emotions of Nowita, the sweet singer, a student at the Female Seminary ("Nowita, the Sweet Singer," 1900). Anderson draws an analogy between the teacher's abuse of Nowita and the federal government's theft of Cherokee lands, leaving the heartbroken Nowita, who expected to marry her sweetheart, "wedded" only to her memories. Wenotah (Irene Campbell Beaulieu [Sioux]) catalogs a long list of outrages, the buffalo "driven . . . away forever, / By white man's avarice," "wigwams burned," land stolen, "graves . . . looted, then forsaken," and treaties "diverted / With motives low, unjust, and base / To benefit only the alien race" (1916). James Harris Guy—a talented Chickasaw poet and a tribal police sergeant whose considerable poetic ambitions came to an early end when he was murdered while trying to arrest brutal criminals—blames "the fearful fall" of once "honest and fearless" Indians on the dishonor and lies of "the whiteman" ("Lament of Tishomingo," 1879). Just as skeptically but with more humor, Tso-le-oh-woh (Cherokee) and Leta V. Meyers Smart (Omaha) make fun of federal officials. Tso-le-oh-woh marvels at "How blest we are, we little *reds*," that such loving, "kind-hearted Christian whites" "Will sell their very purses . . . to get to be our nurses," and all with no thought for "The magic of a dollar. *No indeed!*" (1853). Seventy years later, Smart writes poems that make fun of the federal commissioners of Indian Affairs, even turning them into spooky spirits like something out of a poem by Stephen Crane.

Lawyer poets Richard C. Adams and Too-qua-stee (DeWitt Clinton Duncan) give their outrage a legal turn. Adams explains the closed, circular logic of colonialism:

> If the Indian seeks the Government, there his grievance to relate,
> He must first obtain permission from those who rule the State!
> If his rights are there denied him and an attorney he would seek,
> He is sternly then reminded he has no right to speak!
> "For under section so and so, which guides your legal move,
> "You see no attorneys can appear for you, except if we approve;
> "And if, in our opinion, your claim does not adhere
> "To the interests of the public, then your cause we cannot hear."
>
> ("To the Delaware Indians," 1899)

Adams conveys how the Delawares, like many other Indian nations, were driven into a Kafkaesque house of bureaucratic mirrors, so that whatever they did to deserve their rights or get their rights recognized, the ground beneath them still shifted and the bureaucracy tipped against them. In "Cherokee Memories" (1900), Too-qua-stee recalls an idyllic interlude between the brutality of removal to Indian Territory and the later encroachment onto Indian Territory of white people and culture with their laws and statutes. In those better days, instead of Italian silks and French weaves, the women wore homespun and "The men wore buckskin pants and elkhide shoes." Too-qua-stee/Duncan envisions an outraged Lord upbraiding white men for their misguided sense of legal entitlement:

> Go tell those white men, I, the Lord of Hosts,
> Have marked their high presumption, heard their boasts.
> Observe their laws; their government is might
> Enthroned to rule, instead of perfect right.
> Could I have taught them such gross heresy,
> As "Greatest good to greatest number" be?
> Has shipwrecked crew, with gnawing famine pressed,

A right to slaughter one to feed the rest?
Should just minorities be made to yield
That wrong majorities may be upheld?
In nature, is this not the rule that brutes
Observe in settling up their fierce disputes?

In less legal domains, Duncan's Lord is no less stunned by white presumption and vanity:

Go tell those white men not to be so proud;
'Twas I that hid the lightning in the cloud.
That twice ten thousand years, or thereabout,
Should pass ere they could find the secret out,
Shows dullness quite enough to chill their pride
And make their swelling vanity subside.
Steam, too, I made; its power was nothing hid;
From age to age it shook the kettle's lid
Full in their view; but never could they see it,
Till chance vouchsafed from mystery to free it.
The art of printing, too, is all my own,
Lo! every foot of living thing had shown,
(I ordered so) as long as time had run,
How easily the printing job was done;
Yet time's last grain of sand had well nigh sped,
Ere their dull wit these signs correctly read;
Ere Gutenberg, by chance, could take the hint,
And fumbling set a thought in clumsy print.

("The White Man's Burden," 1899)

As it happens, Gutenberg's originality came from inventing moveable type, not print, but the larger point remains that Too-qua-stee is not impressed.

Whites have company in their colonialist abuse of Indians, for they sometimes encourage or recruit corrupt Indians. In "The Indian Game" (1922), Wa Wa Chaw (Payomkowishum, Luiseño) spoofs corrupt Indian leaders who join corrupt whites to play the "Indian Game" and take the whites' payoffs. Government officials pretend or abuse Indian friendship, and "Heap-chiefs share the Pale-face leaf," she complains, in her satirical take-off on Indian speech—or on clichéd, non-Indian ideas of Indian speech.

Carlos Montezuma, who was probably the first Indian graduate of my own university, the University of Illinois, takes on the United States government with special fury. In "Indian Office" (1916), he offers a long list of travesties from the Office of Indian Affairs (now called the Bureau of Indian Affairs), including "Keeping the Indians as wards," "caging the Indians on reservations," "opening Indians' land for settlers," "Reimbursement Funds (Government Mortgage)," "dams built on reservations," "Giving five or ten acres of irrigation land to the Indian and taking the rest of his land away for land-grabbers," "selling the Indians' surplus (?) land" (Montezuma's question mark challenges the very concept of surplus land), disposing "of the Indians' mineral lands," "selling the timber land of the Indians," sending children away to schools, and generally discriminating and "doing everything for the Indians without their consent." As Montezuma puts it—patriarchally—in another poem, "Steady, Indians, Steady!" (1917):

They have taken your country,
They have taken your manhood,
They have imprisoned you,
They have made you wards,
They have stunted your faculties.

Taking the country comes first on Montezuma's list. If there is one issue in Indian-white conflict that comes up most often and most passionately, it is "removal," the conventional euphemism for the forced expulsion of Indian nations from their lands. Many poems lament removal, not only the famous Cherokee Trail of Tears but other expulsions as well, including repeated removals in the 1830s, 1840s, and beyond as the relentless white hunger for other people's land pushed Indian nations from one promised refuge to another. On the eve of removal, in 1838, an unnamed Cherokee—probably the much-admired Jesse Bushyhead—bids his homeland goodbye:

Adieu ye scenes of early sports,
  A last, long sad adieu;
Ye hills and dales and groves and brooks,
  This is our last review. . . .

Adieu the land that gave me birth,
  Thou God that rules the sky,
Protect that little spot of earth
  In which our fathers lie.

Tread lightly on the sleeping dead,
  Proud millions that intrude,
Lest, on your ashes be the tread
  Of millions still more rude.

("The Indian's Farewell")

In similar words, William Walker, forced with his people to leave Ohio a few years later in 1843, wrote the following lines in Wyandot (rendered here in his English translation—the original Wyandot has not survived) as he prepared to leave his home:

Farewell, ye tall oaks, in whose pleasant green shade
I've sported in childhood, in innocence played,

My dog and my hatchet, my arrow and bow,
Are still in remembrance, alas! I must go. . . .

Sandusky, Tyamochtee, and Broken Sword streams,
No more shall I see you except in my dreams.
Farewell to the marshes where cranberries grow,
O'er the great Mississippi, alas! I must go. . . .

Let me go to the wildwood, my own native home.
Where the wild deer and elk and buffalo roam,
Where the tall cedars are and the bright waters flow,
Far away from the pale-face, oh, there let me go.

("The Wyandot's Farewell")

Bushyhead and Walker associate their homeland with the personal past of their own childhood play and with its flora and fauna, its earth and its waters. While Walker wants to shun the white interlopers altogether, Bushyhead, forced to leave behind his ancestors' graves, pauses first to lay down something like a golden rule for invaders: they had better "tread lightly on the sleeping dead," literally as well as figuratively, he warns, or their own descendants and other interlopers will follow their model and do unto them as they have done to the Cherokees. Similarly, in a later poem, Arsenius Chaleco (Yuma) warns whites to rein in their vanity, for they too may yet perish and find themselves, like Indians, the forgotten ruins of an ominous future ("The Indian Requiem," 1924).

In yet another similar poem, Israel Folsom, a Choctaw, writing just before the removal of 1831–1835, or later recalling how he felt as he was about to begin the long, forced journey, asks—with sardonic incredulity at the hypocrisy of whites who promised that Indians could keep their land as long as the grass shall grow and the waters run—

Have the waters ceased to flow?
Have the forests ceased to grow?
Why do our brothers bid us go
  From our native home?

Here in infancy we played,
Here our happy wigwam made,
Here our fathers' graves are laid,—
  Must we leave them all?

("Lo! The Poor Indian's Hope")

As Bushyhead appeals to a larger justice in the universe that will eventually catch up with the invaders, so Folsom concludes:

Whiteman, tell us, God on high—
So pure and bright in yonder sky,—

> Will not then His searching eye
>   See the Indians' wrong?

Adams, a Delaware, strikes many of the same notes. The Delawares were repeatedly removed, and Adams calls attention to the series of broken promises as one removal and broken promise piled on top of another:

> With sorrow, grief and suffering, we were forced at last to go,
> From the graves of our forefathers to a land we did not know.
> But this was now guaranteed to us, "as long as water shall run,"
> Yet on they pushed us, on and on toward the setting sun!
>
> "And this will be the last move," they tell us, if we go;
> "You will hold the country this time as long as grass shall grow.
>
> ("To the Delaware Indians," 1899)

As James Harris Guy sums up the dilemma,

> The white man wants the Indian's home,
>   He envies them their land;
> And with his sweetest words he comes
>   To get it, if he can.
>
> And if we will not give our lands,
>   And plainly tell him so,
> He then goes back, calls up his clans,
>   And says, "let's make them go."
>
> ("The White Man Wants the Indian's Home," 1878)

Guy's curious choice of the word "clans," a category of identity central to the self-definition of many Indian peoples, ironically casts whites as not so different from Indians as the whites like to believe, although still far more presumptuous and greedy.

Such poems set out to lock in a cultural memory, to make it impossible to lose the recollection of the land and the lives that were lost and changed during removal. In 1848, nine years after the Cherokee Trail of Tears, Te-con-ees-kee cannot even let go of the name of his homeland, Georgia: "Though far from thee Georgia in exile I roam, / My heart in thy mountain land still has its home."

> Georgia, o Georgia there is a stain on thy name!
> And ages to come will yet blush for thy shame,
> While the child of the Cherokee exile unborn,
> The results of thy violence deeply will mourn. . . .
> For this comes the name of the land of my birth,
> On my ear as the sound of a curse on the earth.

Over seventy years later, Ruth Margaret Muskrat, the "child of the Cherokee exile" foreseen by Te-con-ees-kee, lives up to his anguished prophecy as she recalls "The Trail of Tears" (1922):

> In the night they shriek and moan,
> In the dark the tall pines moan
> As they guard the dismal trail.
> The Cherokees say it is the groan,
> Every shriek an echoed groan
> Of their forefathers that fell
> With broken hopes and bitter fears
> On that weary trail of tears.

Through repetition where we might expect rhyme, and repetition combined with rhyme—moan and moan, groan and groan—Muskrat burns in the memory of a suffering that the surrounding non-Indian world would rather see as inevitable, inconsequential. But for Muskrat and the Cherokee communal remembrance she insists on, even the pine trees uphold memory.

Poems About Land

The despair and anger over removal draws on and contributes to a larger pattern of Indian people's cultural and emotional commitment to their land. In that context, even poems that might sound like routinely Romantic evocations of the landscape take on specially Indian meaning. To Alfred C. Gillis, for example, the rivers are not mere rivers. In "Where Sleep the Wintoon Dead" (1924), the Sacramento and McCloud Rivers in northern California, "Far from the white man's tread," mark the graves where his ancestors "sleep the sleep of the dead." In a poem read to Cherokee students after removal in 1855, C. H. Campbell seems anxious over the pressure to realign Cherokee ideas about land and make them fit dominating white ideas about land:

> The *pale face* now are strong, and *we* are *free*;
> As *they* have progress made, so *we* must do—
> Must learn to cultivate the mind, the soil,
> And reconcile ourselves to honored toil.

With an intense feeling of *we* the Cherokees versus *they* the whites, Campbell toes the line of typically white pleas for Indian progress. Such pleas defined progress through anti-Indian myths, calling for Indians to become farmers, as if Cherokees had not farmed for centuries, and calling for Indians to work hard, as if they had not worked hard before. But Campbell walks both sides of the cultural fence, for his remark that whites "have progress made" looks down on whites with a condescension not anticipated in the usual white ways of thinking.

In 1887, Congress passed the General Allotment Act, better known as the Dawes Act after its chief sponsor, Senator Henry L. Dawes. The Dawes Act called for redistributing communally owned reservation lands by "allotting" parcels of land to individual Indians, who would be made citizens once they received their allotments. The Act ended communal land ownership and "opened" "surplus" land—meaning unallotted Indian land—to settlers and speculators, that is, to white people. Even allotted lands could eventually be sold, and white people were usually best positioned to do the buying. Troubled by such abuses, Alex Posey (Muskogee/Creek) resented the corrupt officials who administered the Dawes Act. "Ye men of Dawes," he wrote, "avaunt! / Return from whence ye came!" To Posey, federal officials might "strut majestically" but their talk was still "As sleek as ratpaths." Posey was an unusual figure, alert to opposite perspectives on allotment. Much as he resented the "men of Dawes," he ended up working with them. Like many Indians who identified with what they were pressured to see as progress, Posey supported allotment, even while he poured scorn on the corruption that came with it (Littlefield, *Alex Posey*). The Dawes Act's advocates and defenders envisioned it as making Indians into citizens and bringing Indian people into the mainstream economy, but its actual effect was to devastate reservation communities and traditions, casting most reservation land into white hands. This history of struggle over land, even beyond the trauma of removal, drives a great many poems.

Given the centrality of land to the self-conception of most Indian peoples, including the history of removal and the more conniving, indirect removal of the Dawes Act, it is hard to know how to read "A New Citizen," written in 1887 by Elsie Fuller, a sixteen- or seventeen-year-old Omaha, after the passage of the Dawes Act:

> Now I am a citizen!
> They've given us new laws,
> Just as were made
> By Senator Dawes.
>
> We need not live on rations [promised by treaties],
> Why? there is no cause,
> For "Indians are citizens,"
> Said Senator Dawes.
>
> Just give us a chance,
> We never will pause.
> Till we are good citizens
> Like Senator Dawes.
>
> Now we are citizens,
> We all give him applause—
> So three cheers, my friends,
> For Senator Dawes!

Perhaps Fuller is taking what was called a "progressive" stance or, in more accurate terms, an assimilationist stance (matching the views in the school newspaper that published her poem). Perhaps, that is, she is genuinely thanking Senator Dawes for disavowing treaty obligations—such as the commitment to provide rations, as well as the commitment to respect Indian nations' ownership of Indian lands. Or perhaps, dripping with sarcasm and cleverly defying the views of her school newspaper, she scorns Senator Dawes and everything that he represents for Indian people. Though no one would call Fuller's effusion great poetry, by the usual meaning of such terms, whether we see it as naïve or as sly it showcases a culturally, historically resonant impasse between opposite meanings. In that way it evokes the intense debates about allotment across many Indian communities as, in the ensuing decades, the federal government imposed devastating allotment policies on one Indian nation after another. As Posey put the question in 1894, with his characteristic humor playing off Hamlet's famous soliloquy,

To allot, or not to allot, that is the
Question; whether 'tis nobler in the mind to
Suffer the country to lie in common as it is,
Or to divide it up and give each man
His share pro rata, and by dividing
End this sea of troubles? To allot, divide,
Perchance to end in statehood;
Ah, there's the rub!

("To allot, or not to allot")

Posey's "On the Capture and Imprisonment of Crazy Snake, January, 1901" and Too-qua-stee's "Truth Is Mortal" (1901) lament the arrest of Chitto Harjo (in English, Crazy Snake), the legendary Muskogee (Creek) anti-allotment leader. In Posey's words:

Down with him! chain him! bind him fast!
    Slam to the iron door and turn the key!
The one true Creek, perhaps the last
    To dare declare, "You have wronged me!"

It's one thing when Posey romanticizes the world of birds, animals, flowers, and rivers in his nature poems, poems dedicated to finding lyricism in the lands that were about to be allotted. It's another thing when he romanticizes a person, Chitto Harjo, as "the one true Creek," another in the ironically endless line of the last of the Mohicans, as if Chitto Harjo's heroic objection to specific changes meant that he somehow lived outside the inevitable world of change that everyone lives in. Even so, at least for this reader, the romanticizing cliché fades amid the high drama and emphatic rhythms in Posey's sarcastic mockery. Colonialist violence and power finally sound petty next to the heroic courage of those who stand up against all odds for what they believe.

In "Indian Territory at World's Fair" (1904), Too-qua-stee, like Posey, finds the changes in Indian country driving him to sarcasm. He laments the impending loss of Indian Territory as Oklahoma was about to be granted statehood, a change closely tied to allotment, and a change that forfeited the sovereignty of Indian nations, including sovereignty over land. With his bitterest sarcasm, he maternalizes Indian Territory and congratulates her for supplanting her (implicitly Indian) children with a second set of (implicitly mostly white) children, who can join "that mighty group" of mostly white states:

> Thy charms shall be by other loves caressed;
> A new-born race shall revel on thy breast. . . .
> Ah! grandest glories wait upon thy touch,
> When thou becom'st a state, or something such.

The move to statehood went hand in hand with wild speculation over Indian lands newly put up for purchase. In that context, Joseph M. La Hay's "Consolation" (1905) pokes fun at a white friend, a speculator who covets the land of a Cherokee freedman (that is, a black Cherokee)—both of them actual, nonfictional people. The freedman defies the speculator by selling his land to someone else. La Hay seems to think it funny that someone he calls a "coon" outsmarts a powerful white lawyer. Compared to the sneering fury of Too-qua-stee, La Hay's poem takes capitalist speculation and statehood merely as an occasion for amusement. If for Too-qua-stee the world has turned upside down, for La Hay—a Cherokee who left only this one poem—a black man's ascendancy seems funny, as if to suggest that it is only fleeting and cannot challenge the accustomed hierarchy of power, which La Hay does not question. Too-qua-stee's anger, however, seems more typical of those poets who directly address politics and economics.

Poems About the Condition of the World, Poems About Nature

The poets speak not only to local and national topics, as we might expect, but also to international culture and controversies. In one of the earliest poems, from 1822, Delaware Adin C. Gibbs describes his school, the Cornwall Seminary in Connecticut, which had students from twelve nations speaking thirteen languages "But mostly of the *Cherokees*, / The *Angloes*, and the Owhyhees" (Hawaiians). Posey, DeWitt Clinton Duncan/Too-qua-stee, and J. C. Duncan allude to the wars in Cuba and the Philippines, with Posey proclaiming in 1896 that "Cuba shall be free" and with the others, a few years later in the fighting, looking skeptically at the onset of American imperialism.

Indeed, in terms not always pointed to conflict between Indians and whites, the poems often take a broadly oppositional stance, protesting cultural habits and assumptions that came to dominate American culture, perhaps afflicting Indians especially, but also burdening the nation at large. "In UNCLE SAM'S dominion," Posey laments, "A few own all the 'dust.' / They rule by combination / And trade by forming trusts." Less concretely, but more grimly, James Roane Gregory, a brilliant Yuchi whose poetry sometimes gets tangled in awkward and marginally intelligible syntax, wrote a poem at the turn of the century, in 1900, that bears comparison to Thomas Hardy's famously grim yet mysterious poem for the change of centuries in 1900, "The Darkling Thrush." "The land's sharp features seemed to be / The Century's corpse outleant," Hardy writes (Hardy 150). Gregory's poem, called "Nineteenth Century Finality," begins powerfully and then grows hard to untangle. Here it is in its entirety:

Nineteen hundred and it rains fire and blood,
Fast filling up hell and the grave;
A million lives trampled in gory mud,
They kill to kill—killing to save.

Great wars fought for paradise by the lost,
Hark! Widows' cries and orphans' wails!
God of Love! Pierce our hearts with cold death frost!
Crown Jesus Christ a stone, God Baal!

The love of God for man deified him,
The gentiles glorified his name.
The Roman and the Jew crucified him,
Science covers His love with shame.

To Gregory's thinking, apparently, people have crowned Jesus with a stone—or like a stone?—and conflated him with Baal, even while God deifies man in the form of Jesus. While Christians glorify Jesus, Gregory blames "The Roman and the Jew" for crucifying Jesus and in effect figuring the terrible future of a science that teaches how to rain fire and blood. Gregory sees scientific modernity as corrupting the desire to save, converting the compassion of saving grace into a rationalization of modern brutality. No less apocalyptic, at the end of the century, is Too-qua-stee/Duncan's 1899 "A Vision of the End," a scathing, almost Swiftian nightmare of catastrophe that begins

I once beheld the end of time!
Its stream has ceased to be.
The drifting years, all soiled with crime,
Lay in a filthy sea.

At the inverse of Duncan's filthy apocalypse of "reeking waste" where "all that men were wont to prize . . . / In slimy undulations roiled," where "government, a monstrous form . . . / On grimy billows rode," and where "all the monsters ever bred . . . / Lay scattered, floating, dead," other Indian poets, especially Posey, wax lyrical over nature in the familiar tradition of Euro-American Romantic poetry. John Rollin Ridge's magnificent "Mount Shasta" (1854) echoes Percy Bysshe Shelley's "Mont Blanc," and Posey's stirring "Tulledega" echoes passages in Wordsworth's "The Prelude," such as "The Boy of Winander" episode. More generally, Schoolcraft, Ridge, Posey, and others continue the Romantic tradition by writing about flowers, birds, rivers, and the landscape. The land, as we have noted, often carries intense meaning for Indian poets who write out of traditions that see their cosmology wedded with the land of their origin and their ancestors. Ridge's California poems mark an exception, however, for Ridge, a Cherokee, grew up in Georgia before his family's removal to Arkansas and then his own flight to California. When he writes of the California landscape, therefore, he writes of a world that is not the world of his family or ancestors, though his attunement to the land may still owe to a Cherokee or more broadly Native heritage of thinking through landscape. It may also owe to the self-consciousness about landscape that forced exile can provoke, as, again, in the words of Ridge's fellow Cherokee Te-con-ees-kee: "Though far from thee Georgia in exile I roam, / My heart in thy mountain land still has its home." For many poets, such preoccupations merge Native traditions with the traditions of Euro-American Romanticism.

In Jane Johnston Schoolcraft's romantic nature poems, for example, some of them written in Anishinaabemowin, the natural world speaks to her. She recalls that when she returned from Europe to her native land and saw her first pine trees, it dawned on her that she saw no pine trees in Europe, and then suddenly she felt the pine tree welcoming her home:

Mes ah nah, shi egwuh tah gwish en aung
Sin da mik ke aum baun
Kag ait suh, ne meen wain dum
Me nah wau, wau bun dah maun
Gi yut wi au, wau bun dah maun een
Shing wauk, shing wauk nosa
Shi e gwuh ke do dis an naun.

Ah beauteous tree! ah happy sight!
That greets me on my native strand
And hails me, with a friend's delight,
To my own dear bright mother land
Oh 'tis to me a heart-sweet scene,
The pine—the pine! that's ever green.

("To the Pine Tree")

When she translates the poem into English, Schoolcraft revises it to fit English rhythm and rhyme. But first she imagines the Anishinaabe version by drawing on the model of English or Euro-American poetry, writing in what had been an oral language and shaping it into rhyming lines that mix the syntactical patterns of Anishinaabemowin with the syntactical patterns of English.[2] Schoolcraft's Anishinaabe poems are the first-known poems written in an American Indian language, in this case a language that centers on distinctions between animate and inanimate. "Zhingwaak" (Schoolcraft's "shing wauk") is animate, and even in Schoolcraft's English the pine tree emerges as animate. It "greets" her and "hails" her with a Romantic and with an Anishinaabe accent. The pattern of an animate, articulate natural world continues in some of Schoolcraft's other poems. In "The Miscodeed," for example, the little pink flower (the miscodeed) is the "first to greet the eyes of men / In early spring," with its "pretty head / Oft peeping out." In a similar, if more explicit vein, some eighty years later, Hen-toh speaks to the coyote as an equal who can speak back in turn: "Yo-ho, Little Medicine Brother in gray, / Yo-ho, I am list'ning to your call" ("Coyote").

At times, the lyricism may seem forced, as in Gillis's "The Shasta Lily" (1923):

> Fragrant, perfumed, rich and rare,
> Wondrous sweet beyond compare,
> I fain would pluck thee from thy stem,
> O, thou priceless mountain gem.

The heavily end-stopped lines complete themselves by butting into a wall of one-syllable end rhymes that Gillis calls up to fill out the rhyme and the rough meter, comparing the Shasta Lily to other flowers by resorting, paradoxically, to the cliché that it lies beyond comparison. Yet the rough meter (beginning the generally iambic pattern with trochees in lines 1, 2, and 4) has its own version of grace, arguably more lyrical than the neatly iambic tetrameter third line, and Gillis places his poem in a specifically local and tribal context. He follows the title, "The Shasta Lily," with the name of the lily in the Wintun language, the Den-Hu-Luly, and he follows the poem with a note telling how the Wintu people identify this flower with their land and history.

D'Arcy McNickle's "The Mountains" (Cree, Confederated Salish and Kootenai, 1925) makes no direct reference to anything Indian, but readers of his great novel *The Surrounded* (1936) will recognize the mountain setting from the novel. They will also recall how, for the Salish characters in *The Surrounded*, the mountain scenes reverberate with Salish memory and tradition and with a sense of continuing but eventually dashed hopes for a refuge from aggressive white settlers and federal officials. In that sense, a wider context from McNickle's writing helps populate the locally Indian meanings of his poem's mountain landscape.

While Choctaw Mary Cornelia Hartshorne's "April Will Come" (1928) does not call on the same local meaning, she deftly handles the language of nature poetry:

> April will come, and with it April rain
> Singing among young oak leaves; the refrain
> Of it will lie upon the opalescent mist
> Like bells of Angelus. Green bugle vine will twist

And coil itself around the trunks of trees long dead;
And moistened grasses, crushed beneath one's tread,
Will fill the hazy air with pungent scents,
Stirring the dream-fraught earth from somnolence.

Opening a predominantly iambic pattern with insistent trochees (April, Singing), as Gillis did earlier, Hartshorne deftly blends enjambed rhythms (lines that end without a pause, as in lines 1–4) with caesuras (strong pauses in the middle of a line, as in lines 2 and 4). Sometimes, she rhymes single-syllable with multi-syllable words, and she lets a caesura anchor internal rhyme (the near rhyme of mist and twist with angelus). Such language has a flexibility that can speak over the fence dividing an age that expects rhyme and meter from an age that often finds them off-puttingly artificial.

Lynn Riggs's style perhaps comes the closest to patterns familiar to dedicated readers of contemporary poetry, partly because he is among the most recent poets in this collection and partly because he is the poet collected here who did the most to join mainstream, elite literary culture, associating with mainstream writers and publishing in elite, mainstream journals. Riggs works with traditional forms, especially rhyme, but with the lightly carried touch of a later age, as in "A Letter":

I don't know why I should be writing to you,
I don't know why I should be writing to anyone:
Nella has brought me yellow calendulas,
In my neighbor's garden is sun.

In my neighbor's garden chickens, like snow,
Drift in the alfalfa. Bees are humming;
A pink dress, a blue wagon play in the road;
Guitars are strumming.

Guitars are saying the same things
They said last night—in a different key.
What they have said I know—so their strumming
Means nothing to me.

Nothing to me is the pale pride of Lucinda
Washing her hair—nothing to anyone:
Here in a black bowl are calendulas,
In my neighbor's garden, sun.

Riggs sets a base of simple, vernacular vocabulary without a conspicuously poetic sound, and then, perhaps in an echo of Wallace Stevens, he rotates on the vernacular axis and turns to the suddenly lyrical calendulas and the sudden appearance and disappearance of Nella and Lucinda, draped in the lyrically liquid l's of their names and the artful splashes of yellow, pink, blue, and black, complete with a background of strumming guitars. In unmetered stanzas, Riggs offers the familiarity of repetition paced by rhyme: abcb, dede, fgfg, hbcb. With a few near rhymes (snow with road and things with strumming) and a pattern that slaloms beyond the predictable just enough to keep fresh while staying within the predictable just enough to suggest completion and recognition, each line from the first stanza meets its match or its near match elsewhere in the poem (lines 1 and 2, lines 3 and 15, and lines 4, 5, and 16), while the last line of a stanza finds an echo in the first line of the next stanza.

In "The Vandals," Riggs turns the lyricism of nature in an environmentalist direction, lamenting the way miners scrape and blast the landscape. Against such devastation, the motions of bird and beast may sound "Like protestation shrunk to song," he concludes, "Yet all that horde were without tears / Or cognizance of any wrong." The birds and beasts, like the oblivious spider in Robert Frost's "Range-Finding," cannot comprehend the scale of human destruction and are not up to the task of calling it to a halt. With his typical indirectness, Riggs thus seems to ask whether humanity itself has any hope of staunching the devastation it wreaks. In "Change," he sees a far wider devastation. "This is the way of things in this mad world," he begins. "Summer is wrenched at its bright root and whirled / . . . Cones bleed and fall; . . . / . . . the tawny river / Breaks from its bed to scar the sand by night." "Change" is Riggs's version of the prophecy W. B. Yeats offers in "The Second Coming," as finally Riggs steps aside from his characteristic gentleness and indirection to proclaim that "all form / Crumbles like stones of cities."

At such a moment, Riggs takes on the apocalyptic sound of Too-qua-stee and James Roane Gregory. More typically, and unlike most of the other poets in this book, Riggs favors the indirection that suits an audience already committed to poetry, especially to modern poetry. His poems are like the shadow he compares himself to in "Shadow on Snow": "I, a shadow, thinking as I go, / . . . I, a shadow, moving across the snow."

Poems About Love and War

As we might expect, many of the poems in this book address the traditional topics of poetry. Besides nature poems, there are poems about language and poems about heterosexual love of many kinds, and here and there a comic poem. Poems in local dialect, a popular form in the late nineteenth and early twentieth centuries, often record—with a mixture of affection and humor—how the grammar and syntax of Indian languages such as Posey's Creek or Hen-toh's Wyandot influenced Indian English. Though there was nothing unusual about writing in local dialect, for Indian poets it provided a way to translate the liveliness of Indian oral tradition into the European-derived form of written poetry.

Some of the love poems imply a cross-racial attraction, with an Indian speaker romanticizing blue eyes or golden hair without a trace of self-questioning. Many of Ridge's poems fit that formula. "The Stolen White Girl" describes an Indian capturing a white, a popular genre in prose by whites, but Ridge's poem tells the tale from the Indian captor's perspective. Even so, it repeats white fantasies of an Indian man stealing away a blue-eyed damsel. Against the convention of captivity narratives, however, this blue-eyed damsel has earlier fallen in love with her dark captor. In "False, but Beautiful," the habit of imagining a conventionally white lover leads Ridge to give a "snowy arm" even to a lover introduced as "Dark as a demon's dream." But in another of his poems a dark man warns his implicitly white lover of "the coming storm": "my dark doom thou too must share— / . . . And if my portion is despair, / Such too must be thy state" ("The Dark One to His Love," 1848). In a similar vein, the most dwelled-on cross-racial love story is the long, cautionary tragedy of Mabel Washbourne Anderson's "Nowita, the Sweet Singer" (1900), who wastes away after falling in love with the white man who abandons her. I have found at most one uncloseted same-sex love poem, the quirky Wa Wa Chaw's "In Memory of My Homosexual Friend: Imaginary Love. . . ." (date uncertain), though readers might notice a closeted feeling in some of Riggs's poems.[3] Ridge's "The Man of Memory" (1848) spins a remarkable variation on the history of love poems, describing an old man who cannot free himself from a torturing memory of having raped his sweetheart: "He madly used his conscious power / To make that trusting girl his passions' prey." While Ridge's poem seems partly like a young man's rape fantasy, defending against the fantasy by making the rapist wallow in guilt, the poem's reconsideration of patriarchal privilege can reverberate with later readers influenced by the way feminists have intensified the critique of rape.

In Ridge's remarkable poem love or violence can have to do with land and war. It seems an odd poem for a twenty-one-year-old to publish, and a newly married twenty-one-year-old at that, but even at that age Ridge felt haunted by his own memory of violence. For at the age of twelve he watched as twenty-five Cherokees from the anti-treaty John Ross party murdered his father, John Ridge, in an organized vendetta against the Ridge party for signing the 1835 Treaty of New Ochota. In that treaty, John Ridge and his allies—under enormous pressure—agreed to give up Cherokee lands and move the Cherokee people into exile in the west. As John Rollin Ridge later recalled in a letter included with his posthumous book of poems, the assassination "darkened my mind with an eternal shadow" (Ridge 7). (On John Rollin Ridge's life, see Parins. For poems falsely attributed to his father, John Ridge, see the list of "Notable False Attributions" at the back of this volume. Hard feelings between descendants of the Ross and Ridge parties sometimes continue today.)

Of course, there are many differences between the assassination and the poem. In one case, the elderly "man of memory" in Ridge's poem recalls an act of sexual violence that he himself committed. In the other case, Ridge witnessed others commit political violence on his father. Still, the political violence had to do with land, and land and love have much to do with each other. We sometimes love a particular land, and we often associate love with the land where we love. We also commonly eroticize landscape and conflate the theft and abuse of land, the rape of land, with the rape of women. In the same way, more broadly following the trail of violence and trauma, we might conflate one form or instance of violence with another or one violence-haunted memory with another. Drawing on Freud's insight in "Mourning and Melancholia" that when a loved one dies we feel—unconsciously and often in some ways consciously—somehow responsible, somehow at fault or guilty, it seems plausible to suppose that the young Ridge, witnessing the brutal murder of his father and living under the pall of its melodramatic notoriety, would wonder why *him*. What did he do to cause or deserve this violence? From there—admittedly at the risk of oversimplifying the poem, but without claiming that the poem reduces to this one skein of suggestiveness—it seems that Ridge's poem partly takes his own haunting by violence and projects it outward onto another, conflates the haunting memories of the rape of the land and the violence against his family with a rape of the beloved. He seems to project the burden of living under a haunting memory of witnessed violence onto the imagination of what it might be like to live with such a haunting, not just for one decade but for many decades. More largely, the haunting memory is not only Ridge's. His personal and familial memory registers a larger memory and trauma of the Cherokee people and of all peoples forced into exile, forced into arguments with each other and within themselves over how to respond to the colonialist pressure to give up their lands and, more largely, to give up their culture and heritage. Thus Ridge's poem about men trying to reimagine their relations with women itself offers a haunting metaphor both of potentially reimagined gender relations and of a people trying to find ways to reimagine its relation to a history of trauma.

Among the many ways Indian people have found to mediate that trauma, both the history of dispossession and the related sense of threatened masculinity and femininity, Indian men have enlisted in the armed services in disproportionate numbers. But while at least four poets in this volume fought for the Confederacy (W. P. Boudinot, Lipe, Adair, and Martin) and one for the Union (Gregory), and others took sides, I have found only one poem about the Civil War, Ridge's Unionist "Poem" ("All hail the fairest . . . "), which has more to do with the war's politics than with its fighting. Poems about World War I, however, echo the tradition of military service in many Indian communities. In "The Doughboy" (1925), Choctaw Ben D. Locke takes pride in continuing a warrior tradition, yet he believes that the Indian soldier "Stands as a hero undaunted / To a race fast fading from sight." Locke buys into the myth that Indians are vanishing, "on the brink of the abyss," and so for him the tradition he celebrates has run to the end of its course. Carlos Montezuma, by contrast, sees the war and its slaughter as proof that the vaunted "civilization" is "the worst savagery." "Civilization," he writes, "thou art great, thou canst raise millions to slaughter, / Tear to pieces thy brother in the air," but it all comes down to "the Almighty dollar," to "might and not right" ("Civilization," 1917). Writing to Indian readers, Montezuma warns:

> The War Craze is on.
> If you want to fight—fight—
> But let no one force you in. . . .
> They have taken your country,
> They have taken your manhood,
> They have imprisoned you,
> They have made you wards. . . .
> You are not an American citizen—
> You are an Indian;
> You are nothing and that is all. . . .
> Redskins, *true Americans*, you have a fight with those whom you
> wish to fight for.
>
> ("Steady, Indians, Steady!" 1917)

Montezuma's polarizing repetition (the anaphora of "They . . . , They . . . , They . . . " versus "You . . . , You . . . , You . . . ") calls up Indian pride, and in that way it matches the work of a soldier poet like Locke or Thomas Dewey Slinker. But Montezuma tries to recruit Indian pride to resist the federal authority that Locke and Slinker defend.

Poems About Christianity

In something like the same way that some poets take pride in World War I while others—or at least Montezuma—cast it in doubt, some of the poets take pride in Christianity while others look at it with skepticism. Still others, however, hedge their bets and take both stances, more or less subtly but in line with widespread patterns of Native religious syncretism. Indian people, like other people, have always built their own cultures from what they find around them as well as from what they imagine and believe on their own, without necessarily seeing a division between those two paths. Even the Puritan Eleazar refers to pagan Greeks and their god Apollo before turning to more orthodox Christian sentiments. For Eleazar, ancient Greek beliefs might echo or stand in for Native versions of non-Christian beliefs. Other poems fit more snugly in traditional Christian patterns, as when Hartshorne addresses Christ directly to say that "within your eyes / The tender mercy of your Father lies" ("Three Poems of Christmas Eve") or when Schoolcraft asks us "With joyful hearts, and pious lays, / To join the glorious Maker's praise" ("Lines to a Friend Asleep"). On the other hand, the irrepressible DeWitt Clinton Duncan/Too-qua-stee, who ends "The Dead Nation" by rhyming "Christ" with "priced," proclaims that he would "drive old Claus with his load of cheap goods / If I could, to the place where he ought to go— / To freeze to death in the cold polar woods" ("A Christmas Song"). For the place where St. Nicholas ought to go, Too-qua-stee's pause allows us to fill in the name of the hot place before he rounds out the stanza with a hardly less forbidding cold place. J. C. Duncan is less jocular and, if less eloquent, nevertheless more direct when he tells the "White man" to

Return our land and moneys,
  Then Christianity take,
Return us to our innocence,
  We never burned at stakes.

("The Red Man's Burden," 1899)

It is hard to tell whether the last line means that Indians never burned their innocence, that Cherokees never burned Christians, or, as the syntax but not the sense seems to suggest, never burned themselves, never, in effect, cooperated with what amounts to an inquisition.

Some poets blame white Christians for not living up to the Christianity they preach. In "The Dead Nation," Too-qua-stee says wryly that the Cherokee Nation will have to give way to civilization—"And so did Socrates and Jesus Christ" ("The Dead Nation"). Richard C. Adams might seem to want it both ways, demurring that "I do not blame the Christians, if Christians true they be," but he uses his accusation of false Christianity as a passport to decry Christians more largely. He sees Christians as hypocrites: "'This is a Christian Nation,' they oft with pride maintain, / And even on their money their faith they do proclaim." But he also sees Christians, if not Christianity itself, as complicit with colonialism from the get-go, in part because, as so often, it comes down to land:

. . . there came some pilgrims from a far and distant shore,
As they said "with Christian motives," our country to explore;
For us, "a poor heathen nation," their hearts were truly sad;
And to save us from "the infernal powers" they'd be very glad.
But to provide the daily bread of those who laid the plan,
Well, of course, we'd be expected to give them plenty of land.

("To the Delaware Indians")

When Indian poets criticize whites' theft of land, white civilization, or white Christianity, they step outside their colonially assigned roles as ethnographic representatives of their own cultures. Instead, as participant observers in the surrounding white-majority world, they offer their own ethnographic account of the dominant culture, but without the usual pose of ethnographic neutrality. Given the routine of ethnographic thinking when it comes to representing Indian cultures, that is, the sense of obligation to explain Indian cultures more or less from scratch to an audience that knows little about the topic, it may seem remarkable that Indian poets typically refuse to take up the role of what Mary

Louise Pratt has called auto-ethnographers, writers who explain their own cultures from the privileged position of insiders, reproducing or mimicking the way that anthropologists, journalists, and travel writers typically described Indian cultures. Instead of writing to serve colonialist curiosity, Indian poets write for their own purposes, both politically and aesthetically.

Poems About Other Peoples, Poems About Internalized and Externalized Racism

On the other hand, occasionally the poets write about another Indian culture besides their own. In an extreme case, Ridge succumbs to the boilerplate prejudices around him among California settlers and condescends to California Indians. More typically, writing about other Indian peoples leads to an ethnographic approach. "Whence comes this mystic night-song?" asks the Wyandot Hen-toh, to prompt his metrical explanation that "'Tis the An-gu, the Kat-ci-na, 'tis the Hopi's song of prayer" ("A Desert Memory," 1906). Similarly, Hen-toh adopts the voice of a Navajo weaver who explains who Navajos are, prompting a narrative of Navajo origins and beliefs ("The Song of a Navajo Weaver," 1906). In a later, almost Imagist style, the more restrained Riggs, an Oklahoma Cherokee who lived for awhile in Santa Fe, describes a corn dance at Santo Domingo Pueblo in New Mexico, with Koshari (sacred Pueblo clowns) who "glide, halt, grimace, grin, / And turn" while

> Beyond
> The baking roofs,
> A barren mountain points
> Still higher, though its feet are white
> With bloom.
>
> ("Santo Domingo Corn Dance," 1930)

Typically, then, in a pattern that might provoke a smile of amused recognition from many Indian readers, in these relatively early years of Indian poetry, the poets who write about Indian peoples other than their own are displaced Southeasterners from Indian Territory (later Oklahoma) writing about peoples from the Southwest. Robbed of the lands that anchored their heritage, and forced to move to what eventually became Oklahoma, the still prideful Southeasterners often feel self-conscious about their racially mixed heritage and cultures. In that context, they can cast romanticizing eyes on the culturally more conservative peoples of the Southwest, peoples more successful at retaining their lands, languages, homes, and religions. They can see the Southwestern peoples as icons of a genuine Indianness that the surrounding colonialist thinking may lead Oklahoma Indians to see as more genuine or more authentic, even when such comparisons trade on oversimplifying clichés about both Southwestern and Southeastern traditions. Such clichés would be hard to resist. "Where the breezes blow full of invigoration," explains the Cherokee Muskrat, "There lies an Indian reservation," as if writing for people who need to be introduced to the fact of the reservation in the first place, though—unlike Hen-toh or Riggs—as Muskrat goes on to linger lyrically over an Apache reservation she does not get into matters that ring specifically as Southwestern. Instead, she describes generic Indians with tepees, papooses, and, in perhaps the stubbornest cliché, a yearning "for the tale to be told / Of a race that is dying" ("The Apache Reservation," 1922).

Such clichés run widely through these poems and can raise obstacles and questions for later readers. Depending on their experience, later readers often believe in the same clichés, more or less unwittingly, but many readers now respond to clichés about Indians with resentment or scorn. These poems can help us look—perhaps sympathetically, perhaps not always or only sympathetically—at the history of how Indian people can get drawn into anti-Indian ways of thinking from the general culture and find themselves taking those ways of thinking for granted, even against what today we might see as Indian people's own best interests. As we have noted, for example, many love poems take for granted the ideal of a blue-eyed or golden-haired lover. Even a proud poem like Hen-toh's homage to Pontiac can refer to Indian people as "primitive" or describe Pontiac—the famous eighteenth-century Odawa (Ottawa) leader—as "untaught" ("Pontiac"). While recognizing Pontiac's vast knowledge, Hen-toh—in the usual way of the dominant culture—writes as if only school learning counts as education. Perhaps the most pervasive cliché, however, echoed in Hen-toh's reference to Pontiac's people as "scattered remnants of thy valiant race" and in the Montaukett Olivia Ward Bush-Banks' reference to a "scattered remnant" that "Sinks beneath Oblivion's Wave" ("On the Long Island Indian," 1890), is the stubborn myth of the vanishing Indian, immortalized in James Fenimore Cooper's title *The Last of the Mohicans.*

An anonymous Cherokee poem from 1871 seems devoted to the myth of the vanishing Indian:

> Faster and fiercer rolls the tide
> That follows on our track. . . .
>
> There is no hope; the red man's fate
> Is fixed beyond control,
> And soon above each hearth and home
> The mighty waves will roll.
>
> Why is it thus, are we accurst
> And will oblivion's gloom,
> Give back no ray to tell us why
> Extinction is our doom?
>
> ("Faster and fiercer rolls the tide")

To this poet, the Cherokee and Indian future looks hopeless: the Euro-American flood dooms Indian people to extinction. In a variety of ways, other poets see Indian people as disappearing but use the language of disappearance to describe what sometimes sounds more like change than like disappearance.

In powerfully repetitive rhythms, Muskrat's "Sentenced *(A Dirge)*" (1921) drums a resignation to vanishing together with an outrage at the colonialist conquest:

> They have come, they have come,
> Out of the unknown they have come;
> Out of the great sea they have come;
> Dazzling and conquering the white man has come
> To make this land his home.

Perhaps the word "dazzling" sneers at the white man's vanity, but amid the drumbeat of resignation it is hard to tell. By the last stanza, though, Muskrat leaves no uncertainty about whether she likes the conquest she feels resigned to:

> They have won, they have won,
> Thru fraud and thru warfare they have won,
> Our council and burial grounds they have won,
> Our birthright for pottage the white man has won,
> And the red man must perish alone.

With its whiff of a sneer and its insistently rhythmical witnessing, Muskrat's lyrical testimony gives the lie to her claim about perishing, but only barely.

In "The Conquered Race" (1927), Sunshine Rider (the pen name of a Cherokee artist, performer, and writer) describes "an aged chieftain" mourning—at sunset, no less—that "the White Man's ways" have led to the Indians' demise, but in response, a "Paleface spoke with sympathy," arguing that because Indian "young will learn" and take on the role of citizens, "the modern Redman" will rise "wide awake!" His pride stirred by the Paleface's response, the chieftain "leaped to life," only then to fall "foremost on the earth-beaten sod," as if to suggest that proud though he may be, he and the time he represents are irrevocably doomed. In a sense, then, for Sunshine Rider, Indians may seem conquered and ready to vanish into the past, but from our later perspective we might reinterpret the point—and this is very much a poem with a point—as suggesting that one kind of Indian will fade into the past but another kind will live on. Montezuma seems to understand the point exactly, if less melodramatically, when he insists in the title of one of his poems that "Changing Is Not Vanishing."

Poets like Sunshine Rider are more typical. They negotiate a fraught position between, on one hand, the anonymous "Faster and fiercer rolls the tide," which without realizing it gives in to what we today call internalized racism, and, on the other hand, Montezuma's defiance, which likely rings more accurately to Indian readers in the twenty-first century. That vexed spot between opposite understandings of change spins poignantly through a more or less dactylic poem to the Carlisle graduating class of 1895 from the Cherokee Samuel Sixkiller, "the class poet":

> Farewell to dear class, to friends and to strangers,
> Assembling here in our honor today,
> To help Nature's children—the wildflower rangers,
> And make pure Americans from ocean to bay.
>
> . . . . .
>
> When shall the culture, the art and refinement
> Drive from our minds, roving thoughts of the past?
> Shall broad education, or savage confinement,
> Conquer the Red Man now fading so fast?

We might suppose that Sixkiller gives in to a demeaning view of Indians as wholeheartedly as the anonymous poet of 1871, for Sixkiller's poem repeats the full range of demeaning views that were drummed into the ears of Carlisle students.[4] It is troublesome enough when Gillis refers to Indian toddlers as "nature's children" ("To the Wenem Mame River," 1924) or Blue Feather refers to Indians as "Happy and free, just children of nature" ("The Lone Tee-Pee," 1921). But it is more striking when Sixkiller, combining two stereotypes, conflates Indian people with nature and at the same time trades on the dominant culture's infantilizing of Indian people by referring to the Carlisle graduating class—excitedly on the verge of adulthood and leadership—as children. He sees Indians as Nature's wildflowers, versus the "art and refinement" offered by Carlisle. For Sixkiller, Indians are fit for nostalgia, figured here, as so often, in sunsets and images of noble but vanishing masculinity "when the sun in his glory, / Shall shine on the last of the noble Red Man." The idea in *The Last of the Mohicans* title was already a cliché when James Fenimore Cooper's novel came out in 1826, but somehow those hardy last Indians were still busy dying in 1895 and, while supposedly always fading into the sunset, have managed to stay around ever since.

And in some ways that ability to keep living by dying is Sixkiller's point, whether he knows it or not. For when Sixkiller repeats the boilerplate stereotypes that demean him and his fellow students, he also uses stereotypes to move beyond stereotypes. Maybe, in some ways, when an Indian student repeats back what the Carlisle teachers and the dominant culture say about Indians, it is mere repetition, but in some ways maybe it is also repetition with a difference. To be sure, it can disturb us to see an Indian repeating the clichés of a dominant culture that refuses to recognize contemporary Indian people, if we think of Sixkiller and his fellow students—who may have been the ones who chose him as their class poet—caught in the pressure to parrot and perhaps to believe what their teachers tell them. But maybe in some ways Sixkiller's poem veers toward—or at least invites us to ask whether it veers toward—survival skills and even mimicry, a strategy of living on instead of fading into the sunset and dying.[5] Sixkiller says what the Carlisle teachers and administrators want to hear, but that does not mean that he thinks what they want him to think. Nor does it mean that his fellow students believe that he thinks what the poem says. He might have given them reason to know better. They might have known better about how most of them thought. When Sixkiller asks "Shall broad education, or savage confinement, / Conquer the Red Man now fading so fast?" he might mean savage confinement as opposed to broad education, suggesting that before coming to Carlisle he and his fellow students were confined by savagery. Nevertheless, he might mean—or regardless of his intentions, his words can mean—that the arguably not-so-broad education he receives at Carlisle is itself partly a new version of savage confinement. In that case, his poem would surreptitiously turn the language of Carlisle against itself.

A little more boldly, in a poem the next year by one of Sixkiller's classmates, Oneida Melinda Metoxen refers to "Iceland's voyagers, so bold" who "First discovered . . . America" ("Iceland"). But then, under the cover of her need to fill out the rhyme, she adds a dash and a few more words that sneak in an editorially ironic qualifier: "—so we're told." In such ways, school authorities sometimes seem to have slipped, publishing poems by their students that deliberately, as with Metoxen, or perhaps not, as with Sixkiller, smuggle in sentiments that undermine the school's authority. Writing a poem to his teacher the year after he graduates, and not knowing that his teacher would publish the poem, Sixkiller worries that the promises of Carlisle aren't panning out back home in Indian Territory. He can't find a job, and he finds himself getting "down in the face" and "mighty tired" "With nothing much to do." It is surprising that Carlisle printed such a poem, but Sixkiller surrounds his worries with praise for Carlisle and sighs for its "big and cosy nest." Ironically, he feels homesick for school, so uncritically homesick that he can point out—without quite recognizing—how going away to school might have contributed to his worry that back home life now "goes pretty slow" ("[My First Winter Out of School"]).

If we have at least an inkling of reason to doubt how fully Sixkiller submits to Carlisle's demeaning agenda of assimilation, there can be little doubt a generation later about Frank (Francis) Verigan's poem "Be a Carlisle Student" (Tlingit, 1917):

> Say Chief: Just a minute of your time is all I pray. . . .
> Tho I know you'll scorn these verses, it is just the talk you loathe.
> But take it for it's something that must come—
> Be a Carlisle Student, not a reservation bum. . . .
> Look your best you'll then feel better, there's noble blood in all
>   your veins,
> You're the hope of all your people—show them something for
>   their pains.
> Don't be helpless, hopeless, useless, getting by with old time bluff,

Strike a gait with business to it, if there's evil treat it rough.
Take a bulldog grip—make something come—
Be a Carlisle Student, not a reservation bum.

Probably Verigan is joking, at least a little, with his fellow students when he begins with "Chief," the pet name that many non-Indians apply to Indian men, trying to make Indian people and culture fit the colonizers' need to oversimplify Indian variety and Indian leadership. But the poem then funnels its slippery energies into the astonishing refrain that fills out the title and ends each stanza with its snappy conclusive rhyme: "Be a Carlisle Student, not a reservation bum." To live up to Verigan's ideal, and presumably the ideal of the Carlisle authorities who allowed his poem to appear in *The Carlisle Arrow and Red Man*, apparently means not to mope around in hopeless idleness and instead to take up the world of energetic business. In that way, Verigan abides by a common stereotype that runs widely through American culture and even through Indian-written fiction, the stereotype of restless young Indian men with nothing to do who supposedly waste away their lives by refusing to go along with the colonialist business ethic. That stereotype draws on the at least questionable assumption that colonization removed the precolonial roles of Indian men without producing anything like the same displacement for Indian women.[6] From such a perspective, Indians' own ways of doing are invisible. And therefore, from such a perspective, when young Indians do not go along with colonialist expectations, they look as if they're doing nothing at all. From such a perspective, an Indian without a job and a business gait that fits standard-issue white aspirations is simply a bum.

Yet we might wonder what makes Verigan write this poem, besides the ordinary student desire to say and perhaps to believe what students hear from their teachers. He must sense that some of the Carlisle students want to be what he reads—or misreads—as a reservation bum. He may believe that many Carlisle students, after leaving Carlisle, turn into reservation bums. After all, if some students embrace what their teachers tell them, other students resent what their teachers say and even rebel against it, either in school or after they get out of school. Verigan addresses his fellow students directly, as "you," realizing that some of the other Carlisle students will see his sentiments as "just the talk you loathe." Maybe the students who loathe Verigan's ideas and the ideas of the Carlisle authorities simply follow the familiar, and familiarly adolescent, path of resisting authority. Or maybe some of them think through the issue more programmatically and see Verigan's sentiments not merely as encouraging responsibility but also, at least partly, as colonialist. As cultural studies scholars have argued, we might be wary of seeing adolescent and political models of resistance as at odds with each other. Sometimes, adolescent recalcitrance can encourage programmatic, theorized resistance.

In these lights, I hope that we can look at the internalized racism in many of the poems with thoughtfulness about the poets' uncertain position and the history that it helps make visible. I hope that we can view the poets without harsh judgment and with, instead, a sense of the contradictions and pressures swirling around and within them.[7] But difficult as it may have been for many of these poets to see their way entirely outside internalized racism, some of them saw right through it. Broken Wing Bird, echoing Shakespeare's Shylock's perplexity at anti-Semitism, asks "Why? Why? Why?" people suppose that Indians must be irresponsible with "eyes, but not for seeing," "feet, but not for walking," and "a tongue, but not for talking" (1921). In "Changing Is Not Vanishing" (1916), Montezuma, though he was a friend of Carlisle and worked there as a physician for two and a half years, programmatically attacks the colonialist assumptions that underlie many of the other poets' internalized racism:

> Who says the Indian race is vanishing?
> The Indians will not vanish.
> The feathers, paint and moccasin will vanish, but the Indians,—
> never! . . .
> He has changed externally but he has not vanished.
> He is an industrial and commercial man, competing with the
> world; he has not vanished....
> The Indian race vanishing? No, never! The race will live on and
> prosper forever.

In long lines reminiscent of Walt Whitman but with rhetoric like a stump speech, Montezuma finds a way to extol industry and commerce without chastising Indians whose idea of industry and commerce might not match the business gait, the colonialist control of the body and its actions, that looms so large for Carlisle's authorities. Implicitly addressing a touchy topic, he recognizes that a steadily increasing number and proportion of Indian people will have non-Indian as well as Indian ancestors: "Just as long as there is a drop of human blood in America, the Indians will not vanish." More to the point, he recognizes that for Indians to have non-Indian ancestors does not make them less Indian, a concept that remains difficult for many non-Indians to process, and that Indians themselves are sometimes pressured to deny. Indeed, it would be impossible to live without change, but the dominant culture typically supposes that change threatens the authenticity of the rest of the world (but not of the dominant culture), not recognizing that the static signifiers of authenticity (concepts and expressions like nature's children, "Chief," or vanishing into the sunset) are constructions of the colonizers' fantasies. The colonizers project those static models of authenticity and masculinity onto colonized peoples as a way of denying the colonized peoples' ongoing life and resistance to colonialist authority.

Both John Rollin Ridge and Arsenius Chaleco (Yuma) lament the vanishing of Indians by discovering the remains of Indians past. Ridge sees the era of Indians as irrevocably in the past and gone:

A thousand cities
Stand, where once thy nation's wigwams stood,—
And num'rous palaces of giant strength
Are floating down the streams where long ago
Thy bark canoe was gliding. All is changed.

("An Indian's Grave," 1847)

For Ridge, whose majestic rhythms and laments sometimes make him sound, as noted earlier, like an American Shelley, the message of Shelley's "Ozymandias" and "Mutability" speaks of the transience of Indians but not the transience of whites. For Ridge, at least in this poem, the world of whites has conquered. The steamboat palaces seem like the pinnacle of civilization, free from the winds of mortality that sweep Indians off into the dusty mutabilities of time. Chaleco, by contrast, can take the critical skepticism he brings to Indians and turn it back on whites. He laments the vanishing of Indians, lingering lyrically over a colonialist plow that churns up the "mouldering bone[s]" of a warrior and his mourners, including his wife and their child, who "little thought . . . / That through their graves would cut the plow." But then Chaleco faces the conquering wielders of the plow and points the myth of vanishing Indians back at them:

But I behold a fearful sign
To which the white man's eyes are blind,
Their race may vanish hence like mine
And leave no trace behind,

Save ruins o'er the region spread,
And tall white stones above the dead.
And realms our tribes were crushed to get
May be our barren desert yet.

("The Indian Requiem," 1924)

Chaleco may continue to think from within the myth of vanishing, but he takes it outside internalized racism by turning it back on the conquerors. In effect, he accuses the colonizers of vanity and self-delusion to go along with their habit of stealing land. Releasing Indians from the special burden that colonialism imagines for indigenous peoples, he proposes that no people escapes change, that no people escapes the mutability of time.

Just as the poems sometimes succumb to internalized racism—and it would be unfair to expect that any group of writers could remain immune to such a thing—so, as predictably, a few of them also succumb to what we might call externalized racism. That is, instead of learning from the racism that Indian people face, they deflect racism onto African Americans, as we saw already in Joseph M. La Hay's portrait of a Cherokee freedman. Richard C. Adams resents that white Americans acknowledge the rights of "The foreigner from Europe's shore or" what he calls "the ignorant African" ("To the Delaware Indians") without acknowledging the rights of Indians. In something like a verbal blackface, Posey's "A Freedman Rhyme" (1905) corrupts his skill at writing in dialect to try on what he supposes is a black voice. As so often, the issue comes down to land. Satirically, Posey mouths crude, minstrel stereotypes of black speech to protest that black Creeks can receive allotments of land that he would rather save for non-black Creeks:

> You bettah lẹf' dat watermelon 'lone
> An' go look up some vacant lan'
> Fer all dem chillun what you t'ink is yone. . . .
> Bettah hum Yo'se'r, nigger.

Posey can write funny poems, but in this poem his humor falls flat.

The work of, to say the least, a far lesser poet, Joseph Lynch Martin, survives in two poems from the *Cherokee Advocate*. In one of those poems, "Stanzas by Uncle Joe" (1891), Martin—perhaps anticipating his death seven months later—begins by saying "To my dear nieces three: / Ellen, Ann and Cherokee." After going on to describe each niece, he writes:

> I love you children, oh, so well!
> Better far than I can ever tell.
> The reason why I love you so good,
> Is because, within your veins runs my blood.

After that not terribly artful eye-rhyme (pairing "good" with "blood"), he then praises the nieces and their piety and concludes with "a parting word before we go: / In your prayers ever remember your Uncle Joe," an unsurprising finish to a seemingly unremarkable poem. But "Stanzas by Uncle Joe" may gain more interest if we bring it into dialogue with Martin's other surviving poem, "A Dream" (1881), which retells the story of Eve and Adam. While it too may seem unremarkable, it has more spunk. Eve and Adam taste of the fatal fruit, and then:

> Long in the evening old master come,
> He soon found out what the devil had done.
> He called up Adam, he called up Eve,
> Here they come with aprons made of leaves.
> Old master asked Adam what made him hide,
> Daddy, said Adam, because I have lied.
> Adam got scared, laid it all on Eve,
> Eve said it was the devil she believed.
> Old master got mad, raised a big fuss,
> And made the old devil git down in the dust.

> He drove out Adam, he drove out Eve
> And told the old devil he could bite him on his heel. . . .

The poem's pleasure in repeating "old master," a colloquial term for a plantation slave master, led me to suspect that Martin owned slaves and that his patronizing attitude to Adam and Eve, self-importantly ventriloquized by routing it through God, stands in, however indirectly, for a patronizing attitude to his slaves and former slaves and their descendants. It seems meaningful that the poem itself raised that suspicion before I researched Martin, who turns out to have owned a lavish plantation with over a hundred slaves and to have fought in the Civil War as a Confederate officer. Lucy Allen, a descendant through one of his slaves, has been a leading figure in the controversial twenty-first-century efforts of black Cherokees to convince the Cherokee Nation to reacknowledge their status as Cherokees. Thus when Martin praises his nieces because his blood runs through their veins, readers of the *Cherokee Advocate* must have enjoyed what amounts to a wink over an open secret. They would have recognized Ellen, Ann, and Cherokee as Martin's nieces, but they would also have known that there were other people with Martin's blood in their veins whom he did not "love . . . so good," at least not in the same way, for he had many children by his slaves (Geller, Cornsilk). Martin might even have intended the joke. Though for later readers the joke might come across as more interesting than funny, it may have been a joke on Martin as well as by Martin, for in those years, the *Cherokee Advocate* usually published poems (not necessarily by Indian people) on p. 1, but they put "Stanzas by Uncle Joe" on p. 2—and they published it on April Fool's Day.

While some things change if we cross from Cherokees back to Creeks, the questions around Martin's poems may turn us back to Posey's disconcerting humor. When Posey puts on blackface and has his imaginary Creek freedman say that blacks had better hurry to get their allotments of land "Fer all dem chillun what you t'ink is yone," such lines, however unwittingly, can suppress the knowledge that in Indian Country the sexually peripatetic fathers of first-generation so-called mixed-race African American children by multiple women were more likely to be Indian than African American. While some mixed-race black and Indian children, especially among the economically less prosperous, were the children of consensual relations, Posey's sneering can also suppress the recognition that many of them were the children of rape by Indian slaveowners. In that sense, what I am calling externalized racism projects onto others the internalized racism that Posey, and perhaps others he can represent, want to repress in their own culture. Such repression, centrally involving Martin's descendants, continues in the twenty-first century through the resurging controversy over the rights of descendants of Cherokee freedmen.

In the frightening case of the brutal Yuchi murderer, rapist, and robber Rufus Buck, who led his gang on a rampage across the Creek Nation in 1895, the self-hate that contributed to such crimes turned oddly gentle at the last moment. After he and his gang were sent to the gallows by the famous hanging Judge Parker in 1896, Buck left a farewell poem in his cell, scrawled on the back of a photograph of his mother:

> I,dremPT, I,wAs,in,heAven,
> Among, THe,AnGels,fAir;
> I'd, neAr,seen,none,so,HAndsome,
> THAT,TWine,in,golden,HAIR;
>
> . . . . .
>
> gooD.BymyDear.Wife, anD.MoTHer
> all.so. My.sIsTers

While waiting for their execution the gang spent much of their time singing hymns ("Five Strung Up"). Less roughly than we might expect, Buck's barely literate poem draws on the rhythm of hymns and ballads (alternating lines of iambic tetrameter and iambic trimeter). Somehow, Buck must have felt that poetry would ennoble his feelings and testify to something like remorse. Marginally literate, not-so-literary poets or versifiers like Martin and Buck might not match the traditional model of poetry fit for anthologies, but they help provide a picture of the roles that poetry played in everyday culture, a model of the respect it commanded and the appeal it held as a way—now often lost as cultural habits have changed—for ordinary people to speak to each other.

Of course, more literary poets of varying skill, cultural insight, and representativeness make up the bulk of this volume, including the only certainly African American and Indian poet I have found, Olivia Ward Bush-Banks.[8] And while the poets in this volume sometimes get snared in the self-defeating lingo of disrespect for Indian people that they find around them, they can stand up to it as well. In "Fallen Leaves" (1927), Hartshorne recalls how she has "heard the white sages" say that her people have lost "their hour / Of dominion," that their "brief time of blooming" has "shattered; / Like the leaves of the oak tree its people are scattered." But she observes, lyrically, that leaves have a rhythm, that they come and go as the seasons change. In effect, she agrees with Montezuma that changing is not vanishing. In that light, like so many of these poets, both those who expect Indian people to vanish and those who expect better things, Hartshorne risks predicting the future. In the "leaves, soon to be crumpled and broken," she also sees "the gradual unfolding / Of brilliance and strength."

Poetry and Indian Identity: Indian Poetry as a Category

Critics of poetry have often struggled to understand the relation between poetry and national or racial identity. But there is no one-size-fits-all answer. Traditionally, following the model of Virgil's *Aeneid*, epic poetry in the European tradition set out to establish stories that built and authorized the nation, national identity, and national pride. More recently, in the Black Arts Movement of the late 1960s and early 1970s, African American writers tried to find or invent a specifically Black Aesthetic that could represent the transhistorical ethos—or even just the immediate needs—of African Americans or, yet more ambitiously, of Blacks across Africa and the Black diaspora. Contemporary critics of Indian literature sometimes make claims about Indian writing at large or, more modestly, yearn for ways of reading that pay particular heed to the specific histories and needs of individual Indian nations. In a broader cultural and legal setting that threatens the sovereignty of Indian peoples, it seems sensible that, directly and indirectly, Indian writing might rise in defense of sovereignty and nationality. The combination of a vulnerable position and a proud history encourages Indian peoples to see their own sovereignty as a lever to uphold their past and shape their future. At the same time, many critics look at race and nationality with suspicion. They fear that generalizations about any one race carry less force as reliable descriptions than as ways of pressuring the diverse members of a race to conform to someone's idea, well intentioned or not, of what they should be. They fear that nationalism becomes not only a way of trying to be one identity but also a way of suppressing or combating other identities within the same people.

Yet, in a partly postcolonial age, it can seem as if the nation only comes under suspicion once the world beyond the colonial powers gets access to it. And it can seem that race comes under suspicion only after the calls from historically less powerful races for their piece of the pie reach a point where the more powerful can no longer refuse to listen. In these still shifting contexts, what does it mean to propose a category such as "Indian poetry"? While some might suppose that we would do better to read poetry with no concern for who wrote it, that argument is moot, because—apart from the occasional brief experiment with calculated ignorance—it is impossible to read poetry without regard for who wrote it. Who did the writing influences what we read and how we read. It also influences what literary history chooses, in effect, not to read. Thus far, such little awareness as there has been of the category of Indian poetry has, for these early poems, done less to call attention to them than it has to erase them from literary history. To recover these poems and thus to have the chance to read Indian poetry in the first place, it has been necessary to think of these works as Indian poetry. As I hope that this introduction can show, that does not mean that Indian poetry is any one specific thing. On the other hand, it can mean that Indian poetry often disperses across particular and identifiable patterns, including the patterns discussed here.

But thankfully, readers will not find the ideas in this introduction the end of the story. Instead, this introduction and the poems that follow it can invite readers, not least Indian readers, to continue the discussion of early Indian poetry, to find more of it than I have found here, and to take it in directions that this introduction does not anticipate. As the poems in this volume often try to predict the future of Indian people, they register a sense of pressure to predict that future. Such pressure to predict implies a sense that Indian futures are in doubt. When Indian people are subjected to intense pressures to assimilate, the need and desire to wonder about the future threaten to bring despair but also offer the possibility of hope. As we look back over the history of early Indian poetry and how close we came to losing it, and as we now have the chance to begin a discussion that may take readers of Indian poetry into many and previously unimagined directions, perhaps that precarious exchange of despair for hope can guide us as we ponder the many ways that changing is not vanishing.

Note on Procedures

Readers may ask how, in choosing poetry by American Indians, I determined who is an Indian. Sometimes, the question of who is an Indian is dauntingly intricate, but it has not proved so intricate for the purposes of this book. For the present purposes, an Indian is someone recognized by other Indians as Indian. Most of the poets in this book were very much involved in specific Indian communities. Understanding Indianness as cultural rather than biological, I do not distinguish between those who supposedly were so-called pure or full bloods and those who were so-called mixed bloods. In that way this volume varies from traditional practice while joining what is arguably an emerging practice. I have not included poems that appeared in more or less Indian newspapers and magazines with no indication that the writer was Indian. Indian-edited and Indian-focused newspapers and magazines routinely published poetry by non-Indians. Though sometimes scholars or antiquarians presume that the writers of such poems were Indian, in many cases they demonstrably were not Indian. When a writer was Indian, the newspaper or magazine usually said so.

That nevertheless leaves several uncertain cases of writers who had conspicuously Indian names and published in Indian journals. When I have included such writers (Blue Feather, Broken Wing Bird, and Sunhair), I have acknowledged the uncertainty. It is possible that they were non-Indian "friends of the Indian" who took on Indian-sounding names.

In choosing the poems, I ruled out choosing songs, including hymns. Songs are sometimes seen as poetry. While I have no objection to seeing songs as poems, there remains a difference between texts composed primarily for the reading eye and texts composed in melody and primarily for the listening ear, often composed orally rather than through writing. Indian songs from these years are already widely available, and the conflation of Indian songs with poetry has tended, like the phony Indian poetry, to push out Indian poems that are not songs, contributing to the sense that there was no Indian poetry (in the narrower sense of the term poetry). Readers who want to find songs will have no trouble finding them. But until this volume, readers who want to find the poetry have had nowhere to go. (Nevertheless, some poems, following common practice, have words like "song" or "lullaby" in the title, and that has not kept them out of this volume, depending on whether they present themselves primarily as poetry or primarily as music. If they present themselves primarily as poetry, I have considered them for this volume.)

I have not found any surviving poems between Eleazar's elegy of 1678 and the earliest dated poems of Jane Schoolcraft, which come from 1815 (though the earliest Schoolcraft poem included in this volume comes from 1820). I hope that the gap between 1678 and 1815 can represent the poems we have lost from those years and encourage readers to find some of those poems and to learn about the Indian people who wrote them. If Benjamin Larnell, as Harvard president John Leverett believed, was writing "extraordinary" poems before he died in 1714, then perhaps Larnell's work and the work of others whom he might represent can still be recovered or, at least, remembered.

The poets are arranged in rough chronological sequence (apart from the separate set of school poems), according to when the individual poets "flourished" in their work or career as a poet. For each poet, the poems appear in the sequence of their publication, or when they were not published in their own time, then in the sequence of their composition, so far as the dates of composition are known. Except where explained otherwise, dates after the poems are the date of first publication and are followed, where applicable, by the dates of revised versions. Sources for the poems are listed in the bibliography. When a head note provides little or no information about a poet, that indicates that little, or nothing, or nothing of relevance is known. The head notes also identify distinguished relatives of the poets, though that can have the effect of favoring male relatives, who tended to have more opportunity for public distinction or more opportunity for their public distinction to be recorded. The names of Indian nations and peoples often present a challenge, as there are often different terms and spellings for more or less the same people. When in doubt, I have followed the terms used by the poet, while otherwise generally following more familiar or more favored spellings from our own time and, where helpful, providing alternative names as well. For readers unfamiliar with the names of Indian peoples and their variations, it may help to say here that the increasingly favored term Mvskoge or Muscogee (and similar spellings of the same word) refers to the same people as the term Creek. Similarly, the increasingly favored term Anishinaabe refers to the same people (at least for the purposes of this book) as Ojibwe and Chippewa (and similar spellings of the same words). And the term Odawa is increasingly favored over the term Ottawa. The variety of terms for the same people can lead to confusion, but consistency would also lead to confusion, and at least the inconsistency helps tell the story of variation and change.

Many of the writers in this book also had more than one name. Some used their name in English and their name in a Native language, and some also went by a translation of their Native name into English. While I have some concern that using the Native names can play into the exoticism that shapes some people's perception of American Indians, I also believe that we need to get past that sense of exoticism and recognize the routine of American Indian languages. Therefore, I have used the names the writers themselves usually used for their writing or at least for their poetry or their public persona. Sometimes, as a way of acknowledging a writer's inconsistency on this matter and taking seriously what that inconsistency may represent, I have used more than one name for the same writer.

Notes

1. On the prevalence of newspaper poetry, see Paula Bernat Bennett, ed., *Nineteenth-Century American Women Poets*, as well as Bennett, *Poets in the Public Sphere.* Since newspapers often published poems anonymously, some newspaper poems written by Indian people will probably never be identified as written by Indians. On Cherokee literature, see especially Daniel Heath Justice. That even Justice's excellent history of Cherokee literature, *Our Fire Survives the Storm.* does not address the large body of Cherokee poetry shows how little knowledge there has been of the history of American Indian poetry, even among well-informed scholars. (Justice discusses Riggs, but for his plays, not his poetry.)
2. I owe this observation about Schoolcraft's syntax to Margaret Noori, who teaches Anishinaabe language and literature at the University of Michigan, and to John Nichols, who teaches Anishinaabe language and literature at the University of Minnesota.
3. For a reading of Riggs's plays and life as closeting his gay desire, see Craig S. Womack, *Red on Red*, 271–303.
4. Amelia V. Katanski describes how the Carlisle Indian School used its printing press to discipline the thinking of Indian students (chaps. 2–3). (Katanski does not discuss the poems by Indian students included in Carlisle publications.)
5. On anticolonial mimicry, see the classic discussion by Homi K. Bhabha, and on Bhabha's view of mimicry, see Parker, *How to Interpret Literature*, 253–55.
6. For a discussion of this stereotype in Indian writing, see Parker, *The Invention of Native American Literature.*
7. One vexed issue requires special notice. Namely, some of the poems use the word "squaw," which many readers in later times see as derogatory, often as extremely derogatory. While the word's origins—despite widespread misinformation to the contrary—are probably not derogatory, and recent years have seen considerable debate over the word's history, there is no doubt that it is often used in derogatory ways. Nevertheless, the poets in this book do not intend it as derogatory.
8. I await with interest work in progress about Ann Plato by Ron Welburn. Plato, an African American writer who was born about 1820 and lived in Hartford, Connecticut, published a book of essays and poems in 1841. Based on extensive historical research, Welburn argues that Plato was Indian as well as African American. In Plato's poem "The Natives of America," the speaker's father recounts the history of his Indian ancestors (Plato, 110–12). If Plato herself is the speaker, then the poem indicates that she was Indian as well as African American.

POEMS

Eleazar

Eleazar was a senior at Harvard College in 1678. As there is no record of him graduating, he may have died before he could graduate. The influential Boston minister Cotton Mather published Eleazar's only surviving poem in Mather's most famous book, *Magnalia Christi Americana* (1702). After a short biography of Thomas Thacher, a Puritan minister known for his medical knowledge and skill in languages, Mather introduced Eleazar's poem in the following words: "And because the Nation and Quality of the *Author*, will make the Composure to become a Curiosity, I will here, for an *Epitaph*, insert an Elegy, which was composed upon this Occasion [Thacher's death], by an *Indian Youth*, who was then a Student of *Harvard* Colledge. (His Name was, *Eleazar*)."

As Mather graduated from Harvard in 1678, he would have known Eleazar. But we have no information about Eleazar beyond what we can find in Mather's brief comment and Eleazar's one surviving poem, written in Latin and Greek. (One scholar says that Eleazar studied with Thacher and then died from disease while still a student, but those must be suppositions, for no source is cited; Peyer, *Tutor'd Mind* 50). For more about the early Indian students at Harvard, see the introduction to this volume.

Assessments of Eleazar's poem have varied. An anonymous contributor to the *Boston Monthly Magazine* of 1825 wrote that Eleazar's elegy, "if not of pure latinity, is quite as good as can be produced at the present day by the commonality of students of Eleazer's [sic] standing" (Anonymous, "The aborigines" 244). The same writer then added: "The Latin is by no means a specimen of refined classical composition, though free from inaccuracy in the metre. It serves, however, to demonstrate the progress in classical learning, of which the aboriginal inhabitants are capable" (247). One later scholar calls the poem "undistinguished" (Rosenwald 307), while another says that Eleazar's "elegy is very well composed, with proper restraint, good taste, and a well ordered sequence of images and ideas" (Jantz 98).

The English translation of Eleazar's poem provided here was prepared for this volume by Ann Hubert and the editor. For more information, see the Textual Notes.

In obitum Viri verè Reverendi D. Thomae Thacheri, Qui Ad Dom. ex hâc Vitâ migravit, 18.8.1678

Tentabo Illustrem, tristi memorare dolore,
  Quem Lacrymis repetunt Tempora, nostra, Virum.
Memnona sic Mater, Mater ploravit Achillem,
  Justis cum Lacrymis, cumque Dolore gravi.
Mens stupet, ora silent, justum nunc palma recusat
  Officium: Quid? Opem Tristis Apollo negat?
Ast *Thachere* Tuus conabor dicere laudes
  Laudes Virtutis, quae super Astra volat.
Consultis Rerum Dominis, Gentique togatae
  Nota fuit virtus, ac tua Sancta Fides. 10

Vivis post Funus; Faelix post Fata; *Jaces Tu*?
Sed *Stellas* inter *Gloria* nempe *Jaces.*
Mens Tua jam caelos repetit; Victoria parta est:
Iam Tuus est Christus, quod meruitque tuum,
Hic Finis Crucis; magnorum haec meta malorum;
Ulterius non quo progrediatur erit.
Crux jam cassa manes; requiescunt ossa Sepulchro;
Mors moritur; Vitae Vita Beata redit.
Quum tuba per Densas sonitum dabit ultima Nubes,
Cum Domino Rediens Ferrea Sceptra geres. 20
Caelos tum scandes, ubi Patria Vero piorum;
Praevius hanc patriam nunc tibi *Jesus* adit.
Illic vera Quies; illic sine fine voluptas;
Gaudia & Humanis non referenda sonis.

Σῶμ᾽ἔχει ἡ κόνις, ἐπί γῆς τ᾽ὄνομ᾽οὔποτ᾽ὀλεῖται,
Κλεινὸν ἐν ἡμετέροις κ᾽ἐσομενοῖσι χρόνοις
Ψυχὴ δ᾽ἐκ ῥεθέων πταμένη, βῆ οὔρανον αἰπύν,
Μιχθεῖσ᾽ἀθάνατος πνεύμασιν ἀθανάτοις.

[written 1678, published 1702]

At the bottom of the poem appear the words "*Eleazar*, Iudus Senior Sophista." *Iudus* is presumably a typographical error for *Indus*, and *Senior Sophista* means that Eleazar was in his fourth year of study at the college, what today is called a senior. (The term leads to confusion because at Cambridge University it meant the third year of study.) 3 ***Memnona* sic Mater, Mater ploravit Achillem:** Kaiser ("Thirteen" 359) notes a source for this line in Ovid: "Memnona si mater, mater ploravit Achillem" (*Amores* 3.9.1). 7 **Tuus:** while we might wonder if *Tuus* is Eleazar's or the typesetter's error for *Tuas*, *Tuus* fits a pattern of personalizing figurative language that includes *Gloria* in line 12 and *Crux* in line 17. Such a pattern argues against the possible emendations of *Tuus* to *Tuas* and of *manes* to *manet*, especially because the meter requires that *Gloria* is in the nominative and not in the ablative case. Thus the present translation reads "as yours . . . sing praises" instead of "sing your praises" (line 7), "as glory" instead of "in glory" (line 12), and "You, cross" instead of "The cross" (line 17). 11 **Vivit post Funus:** Kaiser notes that this line plays off "the common Latin sentiment 'Vivit post funera virtus,' an adaptation of Euripedes, *Fragment* 734" ("Thirteen" 359).

ENGLISH TRANSLATION

On the death of that truly venerable man D. Thomas Thacher, who moved on to the Lord from this life, 18 of August, 1678

I will attempt to remember with sorrowful grief that illustrious
Man whom our times recall with tears.
So a mother wept over Memnon, so a mother wept over Achilles,
With righteous tears, and with weighty grief.
The mind is senseless, the mouth is silent, now the hand refuses this just
Office: Why? Does sad Apollo deny help?

In obitum Viri verè Reverendi

D. THOMÆ THACHERI,

QUI AD

Dom. ex hâc Vitâ migravit, 18. 8. 1678.

Tentabo Illuſtrem, triſti memorare dolore,
Quem Lacrymis repetunt Tempora, noſtra; Virum.
Memnona *ſic Mater, Mater ploravit Achillem,*
Juſtis cum Lacrymis, cumque Dolore gravi.
Mens ſtupet; ora ſilent, juſtum nunc palmo recuſat
Officium : Quid? Opem Triſtis Apollo negat?
Aſt Thachere *Tuus conabor dicere laudes,*
Laudes Virtutis, quæ ſuper Aſtra volat.
Conſultis Rerum Dominis, Gentiquæ togatæ
Nota fuit virtus, ac tua Sancta Fides.
Vivis poſt Funus; Fælix poſt Fata; Jaces Tu?
Sed Stellas *inter* Gloria *nempe* Jaces.
Mens Tua jam cælos repetit; Victoria parta eſt:
Jam Tuus eſt Chriſtus, quod meruitque tuum.
Hic Finis Crucis; magnorum hæc meta malorum;
Ulterius non quo progrediatur erit.
Crux jam caſſa manes; requieſcunt oſſa Sepulchro;
Mors moritur; Vitæ Vita Beata redit.
Quum tuba per Denſas ſonitum dabit ultima Nubes,
Cum Domino Rediens Ferrea Sceptra geres.
Cæles tum ſcandes, ubi Patria Vera piorum;
Prævius hanc Patriam nunc tibi Jeſus *adit.*
Illic vera Quies; illic ſine fine voluptas;
Gaudia & Humanis non referenda ſonis.

Σῶμ' ἔχει ἡ κονίν, ἀπὶ γῆς τ' ὄνομ' οὔποτ' ὀλεῖται,
Κλεινὸν ἐν ἡμετέροις κ' ἐσσομένοισι χρόνοις·
Ψυχὴ δ' ἐκ ῥεθέων πταμένη, βῆ οὐρανὸν αἰπύν,
Μιχθεῖσ' ἀθάνατος πνεύμασιν ἀθανάτοις.

Eleazar, Judus Senior Sophiſta

Figure 2. Eleazar's elegy for Thomas Thacher, 1678, as it appeared in Cotton Mather, *Magnalia Christi Americana*, Book 3 (London: Thomas Parkhurst, 1702).

But Thacher I, as yours, will try to sing praises,
Praises of virtue, which fly beyond the stars.
To the masters learned in subjects, and to the esteemed ministers
Your virtue was well known, as was your holy faith. 10
Lively after the funeral; happy after death; do you rest?
But you, as glory, truly rest among the stars.
Your soul already returns to the heavens; victory was prepared:
Now Christ is yours, and yours what he merited,
This is the limit of his torment; this is the end of his great hardships;
It will not be further from where he may proceed.
You, cross, now remain empty; the bones rest in the grave;
Death dies: blessed life returns to life.
When the last trumpet will give its sound through the thick clouds,
Returning, you carry iron scepters with the Lord. 20
Then you will climb heavenward, where the home of the truly pious is;
Leading the way to this homeland, Jesus now approaches you.
There is true rest, there is delight without limit.
Joys also not to be repeated by human song.

Dust holds the body, upon earth the name will never perish,
Famous in our times and those to come;
And the soul, flying from the limbs, went to high heaven,
Undying, having been mixed with spirits immortal.

3 **Memnon:** Ethiopian king killed by Achilles in the Trojan War. Memnon's mother Eos, goddess of the dawn, wept for him every morning. 3 **Achilles:** nearly invincible Greek hero in the Trojan War. 6 **Apollo:** Greek god associated with medicine and healing as well as music and poetry. 9 **esteemed ministers:** This phrase offers a guess at how to translate an expression that, translated literally, means *people who wore a toga.* 14 **what he merited:** salvation (as Kaiser notes, "Thirteen" 360). 20 **iron scepters:** figurative, meaning firm authority.

Jane Johnston Schoolcraft, Ojibwe, 1800–1842

Jane Johnston Schoolcraft (her English name) or Bamewawagezhikaquay (her Ojibwe name), Woman of the Sound the Stars Make Rushing Through the Sky, was born in Sault Ste. Marie in what is now the state of Michigan. Schoolcraft's mother, Ozhaguscodaywayquay or Susan Johnston, was a prominent leader and trader and the daughter of Waubojeeg, a war chief famed for leadership in war and civil life as well as for eloquence in story and song. Schoolcraft's father, John Johnston, came from a prominent Scotch-Irish family in the north of Ireland. He left for the United States and Canada in 1790 and set out as a fur trader. After their marriage, Ozhaguscodaywayquay and John Johnston settled in Sault Ste. Marie, where they built a prosperous fur trade business. John Johnston fought with the British in the War of 1812. Apart from visits to Mackinac Island and a trip in 1809–1810 to Ireland and England, Jane Johnston grew up in a world where the only English speakers were her father, her siblings, and the occasional passing fur trader, and where the only other white people were French-speaking men. But her father was a book lover, and she received an extensive English education from his library. She spoke Ojibwe and English in her daily life and raised her children in Ojibwe.

In 1822, federal troops arrived at Sault Ste. Marie with a federal Indian agent, Henry Rowe Schoolcraft. In 1823, Jane and Henry married. Henry wrote and published widely in many fields. Drawing on the knowledge of the Johnston family and his experience as Indian agent, he won fame for his writings about American Indians, especially the Ojibwe. Jane, however, did not publish her own writings, though some of them appeared in a handwritten magazine from 1826–1827 which Henry circulated among friends and which was published in 1962 (Mason). He also drew on her writings for his own publications and published a few of her writings after she died. A full compilation of her writings, based on the surviving manuscripts and with a biography and cultural history, appeared as *The Sound the Stars Make Rushing Through the Sky: The Writings of Jane Johnston Schoolcraft* (2007). It is the source for the poems included here. Readers can find more information about Schoolcraft's other writings in *The Sound the Stars Make*, including poems dated as early as 1815 as well as stories and Schoolcraft's translations of songs from Ojibwe into English. The manuscripts that provide the sources for most of the poems included here sometimes survive in Schoolcraft's own handwriting and sometimes in her husband's copies. He may have tinkered with some of the poems when he copied them, perhaps sometimes with and sometimes without her direction or permission, but she seems to have welcomed his suggestions about her manuscripts.

Schoolcraft's central role in the history of American poetry extends beyond her own poetry, because her stories, as they appeared in Henry Schoolcraft's publications, became a key source for Henry Wadsworth Longfellow's sensational bestseller *The Song of Hiawatha.* Schoolcraft was the first known American Indian literary writer (unless we consider Eleazar), the first known Indian woman writer, and the first known Indian poet (again apart from the Harvard-student Indian poets, whose work has not survived beyond the poem by Eleazar in this volume). She was, as well, the first known American Indian to write out traditional Indian stories and the first known poet to write poems in an American Indian language.

Pensive Hours

The sun had sunk like a glowing ball,
As lonely I sat in my father's hall;
I walk'd to the window, and musing awhile,
The still, pensive moments I sought to beguile:
Just by me, ran smoothly the dark deep stream,
And bright silver rays on its breast did beam;—
And as with mild luster the vestal orb rose,
All nature betokened a holy repose,
Save the Sound of St. Mary's—that softly and clear
Still fell in sweet murmurs upon my pleas'd ear 10
Like the murmur of voices we know to be kind,
Or war's silken banners unfurled to the wind,

Now rising, like shouts of the proud daring foe,
Now falling, like whispers congenial and low.
Amidst such a scene, thoughts arose in my mind;
Of my father, far distant—of life, and mankind;
But slowing, receding—with awe most profound
They rested on God, and his works spread around,
Divine meditation!—and tear drops like dew—
Now moisten'd my hand,—for His mercy I knew: 20
Since even a leaf cannot wither and die,
Unknown to his care, or unseen by his eye;
Oh how much more then, will he hear when we mourn,
And heal the pierced heart that by anguish is torn,
When he sees that the soul to His will loves to bend,
And patiently suffers and waits to the end.
Such thoughts—the lone moments serenely employed,
Creating contentment and peace unalloyed—
Till roused by my harp—which so tremblingly true,
The soft balmy night breeze enchantingly blew, 30
The sounds to my heart as they vibrated clear,
Thrill'd sweetly and carried the melody tried,
Softer and sweeter the harmony rings,
I fanceyed some spirit was touching the strings,
And answered, or seemed to my hopes, thus to say,
Let thy Soul live in hope, mortal:—watch still and pray.
A holy tranquility spread o'er my mind.
At peace with myself, with my God, and mankind.
I felt that my prayers were heard and approv'd,
For the speedy return of my father beloved; 40
For the health I so priz'd, but so seldom enjoyed.
That the time yet in store—should be wisely employed.
And my mind ever feel, as I felt at that time,
So pensively joyful, so humbly sublime.—

[written 1820, published 1962]

7 **vestal orb**: Alluding to the vestal virgins of ancient Rome, "vestal" was a typical poetic term for a chaste woman. 9 **St. Mary's**: the St. Mary's River at Sault Ste. Marie. 12–14: This description probably draws on Schoolcraft's memory of the War of 1812 at Fort Mackinac, though it could also draw on a fabled moment of crisis at Sault Ste. Marie in 1820, when war almost broke out after Sassaba, a pro-British, anti-American chief, raised a British flag in defiance of Lewis Cass's expedition, which had come to assert federal authority and demand a treaty. The outnumbered Cass marched unarmed into the Ojibwe town and trampled on the British flag. Schoolcraft's mother Ozhaguscodaywayquay and brother George then averted war by convincing the local Ojibwe leaders to agree to Cass's treaty. 29 **harp**: An aeolian harp, named for Aeolus, the Greek god of the winds, is a box with gut strings placed in a window and tuned to produce harmony when the wind blows, like a wind chime. It was a popular metaphor of poetic inspiration for Romantic poets, and there is evidence that the Johnstons kept an aeolian harp in their window.

The Contrast

With pen in hand, I shall contrast,
The present moments with the past
And mark difference, not by grains,
But weighed by feelings, joys and pains.
Calm, tranquil—far from fashion's gaze,
Passed all my earliest, happy days
Sweetly flew the golden hours,
In St. Mary's woodland bowers
Or my father's simple hall,
Oped to whomsoe'er might call 10
Pains or cares we seldom knew
All the hours so peaceful flew
Concerts sweet we oft enjoyed,
Books our leisure time employed
Friends on every side appeared
From whose minds no ill I feared
If by chance, one gave me pain
The wish to wound me not again
Quick expressed in accents kind
Cast a joy throughout my mind 20
That, to have been a moment pained,
Seemed like bliss but just attained.
Whene'er in fault, to be reproved,
With gratitude my heart was moved,
So mild and gentle were their words
It seemed as soft as song of birds
For well I knew, that each behest,
Was warmed by love—convincing test.

Thus passed the morning of my days,
My only wish, to gain the praise 30
Of friends I loved, and neighbours kind,
And keep a calm and heavenly mind.
My efforts, kindly were received,
Nor grieved, nor was myself aggrieved.
But ah! how changed is every scene,
Our little hamlet, and the green,
The long rich green, where warriors played,
And often, breezy elm-wood shade.
How changed, since full of strife and fear,
The world hath sent its votaries here. 40
The tree cut down—the cot removed,
The cot the simple Indian loved,

The busy strife of young and old
To gain one sordid bit of gold
By trade's o'er done plethoric moil,
And lawsuits, meetings, courts and toil.

Adieu, to days of homebred ease,
When many a rural care could please,
We trim our sail anew, to steer
By shoals we never knew were here, 50
And with the star flag, raised on high
Discover a new dominion nigh,
And half in joy, half in fear,
Welcome the proud Republic here.

[written 1823 and possibly later, published 2007]

41 cot: cottage. **51 star flag:** Each morning, Army troops raised the U.S. flag at Fort Brady near the Johnston house. **54 proud Republic:** Schoolcraft's husband Henry Rowe Schoolcraft came to Sault Ste. Marie as the official representative of the U.S. republic, thus leading to a conflict between Jane Johnston Schoolcraft's loyalties to the old and her loyalties to the new. For an earlier version of this poem, which does not mention the new republic, see Schoolcraft, *The Sound the Stars Make Rushing Through the Sky.*

Invocation

To my Maternal Grand-father on hearing his descent
from Chippewa ancestors misrepresented

Rise bravest chief! of the mark of the noble deer,
With eagle glance,
Resume thy lance,
And wield again thy warlike spear!
The foes of thy line,
With coward design,
Have dared with black envy to garble the truth,
And stain with a falsehood thy valorous youth.

They say when a child, thou wert ta'en from the Sioux,
And with impotent aim, 10
To lessen thy fame
Thy warlike lineage basely abuse;
For they know that our band,
Tread a far distant land,
And thou noble chieftain art nerveless and dead,
Thy bow all unstrung, and thy proud spirit fled.

Can the sports of thy youth, or thy deeds ever fade?
Or those e'er forget,
Who are mortal men yet,
The scenes where so bravely thou'st lifted the blade, 20
Who have fought by thy side,
And remember thy pride,
When rushing to battle, with valour and ire,
Thou saw'st the fell foes of thy nation expire?

Can the warrior forget how sublimely you rose?
Like a star in the west,
When the sun's sunk to rest,
That shines in bright splendour to dazzle our foes?
Thy arm and thy yell,
Once the tale could repel 30
Which slander invented, and minions detail,
And still shall thy actions refute the false tale.

Rest thou, noblest chief! in thy dark house of clay,
Thy deeds and thy name,
Thy child's child shall proclaim,
And make the dark forests resound with the lay;
Though thy spirit has fled,
To the hills of the dead,
Yet thy name shall be held in my heart's warmest core,
And cherish'd till valour and love be no more. 40

[written 1823, published 1860]

Title: Schoolcraft resents the rumor that her grandfather, the famed Ojibwe war chief Waubojeeg, was Sioux and not Ojibwe (not Chippewa). Waubojeeg had two Sioux half-brothers. 1 **mark of the noble deer:** Waubojeeg's totem, or clan, was the reindeer.

To the Pine Tree

on first seeing it
on returning from Europe

Shing wauk! Shing wauk! nin ge ik id,
Waish kee wau bum ug, shing wauk
Tuh quish in aun nau aub, ain dak nuk i yaun.
Shing wauk, shing wauk No sa
Lhi e gwuh ke do dis au naun
Kau gega way zhau wus co zid.

Mes ah nah, shi egwuh tah gwish en aung
Sin da mik ke aum baun
Kag ait suh, ne meen wain dum
Me nah wau, wau bun dah maun 10
Gi yut wi au, wau bun dah maun een
Shing wauk, shing wauk nosa
Shi e gwuh ke do dis an naun.

Ka ween ga go, kau wau bun duh e yun
Tib isht co, izz henau gooz ze no an
Shing wauk wah zhau wush co zid
Ween Ait ah kwanaudj e we we
Kau ge gay wa zhau soush ko zid

TRANSLATION

The pine! the pine! I eager cried,
The pine, my father! see it stand,
As first that cherished tree I spied,
Returning to my native land.
The pine! the pine! oh lovely scene!
The pine, that is forever green.

Ah beauteous tree! ah happy sight!
That greets me on my native strand
And hails me, with a friend's delight,
To my own dear bright mother land 10
Oh 'tis to me a heart-sweet scene,
The pine—the pine! that's ever green.

Not all the trees of England bright,
Not Erin's lawns of green and light
Are half so sweet to memory's eye,
As this dear type of northern sky
Oh 'tis to me a heart-sweet scene,
The pine—the pine! that ever green.

[2007]

In his "Notes for a Memoir of Mrs. Henry Rowe Schoolcraft," addressed to Anna Jameson, a renowned writer who befriended Jane Schoolcraft and later Elizabeth Barrett Browning and Robert Browning, Henry Rowe Schoolcraft tells the story behind this poem. When Jane Johnston returned from Europe as a child in 1810, "On the home route from Quebec to St. Mary's, her father was impressed with the pleasure she appeared to derive from the scenery of her native country (always a strong point of admiration with her) but when, in crossing the Niagara ridge, in the route from Queenston to Fort Erie, she saw the pine, she could not resist the expression of impassioned admiration. 'There pa! see those pines!' she exclaimed, 'after all I have seen abroad, you have nothing equal to the dear pine.' At a later period, I asked her if she could not recal[l] her feelings at the moment, on which [s]he gave me some lines in the Indian language, of which, you [Jameson] will find a translation appended" (96–97).

Ojibwe text, 1 Shing wauk!: Though it might not matter for this poem, Shingwauk, The Pine (also called Shingwaukonse, Little Pine), was the name of a prominent and eventually revered Ojibwe chief on the Canadian side of Sault Ste. Marie, well known to the Johnstons and Schoolcrafts. On Shingwauk, see especially Janet E. Chute, *Legacy*, and Chute, "Shingwaukonse," including p. 93 for his connection to the Johnston family.

By an *Ojibwa Female* Pen

Invitation to sisters to a walk in the Garden, after a shower

Come, sisters come! the shower's past,
The garden walks are drying fast,
The Sun's bright beams are seen again,
And nought within, can now detain.
The rain drops tremble on the leaves,
Or drip expiring, from the eaves;
But soon the cool and balmy air,
Shall dry the gems that sparkle there,
With whisp'ring breath shake ev'ry spray,
And scatter every cloud away. 10

Thus sisters! shall the breeze of hope,
Through sorrow's clouds a vista ope;
Thus, shall affliction's surly blast,
By faith's bright calm be still'd at last;
Thus, pain and care,—the tear and sigh,
Be chased from every dewy eye;
And life's mix'd scene itself, but cease,
To show us realms of light and peace.

[written by 1826, published 1962]

Lines to a Friend Asleep

Awake my friend! the morning's fine,
Waste not in sleep the day divine;
Nature is clad in best array,
The woods, the fields, the flowers are gay;—
The sun is up, and speeds his march,
O'er heaven's high aërial arch,
His golden beams with lustre fall,
On lake and river, cot and hall;—
The dews are sparkling on each spray,
The birds are chirping sweet and gay, 10

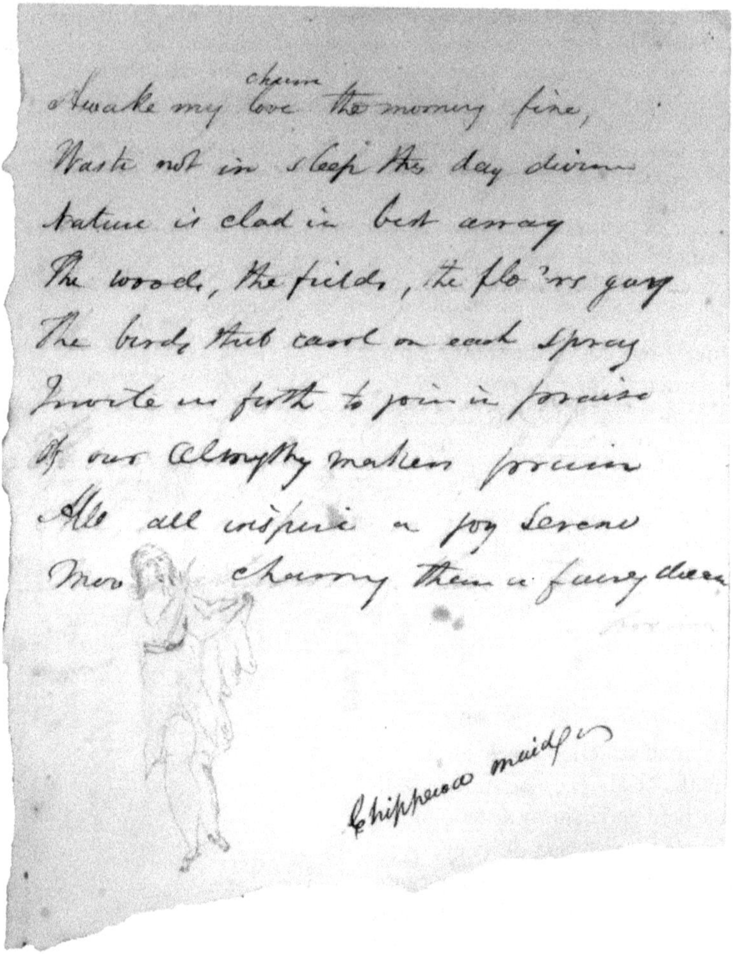

Figure 3. Manuscript of an early draft of Jane Johnston Schoolcraft's "Lines to a Friend Asleep," including a sketch of a dancing "Chippewa maiden." Henry Rowe Schoolcraft Papers, Manuscript Division, Library of Congress, Washington, D.C.

The violet shows its beauteous head,
Within its narrow, figured bed;—
The air is pure, the earth bedight,
With trees and flowers, life and light,
All—all inspires a joyful gleam,
More pleasing than a fairy dream.
Awake! the sweet refreshing scene,
Invites us forth to tread the green,

With joyful hearts, and pious lays,
To join the glorious Maker's praise, 20
The wond'rous works—the paschal lamb,
The holy, high, and just I Am.

[written by 1827, published 1962]

21 paschal: The paschal (Passover) lamb, sacrificed in the Jewish Passover, is often a figure for the sacrificed Jesus, the "Lamb of God" (John 1:29).

To my ever beloved and lamented Son William Henry

Who was it, nestled on my breast,
"And on my cheek sweet kisses prest"
And in whose smile I felt so blest?
Sweet Willy.
Who hail'd my form as home I stept,
And in my arms so eager leapt,
And to my bosom joyous crept?
My Willy.
Who was it, wiped my tearful eye,
And kiss'd away the coming sigh, 10
And smiling bid me say "good boy"?
Sweet Willy.
Who was it, looked divinely fair,
Whilst lisping sweet the evening pray'r,
Guileless and free from earthly care?
My Willy.
Where is that voice attuned to love,
That bid me say "my darling dove"?
But oh! that soul has flown above,
Sweet Willy. 20
Whither has fled the rose's hue?
The lilly's whiteness blending grew,
Upon thy cheek—so fair to view.
My Willy.
Oft have I gaz'd with rapt delight,
Upon those eyes that sparkled bright,
Emitting beams of joy and light!
Sweet Willy.
Oft have I kiss'd that forehead high,
Like polished marble to the eye, 30
And blessing, breathed an anxious sigh.
For Willy.

My son! thy coral lips are pale,
Can I believe the heart-sick tale,
That I, thy loss must ever wail?
My Willy.
The clouds in darkness seemed to low'r,
The storm has past with awful pow'r,
And nipt my tender, beauteous flow'r!
Sweet Willy. 40
But soon my spirit will be free,
And I, my lovely Son shall see,
For God, I know, did this decree!
My Willy.

[written 1827, published 1962]

Title: After a sudden, brief illness, William Henry Schoolcraft died of croup in March 1827 at the age of two years and eight months. Another of Schoolcraft's poems in memory of William Henry, "Sweet Willy," appears below. Seven manuscripts of "To my ever beloved" have survived, and the large number suggests that it played a special role in Schoolcraft's emotions and perhaps in her pride as a poet. The form closely follows the form of Ann Taylor's (1782–1866) once-famous "My Mother" (1804), where the refrain is "My mother" rather than "My Willy." In Taylor's poem, a child addresses its mother, whereas in Schoolcraft's poem, a mother addresses her child. **2**: This line quotes line 3 of Taylor's poem word for word.

To the Miscodeed*

Sweet pink of northern wood and glen,
E'er first to greet the eyes of men
In early spring,—a tender flower
Whilst still the wintry wind hath power.
How welcome, in the sunny glade,
Or hazel copse, thy pretty head
Oft peeping out, whilst still the snow,
Doth here and there, its presence show
Soon leaf and bud quick opening spread
Thy modest petals—white with red 10
Like some sweet cherub—love's kind link,
With dress of white, adorned with pink.

*The C. Virginica.

[2007]

Title: One of the first spring wildflowers, the miscodeed (in Ojibwe; *Claytonia virginica* in Latin), or spring beauty is typically white with pink veins, though sometimes it is all pink. See also Schoolcraft's "Origin of the Miscodeed or the Maid of Taquimenon" (Schoolcraft, *The Sound the Stars Make* 181–83). **11 love's**: the cherubic Cupid, the god of love, often referred to simply as "love."

On Meditation

Sweet meditation now be mine—
The sun has sunk—the stars do shine.
Beautifully the moon doth beam;
Its rays rest on the dark deep stream.
The warblers sweet have ceased to raise,
Their customary songs of praise.
The hum of mortals dies away;
And business ends with closing day.
Mild, calm and peaceful is the scene
My soul's disposed to be serene. 10
Come then soft maid, my faithful friend!
And gently teach me to attend,
With list'ning ear, and open heart,
To truths you always do impart.
Teach me to know when reason's voice,
Disproves my acts—or says rejoice—
Teach me to bend to virtue's sway,
And make me better every day.
Then He who makes the sky above
On me, will sure display his love; 20
While I, each duty do fulfil,
And bow submissive to his will.
Then sweet content shall crown each year,
And nought on earth shall make me fear.

[2007]

Sweet Willy

A hundred moons and more have past,
Since erst upon this day,
They bore thee from my anguished sight,
And from my home away
And pensively they carried thee
And set the burial stone,
And left thy father and myself,
Forsaken and alone.
A hundred moons and more have past
And every year have we, 10
With pious steps gone out to sit
Beneath thy graveyard tree
And often, with remembrance
Of our darling little boy

Repeated—"they that sow in tears
"Shall reap again in joy."
Lo! children are a heritage
A fruit and a reward,
Bestowed in sovreign mercy
By the fecit of the Lord 20
But he, that giveth gifts to men
May take away the same
And righteous is the holy act,
And blessed be his name.
For still it is a mercy,
And a mercy we can view,
For whom the Lord chastiseth
He in love regardeth too.
And sweetly in remembrance
Of our darling little boy 30
Bethink we still, that sorrow's tears
Shall spring in beds of joy.
And aye, that Word is precious
As the apple of the eye
That looketh up to mansions
Which are builded in the sky
That palleth with this scene of tears
And vanities and strife,
And seeketh for that better home
Where truly there is life. 40
I cling no more to life below,
It hath no charm for me,
Yet strive to fill my duty here,
While here below I be.
And often comes the memory
Of my darling little boy,
For he was sown in bitter tears,
And shall be reaped in joy.

[written 1835 or later, published 2007]

1 **A hundred moons and more**: These words set the poem over eight years and four months after William Henry Schoolcraft died in March 1827. **15–16 "they that sow in tears . . .**: after Psalm 125:5: "They that sow in tears shall reap in joy." **17–18 Lo! children . . .**: after Psalm 127:3: "Lo, children are an heritage of the Lord: and the fruit of the womb is his reward." **20 fecit**: made (Latin), in effect meaning "doing." **37 palleth**: covers with a pall (a cloth for covering a coffin).

Lines written at Castle Island, Lake Superior

Here in my native inland sea
From pain and sickness would I flee
And from its shores and island bright
Gather a store of sweet delight.
Lone island of the saltless sea!
How wide, how sweet, how fresh and free
How all transporting—is the view
Of rocks and skies and waters blue
Uniting, as a song's sweet strains
To tell, here nature only reigns. 10
Ah, nature! here forever sway
Far from the haunts of men away
For here, there are no sordid fears,
No crimes, no misery, no tears
No pride of wealth; the heart to fill,
No laws to treat my people ill.

[written 1838, published 2007]

A translation, by Henry Rowe Schoolcraft or Jane Schoolcraft, of a poem in Ojibwe by Jane Johnston Schoolcraft. The Ojibwe version has not survived. In 1838 the Schoolcraft family took a day trip west across Lake Superior along the coast of Michigan's Upper Peninsula. A little north of what is now Marquette, Michigan, they saw what Schoolcraft called Castle Island and what is now called Granite Island. **16 treat:** the word "treat" can evoke the sorry history of treaties between the U.S. government and Indian nations.

On leaving my children John and Jane at School, in the Atlantic states, and preparing to return to the interior

Nyau nin de nain dum
May kow e yaun in
Ain dah nuk ki yaun
Waus sa wa kom eg
Ain dah nuk ki yaun

Ne dau nis ainse e
Ne gwis is ainse e
Ishe nau gun ug wau
Waus sa wa kom eg

She gwau go sha ween 10
Ba sho waud e we
Nin zhe ka we yea

Ishe ez hau jau yaun
Ain dah nuk ke yaun

Ain dah nuk ke yaun
Nin zhe ke we yea
Ishe ke way aun e
Nyau ne gush kain dum

[written 1838 or 1839, published 1851]

[TRANSLATION]

As I am thinking
When I find you
My land
Far in the west
My land

My little daughter
My little son
I leave them behind
Far away land

[emphatically] But soon 10
It is close however
To my home I shall return
That is the way that I am, my being
My land

My land
To my home I shall return
I begin to make my way home
Ahh but I am sad

[2007]

The translation was prepared for *The Sound the Stars Make Rushing Through the Sky* by Dennis Jones, Heidi Stark, and James Vukelich. Henry Rowe Schoolcraft decided to leave his and Jane Johnston Schoolcraft's children, Janee (age eleven) and Johnston (age nine), at eastern boarding schools (not Indian boarding schools). Jane Schoolcraft objected but deferred to her husband's judgment. She wrote this poem after leaving the children at school.

William Walker, Jr., Wyandot, 1800–1874

William Walker, Jr., was born in what is now southeastern Michigan. His mother came from an influential Wyandot family, and his father, a white who was captured and adopted as a child, first by Delawares and then by Wyandots, became a federal sub-agent for the Ohio Indians. Walker went to a mission school in Ohio and then to Kenyon College (Connelley, *Life* 13). He studied Greek, Latin, and French and, besides Wyandot and English, spoke Delaware, Shawnee, Miami, and Potawatomi. In 1826, angry at the pressure on Wyandots to give up their lands in Ohio and move west, he wrote the Methodist minister to the Wyandots: "Oh ye frightened sons of the forest, where can ye find an abiding place to rest your wearied limbs, and sing the songs of your fathers in peace! Unhappy people! never will the whiteman rest till the Pacific Ocean drinks of your blood" (Finley). In 1831, when the Wyandots were offered lands west of Missouri in exchange for their lands in Ohio, Walker led a Wyandot delegation to inspect the western lands and submitted a report rejecting the exchange (Oliphant). In 1835–1836, he was Principal Chief of the Wyandots (Howe 196; Klopfenstein 123–24), and he served for about twenty years as postmaster of Upper Sandusky, Ohio. An influential leader and speaker, he published widely in newspapers, both before and after the Wyandots were finally removed from their lands in 1843. Today his home in Upper Sandusky, Ohio is on the National Register of Historic Places. In 1853, Walker was appointed the first provisional governor of the Nebraska Territory, which included what is now Nebraska and Kansas. A journal he kept in 1845–1854 was published after he died (Connelley, *Provisional*), and in the journal he often quotes poetry. A Democrat, slaveholder (he bought his first slave in 1847; Connelley, *Provisional* 195), and opponent of abolition, he was a member of the controversial 1857 convention in Lecompton, Kansas that called for a pro-slavery constitution for Kansas. Nevertheless, he supported the Union during the Civil War. (Connelley, *Provisional* 5–16; Johannsen. See also Everett, *History of Sandusky County* 17, which includes several details not corroborated elsewhere. For an account highly critical of Walker, see Anderson 75–78.)

["Oh, give me back my bended bow"]

Oh, give me back my bended bow,
  My cap and feather, give them back,
To chase o'er hill the mountain roe,
  Or follow in the otter's track.

You took me from my native wild,
  Where all was bright, and free and blest;
You said the Indian hunter's child
  In classic halls and bowers should rest.

Long have I dwelt within these walls
  And pored o'er ancient pages long. 10
I hate these antiquated halls;
  I hate the Grecian poet's song.

[probably written as a student, approximately in the 1820s,
published 1882 and perhaps earlier]

According to one account, Walker wrote these lines "while at college" (Everett, *History of Sandusky County* 17).

The Wyandot's Farewell

Farewell, ye tall oaks, in whose pleasant green shade
I've sported in childhood, in innocence played,
My dog and my hatchet, my arrow and bow,
Are still in remembrance, alas! I must go.

Adieu, ye dear scenes which bound me like chains,
As on my gay pony I pranced o'er the plains;
The deer and the turkey I tracked in the snow,
O'er the great Mississippi, alas! I must go.

Sandusky, Tyamochtee, and Broken Sword streams,
No more shall I see you except in my dreams. 10
Farewell to the marshes where cranberries grow,
O'er the great Mississippi, alas! I must go.

Dear scenes of my childhood, in memory blest,
I must bid you farewell for the far distant West.
My heart swells with sorrow, my eyes overflow,
O'er the great Mississippi, alas! I must go.

Let me go to the wildwood, my own native home.
Where the wild deer and elk and buffalo roam,
Where the tall cedars are and the bright waters flow,
Far away from the pale-face, oh, there let me go. 20

[written 1843, published 1882 and perhaps earlier]

Title: In 1843, the Wyandots were forced from their home in Ohio. Walker wrote this poem in Wyandot "just before" leaving (Everett, *History of Sandusky County* 17). While the Wyandot version has not survived, the present text is Walker's translation of the poem into English.

Israel Folsom, Choctaw, 1802–1870

Israel Folsom was born in the Choctaw Nation in what is now Mississippi. In 1822, he was a student at the Cornwall School in Connecticut ("Foreign Mission School"; Morse 265, 272, 276–78), described in this volume in a poem by his schoolmate, Adin C. Gibbs. Folsom's brother-in-law was Choctaw diplomat and Chief Peter Pitchlynn, whose poems are included in this volume. Folsom's one known poem recalls the pain of forced removal from his homeland. A Presbyterian minister, he also wrote accounts of Choctaw traditions and history and served several times as a Choctaw delegate to Washington, D.C. In 1864 he was president of the Grand Council of the Sixth Confederate Indian Nation.

Lo! The Poor Indian's Hope

Land where brightest waters flow,
Land where loveliest forest grow*
Where warriors drew the bow,
  Native land farewell.

He who made yon stream and tree,
Made the White, the Red man free,
Gave the Indians' home to be
  'Mid the forest wilds.

Have the waters ceased to flow?
Have the forests ceased to grow? 10
Why do our brothers bid us go
  From our native home?

Here in infancy we played,
Here our happy wigwam made,
Here our fathers' graves are laid,—
  Must we leave them all?

Whiteman, tell us, God on high
So pure and bright in yonder sky,—
Will not then His searching eye
  See the Indians' wrong? 20

*The lands had been promised, by treaty, to the Indians "as long as the grass should grow and water run."

[written perhaps around 1831, published 1875]

Title: refers to a famous passage in Alexander Pope's *An Essay on Man* (1733–34): "Lo! the poor Indian, whose untutor'd mind / Sees God in clouds or hears him in the wind" (Epistle 1, line 99, p. 508). **Note, *The lands had been promised. . . .** : The note appears in the original publication. While the general sense of such phrases accurately reflects the sense of many treaties, and while legend has it that such phrases often appear in treaties, these words do not appear in any treaties with the federal government (Prucha 262–63). Nevertheless, a similar phrase appears in a famous letter from President Andrew Jackson, who was the driving force behind removal. Jackson gave the letter to his agent to the Choctaw Nation, Major David Haley, who gave it to the Choctaw chief David Folsom, a colonel in the United States army commissioned by Jackson, and an older brother of Israel Folsom (Brewer 59). The letter asks Haley to tell the Choctaws that in Indian Territory "their white brethren will not trouble them; they will have no claim to the land, and they can live upon it, they and all their children, as long as grass grows or water runs, in peace and plenty. It will be theirs forever. . . . There, beyond the limits of any State, in possession of land of their own, which they shall possess as long as Grass grows or water runs, I can, and will protect them and be their friend & father" (Abel 372–73, including text of letter at 373, though the text here comes from *The Papers of Andrew Jackson* 494; both versions transcribe Jackson's draft, not the copy sent to David Folsom). Jackson thus used the phrase not for the homeland that he sought to take away from the Choctaws but for Indian Territory where he sought to send them. Folsom's poem, by contrast, uses the phrase for the traditional Choctaw homeland.

An Indian (Jesse Bushyhead?), Cherokee

Preceded by the introductory note from H. F. Buckner reproduced below, this poem was published in the *Indian Advocate* in 1848, when Buckner was a Baptist missionary in Kentucky preparing to move to the Creek Nation. He worked as a missionary in the Creek Nation from 1849 until his death in 1882. The poem was signed simply "An Indian," and Buckner believed it was written by Jesse Bushyhead (1804–1844). A Baptist minister from Tennessee, Bushyhead attended mission schools and a seminary. Though he staunchly opposed removal, he led a contingent of a thousand Cherokees on the Trail of Tears in 1838–1839. Near what is now Westville, Oklahoma, Bushyhead established the Baptist Mission in 1839. He served as Chief Justice of the Cherokee Nation from 1840 to 1844 (Meserve 351). Dennis Wolf Bushyhead (see "I've returned to home and scanty lunch" by Hors de Combat, in this volume, pp. 155–56), later principal chief, was his son. No copy appears to have survived of the issue of the *Athens Courier* that originally published the poem. Buckner refers to the Ocoee Purchase, an area in southeastern Tennessee where an 1836 treaty forced Cherokees, including Bushyhead, to leave their land.

> In looking over an old file of papers, I came across the following touching piece in the Athens Courier, composed by "An Indian" (supposed by many to be Elder Bushyhead, deceased) just before the Cherokees left the Okoee purchase. Should it be as interesting to others as it is to me, it will be worthy of being re-published in the Advocate.
>
> H. F. BUCKNER

The Indian's Farewell

Adieu ye scenes of early sports,
   A last, long sad adieu;
Ye hills and dales and groves and brooks,
   This is our last review.

Tho' oft beneath your fragrant shades,
   When nature bloomed in green,
In soft repose, I've calmly laid
   And viewed the tranquil scene.

Ye merry songsters of the wood
   With music soft and wild, 10
Come chant a lay in mournful mood
   To nature's weeping child.

Hush, hush ye winds, bear not a sound
   Of those sweet notes away;

Sing on sweet minstrel of the grove
Since 'tis thy farewell lay.

It minds my soul of happier days,
It calls up scenes of yore,
When I have listened to those lays
That I must hear no more. 20

Adieu the land that gave me birth,
Thou God that rules the sky,
Protect that little spot of earth
In which our fathers lie.

Tread lightly on the sleeping dead,
Proud millions that intrude,
Lest, on your ashes be the tread
Of millions still more rude.

I see a star in fancy's dream
Bright in the welkin blue, 30
That on my soul sheds hode's faint gleam;
Dear native land, adieu.

[1848]

11 **lay**: song. 30 **welkin**: sky. 31 **hode's**: perhaps a misprint for "home's."

John Rollin Ridge/Yellow Bird, Cherokee, 1827–1867

John Rollin Ridge, whose Cherokee name was Chees-quat-a-law-ny and who often published as Yellow Bird, the English translation of his Cherokee name, was born to a distinguished family in the Cherokee Nation in Georgia. His father John Ridge and grandfather Major Ridge, prosperous farmers and slaveholders, were influential leaders caught in the dispute over how to respond to pressure from the United States to give up Cherokee lands and move west. Though they opposed removal, they finally decided, together with John Ridge's cousins Stand Watie and Elias Boudinot (Buck Watie), editor of the first American Indian newspaper, the *Cherokee Phoenix*, to sign the 1835 Treaty of New Echota, agreeing to remove to Indian Territory. They came to believe that removal was inevitable and that the Cherokees would get better terms by agreeing to give up their land and go west. The Ridge faction was thus dubbed the "Treaty Party," as opposed to the party led by Chief John Ross, which continued to oppose removal and which saw the Ridges as traitors for signing the treaty. In 1836–1837, the Ridges traveled west, over a year before federal troops forced most of the remaining Cherokees west on the notorious Trail of Tears. Then in 1839, all on one night, large contingents of the Ross faction assassinated Major Ridge, John Ridge, and Elias Boudinot. (Stand Watie escaped and lived on to serve as a Confederate general in the Civil War.) Young John Rollin and his mother watched as murderers dragged his father from bed, stabbed him over and over, and then marched and stomped over his still dying body. The memory tormented John Rollin Ridge for the rest of his life.

After the murders, the Ridges fled to Arkansas. By that point, John Rollin had already received an excellent education in Cherokee missionary schools near his home and, as removal approached, in Alabama. His family brought his teacher with them to the west, where his education continued both in school and through a tutor. From 1843 to 1845, he was a student at Great Barrington Academy in Massachusetts. There, and then back in Arkansas, he studied Latin, Greek, and classical literature. After school, he studied law and then began to farm in Indian Territory, but in 1849 he killed a member of the Ross party, probably in self-defense. Fearful of the consequences, he fled again. From Missouri, he planned ways to oppose the Ross party, but in 1850 he left to join the California Gold Rush. In California, Ridge worked as a newspaper editor and journalist. In 1854 he published the first-known novel by an American Indian (and the first novel written in California), *The Life and Adventures of Joaquín Murieta, the Celebrated California Bandit.* Based on actual events and presenting itself as the true story of Murieta, Ridge's tale exposes the brutality of Americans who ruthlessly drove California Mexicans from their land. Murieta's story, as Ridge tells it, echoes the way Americans had earlier driven Cherokees from their lands. Meanwhile, as a committed Democrat, Ridge was active in California politics. With his background as a slaveholder, an opponent of abolition, a Democrat, and a supporter of Stephen Douglas, Ridge furiously opposed Abraham Lincoln and the Republicans during the Civil War but continued to support the Union. After the war, he led the delegation of Southern Cherokees that renegotiated relations with the federal government in Washington, D.C. (Parins)

As a poet, Ridge was a remarkable lyric talent, arguably at least among the several most powerful American poets before Whitman. He seems to have seen the Shelleyan "Mount Shasta" as standing out from the rest of his poems. He included it in *The Life and Adventures of Joaquín Murieta*, and it appeared as the first poem in his book of poems, which his wife published posthumously in 1868, titling it simply *Poems.* Ridge also published many poems in newspapers. He signed his early newspaper poems with the town where they were written, often proudly adding "C.N." for Cherokee Nation. Those include a good number of poems that have not previously been noted in scholarship or bibliographies. Though written at a remarkably young age, the early poems are often among Ridge's best works.

The poems in this volume that are in *Poems* follow that text and appear in the sequence they follow there.

An Indian's Grave

Far in a lonely wood I wandered once,
Where warbling birds of melancholy wing
And music sad, rehearsed their melancholy songs.
All else was silent save the whispering leaves
Strewn by autumnal winds, or here and there
A stream which ever poured a mournful sound

Amid those solitudes so dim, where shadows
Vast and tall, eternal threw their flickering
Darkness. Retrospection sadly turned my mind
To scenes now painted on the map of Time 10
Long past. And as I wandered on, I mused
On greatness fall'n, beauteous things destroyed;
When suddenly my footstep paused before
A mound of moss-grown earth. I wondered,
For a while, what mortal here had found
A resting place? But soon I minded me,
That many years agone a noble race
Had roamed these forest-wilds among, and made
These mountain-fastnesses rebound to shouts
Of liberty untamed, and happiness 20
That knew no bounds. I recollected more,
That, save but a few, they all had fled,
And, fleeing, left some bones behind: The only
Mark that this fair land was once their heritage,
By Nature's gift to her untutored sons.
Then thought I, "This must be the grave of one
Who ranked among the warriors of the
Wilderness!—And when he saw his country
Doomed, his tribe o'erthrown, and his strong arm
Grown weak before his pale-faced foes; and when 30
He knew the hour was come, in which his soul
Must leave the form it once had moved to noble
Deeds, and travel to the hunting-grounds, where erst
His fathers went, he here had dug his grave,
And, singing wild his death-song to the wind,
Sunk down and died!"

Sleep on, dark warrior,
Whoe'er thou art! My hand shall not disturb
The slightest stem that takes its nutriment
From thee. The white man's share may plough some other
Mounds where Red men sleep, round which no mourner 40
Stands in watch to guard the relics of a friend;
But no rude step, and no rude hand shall e'en
Despoil the beauty of this silent spot,
Or sacrilegiously disturb the rest
Of *one* lone Indian form. Sleep on!
The storms that howled around thy head long,
Long ago, and tutored thy stern heart
To agony, have ceased. A thousand cities

Stand, where once thy nation's wigwams stood,—
And num'rous palaces of giant strength 50
Are floating down the streams where long ago
Thy bark canoe was gliding. All is changed.
Then *sleep* thou on! Perchance that peace, denied
In life, within the lonely grave is found.

[1847]

Reflections Irregular

I cast a backward look—how changed
    The scenes of other days!
I walk, a wearied man, estranged
    From youth's delightful ways.
There in the distance rolleth yet
    That stream whose waves my
Boyish bosom oft has met,
    When pleasure lit mine eye.
It rolleth yet, as clear, as bold,
    As pure as it did then; 10
But I have grown in youth-time old,
    And, mixing now with men,
My sobered eye must not attend
To that sweet stream, my early friend!
The music of its waters clear
Must now but seldom reach my ear,
But murmur on still carelessly
To every heedless passer-by.
How often o'er its rugged cliffs I've strayed,
And gaily listened, as its billows played 20
Such deep, low music at their base—
And then such brightening thoughts would trace
Upon the tablet of my mind!
Alas, those days have run their race,
Their joys I nowhere now can find.
    I have no time to think
        Of climbing Glory's sunny mount
    I have no time to drink
        At Learning's bubbling fount!
Now corn and potatoes call me 30
From scenes were wont to enthrall me—
        A weary wight,
        Both day and night

My brain is full of business matters,
Reality has snatched the light,
From fancy's hand, that shone so bright,
And tore the dreams she wove, to tatters!

[1848]

My Harp

Oh must I fling my harp aside,
Nor longer let it soothe my heart?
No! sooner might the tender bride
From th' first night's nuptial chamber part!
No! sooner might the warrior cast
His martial plume of glory down,
Or worshipt monarch fling in dust
His royal sceptre and his crown!

Must all that ever smoothed my way
Along the tedious path of time, 10
Or kept me for some glimpse of day,
Or held my desperate hand from crime;
Must all, that I have loved so dear,
When every other source of joy
Had fled, be careless thrown away
As if it were some idle toy?

Oh no—that harp may all be rough
And grating to another's ear—
So let it be—it is enough
That unto me it still is dear! 20
If, in the silent midnight, I
Have oft my weeping heart beguiled,—
If oft when gloom surrounded me,
My spirit o'er its strains have smiled.

It were a folly strange indeed
To cast that solace from my breast!
It were but wishing yet to bleed
Without one certain place of rest;
It were to drink the bitterest gall,
To add but poison to a wound, 30
And find new pangs of sorrowing
Where hitherto they were not found.

It were to plunge within the deep
   Of wilderness and night—where grope
Worse ills than e'er disturbed the sleep
   Of minds forsook of peace and hope!
Oh, tell me not to spurn this harp,
   Although it may not be divine,
For thou hast felt no pangs, as I,
   And my sad soul's unlike to thine. 40

'Tis sweet, when mournfulness enshrouds
   The spirit sorrowing and pale,
And gather round the angry clouds,
   To take the harp and tune its wail.
'Tis sweet, when calmly broods the night,
   To wander forth where waters roll,
And, mingling with the waves its voice,
   To rouse the passions of the soul!

Then, off with ye! who coldly tell
   Me my loved harp to fling away— 50
I'd rather bid all friends *farewell*,
   Than have the folly to obey!
For friends are but a fleeting trust,
   As transient as the evening's blush;
But, true to me in all my moods,
   My harp shall ne'er its soothings hush!

[1848]

Song

Come to the river's side, my love,
   My light canoe is by the shore,—
We'll float upon the tide my love,
   And *thou* shalt hold the dripping oar.

Methinks thy hand could guide so well
   The tiny vessel on its course;
The waves would smooth their crests to thee
   As I have done my spirit's force.

How calmly will we glide my love,
   Through moonlight floating on the deep, 10
Or, loving yet the safer shore,
   Beneath the fringing willows weep.

Again, like some wild duck, we'll skim,
  And scarcely touch the water's face,
While silver streaks our way shall mark,
  And circling lines of beauty trace!

And then the stars shall shine above
  In harmony with those below,
And gazing up, and looking down,
  Give glance for glance, and glow for glow! 20

And then their light shall be our own,
  Commingled with our souls!—and sweet
As those bright stars of Heaven shall be
  Our hearts, which then shall melting meet.

At last we'll reach yon silent isle,
  So calm and green amidst the waves;
So peaceful too, it does not spurn
  The friendly tide its shore that laves.

We'll draw our vessel on the sand,
  And seek the shadow of those trees, 30
Where all alone, and undisturbed,
  We'll talk and love as we may please!

And then thy voice shall be so soft,
  'Twill match the whisper of the leaves,
And then thy breast shall yield its sigh
  So like the wavelet as it heaves!

And oh that eye, so dark and free,
  So like a spirit in itself!
And then that *hand* so white and small
  It would not *shame* the loveliest elf! 40

The world might perish all, for me,
  So that it left that little isle!
The human race might pass away
  If thou wert left me with thy smile!

Then, to the river's side, my love,
  My boat is waiting on its oar—
We'll float upon the tide, my love,
  And gaily reach that islet's shore.

[1848]

Song

I saw her once—her eye's deep light
Fell on my spirit's deeper night,
   The only beam that e'er illumed
Its shadows drear. The glance was slight,
   But oh, what softness it assumed!

I saw her twice—her glance again
Lit up its fire within my brain;
   My thoughts leaped up, like lightning warm,
And felt a sweetness mixed with pain,
   While gath'ring wildly round her form. 10

I saw her thrice—she was alone,
And her deep glance more deeply shone
   Upon my heart with rapture chained,
The thrill was a meteor thrown
   Athwart some sky where darkness reigned!

I saw her yet again—and clear,
But low, her rich tones met my ear;
   They wandered thro' my bosom sad,
As waters thro' a woodland sere,
   That make decay itself seem glad. 20

The fifth time I saw her—and still
She taught my quiv'ring heart to thrill,
   Like some wild hand upon a lyre,
That's borne along, without its will,
   Across the strings of magic fire!

I saw her oft again—, each hour
Enhanced o'er me her conquering power;
   Her image in my thought became
A spirit-planted, fadeless flower;
   And all my music was her name! 30

I loved the earth on which she trod—
More beautiful than if a God
   Had placed immortal foot-prints there!
I loved the world, though dark its load
   Of ills, because *she* breathed its air!

I loved her slightest careless word—
More sweet than matin of the bird
   That scales the Heaven on mounting wing!

It through my maddened pulses stirred,
  As though it were a living thing. 40

Oh, that 'rapt heart's forever gone,
That boweth once to Beauty's throne,
  And feels the bliss her looks inspire;
For, oh, the seeds of death are sown,
  When love assumes its mad empire!

[1848]

8 **My thoughts leaped up**: echoing William Wordsworth's famous "My Heart Leaps Up."

The Man of Memory

The stormy winds are darkly swelling
Around that distant, lonely dwelling;
By the fire-light, all dim and dreary,
Sits an old man, so worn and weary,
  Scarce his frame his tott'ring limbs can bear.
His wrinkled cheeks are poor and shrunken;
His eye yet wild, though deeply sunken;
That withered brow a paleness dresses,
As if it felt Death's cold caresses,
  And o'er it falls his gray and scattered hair! 10

While the fierce storm is outside fighting,
A thousand thoughts his eyes are lighting—
Fierce thoughts, as mad, as dark, as jarring
As the winds, in their wildest warring,
  While they shake his lone dwelling to its base!
See how his phrenzied eye discloses
A misery that ne'er reposes!
See how his crumbling teeth are gnashing,
While deeds gone by are lurid flashing
  Over the withered features of his face! 20

Ah! how the past's his soul enthralling—
The visions of his youth recalling,
Broods he long in age's wintered madness
O'er the loved scenes of former gladness,
  When his frame was strong, and his heart was young;
When with smooth hands, and soft caresses,
He touched so light his maiden's tresses,
In soft, low words her beauty praising,

While her deep eye was downward gazing
To hide the joy all o'er her features flung. 30

He knew—he could not help from seeing—
How deep the love of that fair being
Thus close to him in fondness clinging!
He knew what *hopes* for her were winging
Through the Future's bright and golden way;
He knew for *him* her heart was beating
With a warm passion far from fleeting,
And, knowing this, in one dark hour
He madly used his conscious power
To make that trusting girl his passions' prey. 40

The mem'ry of her daily sighing,
The look she gave him when a'dying,
The piteous glance of that sweet creature,
Informing sadly every feature,
While she said in accents sweet "How couldst thou?"
Long, long that old man's brain has haunted,
In seeking fame, for which he panted,
He could not, could not in his bride prefer
A lowly cot, and humble life with her,
To laurels green that yet might deck his brow. 50

He had thought his feelings to restrain—
He had thought to feel a deep disdain
For love; and in his path of glory
To forget a frail woman's story,
But mem'ry has a chain which will not break!
In manhood's proudest, highest gladness;
E'en in the wine-cup's flowing madness;
In the spirit's softest musing-time,
When scarce we know we are losing time,
Some senses which ought to sleep will yet awake! 60
From the home of his youth he parted,
From the grave of the broken-hearted,
For foreign scenes where mirth and folly
Might cure him of his melancholy,
But alas, he wandered thus in vain.
No varied views of vale or mountain,
No music of the bubbling fountain,
No ancient scene of some old ditty,
Nor town, nor cot, nor prouder city
Had the magic to relieve his pain. 70

His spirit dwelt beneath the shading
Of a thought his sick soul pervading,
And when his sweetest dream was blooming,
Its death his destiny was dooming.
  Forever to his eye was a dying face,
The tenderest reproach expressing—
And when he thought to feel a blessing
In some most unaccustomed feeling,
Lo, eternal mem'ry is revealing
  Still to his eye that sad and dying face! 80

His heart and mind thus sadly riven,
To desperation soon he's driven;
A game, as deep as Falsehood's tissue,
Plays he, and fearless of the issue.
  With men of blood, of crime, of vice, and hate,
With life compressed and frown severe,
He plunges through his black career—
Then growing old, consumed youth's fires,
To a hermit home he far retires,
  A man whose ruthless mem'ry is his Fate! 90

Well may his brow have paleness deeper
Than the face of the tomb's dead sleeper;
Well may that cheek be poor and shrunken,
That eye so wild, and deep, and sunken,
  Flashing savagely beneath its frosty brow!
Well may the stormy winds be swelling
Around that distant, lonely dwelling;
The ruined fabric dark appearing,
The midnight winds so fierce careering,
  Still well, old man, such wretched ones as thou. 100

[1848]

The man twenty feet high, having the features of the Indian race, said to have been recently discovered in a cave somewhere in the Rocky Mountains:

The remnant of a giant race,—
  Who had for game the Mastodon;
The noble features of whose face
  Show him Nature's mightiest son!

A solitary remnant he,
  His tribe departed from the earth—
Unknown to us his origin,
  Deep wrapt in mystery his birth!

He stands in this broad world alone,
  His language, and his nation dead, 10
A friend, companion he has none
  To share his hard and rocky bed,
Or soothe with a cheerful word,
  The grey hairs falling o'er his brow,
His wrinkled visage, dark and stern,
  Oh what must be his mem'ries now?

Perhaps this continent was young,
  When o'er it roamed his long-fled sires,
And wild their horrid war-whoop rung,
  Where they had lit their council-fires. 20
Perhaps the tribes diminutive,
  Who had for game the elk and deer,
Fled oft from that grim, giant band,
  And sought the wilderness for fear!

Ah, well doth he their legends know,
  Their mighty warriors dark and dread—
Whose arms dealt death at every blow—
  Of eagle eye, and monarch tread!
Their tales of love, and private grief,
  Their dark-eyed women nobly formed, 30
Sublimely beautiful, whose glance
  Of love, those iron bosoms warmed!

Perhaps a queenly one and proud,
  From mighty chieftains purely sprung,
Whose hair, like midnight's sweeping cloud,
  Adown her perfect shoulders hung;
Whose eye with passion's spirit beamed,
  Whose glowing bosom wildly heaved
With loftier love than now is known,
  Itself undoubting, and believed. 40

Perhaps that queenly one was his.
  May be, far north, by Erie's lake,
They saw the dawn of their young bliss,
  And there first felt their passions wake.

As free their love, and beautiful
    As those wild scenes around them were;
How lovely she, and he how brave—
    The Eden of the West was there!

No sickly hue was on his cheek,
    And she was not a fragile thing, 50
As lady delicate, and weak,
    With artful accent murmuring;
Ah no—but Nature's majesty
    Around them thrown, they stood in pride,
With lofty look, and chainless soul,
    The giant chieftain and his bride!

Perhaps long centuries have cast
    The shades of thought around that brow;
And since that moment of the past,
    So bright with love and raptures glow, 60
He's seen the puny nations fade
    In generations one by one,
And, as they faded, still hath gazed
    With undimmed eye upon the sun!

How came he here? how fled his race?
    'Tis written on his memory
In characters we cannot trace,
    But broods he o'er them mournfully.
May be against his tribe there came—
    Too long, too fearfully opprest, 70
In countless numbers rising strong—
    The banded nations of the West.

The mighty tribe like lions rose—
    No doubt contended long and well,
But wasted by unnumbered foes,
    In wars continued shock they fell!
But fell as warriors, heroes fall:
    Fell form by form, and clan by clan,
Till marked, a bleeding fugitive,
    Retired far back this last lone man. 80

[1848]

The Dark One to His Love

Not yet, not yet the seeds of grief
Are in thy bosom sown;
Not yet, not yet the autumn-leaf
Of thy young heart is known.
Not yet, not yet thy soul hath caught
The shadow of my own,
Now is thy buoyant voice yet fraught
With that which mars *my* tone.

Oh yet there's freshness on thy heart,
Thy spirit's wing is white, 10
And loves to soar, and dive, and dart,
And bathe itself in light!
But yet that freshness all shall fade,
That wing grow dark as night,
And those high hopes, which now pervade
Thy soul, shall sink from sight!

Though true, I love not to inform
Thee of thy "blighted fate,"
Nor tell thee how the coming storm
Shall make thee desolate. 20
But my dark doom thou too must share—
Thou art my spirit's mate,
And if my portion is despair,
Such too must be thy state.

If thou wouldst be the happy bird,
That greets the flowery spring;
Let not the air thou breath'st be stirred
By the grim raven's wing.
Oh fly, fly from his mad embrace,
Whose bosom bears a sting, 30
Lest from his hand, with fiend-like grace,
He poisoned arrows fling.

Tempt not the soul to darkness given,
I tell thee tis not well:
For his are lightnings of the heaven
And thunder-bolts of hell!
Search not the midnight mysteries
In which his deep thoughts dwell—
Meet not the glance of those sunk eyes
I tell thee tis not well! 40

The cup may sparkle brightly,
Like rich wine, at the brim;
His manly voice be clear and high,
But pause! drink not with him.
His cup is filled with bitter tears,
Wept till the eye was dim,
And colored with the heart's warm blood—
Again, drink not with him!

Oh, if thou lov'st earth's happiness,
And hatest grim despair, 50
In which *thou* seest no loveliness,
Then fair one, oh beware!
Seek not to share the comet's fate,
Which hath a baleful glare,
But let some flow'ret be thy mate,
Whose look is soft and fair.

[1849]

The Still Small Voice

There is a voice more dear to me
Than man or woman's e'er could be—
A "still small voice" that cheers
The woes of these my darker years.

I hear it in the busy crowd,
Distinct, amid confusion loud;
And in the solemn midnight still,
When mem'ries sad my bosom fill.

I hear it midst the social glee,
A voice unheard by all but me; 10
And when my sudden trance is seen,
They wondering ask, what can it mean?

The tones of woman once could cheer,
While woman yet to me was dear,
And sweet were all the dreams of youth,
As aught can be that wanteth truth!

How loved in early manhood's prime,
Ambition's clarion notes sublime!
How musical the tempest's roar,
"That lured to dash me on the shore!" 20

These tones, and more all beautiful,
That did my youthful spirit lull,
Or made my bosom Rapture's throne,
Have passed away, and left me lone.

And now that I can weep no more
The tears that gave relief of yore,
And now, that from my ruined heart
The forms that make me shudder, start;

I gaze above the world around,
And from the deeps of Heaven's profound, 30
A "still small voice" descends to me—
"Thou'rt sad, but I'll remember thee!"

As burns the life-light in me low,
And throws its ashes o'er my brow,
When all else flies, it speaks to me—
"Thou't doomed, but I'll remember thee!"

Then let my brow grow sadder yet,
And mountain-high still rise regret;
Enough for me the voice that cheers
The woes of these my darker years. 40

[1851]

Title: after "a still small voice," 1 Kings 19:12.

The Humboldt Desert

Who journeys o'er the desert now,
  Where sinks engulfed the Humboldt river,
Arrested in its sudden flow,
  But pouring in that depth forever.

As if the famished earth would drink
  Adry the tributes of the mountains,
Yet wither on the water's brink,
  And thirst for still unnumbered fountains.

Who journeys o'er that desert now
  Shall see strange sights, I ween, and ghastly; 10
For he shall trace, awearied, slow,
  Across this waste extended vastly,

The steps of pilgrims westward bound,
  Bound westward to the Land Pacific,

Where hoped-for rest and peace are found,
    And plenty waves her wand prolific.

Along this parched and dreary track,
    Nor leaf, nor blade, nor shrub appeareth;
The sky above doth moisture lack,
    And brazen glare the vision seareth; 20

Nor shadow, save the traveler's own,
    Doth bless with coolness seeming only,
And, save his muffled step alone
    Or desert-bird's wild shriek and lonely,

No sound is heard—a realm of blight,
    Of weird-like silence and a brightness
That maketh but a gloom of light,
    Where glimmer shapes of spectral whiteness!

They are the bones that bleaching lie
    Where fell the wearied beast o'er-driven, 30
And upward cast his dying eye,
    As if in dumb appeal to heaven.

For lengthening miles on miles they lie,
    These sad memorials grim and hoary,
And every whitening heap we spy
    Doth tell some way-worn pilgrim's story.

Hard by each skeleton there stand
    The wheels it drew, or warped or shrunken,
And in the drifted, yielding sand
    The yoke or rusted chain lies sunken. 40

Nor marvel we, if yonder peers,
    From out some scooped-out grave and shallow,
A human head, which fleshless leers
    With look that doth the place unhallow.

Each annual pilgrimage hath strewn
    These monuments unnamed, undated,
Till now were bone but piled on bone,
    And heaped-up wrecks but congregated,

A pyramid would rise as vast
    As one of those old tombs Egyptian, 50
Which speak from distant ages past
    With time-worn, mystic, strange inscription.

But pass we these grim, mouldering things,
Decay shall claim as Time may order,
For, offspring of the mountain springs,
A river rims the desert border;

With margin green and beautiful,
And sparkling waters silver-sounding,
And trees with zephyrs musical,
And answering birds with songs abounding, 60

And velvet flowers of thousand scents,
And clambering vines with blossoms crested;
Twas here the pilgrims pitched their tents,
And from their toilsome travel rested.

Oh sweet such rest to him who faints
Upon the journey long and weary!
And scenes like this the traveler paints,
While dying on the wayside weary.

Sad pilgrims o'er life's desert, *we*,
Our tedious journey onward ever; 70
But rest for us there yet shall be,
When camped upon the HEAVENLY RIVER.

[1867]

Mount Shasta

Behold the dread Mt. Shasta, where it stands
Imperial midst the lesser heights, and, like
Some mighty unimpassioned mind, companionless
And cold. The storms of Heaven may beat in wrath
Against it, but it stands in unpolluted
Grandeur still; and from the rolling mists upheaves
Its tower of pride e'en purer than before.
The wintry showers and white-winged tempests leave
Their frozen tributes on its brow, and it
Doth make of them an everlasting crown. 10
Thus doth it, day by day and age by age,
Defy each stroke of time: still rising highest
Into Heaven!

Aspiring to the eagle's cloudless height,
No human foot has stained its snowy side;
No human breath has dimmed the icy mirror which
It holds unto the moon and stars and sov'reign sun.

We may not grow familiar with the secrets
Of its hoary top, whereon the Genius
Of that mountain builds his glorious throne! 20
Far lifted in the boundless blue, he doth
Encircle, with his gaze supreme, the broad
Dominions of the West, which lie beneath
His feet, in pictures of sublime repose
No artist ever drew. He sees the tall
Gigantic hills arise in silentness
And peace, and in the long review of distance
Range themselves in order grand. He sees the sunlight
Play upon the golden streams which through the valleys
Glide. He hears the music of the great and solemn sea, 30
And overlooks the huge old western wall
To view the birth-place of undying Melody!

Itself all light, save when some loftiest cloud
Doth for a while embrace its cold forbidding
Form, that monarch mountain casts its mighty
Shadow down upon the crownless peaks below,
That, like inferior minds to some great
Spirit, stand in strong contrasted littleness!
All through the long and Summery months of our
Most tranquil year, it points its icy shaft 40
On high, to catch the dazzling beams that fall
In showers of splendor round that crystal cone,
And roll in floods of far magnificence
Away from that lone, vast Reflector in
The dome of Heaven.
Still watchful of the fertile
Vale and undulating plains below, the grass
Grows greener in its shade, and sweeter bloom
The flowers. Strong purifier! From its snowy
Side the breezes cool are wafted to the "peaceful 50
Homes of men," who shelter at its feet, and love
To gaze upon its honored form, aye standing
There the guarantee of health and happiness.
Well might it win communities so blest
To loftier feelings and to nobler thoughts—
The great material symbol of eternal
Things! And well I ween, in after years, how
In the middle of his furrowed track the plowman
In some sultry hour will pause, and wiping
From his brow the dusty sweat, with reverence 60

Gaze upon that hoary peak. The herdsman
Oft will rein his charger in the plain, and drink
Into his inmost soul the calm sublimity;
And little children, playing on the green, shall
Cease their sport, and, turning to that mountain
Old, shall of their mother ask: "Who made it?"
And she shall answer,—"GOD!"

And well this Golden State shall thrive, if like
Its own Mt. Shasta, Sovereign Law shall lift
Itself in purer atmosphere—so high 70
That human feeling, human passion at its base
Shall lie subdued; e'en pity's tears shall on
Its summit freeze; to warm it e'en the sunlight
Of deep sympathy shall fail:
Its pure administration shall be like
The snow immaculate upon that mountain's brow!

[1853, 1854, 1868]

The Atlantic Cable

Let Earth be glad! for that great work is done,
Which makes, at last, the Old and New World one!
Let all mankind rejoice! for time nor space
Shall check the progress of the human race!
Though Nature heaved the Continents apart,
She cast in one great mould the human heart;
She framed on one great plan the human mind
And gave man speech to link him to his kind;
So that, though plains and mountains intervene,
Or oceans, broad and stormy, roll between, 10
If there but be a courier for the thought—
Swift-winged or slow—the land and seas are nought,
And man is nearer to his brother brought.

First, ere the dawn of letters was, or burst
The light of science on the world, men, nurs't
In distant solitudes apart, did send,
Their skin-clad heralds forth to thread the woods,
Scale mountain-peaks, or swim the sudden floods,
And bear their messages of peace or war.

Next, beasts were tamed to drag the rolling car, 20
Or speed the mounted rider on his track;
And then came, too, the vessels, oar-propelled,

Which fled the ocean, as the clouds grew black,
And safe near shore their prudent courses held.
Next came the wingéd ships, which, brave and free,
Did skim the bosom of the bounding sea,
And dared the storms and darkness in their flight,
Yet drifted far before the winds and night,
Or lay within the dead calm's grasp of might.
Then, sea-divided nations nearer came, 30
Stood face to face, spake each the other's name,
In friendship grew, and learned the truth sublime,
That Man is Man in every age and clime!
They nearer were by months and years—but space
Must still be shortened in Improvement's race,
And steam came next to wake the world from sleep,
And launch her black-plumed warriors of the deep;
The which, in calm or storm, rode onward still,
And braved the raging elements at will.
Then distance, which from calms' and storms' delays 40
Grew into months, was shortened into days,
And Science' self declared her wildest dream
Reached not beyond this miracle of steam!
But steam hath not the lightning's wondrous power,
Though, Titan-like, mid Science' sons it tower
And wrestle with the ocean in his wrath,
And sweep the wild waves foaming from its path.
A mightier monarch is that subtler thing,
Which gives to human thought a thought-swift wing;
Which speaks in thunder like a God, 50
Or humbly stoops to kiss the lifted rod;
Ascends to Night's dim, solitary throne,
And clothes it with a splendor not its own—
A ghastly grandeur and a ghostly sheen,
Through which the pale stars tremble as they're seen;
Descends to fire the far horizon's rim,
And paints Mount Etnas in the cloudland grim;
Or, proud to own fair Science' rightful sway,
Low bends along th' electric wire to play,
And, helping out the ever-wondrous plan, 60
Becomes, in sooth, an errand-boy for man!

This Power it was, which, not content with aught
As yet achieved by human will or thought,
Disdained the slow account of months or days,
In navigation of the ocean ways,

And days would shorten into hours, and these
To minutes, in the face of sounding seas.
If Thought might not be borne upon the foam
Of furrowing keel, with speed that Thought should roam,
It then should walk, like light, the ocean's bed, 70
And laugh to scorn the winds and waves o'er head!
Beneath the reach of storm or wreck, down where
The skeletons of men and navies are,
Its silent steps should be; while o'er its path
The monsters of the deep, in sport or wrath,
The waters lashed, till like a pot should boil
The sea, and fierce Arion seize the upcast spoil.

America! to thee belongs the praise
Of this great crowning deed of modern days.
'T was Franklin called the wonder from on high; 80
'T was Morse who bade it on man's errands fly—
'T was he foretold its pathway 'neath the sea:
A daring Field fulfilled the prophecy!
'T was fitting that a great, free land like this,
Should give the lightning's voice to Liberty;
Should wing the heralds of Earth's happiness,
And sing, beneath the ever-sounding sea,
The fair, the bright millennial days to be.

Now may, ere long, the sword be sheathed to rust,
The helmet laid in undistinguished dust; 90
The thund'rous chariot pause in mid career,
Its crimsoned wheels no more through blood to steer;
The red-hoofed steed from fields of death be led,
Or turned to pasture where the armies bled;
For Nation unto Nation soon shall be
Together brought in knitted unity,
And man be bound to man by that strong chain,
Which, linking land to land, and main to main,
Shall vibrate to the voice of Peace, and be
A throbbing heartstring of Humanity! 100

[1868]

77 **Arion**: legendary ancient Greek poet kidnapped by pirates and rescued by dolphins. 80 **Franklin**: Benjamin Franklin, the famous scientist, writer, and politician who proved that lightning is electrical. 81 **Morse**: Samuel F. B. Morse, a painter who invented the telegraph and Morse code. 83 **Field**: Cyrus West Field led the project to lay a telegraph cable across the Atlantic Ocean in 1858 (briefly) and then again in 1866 (more durably).

Humboldt River

The River of Death, as it rolls
With a sound like the wailing of souls!
And guarding their dust, may be seen
The ghosts of the dead by the green
Billowy heaps on the shore—
Dim shapes, as they crouch by the graves,
And wail with the rush of the waves
On seeking the desert before!
Guarding their dust for the morn
Which shall see us, new-born 10
Arise from the womb of the earth—
That, through rain or through dearth,
Through calm or through storm,
Through seasons and times, no part may be lost,
By the ruthless winds tost,
Of the mortal which shall be immortal of form.

No leaf that may bud
By that dark sullen flood;
No flower that may bloom
With its tomb-like perfume, 20
In that region infectious of gloom;
No subtleized breath
That may ripple that River of Death,
Or, vapory, float in the desolate air,
But is watched with a vigilant, miserly care,
Lest it steal from the dust of the dead that are there;
For the elements aye are in league,
With a patience unknowing fatigue,
To scatter mortality's mould,
And sweep from the graves what they hold! 30

I would not, I ween, be the wight
To roam by that river at night,
When the souls are abroad in the glooms;
Enough that the day-time is weird
With the mystical sights that are feared
Mid the silence of moonlighted tombs;
Weird shores with their alkaline white—
That loom in the glare of the light;
Weird bones as they bleach in the sun,
Where the beast from his labors is done; 40
Weird frost-work of poisonous dews

On shrub and on herb, which effuse
The death they have drank to the core;
Weird columns upborne from the floor
Of the white-crusted deserts which boil
With the whirlwind's hot, blasting turmoil!
As ghost-like he glides on his way,
Each ghastly, worn pilgrim looks gray
With the dust the envenomed winds flail;
And the beast he bestrides is as pale 50
As the steed of the vision of John,
With him, the Destroyer, thereon.

Dark river, foul river, 't is well
That into the jaws of thy Hell—
The open-mouthed desert—should fall
Thy waves that so haunt and appal.
'Tis fit that thou seek the profound
Of all-hiding Night underground;
Like the river which nine times around
The realm of grim Erebus wound, 60
To roll in that region of dread—
A Stygian stream of the Dead!

[1860, 1868]

Title: For three hundred miles its banks are one continuous burying ground. Emigrants to California died on its shores by thousands [Ridge's note]. **55 desert:** Sink of the Humboldt [Ridge's note]. **60 Erebus:** ancient Greek god of darkness, and the name of his realm in Hades, the land of the dead. **62 Stygian:** the River Styx winds nine times around Hades.

To a Star Seen at Twilight

Hail solitary star!
That shinest from thy far blue height,
And overlookest Earth
And Heaven, companionless in light!
The rays around thy brow
Are an eternal wreath for thee;
Yet thou'rt not proud, like man,
Though thy broad mirror is the sea,
And thy calm home eternity!

Shine on, night-bosomed star! 10
And through its realms thy soul's eye dart,
And count each age of light,
For their eternal wheel thou art.

Thou dost roll into the past days,
Years, and ages too,
And naught thy giant progress stays.

I love to gaze upon
Thy speaking face, thy calm, fair brow,
And feel my spirit dark
And deep, grow bright and pure as thou. 20
Like thee it stands alone;
Like thee its native home is night,
But there the likeness ends,—
It beams not with thy steady light.
Its upward path is high,
But not so high as thine—thou'rt far
Above the reach of clouds,
Of storms, of wreck, oh lofty star!
I would all men might look
Upon thy pure sublimity, 30
And in their bosoms drink
Thy lovliness and light like me;
For who in all the world
Could gaze upon thee thus, and feel
Aught in his nature base,
Or mean, or low, around him steal!

Shine on companionless
As now thou seem'st. Thou art the throne
Of thy own spirit, star!
And mighty things must be alone. 40
Alone the ocean heaves,
Or calms his bosom into sleep;
Alone each mountain stands
Upon its basis broad and deep;
Alone through heaven the comets sweep,
Those burning worlds which God has thrown
Upon the universe in wrath,
As if he hated them—their path
No stars, no suns may follow, *none*—
'T is great, 't is great to be alone! 50

[1849, 1868]

10–16: these lines come later in the 1849 version, between the present lines 36–37. **11 soul's:** *clear* [1849]. **13–14:** In place of the stanza break here the 1849 version has the following line: *In night revolving,* **22 native:** not in the 1849 version.

The Forgiven Dead

Pale lies she now before me,
Whom late I scorned with bitter sneers,
What spell is this comes o'er me,
That all mine anger disappears?

My yesterday was clouded
With thinking of her cruel wrong—
But, white in death thus shrouded,
I only know *I loved her long!*

'T was not *herself* that wandered;
It was the demon of her brain— 10
I scarce can mourn I squandered
Such love on one whom love hath slain.

For died she not, pain-haunted
That truth she had forsook for gold?
Death, thou hast disenchanted
Her of sin—chaste, beautiful and cold!

But yesterday I wept not,
As pined she on her costly bed;
Well know I now, she slept not
There in peace, till slept she—dead! 20

I do forgive her, wholly;
Ye angels hear me—I forgive!
She lies so sweet and lowly—
She could not bear to sin and live.

To strew her tomb with roses,
Pure-white, as virgins' tombs should be,
I had not thought: but Fate disposes—
Her *soul* was virgin unto *me.*

[1868]

To a Mocking Bird Singing in a Tree

Sing on thou little mocker, sing—
Sarcastic Poet of the bowery clime!
Though full of scoff thy notes are sweet
As ever filled melodious rhyme!
I love thee for thy gracefulness,
And for thy jollity—such happiness!

Oh, I could seize it for my booty
  But that the deed would make thy music less.

Say, now, do not the feathery bands
  Feel hatred for thy songs which mock their own! 10
And as thou passest by, revile
  Thee angrily, with envy in their tone?
Or, are their little breasts too pure
  To know the pangs our human bosoms feel?
Perhaps they love thee for that same,
  And from thy sweetness new heart-gushes steal?

Upon the summit of yon tree
  How gaily thou dost sing! how free from pain.
Oh, would that my sad heart could bound
  With half the Eden rapture of thy strain! 20
I then would mock at every tear
  That falls where sorrow's shaded fountains flow,
And smile at every sigh that heaves
  In dark regret o'er some bewildering woe.

But mine is not thy breast—nor would
  I place within its little core one sting
That goads my own, for all the bliss
  That heartless robbery of thee would bring.
Ah no, still keep thy music power
  The ever radiant glory of thy soul, 30
And let thy voice of melody
  Soar on, as now, abhorrent of control.

May be thou sing'st of heaven sometimes,
  As raptured consciousness vades thy breast;
May be of some far home where love
  O'er bird-land spreads soft cooling shades of rest.
If man, whose voice is far less sweet
  Than thine, looks high for his eternal home,
Oh, say, do not thy dreamings too
  For some green spot and habitation roam? 40

If living thought can never die,
  Why should thine own expire? If there is love
Within thy heart, it must live on,
  Nor less than man's have dwelling-place above;
Thy notes shall then be brighter far
  Than now they be! And I may listen, too,

With finer ear, and clearer soul,
Beneath a shade more soft, a sky more blue.

[1868]

The Rainy Season in California

The rains have come, the winds are shrill,
Dark clouds are trailing near the ground;
The mists have clothed each naked hill,
And all is sad and drear around.

The swollen torrents rapid rush,
Far down the mountain gorges deep;
Now, falling o'er the jagged rocks,
They thunder through the hollows steep.

Now, in a basin boiling round,
They dance in maddest music high, 10
Or, with a sudden leap or bound,
Dash on like bolts of destiny.

From mountain's side to mountain's side,
The chasms vast in vapors lost,
Seem like a sea of darkness wide,
Which fancy dreams can ne'er be crost.

Far off the loftier mountains stand,
Calm, saint-like in their robes of white,
Like heaven-descended spirits grand
Who fill the darkness with their light. 20

Black clouds are rolling round their feet,
And ever strive to higher climb,
But still their mists dissolve in rain,
And reach not to that height sublime.

Gone are the birds with sunny days,
But flowers shall cheer us in their room,
And shrubs that pined in summer rays
Shall top their leafy boughs with bloom.

The grass grows green upon the hills,
(Now wrapt in thickly fallen clouds), 30
Which tall and beautiful shall rise
When they have cast their wintry shrouds.

Then wandering through their thousand vales,
Each flowery bordered path shall lead

To gardens wild, where nature's hand
Hath nurtured all with kindly heed.

Her own voluptuous couch is spread
Beneath the curtains of the sky,
And on her soft and flowery bed
The night looks down with loving eye. 40

But Fancy paints the scene too fast,
For thus she always loves to leave
The bitter present or the past,
And rainbows from the future weave.

Lo! night upon my musings here,
With rapid, stealthy foot hath crept
Unheard amid the sullen sounds
Which o'er my head have lately swept.

The pouring rain upon the roof,
The winds in wild careering bands, 50
Seem bent to see if tempest proof
The building on its basis stands.

The fiend of this dark night and storm
Stands howling at my very door—
I dread to see her haggard form
Break in and pass the threshold o'er.

But hold your own my trusty door!
Yield not an inch to's utmost might,
Nor let the hellish wild uproar
That reigns without come in to-night. 60

It stands—my lonely candle burns,
The single light for miles around;
Reminding me of some last hope
That still will light life's gloom profound.

Howl on ye elemental sprites,
And mutter forth your curses deep,
The anarchy that others frights,
Shall rock me soundly into sleep.

For, oh, I love to slumber 'neath
The tempest's wrathful melody, 70
And dream all night that on its wings
My soul enchanted soareth free.

[1868]

The Harp of Broken Strings

A stranger in a stranger land,
  Too calm to weep, too sad to smile,
I take my harp of broken strings,
  A weary moment to beguile;
And tho' no hope its promise brings,
  And present joy is not for me,
Still o'er that harp I love to bend,
  And feel its broken melody
With all my shattered feelings blend.

I love to hear its funeral voice 10
  Proclaim how sad my lot, how lone;
And when my spirit wilder grows,
  To list its deeper, darker tone.
And when my soul more madly glows
  Above the wrecks that round it lie,
It fills me with a strange delight,
  Past mortal bearing, proud and high,
To feel its music swell to might.

When beats my heart in doubt and awe,
  And Reason pales upon her throne, 20
Ah, then, when no kind voice can cheer
  The lot too desolate, too lone,
Its tones come sweet upon my ear,
  As twilight o'er some landscape fair:
As light upon the wings of night
  (The meteor flashes in the air,
The rising stars) its tones are bright.

And now by Sacramento's stream,
  What mem'ries sweet its music brings—
The vows of love, its smiles and tears, 30
  Hang o'er this harp of broken strings.
It speaks, and midst her blushing fears
  The beauteous one before me stands!
Pure spirit in her downcast eyes,
  And like twin doves her folded hands!

It breathes again—and at my side
  She kneels, with grace divinely rare—
Then showering kisses on my lips,
  She hides our busses with her hair;

Then trembling with delight, she flings 40
  Her beauteous self into my arms,
As if o'erpowered, she sought for wings
  To hide her from her conscious charms!

It breathes once more, and bowed in grief,
  The bloom has left her cheek forever,
While, like my broken harp-strings now,
  Behold her form with feeling quiver!
She turns her face o'errun with tears,
  To him that silent bends above her,
And, by the sweets of other years, 50
  Entreats him still, oh, still to love her!

He loves her still—but darkness falls
  Upon his ruined fortunes now,
And 't is his exile doom to flee.
  The dews, like death, are on his brow,
And cold the pang about his heart;
  Oh, cease—to die is agony:
'T is more than death when loved ones part!

Well may this harp of broken strings
  Seem sweet to me by this lonely shore. 60
When like a spirit it breaks forth,
  And speaks of beauty evermore!
When like a spirit it evokes
  The buried joys of early youth,
And clothes the shrines of early love,
  With all the radiant light of truth!

[1850, 1868]

1 **A stranger in a stranger land**: As an exile from the Cherokee Nation, Ridge identifies here with Moses' description of himself as a stranger in a strange land, which this line echoes from Exodus 2:22.

October Hills

I look upon the purple hills
  That rise in steps to yonder peaks,
And all my soul their silence thrills
  And to my heart their beauty speaks.

What now to me the jars of life,
  Its petty cares, its harder throes?

The hills are free from toil and strife,
And clasp me in their deep repose.

They soothe the pain within my breast
No power but theirs could ever reach, 10
They emblem that eternal rest
We cannot compass in our speech.

From far I feel their secret charm—
From far they shed their healing balm,
And lost to sense of grief or harm
I plunge within their pulseless calm.

How full of peace and strength they stand,
Self-poised and conscious of their weight!
We rise with them, that silent band,
Above the wrecks of Time or Fate; 20

For, mounting from their depths unseen,
Their spirit pierces upward, far,
A soaring pyramid serene,
And lifts us where the angels are.

I would not lose this scene of rest,
Nor shall its dreamy joy depart;
Upon my soul it is imprest,
And pictured in my inmost heart.

[1867, 1868]

The text comes from the 1868 version, except as indicated in the "Textual Notes" to this volume.

To the Beautiful

Oh, blame me not that I am bold,
Nor scorn my too adventurous rhymes,
For how can he be tame or cold
Whose heart hath bloomed in southern climes?

Or who hath lived among the flowers,
Or by those clear perennial streams,
Whose music charms the gliding hours,
Nor gave his soul to passion's dreams?

Why should his heart not love to live
Within the light of beauty's eyes, 10
And all its world of feeling give,
To win from her, her trembling sighs?

Alas, the world may say 't is wrong,
But who can rule the wayward heart?
For we are weak, and nature strong,
And love is our immortal part!

We may not see the rosy mouth,
The laughing eye, the graceful limb,
And bosom, like the sunny south,
With love o'erflowing from the brim. 20

We may not see such loveliness,
Without the wish at least to gaze;
And cold were she, denying this
To him whose every look is praise.

Forgive me, if my heart has erred,
In deeming thou would'st not despise,
And I will cancel every word,
To meet forgiveness from thine eyes.

[1868]

A Night Scene

Unbroken silence! save the melody
That steals on silence unawares, and makes
It seem scarce more than silence still; that takes
Possession of the senses bodily,
And claims the slumbering spirit ere it wakes.

Save this low melody of waves, no sound
Is heard among the circling hills. I sit
And muse alone—the time and place are fit—
And summon spirits from the blue profound,
That answer me and through my vision flit. 10

What beauteous being stands upon yon hill,
With hair night-hued, and brow and bosom white?
Around her floats the evening's loving light—
Her feet are lost amid the shadows soft and still,
But 'gainst the sky her form is pictured to my sight.

How still! how motionless! yet full of life,
As is of music-tones the sleeping string,
As is of grace the blue-bird's resting wing!
She pauses there—each limb with beauty rife—
As if through boundless space her foot might spring. 20

But hark! what tones are filling all the air,
  That drinks them, with the star-light blended now,
  And wavelet-murmurings from below?
Her voice! her harp! swept by the white hand rare
  That moon-like guides the music's tide-like flow.

Strange one! no harp! no voice I've heard like thine,
  No startling beauty like thine own have seen,
  The rounded world and vaulted heaven between.
To gaze on thee 't is madness all divine,
  But o'er the gulf my spirit loves to lean. 30

Thou art what I may ne'er embrace on earth,
  Thou sweetly moulded one, thou heavenly-eyed!
  But if when we do lay these forms aside,
For us new forms among the stars have birth,
  In some sweet world we'll meet, my spirit bride!

Fair worlds, like ripples o'er the watery deep
  When breezes softly o'er the surface play,
  In circles one by one ye stretch away,
Till, lost to human vision's wildest sweep
  Our souls are left to darkness and dismay. 40

[1868]

False, but Beautiful

Dark as a demon's dream is one I love—
In soul—but oh, how beautiful in form!
She glows like Venus throned in joy above,
Or on the crimson couch of Evening warm
Reposing her sweet limbs, her heaving breast
Unveiled to him who lights the golden west!
Ah, me, to be by that soft hand carest,
To feel the twining of that snowy arm,
To drink that sigh with richest love opprest,
To bathe within that sunny sea of smiles, 10
To wander in that wilderness of wiles
And blissful blandishments—it is to thrill
With subtle poison, and to feel the will
Grow weak in that which all the veins doth fill.
Fair sorceress! I know she spreads a net
The strong, the just, the brave to snare; and yet
My soul cannot, for its own sake, forget
The fascinating glance which flings its chain

Around my quivering heart and throbbing brain,
And binds me to my painful destiny, 20
As bird, that soars no more on high,
Hangs trembling on the serpent's doomful eye.

[1868]

To L——on Receiving Her Portrait

Long years have passed, and I have seen thee not,
Save in my waking and my nightly dreams,
When rose our quiet well-remembered cot
In that far land of pleasant woods and streams.

Around my brow the storms of thought have swept,
And o'er my brain their quivering lightnings played,
Yet mem'ry hath survived the shock and kept
Unharmed the impress which thy love has made.

Disease hath fed upon my frame, and I
Have deemed it would be sweet to sleep beneath 10
The sod! I thought of thee, and would not die,
But struggled with my pain and conquer'd death.

Within the shadows of the mountains tall,
Which seemed the wings of grand and gloomy thought,
I've laid me down and dreamed—forgetting all
Save thee and thy sweet holy love unbought.

Deep in the forests lone and dark I've sat,
'Till sense and soul were charmed; and I did take
The voice of streams for thine, and dreaming that
Thyself was there, I wept for joy's own sake. 20

Oft gazing on the Heavens, I've seen thy form
Of loveliness far floating midst the blue,
Or lying on the couch of Evening warm,
Whose blush was like thine own cheeks' rosy hue.

And now that thy fair features meet my eyes,
Presented lifelike by the skill of art,
I feel a thousand raptures bird-like rise,
And form sweet music-circles round my heart.

I look again: alas, those eyes are sad
As lonely stars that in the ocean sit! 30
Reproach me not, sweet orbs! for life has had
Few charms for me since last those eyes I met.

I turn away: I cannot bear those eyes
Of melancholy meaning, calm and deep;
They speak to me of rudely rended ties—
And life's stern task allows no time to weep.

[1868]

The Stolen White Girl

The prairies are broad, and the woodlands are wide
And proud on his steed the wild half-breed may ride,
With the belt round his waist and the knife at his side.
And no white man may claim his beautiful bride.

Though he stole her away from the land of the whites,
Pursuit is in vain, for her bosom delights
In the love that she bears the dark-eyed, the proud,
Whose glance is like starlight beneath a night-cloud.

Far down in the depths of the forest they'll stray,
Where the shadows like night are lingering all day; 10
Where the flowers are springing up wild at their feet,
And the voices of birds in the branches are sweet.

Together they'll roam by the streamlets that run,
O'ershadowed at times then meeting the sun—
The streamlets that soften their varying tune,
As up the blue heavens calm wanders the moon!

The contrast between them is pleasing and rare;
Her sweet eye of blue, and her soft silken hair,
Her beautiful waist, and her bosom of white
That heaves to the touch with a sense of delight; 20

His form more majestic and darker his brow,
Where the sun has imparted its liveliest glow—
An eye that grows brighter with passion's true fire,
As he looks on his loved one with earnest desire.

Oh, never let Sorrow's cloud darken their fate,
The girl of the "pale face," her Indian mate!
But deep in the forest of shadows and flowers,
Let Happiness smile, as she wings their sweet hours.

[1868]

Poem

The waves that murmur at our feet,
  Through many an age had rolled
Ere fortune found her favorite seat
  Within this land of gold.

The Digger, searching for his roots,
  Here roamed the region wide—
Or, wearied with the day's pursuits,
  Slept by this restless tide.

The dream of greatness never rose
  Upon his simple brain; 10
The wealth on which a nation grows,
  And builds its power to reign,

All darkly lay beneath his tread,
  Where many a stream did wind,
Deep slumbering in its yellow bed,
  The charm that rules mankind.

Had he and his dark brethren known
  Of gold the countless worth,
They now beyond that power had grown
  Which sweeps them from the earth. 20

But happier he perchance, by far,
  Still digging for his roots,
Than thousand paler wanderers are
  Whose toil hath had no fruits.

Still following luck's unsteady star,
  Where'er its light hath gleamed,
To many a gulch and burning bar,
  Which proved not what it seemed.

How wearied they have sat them down,
  To watch the passers by— 30
The throng that still 'gainst Fortune's frown,
  Their varied "prospects" try.

Behold the active and the young,
  Whose strength not yet doth fail,
And hear them, with a cheerful tongue,
  Encourage those that quail.

With mournful, melancholly look,
  The broken-hearted come,

Whose souls we read as in a book,
Though shut their lips and dumb! 40

And mark yon aged, trembling one,
How weak his step and slow!
Ah, hear him as he totters on,
Sigh painfully and low!

Far from the peaceful home he left,
In fever-rage for gold—
Of friends, almost of hope bereft,
He now is trebly old.

And Fortune often favors not,
Who most her favors need; 50
Thus he may wander on forgot,
While strong ones gain the meed.

How many hearts like his have pined,
As prisoned bird of air,
For sunny homes they left behind,
And friends who loved them there,

And many a merry heart *shall* pine,
Through long and lonesome years,
And watch the light of life decline
Amidst uncounted tears. 60

Far off among the mountains stern,
Shall thousands meet with blight,
And many a raven lock shall turn
To hairs of frosty white;

And many a lonely grave shall hide
The mouldering form of him
For whom sad eyes are never dried,
With age and sorrow dim.

Yet, though the wayside all be strewn
With sorrows and with graves, 70
The glory of the race is shown
By what it does and braves.

What though the desert's mouldering heaps
Affright the startled eye—
What though in wilds the venturer sleeps,
His bones uncovered lie,

'Tis not the living that have won
Alone the victory:
But each dead soldier, too, has done
His part as loftily. 80

'Tis they—the living *and* the dead—
Who have redeemed our land;
Have cities reared, the arts have spread,
And placed us where we stand.

As led Adventure bold before,
The Arts and Learning came;
And now, behold! upon this shore
They have a place and name.

Where roamed erewhile the rugged bear
Amid these oaks of green, 90
And wandering from his mountain lair
The cougar's steps were seen,

Lo! Peace hath built her quiet nest;
And "mild-eyed Science" roves,
As was her wont when Greece was blest,
In Academic groves.

Oh! tranquil be these shades for aye,
These groves forever green;
And youth and age still bless their day
That here their steps have been. 100

May Learning here still have her seat,
Her empire of the mind;
The home of Genius, Wit's Retreat,
Whate'er is pure refined.

And thus the proudest boast shall be
Of young Ambition crowned—
"The woods of Oakland sheltered me,
Their leaves my brow have bound."

Delivered at Commencement of Oakland College, California, June 6th 1861.

[1868]

4 **this land of gold**: much of the poem addresses the California Gold Rush, which began in 1848. The gold drew a huge influx of settlers who decimated the Indian population through disease, theft of land, and genocide. 5 **Digger**: derogatory term for California Indians. In this poem and other writings, Ridge shows a conflicted response to California Indians, sometimes joining in the prejudices against them and feeling that, as a Cherokee, he was superior.

Erinna

Imagination! rouse thee from repose,
And to our eyes Erinna lost disclose;
Since from the living voice of Time is gone
Her genius-gifted and melodious tone,
And from his starlit page the words are fled
She from her early lyre in wonder shed!
Arouse thee! fling around her fancied form
A glorious hue—a beauty rich and warm.
'Tis done: alone by Lesbos' wave-washed strand
I see her in the pride of beauty stand, 10
Far gazing where the Aegean waters smile
Around her native home and classic isle.
Soft blow the breezes on her snowy brow,
And stir the folds around her limbs that flow;
Her golden hair's luxuriance on her neck
Falls unregarded down—it needs no check,
For who would comb the plumage of the bird,
Or smooth the dimpling waves by Zephyrs stirred?
Her small white hands are linked beneath her zone,
And 'tween her sweetly rounded arms are shown 20
Twin spheres of love and Pleasure's burning throne!
A glow is on her cheeks and fresh her lips
As evening cloud the sun's vermilion tips;
Her clear, bright eye wild wanders o'er the main,
That rolling its blue waves along, a strain
Eternal utters and sublime, to charm
The fair, green isles that o'er its bosom swarm.

Ah, beautiful indeed! What magic gives
The grace that in her every movement lives?
What power unseen is breathing o'er her face, 30
Where every lineament divine we trace?
It is the magic Sorcerer never stole
From science dread—the magic of the soul!
It is the power of Genius, Heaven conferred,
Which, though it be unseen and all unheard,
Imparts its own true beauty to the face,
And lends unto the form its bloom and grace.

Erinna, mid the objects Time has cast
His hand upon, thou standest within the past
In lonely and peculiar loveliness. 40
The child of song, with nature's own impress

Upon thee, yet thy harp is hushed, and no
Sweet strains of thine through distant times shall flow;
Thy voice hath perished sweetly though it sung,
And perished those who on its accents hung.

Thou wert a bird that breathed its soul away
In song, and died—but Echo lost the lay;
Thou wert a star which shone a single night,
But, setting once, returned no more its light.
Thou art a glorious image of the mind 50
Seen through the depths of ages far behind,
Round which our Fancy flings her brightest beams,
While ancient Story faintly aids her dreams.

The friend of Sappho! linked together be
Those names, and never wrecked on Time's wide sea;
And when we read the passion-wildering strain
Of Sappho's muse, that charms the listening brain,
We'll feel Erinna's voice our hearts inspire,
And deem her lovely hand is on the lyre!

[1848, 1868]

Title: Erinna, a native of Lesbos and friend of Sappho, died at the early age of nineteen. She is described as a girl of extraordinary beauty and genius, but her works, all except two or three epigrams, have unfortunately perished. (Poets and Poetry of the Ancients. By Wm. Peter, A.M.). [Ridge's note.]

Modern scholars look with uncertainty on the little we know about Erinna. In 1928, scholars found a fragmentary excerpt from a long poem probably written by Erinna. They now believe that she lived in the fourth century B.C.E., about two and a half centuries after Sappho. No one knows whether the legend of her death at nineteen is accurate. For a summary, see Snyder 88–89; for a comprehensive account, see Neri.)

Lines on a Humming Bird Seen at a Lady's Window

Yon dew-drunk bacchanal
Hath emptied all the roses of their sweets,
And drained the fluent souls
Of all the lilies from their crystal bowls;
And now, on rapid wing he fleets
To where by yonder crystal pane
A lady, young and fair,
Looks out upon the sifting sunlit rain.

That ripe, red mouth he takes
For rarer flower than ever yet was quaffed, 10

And longeth much to sip,
The honey of that warm and dewy lip,
And drain its sweetness at a draught.
Ah, vain, delusive hope! 't is hard,
But, rainbow wing-ed bird,
Thou'rt not alone from those sweet lips debarred.

Now, charm-ed with her eyes,
And dazzled by their more than sunny light,
He winnoweth with his wings
The fineness of the golden mist, and swings, 20
A breathing glory in her sight!
Too happy bird, he's won a smile
From that proud beauty there
Which from his throne an angel might beguile.

How dizzy with delight
He spins his radiant circles in the air!
Now, on their spiral breath
Upborne, he 'scapes th' enchantress underneath
And will not die of joy or of despair—
The joy of her bright eyes, and wild, 30
Despairing e'er to win
The nectar of those lips which on him smiled.

[1868]

Poem

All hail, the fairest, greatest, best of days!
With heaving hearts, and tongues attuned to praise.
Behold, what thousands at thy coming throng,
With bannered pomp, with eloquence and song.
Upon her path impulsive bounds the earth,
As conscious of her deed of grandest birth;
And Time's Recorder, standing in the sun,
To count the orbic periods as they run,
Re-notes the chiefest hour of all the age,
And finds new glory on his blazing page. 10
Oh, well this day may throbbing bosoms beat,
And fervent spirits feel divinest heat,
And young and old, with willing steps and free,
And voices glad as waves of summery sea,
Come forth from cottage and from hall, to fling
On Freedom's shrine the tributes that they bring!

Well might the theme the meanest muse inspire,
To sweep the willing chords with hand of fire,
For, burning in the firmament of fame,
Each name renowned pours down its flood of flame, 20
And deeds come crowding in the path of years,
Till all the Past in one grand scene appears;
And standing midst the wondrous days of old,
We seem, with unveiled vision to behold
What Kings with trembling and with awe surveyed,
The deep foundations of an empire laid.
With Adams and with Washington we see
The growing of the shadowed prophecy,
And watch, elate, the pillared structure rise,
Till, crowned with stars, and domed amid the skies, 30
It fronts the Nations in its strength: and, lo!
Amidst the rapture of the hour aglow,
From yonder far-seen Heaven's supremest heights
Descendeth IMMORTALITY, and writes
Her name upon its constellated brow!
Long years, or bright or dark that tower has stood—
Full many a siege has braved of fire and flood;
Contending factions sweeping at its base at will,
The storms have cleared and left it glorious still.
Through night and darkness has its beacon light 40
Still shone upon the nation's wondering sight;
And when they looked to see its proud dome bend,
And midst the blackening gloom and wreck descend,
It rose, emerging from the tempest's shock,
Like Chimborazo's condor-nesting rock!

But in our dome the eagle builds its nest,
And with our banner flies with armored breast;
Yet, crawling round those pillars white, we've seen
Beneath his perch, those meaner things unclean;
That hissing wind where demigods have trod! 50
They've slimed Mount Vernon's consecrated sod.
In all the nation's highways still we meet
Their coiling shapes, and in the august seat,
Where sat a Washington, but late we found
The meanest reptile of them all inwound.
But now these slimier things their tasks have done,
And in their stead comes forth the monster one,
Their many-headed sire! Yea, Treason rears
Aloft his snaky front, and impious, dares

The high and holy place, where sits enthroned 60
Our country's Genius, with her armies zoned.
Black rolls the cloud o'er friend and foe alike—
But whom, whom shall the bolts of vengeance strike?
Methinks the starry banner that had braved
The regal mistress of the deep, has waved
Where Cortez' banners soared; with victory blest,
Has rippled in the breezes of the west;
In northern hurricane has tost, and known
But triumph in its march from zone to zone,
Shall never sink before you rebel crew— 70
Shall never bow, vile traitors, unto you!

Ah, would those tongues could speak which now are dumb!
For, lo! the evil days have on us come,
And heroes, patriots stand appalled to see
In hands untried the nation's destiny.
Good men and true there are—strong men and bold;
But not, oh, not the mighty men of old!
'T was not till Jackson's heart was dust; till Day
To Night had given the electric brain of Clay;
Till God-like Webster's all imperial mind, 80
From its vast sphere of living light declined,
That Treason, scourged into his den, did dare
Again come forth to foul the shrinking air,
And blot the face of Freedom's soil with births
That Hell shall own too monstrous for the earth's.
And he who stood those men of strength beside,
In heart and brain and breadth of soul allied,
The statesman of a younger time, but tried
In days his elders might have shrunk to see—
The gallant, glorious Douglas, where is he? 90
The hosts that rallied to his battle cry,
And deemed such power was never made to die,
Now weep above the spot whose sods enfold
The man of might this orb shall seldom mould.
He died too soon, but other souls sublime
Shall spring perchance, from out this troublous time,
And, seizing from each silent chieftain's grave
The drooping, mourning standards of the brave,
Their folds unfurl and bear them to the field
Where free-born patriots die but never yield. 100

God of our fathers, grant that such there be!
And round them pour the millions of the free.

Let voice to voice, and hand to hand, and soul
To soul, give answer, and combine, as roll
The waves unto the marching winds that sweep
Cloud-bannered, thunder-armed, upon the deep.
In peace or war still let our Nation stand—
Fair Liberty still haunt her native land,
And long, long after we have sunk to dust,
And crowns and kingdoms failed, as fail they must, 110
And Treason, spreading wide its serpent toils
Has died, self-stung in its own coils—
This frame gigantic of our Nation's might,
Shall loom upon the world's enraptured sight,
Still bearing on its broad, majestic brow,
ESTO PERPETUA!—Eternal be, as now.

Delivered at San Francisco, July 4th, 1861.

[1868]

27 **Adams, Washington**: George Washington and John Adams, the first and second presidents of the United States. 36 **or bright**: whether bright 45 **Chimborazo**: famously high mountain in Ecuador. 51 **Mount Vernon**: home of George Washington. 55 **meanest reptile**: possibly Abraham Lincoln, from Ridge's perspective. 61 **Genius**: spirit. 66 **Cortez**: sixteenth-century Spanish conqueror of Mexico. 78–80 **Jackson, Clay, Webster**: General and later President Andrew Jackson, here addressed respectfully, though he forced the Cherokees from their lands; Henry Clay and Daniel Webster, two of the most influential American orators and statesmen in the first half of the nineteenth century. 116 **Esto Perpetua**: Latin for Let It Be Forever. **Note, July 4**: By July 4, the Civil War had begun. Lincoln became president in March 1861, and the Civil War began in April.

A Scene Along the Rio de las Plumas

With solemn step I trace
A dark and dismal place,
Where moss with trailing ends,
From heavy boughs depends;
Where day resembles night,
And birds of sullen flight
Pierce darkness with their screams;
Where slow and sluggish streams
Crawl through the sleeping woods
And weirdful solitudes. 10
In dreamy languor bound,
Upon their slimy breast
The lolling lilies rest,
And from their depths profound
Strange things, with staring eyes

And uncouth limbs, arise—
A moment gaze with mute surprise
Then sink adown like lead,
And seek their oozy bed.

What looks a spirit there, 20
Snow-white upon the air,
And hov'ring over these
Deep pools and drooping trees,
As if some heavenly sprite
Had come from Day to Night,
Is but the crane that feeds,
When hungered 'mong the reeds;
Or sloughs, flag-margined, wades,
Meandering 'neath the shades,
And makes his vulgar dish 30
Of creeping things and fish.

Yon ermined owl that flits
Through dusky leaves, or sits
In somber silence now
On yonder ivyed bough,
And looks a druid priest—
No higher thoughts inspire
Than lowest wants require,
As how to make his feast,
When lurking mouse or bird 40
Hath from its covert stirred.

Those flaming eyes awake
In yonder thorny brake,
Which dilate as I pass,
Illumining the grass
And lighting darksome ground,
Are not from that profound,
Where cries of woe resound
And Dante's damned abound,
Nor yet the wandering ghouls,— 50
The dread of dead men's souls,—
(Because their flesh he craves,
And digs it from their graves),
But orbs of sinuous snake
Who from the neighboring lake
Or vapor-breeding bog,
His victim soon shall take—

Some luckless dozing frog.
Nor will thy lither shape,
Thou rodent sly escape, 60
If once thine eye hath caught
The fire within that head,
From venomed sources fed,
With fascination fraught.

I reach a dimmer nook,
And warily I look,
For where yon night-shades grow
And baneful blossoms blow,
Beneath the toadstools, well
I know ill-creatures dwell— 70
Tarantula, whose bite
Would strongest heart affright;
The stinging centipede,
Whose hundred-footed speed,
And hundred arm-ed feet
Bring death and danger fleet,
That, with Briarean clasp,
The fated victim grasp,
And scorpion, single-stinged,
Fabled erst as winged, 80
And still reported wide,
If pressed, a suicide.

And here I see—but lo!
I can no further go,
For what's this hum I hear
Which fills the atmosphere,
And drums the tingling ear
Till, half distraught, I reel?
I heard, but now I feel!
Good sakes, what winged forms! 90
What singing, dizzing swarms!
Ten thousand needles flamed
Could not with them be named.

[1868]

Title: The Rio de las Plumas in northern California, now known as the Feather River, an English translation of its Spanish name. **49 Dante's damned**: those consigned to the torments of hell in medieval Italian poet Dante Alighieri's *Inferno*. **77 Briarean**: In ancient Greek mythology, Briareus was one of the three Hecatonchires, giants with fifty heads and a hundred hands.

The Still Small Voice

Alas, how every thing will borrow
Hues, tones, and bitterness from sorrow!
If evening comes with softened ray
To close the eye of dying day;
If morning ushers in the morrow
With dew-drops sprinkled on its way,
'Tis all the same: a voice is whispering from the Past—
"Too late! too late! the doom is set, the die is cast!"

If through the woods my footsteps roam,
Where always they do feel at home, 10
And wandering leisurely I trace
Each streamlet to its rising place,
To hear its music, see its foam,
No tide of sound, no shape of grace
Can hush that solemn voice, that whispering from the Past—
"Too late! too late! the doom is set, the die is cast!"

If o'er some well-loved page I bend
In converse deep as with a friend
Whose kindly tones I love to hear,
That lowly sound will reach my ear, 20
And sadly with my feelings blend
As sigh with sigh and tear with tear!
The mighty thoughts I read all fade before the Past,
Which cries "too late! the doom is set, the die is cast!"

Oh, never hushed that voice will be!
As sadly as the mournful sea,
Where savage silent shores it laves,
And darkness dwells upon its waves,
Do sound its low-breathed tones to me!
The peace my bosom often craves,
Will linger but a moment's space—it flies the Past, 30
Whose voice yet cries "the doom is set, the die is cast!"

A raven-thought is darkly set
Upon my brow—where shades are met
Of grief, of pain, of toil, and care—
The raven-thought of stern despair!
Oh, wherefore are my eyelids wet,
While birds make music on the air?
No ear but mine can catch the breathings of the Past,
"Too late! too late! the doom is set, the die is cast!" 40

Adieu, sweet scenes of other days;
Ye sleep within the past, like rays
Of moonlight on a silent lake.
'T is not within my power to wake
Your slumbers with these feeble lays;
I can but feel my bosom quake
To hear the low but awful fiat of the Past—
"Too late! too late! the doom is set, the die is cast!

[1848, 1851, 1868]

Title: after "a still small voice," 1 Kings 19:12.

Eyes

I sing of eyes, of woman's eyes,
A theme from earliest ages sung,
But which, till all of nature dies,
Shall ever bid the harp be strung.

There is the eye of sober gray,
Which seems to shadow forth regret,
As if the spirit mourned alway
Its starry hopes forever set.

There is the eye of hazel bright,
Which wins and dazzles where it falls, 10
Reviving with its showers of light
The happy bosom it enthralls.

There is the eye of tender blue,
Soft as the heaven at set of sun,
Which many deem is ever true,
And smiles on all but speaks to one.

There is the eye of darker hue,
Which rivals Midnight on her throne;
Now softly bright as streams that through
The shady forests wander lone; 20

Now like a cloud that hides from sight
The beauty of the rolling spheres,
And flashes far with angry light,
Or sinking downwards melts to tears.

As sages loved in ancient days
To read the heavens when darkness fell,

So on those orbs of black we gaze,
And feel our inmost bosoms swell.

As lovely as the worlds that lie
Reposing in the Night's embrace, 30
Is the soft meaning of that eye,
And deeper than the depths of space!

I cease—for all description's vain;
Let each one choose the eye he likes,
That melts the heart or soothes the brain,
Or like the dreaded lightning strikes;

But as for me, I love those eyes,
No matter what their hues may be,
To which the heart's warm feelings rise
In overflowing love to me. 40

Alternate fount of light and tears,
Their smiles are sweet, their sadness too,
And I could joy or grieve for years,
As those fond eyes might bid me do!

[1853, 1868]

Te-con-ees-kee, Cherokee

Nothing is known about Te-con-ees-kee beyond what appears in his two poems published in the *Cherokee Advocate.* From "Though far from thee Georgia in exile I roam," it appears that he came from Georgia, fought with the federal government—perhaps against the Creeks in 1814 at the Battle of Horseshoe Bend—and later left his home as part of the forced removal of Cherokees to the west. At least several Cherokees named Te-con-ees-kee (in various spellings) appear briefly in records within the right time frame, but without substantial information about them and without providing a way of differentiating among various people with the same name.

[This poem was introduced with the following note above its title:]
Te-con-ees-kee is mistaken as to the name of the Female Seminary. It was suggested by one and approved by many, that the name be Pocahonta &c., but the Executive preferred the following, which the institution will bear—Cherokee Female Seminary.

The following lines, however, are none the less acceptable and becoming. We give them a place with pleasure.

Suggested by the report, in the Advocate, of the laying of the corner stone of the Pocahontas Female Seminary—Cherokee Nation

From the fair land of her heart's fond devotion,
The daughter of the Chieftain was borne o'er the wave,
To a far away Isle mid the mists of the Ocean;
And a winter was left on the heart of the Brave:
How oft repeated! perhaps in a while,
The spring bird of Powhatan will come from the Isle.

Years passed, and the clods of the vale of Virginia,
Where James river rolls its tide, lay o'er the dead;
The Chief in the grave was reposing, nor seen ye,
That daughter in sorrow recline o'er his bed; 10
The father had waited, and watched, but the while,
The Bird of Powhatan came not from the Isle.

No more to the land of her youthful devotion—
From her seaward bower she returned o'er the wave,
For in that far away Isle of the Ocean,
The hand of the stranger had made her a grave.
He perhaps, a tear, over her memory shed,
But O! there was no Indian to weep by the dead.

Years passed, still along on wings of time stealing
Away to the shades of eternity past; 20
And o'er the memory of the brave and the feeling
There were shades from the night of forgetfulness cast.
Time's hand e'en the name from the marble had smitten;
That marked the lone grave in the Isle of the Britain.

But a spirit comes up from the shadow of years,
That word of the past, from that realm to reclaim,—
The name, Pocahontas the Cherokee hears,
And Tahlequah's valley re-echoes the name,
Where the cheer on the vale arose loudest, they placed,
That name that was brought from the years of the past. 30

How meet, that from this valley the welcome arose,
"To the sky" that a boon it its beauty unfurls,
For where would the daughter of Powhatan repose,
In remembrance but here with Cherokee girls,
Here, here on their hearts let their memory be written,
Who sleeps far away in the Isle of the Britain.

The earth wounded stranger that wandered abroad,
   To a nature of fire and feeling allied,
The cruel may censure, the unmeaning applaud,
   But let not the full feeling of heart be denied, 40
By you to her memory whose name of past years,
This Dome on the valley of Tahlequah bears.

[1848]

2 **daughter of the Chieftain**: Pocahontas was the daughter of Wahunsenacawh, better known as Powhatan, the powerful leader (weroance or chief) of the Powhatan people and the Powhatan confederacy in what is now eastern Virginia, near where the British built Jamestown in 1607. British colonists captured Pocahontas in 1613. In 1614 she married the colonist John Rolfe, and the following year she and her husband traveled to Great Britain, where she died from smallpox in 1617. **28 Tahlequah**: capital of the Cherokee Nation in Indian Territory. **42 Dome**: the original building of the Cherokee Female Seminary had a modest dome at its center.

["Though far from thee Georgia in exile I roam"]

Though far from thee Georgia in exile I roam,
My heart in thy mountain land still has its home;
Would I ask the wretch in captivity borne,
From the home of his heritage why he would mourn;
Far in flown years those scenes of *my* sorrow recede,
Yet still must my heart in its bitterness bleed,
Still must the name of the land of my birth,
Alight on my ear as a curse on the earth:
Georgia, O Georgia! there is that in thy name,
To my heart that within enkindles a flame; 10
An anguish debaring the tears from the eyes,
But my heart may not here in its bitterness rise,
I remember thee fondly thou land of birth,
While the sports of my childhood, the scenes of my mirth,
And even the sorrows of manhood appear,
With all of their bitterness still to endear,
That remembrance the more, to the heart that now bleeds,
The more, that those scenes of my sorrow recede:
I love thee still Georgia, thy mountain land gave
Me birth, and my father has in it his grave, 20
Thy mountain stream sings to the peaceful repose,
Of my children that sleep where it warbling flows,
And though I'm now an alien and stranger to thee,
For these thou art fondly remembered by me;
O! Land of the home of my heart, did they well,
The first born of thy mountains from thee to expel?
Knew you who spoiled us the hearts of that race,

You trampled to the dust, and expelled from your face?
Can time from the heart of the red-man erase,
The feelings his pride may not deign to express, 30
But that awake too oft in the thoughts of his breast,
When its better emotions would wish them at rest;
Was there kindness toward thee in his heart, and a trust,
That led him to deem thee e'en more than thou wast;
That led him to look to a brother, than he
More favored, who his guide and his guardian would be,
How did you requite then that bosom all feeling?
He met thee all courteous, but you saw him not kneeling,
Must you have him more humbly to bow at thy beck?
That you fastened the fetters of force on his neck? 40
Georgia, o Georgia there is a stain on thy name!
And ages to come will yet blush for thy shame,
While the child of the Cherokee exile unborn,
The results of thy violence deeply will mourn,
He who with his country on the foeman has rushed,
And in the chances of war has before him been crushed,
Feels not in his fall the deep wounds that belong
To him who receives from a brother a wrong;
My blood in the heat of the battle was shed;
But 'twas in the battles of my brother that I bled; 50
Then sought I, in peace, in the land of my birth,
Beside him a home, but was spurned from the earth;
For this has my heart thus in bitterness bled,
And *will* bleed, though those scenes of my sorrow have fled,
For this comes the name of the land of my birth,
On my ear as the sound of a curse on the earth.
But peace to thee Georgia, though this must be so,
Peace to thy Highlands, and the streamlets that flow
From thence mid the scenes of my joys and my sorrows;
Peace be to thee while remembrance for me borrows, 60
The weeds of the mourner from every loved scene,
On mountain and vale where my footstep has been,
O for the memory of the once loved that thou hast,
In the graves of thy mountains, my peace on thee rest.

[1848]

49 **My blood . . . was shed / . . . in the battles of my brother**: suggesting that Te-con-ees-kee fought for the United States before the United States forced him from his land. 61 **weeds**: clothes worn for mourning.

Si-tu-a-kee, Jr., Cherokee

At its publication, this poem was attributed to Si-tu-a-kee, Jr., perhaps the same Situakee (or Situwakee) who later fought for the Confederacy in the Civil War, and perhaps related to the Cherokee chief and judge Situakee who led a large contingent of Cherokees on the Trail of Tears in 1838 and 1839 (Starr 103, G. Foreman 311).

To the Tahlequah Gals

Farewell, oh many are the hours,
Of friendship we have known—
And many are the gentle words,
And breathed in gentlest tone.

That you have kindly spoken, when,
No thought of parting rose,
To cloud our dream of happiness,
And warn us of its close.

Farewell, our intercourse has been,
Unbroken by a——words; 10
No look of coldness ever yet,
Our bosom's peace has stirr'd.

But evenly and truthfully,
The hours have past us by—
And now, I cannot say—farewell,
Save with a tearful eye.

But still farewell, and when afar
From one who loved thee ever,
Oh let not time, nor change, nor aught,
Our friendship's bright chain sever; 20

But keep its links as pure and bright,
As ever in time gone by—
And if 'tis ordered that we meet
No more beneath the sky.

[1850]

Title: Tahlequah was the capital of the Cherokee Nation in Indian Territory. **10 ——words**: the long dash is clearly a long dash, but the letters between *w* and *s* are too faintly printed to be certainly transcribed.

William Penn Boudinot, Cherokee, 1830–1898

Born in the Eastern Cherokee Nation, William Penn Boudinot (the last syllable is pronounced like the word *knot*) came from a legendary Cherokee family. His father was Elias Boudinot, who edited the *Cherokee Phoenix*, the first American Indian newspaper. His brother was the well known politician and editor Elias Cornelius Boudinot. Stand Watie, the famous Cherokee Confederate general, was their father's brother, and Chief John Ridge was their father's cousin, so that William Penn Boudinot was also related to Ridge's son John Rollin Ridge, whose poetry appears in this volume. After Elias Boudinot and John Ridge were assassinated in 1839 for signing (with great reluctance) the Treaty of New Echota, which authorized the Cherokees' removal from their homeland, William Penn Boudinot went to school in Vermont and Connecticut and then worked as a jewelry engraver in Philadelphia. Returning to Indian Territory, he began public service as a clerk of the Cherokee National Committee (the Cherokee Senate). During the Civil War, he fought with the Confederates under Stand Watie. Later, he was a leader of the Cherokee National Party, editor of the *Cherokee Advocate*, supervisor of schools, executive secretary to Chief Dennis Bushyhead, and a Cherokee delegate to Washington, D.C. As a lawyer, he played a key role in shaping Cherokee law. He disappeared in 1898 while seeking treatment for a morphine addiction, probably jumping or falling from a ship in Lake Michigan. William Penn Boudinot's one published poem, included here, which he signed "CHEROKEE" and "Tahlequah" (the capital of the Cherokee Nation), was frequently reprinted. (O'Beirne and O'Beirne 267–69; Littlefield and Parins, *Biobibliography, Supplement* 180; Parins, *Elias Cornelius Boudinot* 18, 213)

["There is a spectre ever haunting"]

"That they may learn what they are, whence they come
and whither they must return." —MCDONOUGH

There is a spectre ever haunting
All the living things of earth;
Like a shadow dark attending
Every mortal from his birth,
And its likeness is a demon's;
Horrible with mocking mirth.

And it never sleeps nor tires,
Never turns away its eye,
Which is always fixed and greedy,
Gazing on us ardently— 10
When at night we sleep it watcheth
At our bedside standing by.

Low it croucheth by the cradle
Where the new-born infant sleeps,

Watching with the watchful mother
When it smiles and when it weeps;
Unseen, silent, absent never,
'Round the dreaming babe it creeps.

Thus from life's first faint beginning
Till the dreaded Close appears 20
Does this still, unknown companion
Dog us through our flying years—
And it mocks our silly pleasures
As it mocks our useless tears.

Just behind us all it moveth
With a still and stealthy tread,
As it followed unseen millions
Who once lived like us 'tis said;
As we wander to the region
Whither *they* have darkly fled. 30

Few hath ever seen this spectre,—
Caught its desolating eye,
When the dews of life's fresh morning
Stir the heart with feelings high,
And the Evening and the Darkness
Seemeth never to be nigh.

But unconscious as we travel,
Lo, our day hath passed its noon;
And we startle at the sinking
Of our onward Sun so soon; 40
And the mournful Night approacheth
Which is lighted by no moon.

Then, when love nor fame nor pleasure
Warms the heart to dim the sight—
When at last the mental vision
Pierces through the mental night,—
Then we know the dark attendant
Of our feeble, failing flight.

And we feel his icy fingers
Tracing wrinkles on the brow; 50
While his breath so cold and deadly
Turns the raven hair to snow;
As we hobble on our journey
With a stumbling step and slow.

"Whither," pleads the weary trembler,
  "Whither, whither do we fly?"
But the Night now o'er them closing
  Shuts the scene from human eye.
Clear is heard the faint voice pleading,
  Never, never, the reply. 60

* * * * * *

On the footsteps of each mortal,
  From his first to latest date,
When he joys, or loves, or sorrows
  Wretched—happy—humble—great—
Mocking glides this silent Phantom;
  Child of clay, it is thy *Fate.*

Like the helpless clouds of Heaven
  Borne upon the unseen wind—
Leaving nought that telleth after
  Token, sign or trace behind,— 70
Swiftly thus on Fate's broad pinions
  Fly the millions of mankind.

[1851]

McDonough: John McDonogh (1779–1850) was born in Baltimore and later lived in and near New Orleans. A white slaveowner, he arranged for his slaves to earn their freedom through years of work. His will left his fortune from a prosperous shipping business to schools for poor whites and freed blacks in Baltimore and New Orleans. The epigraph roughly quotes from McDonogh's will, which asks the students to plant flowers on his grave. "This little act will . . . open their young and susceptible hearts, to gratitude and love, for their Divine Creator, for having raised up, as the humble instrument of his bounty to them . . . a poor, frail, worm of earth, like me; and teach them at the same time, 'What they are, whither they came, and whence they must return'" (McDonogh 32). The source of McDonogh's quotation remains unidentified. **31 Few**: *None* in the 1859 and May 1889 reprintings. **60**: echoing Edgar Allan Poe's "The Raven," apparently also referred to in line 52. In the 1899 reprinting in *Twin Territories*, the editor noted (with exaggeration) that the poem "is written in the weird style of Poe's immortal 'Raven.'" **67**: Here the 1899 printings include an additional stanza: "Just behind us all it moveth, / With a still and stealthy tread; / As it followed unseen millions, / Who once lived like us, 'tis said; / As we wander to the region, / Where, forgotten, they have fled."

Tso-le-oh-woh, Cherokee

While nothing is known about the writer of these two poems, they are themselves extraordinary testimony. (The spelling of the poet's name varies. "A Red Man's Thoughts" is signed Tsoo-le-oh-wah, and "What an Indian Thought When He Saw the Comet" is signed Tso-le-oh-woh.)

A Red Man's Thoughts

Suggested by the eagerness and the multitude of the applicants for Indian Superintendencies and Agencies

'Tis strange to think how hard they love us—
These kind-hearted Christian whites
Tho' "by nature so far above us"
Stooping each his fondness plights.

How blest we are, we little *reds*
To get such great attentions—
Pure love for us has addled heads
Of most superb pretentions.

These good old souls along the line
Will sell their very purses— 10
Take long travels—grow quite divine—
To get to be our nurses.

Of dimes and cents they never dream
Or stoop to flatt'ries hollow;
O'er their proud souls doth never gleam
The magic of a dollar. *No indeed!*

They kneeling plead for our poor race
All elbowing off th' others,
With streaming eyes they stretch their grace
To get to be our "fathers." 20

We are but children at the most,
Poor, weakly, red and puny,
But for our dear sakes to brave the worst,
Indeed 'tis "sorter" funny.

They leave their homes and all that's dear—
Go to the Fed'ral City—
Yet oft, Uncle Sam! *he* will not hear,
Indeed it is a pity.

If he but knew how hard they loved us—
How all their examples past 30
Have so moralized and improved us,
That now we are wond'rous blest.

He would not—could not thus mistreat them,
He would hush their plaintive cries

The whole colony! he would greet them!
  Drying tears with Agencies.

Before a *one* should miss a berth
  As needs he'd make another
Till every Indian on the earth
  Should have a sep'rate "father." 40

And this I think he ought to do
  'Tis only what they merit
Where'er there's a good on this broad earth
  "*They* have a right" to share it!

[1853]

applicants for Indian Superintendencies and Agencies: white men seeking appointments from the United States government to positions of responsibility over Indians and over federal funding for Indian concerns. **11 divine**: religious. **18 others**: other officials and, implicitly, other profiteers. **20 "fathers"**: government agents often referred to themselves, the federal government, or the president as the Indians' father, thus addressing Indians and their leaders as children. **36 with Agencies**: by appointing the pleaders to serve as agents, and perhaps with a pun on agents' eyes.

What an Indian Thought When He Saw the Comet

Flaming wonderer! that dost leave vaunting, proud
Ambition boasting its lightning fringed
Immensity—cleaving wings, gaudy dipp'd
In sunset's blossoming splendors bright and
Tinsel fire, with puny flight fluttering
Far behind! Thou that art cloth'd in mistery
More startling and more glorious than thine own
Encircling fires—profound as the oceans
Of shoreless space through which now thou flyest!
Art thou some erring world now deep engulph'd 10
In hellish, Judgement fires, with phrenzied ire
And fury hot, like some dread sky rocket
Of Eternity, flaming, vast, plunging
Thro' immensity, scatt'ring in thy track
The wrathful fires of thine own damnation
Or wingest thou with direful speed, the ear
Of some flaming god of far off systems
Within these skies unheard of and unknown?
Ye Gods! How proud the thought to mount this orb
Of fire—boom thro' the breathless oceans vast 20
Of big immensity—quickly leaving
Far behind all that for long ages gone

able chief clerk of the Indian Bureau, Commissioner *ad interim*

For the Cherokee Advocate.

What an Indian thought when he saw the Comet.

Flaming wonderer! that dost leave vaunting, proud,
Ambition boasting its lightning fringed,
Immensity—cleaving wings, gaudy dipp'd
In sunset's blossoming splendors bright and
Tinsel fire, with puny flight fluttering
Far behind! Thou that art cloth'd in mistery
More startling and more glorious than thine own
Encircling fires—profound as the oceans
Of shore less space through which now thou flyest!
Art thou some erring world now deep engulph'd
In hellish, Judgement fires, with phrezried ire
And fury hot, like some dread sky rocket
Of Eternity, flaming, vast, plunging
Thro' immensity, scatt'ring in thy track
The wrath full fires of thine own dam nation
Or wingest thou with dire full speed, the car
Of some flaming god off far of systems
Within these skies unheard of and unknown?
Ye Gods! How proud the thought to mount this orb
Of fire—boom thro' the breathless oceans vast
Of big immensity—quickly leaving
Far behind all that for long ages gone
Dull, gray headed dames, have prated of—
Travel far off mystic eternities—
Then proudly, on this little twisting ball
Returning once more set foot, glowing with
The splendors of a vast intelligence—
Frizzling little, puny humanity
Into icy horrors—bursting the big
Wide—spread eye ball of dismay—to recount
Dire full regious travers'd and wonders seen!
Why I'd be as great a man as Fremont
Who cross'd the Rocky Mountains, did'nt freeze
And's got a gold mine!

TSO-LE-OH-WOH.

MORTUARY.

We furnish below a tabular statement of the mortality of the city, since

Figure 4. Tso-le-oh-woh's "What an Indian Thought When He Saw the Comet" as it appeared in the *Cherokee Advocate*, 28 September 1853, just after the Klinkerfues comet flew across Indian Territory and the United States.

Dull, gray headed dames have prated of—
Travel far off mystic eternities—
Then proudly, on this little twisting ball
Returning once more set foot, glowing with
The splendors of a vast intelligence—
Frizzling little, puny humanity
Into icy horrors—bursting the big
Wide-spread eyeball of dismay—to recount 30
Direful regions travers'd and wonders seen!
Why I'd be as great a man as Fremont
Who cross'd the Rocky Mountains, didn't freeze
And's got a gold mine!

[1853]

Title: The Klinkerfues comet passed through the skies just before this poem was published in 1853.

C. H. Campbell, Cherokee

In the 1 August 1855 issue of *The Wreath of Cherokee Rose Buds*, the student newspaper of the Cherokee Female Seminary, an article recounted the celebration of the fourth anniversary of the opening of the Cherokee Female Seminary and the Cherokee Male Seminary on 7 May. The article included the following coy paragraph introducing these lines: "There was also a poem by Mr. C. H. Campbell, with which we would be very glad to please our readers, but it is not in our possession. However, we have taken the liberty to purloin a few lines from a copy that we have seen, and as we have so frankly acknowledged our misdemeanor, we hope the gentleman will pardon us."

["Our tribe could once of many warriors boast"]

Our tribe could once of many *warriors* boast,
When first the *pale face* came upon our coast;
But *war* is not the business *now* of life,
For we have long ceased from bloody strife.
The *pale face* now are strong, and *we* are *free;*
As *they* have progress made, so *we* must do—
Must learn to cultivate the mind, the soil,
And reconcile ourselves to honored toil.
We otherwise can ne'er expect to be
A prosperous people, virtuous, happy, free. 10

[1855]

6 so *we* must do: The end of this line oddly breaks the poem's pattern of rhymed couplets, and its awkward language offers no compensating gain in force or eloquence. The broken pattern raises the possibility that the words were incorrectly transcribed from the purloined manuscript. Perhaps the line ended with something like "so must we" (rhyming "we" with "free"), or perhaps, in keeping with the iambic pentameter that runs through most of the lines, it ended with something like "so now must we."

Former Student of the Cherokee Male Seminary, Cherokee

The poet of "The Rose of Cherokee" signed the poem only as "A former student of the Male Sem."

The Rose of Cherokee

Though Beauty deck the Spring in flowers
Like Rainbows sleeping in the green,
Or soft though moonlight's dewy showers
May star-like glitter o'er the scene;
Though passions young and warm may spring
With rapture through the thrilling heart,—
Though Earth and Sea their treasures bring
Combined with all that's prized in Art—
Still, wanton Nature's dark-eyed child,
Is far more dear to me— 10
The sweetest flow'r that gems the wild
Is the Rose of Cherokee.

Though far away 'neath orient skies
Where clouds come not, nor sweeps the storm,
The maid may blush in roseate dyes
Like hues upon the angel's form;
The flashing light of jeweled fire
Tho' wealth may shower o'er neck and arm,
Though soft, voluptuous, gay attire
May heighten every dazzling charm,— 20
Still, wanton Nature's dark-eyed child,
Is far more dear to me—
The sweetest flower that gems the wild
Is the Rose of Cherokee.

Though gorgeous flowers flame o'er their bed
Adorned by Art's surpassing taste,

Their fragrance and their blush-light shed
When by the lips of Rose are placed;
Though wild flowers spangling every green
Woo all the stars from Heaven's blue deep 30
Till eyes of love melt o'er the scene,
And tears of bliss in silence weep—
Still, wanton Nature's dark-eyed child
Is far more bright to me—
The sweetest flow'r that gems the wild
Is the Rose of Cherokee.

She is a gay and artless sprite.
Her eye is glad, and happiness
Plays round her lips a rosy light,
Bright with the conscious power to bless 40
Her heart's as pure, as wild, as free
As yonder streamlet leaping bright—
Her soul's a gem of purity,
And warm as loveliest star of night—
Yes! wanton Nature's dark-eyed child
The jewel is for me—
The sweetest flower that gems the wild
Is the Rose of Cherokee.

[1855]

9-12: The chorus echoes the folk song "The Yellow Rose of Texas," which dates from the 1830s. Both use ballad meter to praise a woman—in one case a Cherokee and in the other case a light-skinned (yellow) African American—as a rose and as the "sweetest" woman for "me."

Joshua Ross, Cherokee, 1833–1924

Born in the Cherokee Nation in Alabama, Joshua Ross was a nephew of Chief John Ross and a grandson of Assistant Chief George Lowry. After the Cherokees were forced from their lands, he attended schools in Indian Territory and Arkansas and then graduated from the Cherokee Male Seminary in 1855 and from Emory and Henry College in Virginia in 1860. He taught at the Cherokee Female Seminary and the Cherokee Male Seminary. Admired for his wide learning, he clerked in a store, eventually opened his own store at Muskogee in the Muskogee (Creek) Nation, and served as a member of the Cherokee National Council, where he supported the Confederacy during the Civil War. He represented the Cherokee Nation at the General Council of the Indian Territory at Okmulgee in 1870–1875 and was an organizer of the Indian International Fair at

Muskogee. Ross signed his poems as "The Wanderer," except for the poem called "The Wanderer," which he signed "Z." (Wright 12)

My Ruling Star

I gazed upon a lovely star,
  That kindly beamed on me,
Until I loved and worshiped it,
  E'en to idolatry!

The countless gems that round it shone,
  Grew pale beneath its light,
Until it seemed to shine alone,
  The only orb of night!

When passing clouds obscured its light,
  Exquisite was the pain 10
That seized upon my trembling heart,
  Until it gleamed again!

Beneath its pure enchanting light,
  I walked in virtue's way;
Life seemed renewed—such holy power,
  Was in each heavenly ray!

But lo! a black unseemly cloud,
  Most hideous to the eye,
Eclipsed my pure and lovely star,
  And darkness robed the sky! 20

Then hope's bright torch, grew pale and dim,
  And madness seized my brain—
That monster foul black grim despair,
  O'er all things seemed to reign.

Thus wrapped in gloom I lonely walk
  Life's dark and dreary way,
Still longing to behold again
  One pure inspiring ray.

Oh! lovely gem, appear again!
  In smiles of sparkling light, 30
And dissipate those gloomy clouds,
  This dark oppressive night.

[1855]

Sequoyah

O'er Sequoyah's lonely grave
The forest oaks their branches wave;
No guide is known to point the place
Where sleeps the Cadmus of his race,
Neglected son of genius rest—
No marble presses on thy breast;
But when the Nation fades away
Before the mighty Saxon sway;
When high upon the list of fame
In letters bright shall stand thy name; 10
The learned have your powers admired
And some have thought you were inspired;
Like to that mighty seer of old,
Before whose eye the future rolled;
Who saw great nations rise and fall
And read the writing on the wall;
Now all are loud in praising thee,
But when you lived seemed not to see,
Aught in the gifted forest child
Above the common Indian wild; 20
So thou didst to the deep wood fly
In solitude alone to die;
No well loved hand or sister dear
To wipe away the last sad tear.

[1856]

Title: Sequoyah (1767–1843), revered Cherokee silversmith who invented the Cherokee writing system, a syllabary rather than an alphabet. 4 **Cadmus**: ancient Phoenician prince said to have brought the alphabet from Phoenicia to Greece. 13 **mighty seer of old**: Daniel, chap. 5.

The Wanderer

1. As proudly the steamer is gliding along
I'll try for a moment to write me a song;
The measure I'll suit to some sorrowful air
Like the tune of a love ditty sung by the fair.

2. For I from my home am far, *far* away,
Rocked by the waves and laved by the spray;
How many reflections come crowding my mind
Of the scenes of my boyhood all left behind.

3. But *these* are the hills my forefathers saw,
When justice was done without aid of the law, 10
And this is the stream so broad and so blue
Whose waters floated my brother's canoe.

4. No wonder our fathers were loth to depart
From these beautiful scenes so cherished at heart
But let not the children repent of the day
When the fathers from home were driven away.

5. The country they have, more beautiful still
Is ample enough with rich lands to till;
The climate is wholesome the fountains are pure,
And some are medicinal, for sickness a cure. 20

6. The shades of the evening are gathering around
And heavier and deeper the waters dull sound
The mountains grow dim in the distance afar
And the waters reflect the bright evening star.

7. Long have I looked toward my home in the West
Now weary of watching I'll go to my rest
For the twilight of even has deepened to night,
And every fond object has faded from my sight.

8. But memory unfolding forever shall be
Of my Cherokee home, so dear to me— 30
The streamlets are beautiful, the landscapes are fair,
I'll go to my berth and dream of them there.

[1856]

10 **justice was done without aid of the law**: the forced removal of the Cherokee people. 12 **Whose**: this word is not legible in the copy seen by the editor but appears to begin with *W* and end with *e*.

On a Lady's Eyes

Lady, there is a light divine
Beaming from those eyes of thine;
Their brilliant light surpasses far,
Evening's pure effulgent star.
Though loved ones wander far from thee
Forgotten, thou canst never be;
Nor will they from thee falsely stray,
Pursuing vice or folly's way;
For all things lovely, pure and bright,
Will call to mind the chastening light 10
That sparkles in fair —— eye,

And lifts the soul to scenes on high.

Ye guardian spirits hover near,
And suffer not one burning tear
To dim those orbs now shining bright,
So full of hope and fond delight.
Fair lady, if our mother Eve
Had eyes like thine, we would not grieve
For Eden lost. No, it would be
Our own in all its purity: 20
For when the 'snake' had seen those eyes,
He would have fled from Paradise;
His envy would have passed away
Beneath each pure enchanting ray.

[1859]

11 **fair —— eye**: The dash coyly stands in for the lady's name followed by an apostrophe and the letter *s*, for example, Liza's, Sara's, etc.

Peter Perkins Pitchlynn, Choctaw, 1806–1881

Peter Pitchlynn was born into a prosperous slaveholding family in the Choctaw Nation in what is now Mississippi. He attended four or five schools, though none of them for long, beginning with mission schools in Tennessee, then the Choctaw Academy in Kentucky and the University of Nashville in Tennessee. Renowned Choctaw leader and district Chief David Folsom and his brother Israel Folsom, who has a poem in this volume, were Pitchlynn's relatives as well as brothers of his first wife. Pitchlynn was centrally involved in Choctaw politics in many ways over many years, often blending his own interests with the interests of the Choctaw Nation that he also served. He played key roles in writing the Choctaw constitution in 1826 and again in 1834, in writing Choctaw laws over many years, and in negotiating the Treaty of Dancing Rabbit in 1830, which forced the Choctaws to leave their homeland. He also played key roles in armed opposition to the same treaty, in founding the Choctaw educational system in Indian Territory, and in many additional treaties and negotiations with the United States, often representing the Choctaws in Washington, D.C. In 1831 he was elected district chief, and in 1831–1832 he led a party of over 400 Choctaws on the forced removal to Indian Territory. There he built a large plantation with many slaves. After 1853, he lived mostly in Washington, representing Choctaw interests. During the Civil War, however, when he failed to convince the Choctaw Nation to support the Union, he returned to his plantation. Then in 1864, with the Confederacy losing the war, Pitchlynn was elected principal chief. He helped negotiate the surrender of Choctaw troops and, in 1866, after leaving his position as chief, he helped negotiate the treaty that restored relations with the federal government. (Baird)

Song of the Choctaw Girl

I'm looking on the mountain,
I'm gazing o'er the plain;
I love the friends around me,
But wish for home again!

I hear their tones of kindness,
They soothe my every pain;
I know they love me truly—
I wish for home again!

My mother's grave is yonder,
And there it must remain; 10
My father's care is tender,
I wish for home again!

My sisters and my brothers—
Alas! it may be vain,
This longing for beloved ones—
I wish for home again.

O, take me to my Nation,
And let me there remain;
This other world is strange, strange—
I wish for home again 20

Give me the western forest—
The mountain, stream and plain,
The shaded lawns of childhood—
Give me my home again!

The free breeze of the prairie
The wild bird's joyous strain,
The tree my father planted—
O, take me home again!

The sunshine and the flowers,
My mother's grave again, 30
Give me my race and kindred—
O, take me home again!

[undated, probably 1850s, published 1972]

Title: Pitchlynn wrote this poem for his daughter Rhoda when she visited him in Washington, D.C., while on vacation from school in Virginia (Baird 90). Rhoda was born in 1840, suggesting that the poem was written in the 1850s.

["Will you go with me"]

Will you go with me
To my home in the West,
To the land of the mountains,
To the land of the prairies,
To the land of the setting sun,
Far away toward the setting sun.

I say will you go with me,
And be mine for me to love,
& for me to protect, cherish & love,
To be mine in heart & soul, 10
For me to love among the flowers,
Love among the songs of birds.

Will you go with me
To my home in the forest,
To my home thats far away,—
Far beyond the Mississippi,—
In a pleasant valley is my home,
And, Oh will you go with me?

I would not have thee to go
To my home in the forest, 20
If I loved thee not as a man,
If I could not protect thee as a man
If I could not make thee as a man,
My loving my dear my happy wife.
Will you go with me?

[undated, probably 1856 or 1857, published 1972]

The manuscript has crossed-out words and lines not recorded here. 1 **you**: probably addressed to Carolyn Eckloff Lombardi, whom Pitchlynn courted in 1856 and 1857 and who became his second wife. His first wife, Rhoda Folsom Pitchlynn, died in 1844 (Baird 24, 94, 134).

John Gunter Lipe, Cherokee, 1844–1862

John Gunter Lipe fought with the Confederate Army under the famous Cherokee Brigadier General Stand Watie and was killed in action in 1862. In February 1861, months before the Civil War began, he wrote this poem in the autograph album of Victoria Hicks, who later married his older brother. (Starr 144, 571)

To Miss Vic

I stand at the portal and knock,
And tearfully, prayerfully wait.
O! who will unfasten the lock,
And open the beautiful gate?

Forever and ever and ever,
Must I linger and suffer alone?
Are there none that are able to sever,
The fetters that keep me from home?

My spirit is lonely and weary,
I long for the beautiful streets.
The world is so chilly and dreary,
And bleeding and torn are my feet.
Tahlequah, Cherokee Nation.

[written 1861, published 1921]

Anonymous Cherokee

This poem from the *Cherokee Advocate* was signed "Cherokee." It seems reasonable to trust the *Advocate*'s attribution of the poem to a Cherokee writer.

["Faster and fiercer rolls the tide"]

Faster and fiercer rolls the tide
That follows on our track,
And all our prayers cannot avail
To turn the current back.

Onward, still onward, it has rolled,
Advancing like a host
And soon beneath the treach'rous waves
Our nation will be lost,

Westward retreating, ever back,
And ever xxxx the insatiate waves 10
Roll on their hungry tide.
For all around on every side
The thund'ring breakers roar.

Year after year we've watched the flood
 Rush onward in its swell,
And faithful hearts and hands have wrought
 Its volume to repel.

But barriers we thought were built
 On truth's Eternal Rock,
Have crumbled from their sandy base 20
 Before the billow's shock.

Honor has shrieked, and Pity cried,
 And Justice pled in vain,
But, "Onward, onward," is replied
 Back from the surging main.

There is no hope; the red man's fate
 Is fixed beyond control,
And soon above each hearth and home
 The mighty waves will roll.

Why is it thus, are we accurst 30
 And will oblivion's gloom,
Give back no ray to tell us why
 Extinction is our doom?

From out the graves of ages gone
 No voices speak our name,
No marble tongues, nor storied piles,
 Our ancient deeds proclaim.

Beyond our few historic years,
 Tradition's flickering light,
But serves to throw around our past 40
 A deeper, blacker, night.

We only know we are hasting on,
 Towards the spirit land,
And in its peaceful shades no more
 Will feel oppression's hand.

[1871]

10 xxxx: illegible word.

David J. Brown, Cherokee, born about 1856, died 1879

David J. (Cookee) Brown graduated from the Cherokee Male Seminary in 1878 and the next year was shot and killed in Muskogee, Indian Territory.

Sequoyah

Thou Cadmus of thy race!
 Thou giant of thy age!
In every heart a place,
 In history a living page:
The Juggernaut chariot time,
 May crush as she doth give;
But a noble name like thine,
 Shall ever with kee-too-wah live.

Orion like thou dost stand,
 In every age and clime, 10
With intellect as grand,
 As ever shown by time;
Twas thy hand lit the spark,
 That heavenward flashed its ray,
Revealing the shining mark,
 The straight and narrow way.

Ignorance and superstitious awe,
 From high pedestals toppled o'er,
Whereas the ancient giver of law,
 Smiting, thou mad'st the waters pour; 20
Stand thou didst on Pisgah's height,
 And gazed into the future's deep,
But day was ne'er unclasped from night,
 E'er thy spirit silently fell asleep.

[1879]

Title: Sequoyah (1767–1843), revered Cherokee silversmith who invented the Cherokee writing system, a syllabary rather than an alphabet. 1 **Cadmus**: ancient Phoenician prince said to have brought the alphabet from Phoenicia to Greece. 5 **Juggernaut**: a Hindu god known for his car or chariot. British accounts mistakenly supposed that the car of the Juggernaut ran over believers, leading to the term Juggernaut for a crushing, unstoppable force. 8 **kee-too-wah**: variously spelled name of the ancient, original Cherokee city and the spiritual center of the Cherokee people, as well as a term that can represent the Cherokee people at large. Brown published a song called "Kee-too-wah." 9 **Orion**: giant ancient Greek hunter known for his beauty and for transforming into one of the easiest-to-see constellations in the night sky. 21 **Pisgah's height**: Pisgah is a high place or mountain in the Old Testament. Moses first saw the promised land from Pisgah (Deuteronomy 34.1).

James Harris Guy, Chickasaw, died 1885

James Harris Guy, from Boggy Depot, Indian Territory, was a nephew of Cyrus Harris, the first elected governor of the Chickasaw Nation, who served as governor for five terms. Guy was also a brother of William Malcolm Guy, who held many offices in the Chickasaw Nation, including governor from 1886-1888. A deputy U.S. marshal and a sergeant in the Chickasaw Indian Police, James Guy was shot and killed while trying to arrest a gang of outlaws. At the time of his death, he had agreed to publish a book of legends and poems, but no poems (or legends) written by him are known beyond the four poems reprinted here. Guy published the first two of the poems included here with letters to the editor of *The Council Fire*, edited by former Oregon Superintendent of Indian Affairs Alfred B. Meacham. Those poems appear here as they originally were published, with Guy's letters. (J. B. Meserve, "Governor"; O'Beirne; Roff; "Some Chickasaw Indian Lore")

["The white man wants the Indian's home"]

TISHOMINGO, C. N., I. T., June 17th, 1878.
A. B. MEACHAM, Washington, D.C.

Dear Sir:—To-day I picked up two copies of your *Council Fire*, being the first I have seen. I am a Chickasaw Indian, and in spite of the expressed contempt by the white man, I am glad of it. Are we not equal? Surely God made us so mentally as well as physically. If we stand behind the whites to-day in education, is it our fault? No! had the United States Government kept its pledges toward us, our schools would all now be in full operation.

There is sorrow in the Indian's home to-day. They (the whites) say our land is "too good" for us; it is only fit for the whites. And unless brave men like you stand up for us, sooner or later we perish from the face of the earth, *because we are Indians.* I did not know before that there was a white man brave enough to stand up and say in the Capital, "the Indian has been wronged." But he has been wronged, and bitterly wronged. It speaks volumes when a Senator can in the Senate-room challenge his people to produce one single instance of an Indian treaty being carried out faithfully towards the Indians.

Will you answer this? Have the five civilized nations done anything against the United States government since the Rebellion? If not, why is the United States continually trying to gain our lands? for all these Territorial bills are nothing else but levers brought to bear on the destruction of the Indians' titles. Will you, and brave men like you, allow this? We are trying to live godly lives; but sometimes I feel like an old Chickasaw Indian to whom I was describing Heaven. Among other things I told him all would be brothers; that we should all live together in peace. Judge of my astonishment when he replied, "Is the white man going there?" I told him yes. Then he said, "I do not want to go there then, for he would always be saying 'Indian got no right there; heaven too good for Indian; white man wants it all; so Indian have to go." And he refused to listen to me any longer. Tell your government we are not drunkards or thieves; that we are doing the best we can for ourselves.

I send you a few lines expressing the sentiment of my people:

The white man wants the Indian's home,
He envies them their land;
And with his sweetest words he comes
To get it, if he can.

And if we will not give our lands,
And plainly tell him so,
He then goes back, calls up his clans,
And says, "let's make them go."

The question in the Indian's mind
Is, where are we to go? 10
No other country can we find;
'Tis filled up with our foe.

We do not want one foot of land
The white man calls his own;
We ask of nothing at his hands,
Save to be let alone.

Send me a copy of the paper and I will forward you a dollar.—

[1878]

C. N., I. T.: Chickasaw Nation, Indian Territory. **When a Senator . . .** : perhaps a reference to remarks by Senator Richard Yates of Illinois in 1869. **five civilized nations**: a common term for the Cherokee, Chickasaw, Choctaw, Muskogee (Creek), and Seminoles. **since the rebellion**: since the Civil War. Many Indians from Indian Territory, including Guy's brother William and possibly Guy as well, fought with the Confederacy.

The Lament of Tishomingo

TISHOMINGO, C. N., INDIAN TERRITORY,
December 12th, 1878

Editor *Council Fire*:

Dear Sir:—I suppose ere this you have the report of the committee, misnamed the "Investigating Committee," sent to take the lands from the civilized Indians. Why is it, Mr. Meacham, that we must be so persecuted? Is it not enough that we must give up our beautiful homes east of the Mississippi and come to a wild country to live? Must we even now surrender our homes here, in spite of the many promises to the contrary by the Government?

Mr. Meacham, the Senatorial Committee is simply mistaken when they say they did not meet with a cordial reception on their visit to this country. The different capitals of the Indians are all located miles away from the railroad. Did the Committee expect the Indians to violate their laws by taking their records to the railroad? If so, they have mistaken their men; for the Indian thinks more of his oath of office than of his private interests.

The petition gotten up in the cities along the railroad for the United States to organize a Territorial government among us, has not a sympathiser except those who have claims on bonds sold by the railroad upon lands belonging to the Indians, and granted to the railroad by the United States. We have five papers in the Territory, and three of them favor giving up the lands; but let us look a little closer. The *Cherokee Advocate* is published by the Cherokee Nation, and is a faithful exponent of the Indian people. The same can be said of the *Indian Journal*, published by the Creeks at Muskogee. The next, called the *Star Vindicator*, at McAlester, is owned by two white men, one of whom has a citizen's right by marriage, and have received bonds for their advertisements of the M. K. & T. R. R. The Atoka *Independent* and Caddo *Free Press* are both owned by white men, and are servants of the same master. They are afraid to say their souls are their own. They are not satisfied with being allowed to live here without being taxed, but must raise the cry of "open the country." The Indians have stood much, as the records of the past show; but until all past claims are settled, we will never agree to divide our lands. "An Indian never forgets," and we have our past to warn us; and if the United States Government concludes that "might makes right," and pays no attention to its promises, the Indians will only yield at the cost of their lives, and will die as men rather than yield to the power of a government that will not keep its faith. We ask you and other men, who are not slaves, to show to the world this fact, *if you let us alone, we will, in time, divide our lands ourselves.* It will cost the United States more to subdue us than the land would sell for in the open markets of the world. Help us! we need your help.

I will close with the following:

The Lament of Tishomingo

From the door of my cabin I sit and gaze,
  With sad and tearful face,

As memory brings forth those other days,
And the fearful fall of my race.

For you must know I come from a band
Of honest and fearless men,
And when we in friendship gave our hand,
You need not have feared us then.

But they say we are changed entirely now,
From what we were in the days of Penn, 10
And the suggestion arises why and how
Are we changed from what we were then.

As long as the whiteman kept his word,
As *men* should always do
The vows of friendship were often heard,
For we were honest and true.

But there has dawned a day of deepest woe
Upon us and the white man's sight;
For the white man's honor has fallen so low
That evil has conquered the right. 20

—*A Chickasaw.*

Will send you some subscriptions in a few days.
Respectfully Yours, JAMES H. GUY,
Tishomingo, C.N.

[1879]

Title: Tishomingo was a revered Chickasaw war chief from the late eighteenth century through the time of removal in the 1830s. Though he fought with the United States, when he was over a hundred years old the United States forced him and his people to leave their homes and travel the Trail of Tears to Indian Territory. **M. K. & T. R. R.**: Missouri, Kansas and Texas Railroad. **10 Penn**: probably William Penn, the founder of Pennsylvania, known for his treaties and peaceful relations with Indian peoples, though not with the Chickasaws. Tishomingo visited Philadelphia, Pennsylvania, and perhaps Guy chose Penn's name to fit the rhyme.

Old Boggy Depot

A gifted soul—the product of the Boggy Depot environment—was that of James H. Guy, a younger brother of Gov. William M. Guy, of the Choctaw nation. In 1881, some years after the abandonment of Boggy Depot, he re-visited the scenes of his boyhood life. It was a dreary, rainy day—one well calculated to inspire a feeling of melancholy reminiscence—and he poured out his feeling in a few brief verses which are well worthy of preservation in the literature of Oklahoma.

I came here today, in the cold, stormy rain,
And walked the old streets as of yore,
Past its weather-beaten houses, with weather-worn pane,
And with rickety, rat-haunted floor.

Old Town, you loom up like a gust in the gale,
That gibbers and groans in the blast,
And you speak with a dreary, wearisome tale
Of my all but forgotten past.

The houses so lone, once so cheerful and gay,
Where the light-footed dancers whirled round— 10
My heart cries with anguish, my friends, where are they?
And echo replies in the ground.

On the streets, now deserted and dead,
The wealth of the country once poured,
And daily the ships of the prairie streamed here
With the wares of our merchants aboard.

O, my father's old home, you will soon tumble down,
For your timbers are crumbling away;
But your record is writ in the heart of the town
And your glory abideth for aye. 20

Old Town, you are dead and your greatness is gone,
Like the merchants who stood in your doors,
And only the graves on the hillside, so lone,
Tell aught of the life that was yours.

[written about 1881, published 1927]

Title: After the railroad arrived in 1872 and bypassed the thriving Chickasaw and Choctaw town of Boggy Depot, the town emptied out. Today it is known as a ghost town. **Note, A gifted soul . . .** : This note appears in the original printing of 1927; William M. Guy was Governor of the Chickasaw nation, not the Choctaw nation.

Fort Arbuckle

The day has been long and dreary;
I halt with the sitting sun
To gaze on the open world,
And the work that the years have done;
And a vision rises before me,
Of the past as it hath been,
And all that the rolling hills have heard,
And the bright-eyed stars have seen.

Full many a thrilling story
 Could the echoing rocks repeat, 10
And methinks I hear in the forest
 The tramp of hurrying feet.
The yells of the great Commanche
 Ring once more in my ear,
And files of the ghostly warriors
 Appear and disappear.

I see the dusky phantoms
 Rise from their graves to-day,
With the war paint still upon them
 As they started for the fray; 20
They scorned the white man's promise
 And refused to be his slaves,
But their ranks were few and feeble,
 And the sun sets on their graves.

Once more from the hill above me
 The painted warriors ride,
And fall upon Fort Arbuckle
 Like rocks from the mountain side;
But now the bow and the quiver
 Give place to the plodding plow, 30
A bible, a hut, a handful of corn
 And a Christian's broken vow.

Oh, mystical Fort Arbuckle,
 The sun is falling aslant,
And a friend stands out in his doorway;
 God speed thee, Thomas Grant;
For thou hast ever a seat at thy board,
 And in thy heart a place,
For him who would sing the wide world o'er
 The songs of a ruined race. 40

[written 1885 or earlier, published 1891]

Title: Federal troops built Fort Arbuckle in 1851 near the present Hoover, Oklahoma, to protect Texas settlers, the Chickasaw Nation, and settlers en route to California from Comanche, Kiowa, and Cheyenne raiders. It was abandoned in 1870 (Morrison, Norris). **36 Thomas Grant**: When Fort Arbuckle was abandoned, Thomas Grant bought the fort site from the Chickasaw nation (Sharp et al. 81).

John Lynch Adair, Cherokee, 1828–1896

Born in the Cherokee Nation in Georgia, Adair was forcibly removed west in 1839. His sister died during the removal. Raised by wealthy slave-owning relatives after his parents died, he took a strong interest in studying the classics, especially Latin. Adair fought as a captain in the Confederate Army and after the war served in many offices for the Cherokee Nation, including national auditor, clerk of the Cherokee Senate, executive councilor under Chief Louis Downing, delegate to Washington, member of the board of education, assistant executive secretary under Chief Dennis Bushyhead, secretary under Chief Joel B. Mayes, and editor of the *Cherokee Advocate*. He also edited four other newspapers: the *Daily Indian Chieftain*, the *Indian Chieftain*, the *Talequah Courier*, and the *World*. (O'Beirne and O'Beirne 463; Littlefield and Parins, *Biobibliography* 203; Littlefield and Parins, *Native American Writing in the Southeast* 14)

Hec Dies

An Imitation

He who looks just beyond
The day,
That closes o'er life's sun-set hills,
First of spring emeralds, and beryls
Of autumn next, and winter's snows
Further on, knows or good as knows,
That far these hills beyond
Is day.—

That all this fretful scene
To day, 10
Is but little more than a dream;
And of events this turbid stream,
Beginning—ah where?—and ending—
Ah where?—and forever wending
Is not a real scene
To day.—

That we'll lie down to dream
Some day,
And weary, we would have it night
While the sun is high, warm and bright; 20
Will wake from sleep to find,
That all we've seen and left behind,
Was nothing but a dream,
That day.—

Wonder how long we've slept
That day;
Think we've been dreaming, nothing more,
And to some one, who went before
To sleep, will wish to tell our dreams
Of strange and unknown scenes, 30
We beheld as we slept
That day.—

That our loved ones we'll see,
That day,
Who had grown weary and had slept,
And in their dreams had laughed and wept
O'er scenes that were so real,
That nothing could be ideal,
Of what they seemed to see,
That day.— 40

Believe we were dreaming,
The day,
We thought was something more than sleep—
It was so cold, calm and deep—
In which they lay; and sorrow's tears
We'll think were strange, and so the fears,
That made sad our dreaming,
That day.—

That we realize,
That day, 50
Hope's sweetest fruits, love's fondest dreams,
And so the momentary gleams
We have of better things, which come
From the stars, or it may be some
Place we will realize,
that day.

[1877]

Title: Latin for This Day. **4 beryls**: a mineral with emerald and aquamarine gems.

"Joy Returneth with the Morning"

A great storm had blown out the stars,
And the winds, rushing from their caves,
Lashed the sea into mountain waves,
And the ship, under bending spars,

In utter darkness plowed the deep.
Unto Him whom the winds obeyed
On Galilee, I humbly prayed,
That in His keeping I might sleep.

In a haven calm and bright
With tropic sunshine, where the scent 10
Of orange bloom made redolent
The breeze that was so soft and light
That there scarcely a wavelet broke
Upon the bosom of the bay,
Where next morning our good ship lay,
To glad consciousness I awoke.

So may it be, Good Lord of all,
When in darkness sinks my sun,
And my stars go out, one by one;
To as calm a sleep may I fall, 20
And that which only faith had been,
Awake to find a truth to be,
Where no white sails go out to sea,
But are forever coming in.

[1889]

Title: from Psalm 30.5: "weeping may endure for a night, but joy cometh in the morning."

John Palmer, Chemakum, Skokomish, born about 1847, died 1881

John Foster Palmer, probably the same John Palmer who wrote this poem, was born in Fort Townsend in what is now the state of Washington. A Chemakum, he moved to San Francisco in 1859 with a family that took him in after his father died, and then he traveled to the Amur River in Russian Manchuria, where he spent several years. Returning to the United States, he worked at the Makah Reservation and then in 1868 moved to the Skokomish Reservation, where he served as a government interpreter for eight years. He spoke Twana (Skokomish), Nisqually, Clallam, Chinook jargon, Russian, and English. Palmer was described, with admiration, as having "a library worth fifty dollars" and subscribing to "several newspapers and magazines, both eastern and western." He was said to have gone to school for only two weeks (Eells 189), whereas the writer of this poem was said to have attended a local school. Possibly one of those accounts is in error, as no record of another Skokomish John Palmer has turned up thus far. He would not have had a son with the same name, since he had no children. The leading Indian organizer of the local church, he died in an accident while working in a saw-mill. (Eells 188–90, 231–32)

The following note precedes the poem: "Here is another specimen of Indian composition. We make no apology. We propose to show by giving *verbatim* Indian productions, that the Indian is capable, emotional, poetical, and a hopeful subject for education. This production is full of tender sympathy. John Palmer was a pupil in one of our agency schools. His sister was married a few months since, and when leaving home said, 'Brother John remember me.'"

[I Remember You]

Yes, sister, I do always remember you,
In everything I do, I remember you.
When I get up in the morning then I remember you.

I go to milk the cows and feed the chicks,
Then I think why Martha would have helped
If she were here, then, sister, I remember you.

In meals, in our breakfast, dinner and supper,
While thanking God for our daily food,
I say to Him be with our friends who are
Far away, then, sister, I remember you. 10

And in our daily prayers, morning and evening,
I ask God to bless you and take care of you,
Make you useful and make you humble as Martha
Of the New Testament times,
Then, Martha, I remember you.

When I cross the elbow of Hood's canal on the bay,
The bay was calm, the water was clear as glass,
The shadow of the shore looked natural,
Then, sister, I remember you.

The white logs that shined on shore, and 20
The white, black and brown horses and
Cattle that moved along the shore,
How plain and natural they looked
In the shadow in water,
Then, sister, I remember you.

And when I come on shore,
I get on the spit or point, I look
And see the beautiful flowers;
I kneel down to smell them, the
Sweetness goes down into my heart, 30
I say how sweet they are,

They are as sweet as my sister.
Then, Martha, I remember you.

And as I come back the tide is low,
So I have to take for the water to drag
My little canoe, and as the current is so swift
Rob Roy is so hard to manage.
Then, sister, I remember you.

Rob Roy turns to right and left side,
And will not make me go fast, while 40
The painter or the rope that is fastened
To Rob Roy is scratching and cutting
My shoulder, then I would say if sister
Were here, I could say, keep Rob Roy
Straight, sister.
Then, Martha, I remember you.

Oh! Puget Sound, September warm,
And how pleasant art thou.
Thou bringest the Indian Summer
In some parts of thee, 50
How my heart throbs to think that
It is vacation month, how I think that
We shall have a pleasant time.
Then, sister, I remember you.

And when I come from my work
I sing in Indian song as I walk
All along the river bank, I say in my
Song, Martha, Martha, I mourn for thee.
Then, sister, I remember you.

As I sing these songs for thee, 60
I sing as loud as I can, I stop and
Listen to the echo, I hear it on
Both sides on the banks of the river,
I make both banks to ring with
The echo of my song.
Then, sister, I remember you.

And now, sister, the Lord may bless you
And take care of thee and thy husband,
May you live long and happy life.
Pray to God to take care of you and 70
I will pray to Him for you and me,

Then, sister, I will remember you
Always, so you must remember me
So I can remember you.

[1880]

37 **Rob Roy**: named for the legendary Scottish outlaw and folk hero (1671–1734).

Joseph Lynch Martin, Cherokee, 1817–1891

Joseph Lynch Martin, son of the first Chief Justice of the Supreme Court of the Cherokee Nation, was born in the Cherokee Nation in Georgia. He went to school at Cherokee mission schools and in St. Louis. In 1839, he survived forced removal to Indian Territory. There he built a huge, lavish plantation called Green Briar near the present Strang, Oklahoma. He owned over a hundred slaves and fought as a cavalry officer in the Confederate Army under the famous Cherokee Brigadier General Stand Watie. Martin married five times and also had many children by his slaves. ("Obituary"; Littlefield and Parins, *Biobibliography* 267; Geller; Cornsilk)

A Dream

BY GREEN BRIER JOE

I went to a garden to get me some leaves,
And there I saw old mother Eve.
She was looking at the fruit and looking at the tree,
And said, the fruit looks mighty good to me.
To eat this fruit will make me wise.
Oh, how I want to open my eyes.
But old master says nay, and I must obey,
Yet the fruit looks so good and sweet to-day.
The old serpent was there and told her to eat,
The old cuss told her she would find it good meat. 10
She took of the fruit and did eat some,
And the old serpent thought it mighty pretty fun.
She gave to Adam and he did eat,
The old man said he found it good meat.
After they had eat they found they had done wrong,
The took to the brush and the devil went along.
Adam found out as they went along,
That they lacked a garment in the shape of a gown.
Adam gathered leaves and made them a gown,
He sewed the leaves together while sitting on the groun. 20

Long in the evening old master come,
He soon found out what the devil had done.
He called up Adam, he called up Eve,
Here they come with aprons made of leaves.
Old master asked Adam what made him hide,
Daddy, said Adam, because I have lied.
Adam got scared, laid it all on Eve,
Eve said it was the devil she believed.
Old master got mad, raised a big fuss,
And made the old devil git down in the dust. 30
He drove out Adam, he drove out Eve,
And told the old devil he could bite him on his heel,
Then talked to Eve, this to her said,
She could bang the devil on top of his head.
The old folks left, looking very sad
And the devil crawled off and seemed very mad.
He gave the devil a coat, the color it was brown,
The devil looked so mean crawling on the ground.
I then heard a voice, and this is what it said,
You must not believe the devil is dead. 40
Old master fixed this thing up, done it mighty fast,
And if you don't mind the devil will git you all at last.

[1881]

Stanzas by Uncle Joe

To my dear nieces three:
Ellen, Ann and Cherokee.
Cherokee, a matron, and Ann, a teacher;
Ellen, wife of Thompson Joe a preacher.

Cherokee cuts for the children and makes their clothing.
Ann does the teaching, training, and the moulding;
Ellen gives a helping hand
And does the very best she can.

I love you children, oh, so well!
Better far than I can ever tell. 10
The reason why I love you so good,
Is because, within your veins runs my blood.

Your calling is good, there is no better,
Than to learn the Indian youth his letter
And teach him the road by Jesus given—
The narrow way that leads to Heaven.

When your work is over here below,
You will wear the robes that's white as snow,
And now a parting word before we go:
In your prayers ever remember your Uncle Joe. 20
Your Uncle,
JOE L. MARTIN

[1891]

1–2 nieces three: / Ellen, Ann and Cherokee: Martin's father had sixteen acknowledged children by two wives on separate plantations in Georgia, so Martin had many nieces, including nieces named Cherokee (who also had a daughter named Cherokee), Mary Ellen, Ellen (who had a daughter named Anna), and Mary Ann (who had daughters named Mary Ann and Cherokee).

Wenonah

Wenonah, though possibly a pseudonym, is a common name for Indian women. The one poem attributed to her indicates that this particular Wenonah was a talented poet. She signed her poem "Oowala, I.T., Nov. 14, 1886." Oowala was in the Cherokee Nation in Indian Territory (I.T.), now Oklahoma.

Thanksgiving

Under the cool, white snowdrifts
The old year slippeth to die,
And her voice trembles off into music
That swoops through the opening sky.

All the sweet tones and all the discordant,
That the days of her passage have known,
Blend into melodious praises,
That reach to the heights of the throne.

For the poor fragile things that have perished;
For the beautiful things that remain; 10
For joy's sunny chaplet and favor;
For the gall, and the thorns and the pain;

For all, Gracious Father, we thank Thee,
For wounding and healing alike;
For peace and for battle, rest and discomfort;
For day, and aye—for the night.

Let our hearts mount up to the Father,
On the quivering wings of desire;
Give us, Lord, for the year that's to follow,
Strength to labor, endure and aspire. 20

[1886]

Hors de Combat, Cherokee

An unidentified Cherokee published this poem under the pen name "Hors de Combat," a French expression that translates literally as "out of the fight," meaning wounded, sick, or captured soldiers who can no longer fight.

["I've returned to home and scanty lunch"]

I've returned to home and scanty lunch,
From electioneering for Rabbit Bunch;
I've rode and walked and laughed and sung,
But everybody's says Rabbit's hamstrung.
I met one man that I tried to fix,
But he said, he's right were it not for the Dicks,
He said they were so full of their tricks
That he could not with the Rabbits mix.
He said, again, they'd blowed it round
That none but Rabbits could be found; 10
And when the Rabbit as chieftain towered,
They, themselves, would have the power.
Then I went over to Salasaw creek
And there I met one awful "stick":
He said he would for the Rabbit speak
And to his party he'd ever stick.
And farther on, near Childer's station,
Was "Rabbit's Voter" in lamentation:
For, said he, we'll lose our places,
If ever our leader lose the races. 20
I then went on to Webbers Falls,
Where judicious "Fair Play" took Rabbit's cause,
He for the darkeys made one call,
But, not now, "Justice" made him squall.
"Fair Play" he said he wanted to prattle,
But he'd admit he'd lost the battle;

His tricks he said the darkies all knew,
And from his Bunch, they all with Drew.
We then went on to Cooweescoowee
Where Taylor once hollowed hoo-e-hoo-e. 30
He said for the Rabbit he'd fought mighty strong,
But through the CHIEFTAIN he found he's wrong.
And so, MR. CHIEFTAIN, I feel mighty sad,
To see our chances are looking so bad,
But if we fail to elect our man,
We'll nominate Bushy and make another stand.

[1887]

2 **Rabbit Bunch**: Prosperous Cherokee farmer and Assistant Principal Chief of the Cherokee Nation. The anti-allotment National Party's candidate for principal chief in 1887, he was narrowly defeated in a divisive and contested election. 6 **Dicks**: possibly referring to men named Richard. 13 **Salasaw creek**: Sallisaw Creek in what is now eastern Oklahoma. 17 **Childer's station**: now Sallisaw, Oklahoma. 27 **darkeys, or darkies**: a now unequivocally derogatory term for African Americans. Many Cherokees owned black slaves until slavery ended in 1865. The status of black Cherokees—Cherokee slaves, former slaves of Cherokees and the descendants of Cherokee slaves—remains controversial to this day. 29 **Cooweescoowee**: Cherokee district named after the Cherokee name of Chief John Ross (1790–1866). 30 **Taylor**: Perhaps Campbell Harrison "Cam" Taylor, a prominent lawyer, or Deputy Sheriff of Cooweescoowee, but there were many Taylors, and this incident has not been identified. 34 **CHIEFTAIN**: The *Indian Chieftain*, the newspaper that published this poem. 36 **Bushy**: Principal Chief Dennis Wolf Bushyhead of the National Party, whose term ended in 1887. Bushyhead supported the rights of black Cherokees. His father was the Rev. Jesse Bushyhead (see "The Indian's Farewell" by "An Indian," probably Bushyhead, in this volume).

Alexander Posey, Creek (Muskogee), 1873–1908

Alex Posey was born and raised in the Creek Nation and rarely traveled beyond it, but he was the most widely recognized American Indian literary writer of his day. Posey's mother came from the prominent Harjo family. Like Posey's father, they were active in local Creek politics, with Posey's mother's father, Pahosa Harjo Phillips, serving in both the House of Warriors (like the U.S. House of Representatives) and the House of Kings (like the U.S. Senate) when Posey was a teenager. Posey grew up speaking Creek until age fourteen, when his father required him to speak English. After that, he went to the Creek national boarding school and did so well in his studies that, after school hours, he began working for—and sometimes running—the local newspaper. The Creek Nation then sponsored him at Bacone Indian University, where he studied Latin and Greek. On his own as well as in school, he read widely in British and American literature, and he began writing poetry. His favorite poet was Robert Burns, who wrote in Scottish dialect, and he also found models in the British Romantics, especially Shelley, and in the American Fireside poets. Soon Posey began to publish poems, stories, essays, and feature articles, first in Bacone publications and then in local newspapers, usually under the pseudonym Chinnubbie Harjo. Local newspapers also reprinted his poems and other writings.

At twenty-two, he was elected to the House of Warriors and found himself centrally involved in Creek politics, but soon he moved away from a politician's role and accepted a series of administrative posts at Creek schools, including Superintendent of the Creek Orphan Asylum, of public instruction for the Creek Nation, of the Creek Nation boarding school, and of the Wetumpka National School. Early in the new century, he started to focus less on writing poetry. In 1902 he bought and took on the editorship of the *Indian Journal*, making him the first American Indian to edit a daily newspaper. Posey began writing a series of fictional newspaper letters in the voice of the imaginary Fus Fixico, a traditional Creek who—with his friends—speaks in Creek-inflected English. National newspapers began reprinting his poems, and national editors sought more poems as well as the Fus Fixico letters, but Posey declined, saying that only local audiences would understand his work. Perhaps he also favored writing for an Indian audience. The satirical Fus Fixico letters are a classic of American humor and of Indian dialect writing, and some of Posey's poems also work with dialect. Dialect writing was popular at the time, and Posey's dialect writing shows unusual skill and a flair for the satirical—undermined, occasionally, by anti-black racism. Many of Posey's writings, including his poems, address the tumultuous issues of contemporary Creek life as the federal government pressured Creeks to allot their lands and pressured Indian Territory to give up the sovereignty of Indian nations in favor of statehood. From 1904 to 1907, Posey left newspaper editing and worked for the Dawes Commission, seeking to enroll conservative Creeks so that they would not lose the chance to receive their allotments.

Posey blended overlapping impulses. He was like traditionalists in his fluency in the Creek language and knowledge of traditional culture and in his respect for those who spoke the language and spoke Creek-inflected English. He was also like traditionalists in his acid criticism of the corrupt federal bureaucracy that oversaw the allotment of communally held lands to individuals, the sale of "surplus" lands, and the sacrifice of Indian sovereignty. He was unlike traditionalists in his belief that the best way to preserve Creek identity was to assimilate, in his willingness to work for the bureaucracy that he criticized, and—near the end of his life—in his decision to join in real estate speculation. At the age of thirty-four, while a rescue crew sought to save him, and while more than a hundred onlookers watched, Posey drowned in a flood of the North Canadian (Oktahutche) River, the same river he had grown up by and often written about, a fate eerily anticipated in "My Fancy," a poem about drowning in the very same river.

In 1910, Minnie H. Posey, Alex Posey's wife, published a collection of his poems. She seems to have revised some of the poems and transcribed some of them incorrectly (Sivils xxiii-xxiv). Meanwhile, few copies of the collection survived, so that even with the growth of interest in Indian writing, Posey remained better known for his Fus Fixico letters, collected in 1993, than for his poems. In 2008, however, Matthew Wynn Sivils published a collection of all Posey's poems, working from the original publications and manuscripts and including many poems that had never been published. This new collection opens the way to a revaluing of Posey's considerable poetic talent. The poems below draw their texts mostly from Sivils's edition and appear in the sequence they follow in that edition, based on the dates of composition so far as they can be determined. Dates or approximate dates are provided when known. (Littlefield, *Alex Posey*)

O, Oblivion!

O, Oblivion, how thou'rt robbed and cheated!
Congress never meets but there is seated
From thy dark abode some politician
With a bill anent the demolition
Of our Indian governments, and gets in
Print, like Curtis and the well-named Dennis Flynn,
And that there man from Colorado—Teller,
I believe, he's called—that wondrous feller
Who thundered by us once aboard a car,
And knew just what we needed here, by Gar! 10
But Dawes will make thee restitution,
Though he violates the Constitution!

[probably 1894]

4 **anent:** about. 6 **Curtis:** U.S. representative Charles Curtis (Kaw). Later a U.S. senator and vice president, Curtis promoted legislation to, as Posey puts it, demolish Indian governments. In Indian Territory, the federal Curtis Act of 1898 authorized the allotment of Indian lands, abolished the courts of tribal nations, and replaced the laws of tribal nations with federal law. By taking power from Indian nations, it prepared the path for Indian Territory and Oklahoma Territory to become the state of Oklahoma in 1907. 6 **Dennis Flynn:** Dennis Thomas Flynn, who served four terms representing Oklahoma Territory in the U.S. Congress, sponsored legislation to help white land seekers acquire Indian lands in Indian Territory. 7 **Teller:** Secretary of the Interior and Senator from Colorado Henry M. Teller. While secretary of the interior, Teller began a Religious Crimes Code that banned Indian ceremonies. 10 **Gar:** euphemism for God, used here comically to keep from swearing. 11 **Dawes:** Senator Henry L. Dawes sponsored the General Allotment Act of 1887, better known as the Dawes Act. It called for redistributing communally owned reservation lands by "allotting" parcels of land to individual Indians. In the process, the Dawes Act ended communal land ownership and "opened" "surplus" land—meaning unallotted Indian land—to settlers and speculators, that is, to white people. Even allotted lands could eventually be sold, and white people were usually best positioned to buy them. The Dawes Act led to a massive loss of land for Indian nations.

Ye Men of Dawes

Ye men of Dawes, avaunt!
    Return from whence ye came!
If ye are godly men—
        I fear ye're not the same—
        Lay down this work of shame!
        This first thing that ye know
Five thous'n' will warp
    Your little conscience so!

Is there no good that ye
    Can do in any state 10

That ye have come among
Us, so precipitate,
For to negotiate?
Lo! has the lurid flame
Of mobs gone out at last,
With crimes by every name?
O man of Dawes, ye talk
As sleek ratpaths 'neath
A crib, or slipp'ry elm
Tree growing on the heath; 20
Ye take all lodgings, faith,
In manner to impress:
Look kind o' sour, as if
In mighty mental stress:

Ye wear duck suits galore
And shoes of patent skin:
Ye strut majestically;
But ye can't lead us in
To any such a sin
As giving aid to ye 30
To sanctify a wrong—
Gives robbery chastity!

[probably 1894]

1 **Dawes**: see note to Posey's "O, Oblivion!" above, line 11. 7 **Five thous'n'**: 5000 dollars. 10 **state**: condition, but also one of the United States, as opposed to Indian Territory, which was not a state. 25 **duck**: duck cloth, a kind of canvas. 26 **patent skin**: glossy leather.

["To allot, or not to allot"]

To allot, or not to allot, that is the
Question; whether 'tis nobler in the mind to
Suffer the country to lie in common as it is,
Or to divide it up and give each man
His share pro rata, and by dividing
End this sea of troubles? To allot, divide,
Perchance to end in statehood;
Ah, there's the rub!

[1894]

Title: The title ponders whether or not to go along with the Dawes Act by allotting communal Indian lands to individual Indians. Allotment was seen as a step to statehood, and statehood would mean sacrificing the sovereignty of Indian nations. Posey plays off Hamlet's famous soliloquy "To be or not to be." Hamlet—in that soliloquy and elsewhere—is often seen as a classic example of indecision.

Wildcat Bill

Whoop a time er two fer me!
  Turn me loose an' let me be!
I'm Wildcat Bill,
  From Grizzle Hill,
A border ranger; never down'd;
  A western hero all around:
A gam'bler, scalper, born a scout;
  A tough; the man ye read about,
From no man's lan';
  Kin rope a bear an' ride a buck; 10
Git full on booze an' run amuck;
  Afeard o' nothin'; hard to beat;
Kin die with my boots upon my feet—
  An' like a man!

[1894]

Note: This poem is Posey's attempt to imitate the speech of the white people then streaming into Indian Territory (Littlefield, *Alex Posey* 70–71).

["In UNCLE SAM'S dominion"]

In UNCLE SAM'S dominion
  A few own all the "dust."
They rule by combination
  And trade by forming trusts.

In the "injun's" own arrangement
  We acknowledge with a sigh,
We can realize derangement,
  Tho' the mote is in our eye.
But in trying to reform us,
  Our great white Uncle, why 10
Don't you firstly pluck the saw-log
  From out your own black eye?

[1895]

Note: Sivils has not confirmed that Posey wrote "[In Uncle SAM'S Dominion]," but he attributes the poem to Posey based on its style and on where and when the poem was published (33). 3 **combination:** cartel, business monopoly. 4 **trusts:** cartels, business monopolies.

Cuba Libre

Forward, Cuba, forward!
  Down with treachery!
Forward! Hang the coward
  For his butchery!—
  Weyler, beast of Spain!

Forward! forward ever!
  Down with tyranny!
Forward! backward never
  From thy enemy!—
  Weyler beast of Spain! 10

On! on! Gomez, triumphantly!
Thou hast the wide world's sympathy!

Maceo, rest thee,
Cuba shall be free!

[1896]

Title: Spanish for "Free Cuba." 5 **Weyler**: General Valeriano Weyler, notoriously brutal Spanish military governor assigned to put down the Cuban rebellion against Spanish rule. 11 **Gomez**: General Máximo Gómez Baez, the revolutionary military leader in Cuba's War of Independence in 1895–1898. 13 **Maceo**: General Antonio Maceo Grajales, Gómez's second in command, killed in 1896 two and a half weeks before Posey's poem was published.

Callie

It was April, and the orchard looked like
White clouds huddled up together, tightly
Tinged with crimson, accounting every zephyr.
Callie, leaning from the window, begged in
Vain that afternoon for just a single
Blossom of the many in my hand. How
Gloriously pretty! and my love was
Deep for Callie; but a boyish heart was
Mine, and I had not the courage then to
Offer any token of affection. 10
And, as she sat there begging; and I stood
There hesitating, with my flowers; all
The while the martins sallied to and fro
Above us; all around the woods were green,
With here and there a glimpse of prairie land
Beyond; and still beyond, the mountains blue,
With cool dark shadows crawling over them.

[2008]

The Squatter's Fence

He sets his posts so far apart
And tacks his barbed wire so slack
In haste to get the [Injun] land
Enclosed and squat him qui'lly down,
Unseen by any, that
His fence when built looks like
A country candy pulling!

[written about 1897, published 2008]

3 **[Injun]**: emendation by Sivils.

To Our Baby, Laughing

If I were dead, sweet one,
    So innocent,
I know you'd laugh the same
    In merriment,
And pat my pallid face
    With chubby hands and fair,
And think me living as
    You'd tangle up my hair.

If I were dead, loved one,
    So young and fair, 10
If I were laid beneath
    The grasses there,
My face would haunt you for
    A while—a day maybe—
And then you would forget,
    And not remember me.

[written about 1897, published 2008]

Title: another manuscript of this poem has the title "To Baby Yahola." Posey's son Yahola Irving Posey was born 29 March 1897.

The Two Clouds

Away out West, one day,
Two clouds were seen astray.

One came up from the sea,
    Afar unto the South,
And drifted wearily.
    One came out of the North.

Away out West that day,
A town was swept away!

[probably 1897]

The Idle Breeze

Like a truant boy, unmindful
Of the herd he keeps, thou, idle
Breeze, hast left the white clouds scattered
All about the sky and wandered
Down to play at leap frog with the
Grass and rest in the branches;
While, one by one, the white clouds stray
Apart and disappear forever.

[written 1897, published 2008]

My Fancy

Why do trees along the river
    Lean so far out o'er the tide?
Very wise men tell me why but
    I am never satisfied:
And so I keep my fancy still,
    That trees lean out to save
The drowning from the clutches of
    The cold, remorseless wave.

[written 1897, published 2008]

In another manuscript of the same poem, there titled "Fancy," line 3 reads "Cold reason tells one why but," and a stanza break comes between lines 4 and 5.

To a Hummingbird

Now here, now there;
    E'er poised somewhere
In sensuous air.
    I only hear, I cannot see
The matchless wings that beareth thee.
    Art thou some frenzied poet's thought,
That God embodied and forgot?

[1897]

To the Crow

Caw, caw, caw,
Thou bird of ebon hue,
Above the slumb'rous valley spread in flight,
On wings that flash defiance back at light,
A speck against the blue,
A-vanishing.

Caw, caw, caw,
Thou bird of common sense,
Far, far in lonely distance leaving me,
Eluded, with a shout of mockery 10
For all my diligence
At evening.

[written 1897, published 2008]

The Bluebird

A winged bit of Indian sky
Strayed hither from its home on high.

[2008]

Coyote

A few days more and then
There'll be no secret glen,
Or hollow, deep and dim,
To hide or shelter him.

And on the prairie far,
Beneath the beacon star
On Evening's dark'ning shore,
I'll hear him nevermore.

For where the tepee smoke
Curled up of yore, the stroke 10
Of hammers ring all day,
And grim Doom shouts, "Make way!"

The immemorial hush
  Is broken by the rush
Of armed enemies
  Unto the utmost seas.

[2008]

Sunset

In coward clouds forgot,
  In yonder's sunset glow,
The day, in battle shot,
  Lies bleeding, weak, and low.

[written 1898, published 2008]

The Legend of the Red Rose

The red rose once was white
  As any flake of snow can be;
The sum of her delight
  Was knowledge of her purity—
  For so the pretty little legend goes.

But, on a luckless day,
  There bloomed outside the garden wall
A common wildwood flower,
  So wondrous sweet and fair and tall,
  That envy flushed the white cheeks of the Rose. 10

[probably written 1898; 1910]

This version of the poem, following Sivils, reproduces the text of Posey's surviving manuscript. In the version published by Minnie H. Posey, which she might have revised, the poem has no stanza break, and lines 5–10 read, "As ev'ry bee and nodding Poppy knows. / But, in a luckless hour, / There bloomed outside the garden wall / A common wildwood flow'r, / So wondrous fair and sweet and tall, / That envy flushed the white face of the Rose!"

To a Morning Warbler

Sing on till light and shadow meet,
  Blithe spirit of the morning air;
I do not know thy name, nor care;
  I only know thy name is sweet,
And that my heart beats thanks to thee,
Made purer by thy minstrelsy.

[1899]

Eyes of Blue and Brown

Two eyes met mine
  Of heav'n's own blue—
Forget-me-nots
  Seen under dew;

My heart straightway
Refused to woo
All other eyes
Except those two.

Days came and went
A whole year thro, 10
And still I loved
Two eyes of blue.

But when one day
Two eyes of brown,
In olive set
Beneath a crown

Of browner hair,
Met mine, behold,
The eyes beneath
The shining gold, 20

Love-lit and loved
In days of yore,
Grew dim, and were
Sky-blue no more!

[written 1898, published 2008]

Flowers

When flowers fade, why do
Their fragrances linger still?
Have they a spirit, too,
That Death can never kill?
Is it their Judgment Day
When from the dark, dark mould
Of April and of May
Their blooms again unfold?

[written 1898, published 2008]

The Deer

From out the folded hills,
That lie beneath a thin blue veil,
There comes a deer to drink
From Limbo's waters in the dale.

Then flies he back into
  The hills, and sitting here, I dream
And watch, as vain as he,
  My image lying in the stream.

[written 1898, published 2008]

4 **Limbo's waters**: the waters of Limbo Creek, near where Posey grew up in the Muskogee Nation.

When Love Is Dead

Who last shall kiss the lips
  Of love when Love is dead?
Who last shall fold her hands
  And pillow soft her head?

Who last shall vigil keep
  Beside her lonely bier?
I ask, and from the dark
  Cold night without, I hear

The mystic answer: "I
  Her mother, Earth, shall press 10
Her lips the last in my
  Infinite tenderness."

[1900]

Say Something

Form something when you'd have men heed;
Don't bark when you have nothing treed.

[2008]

Tulledega

My choice of all choice spots in Indian lands!
Hedged in, shut up by walls of purple hills,
That swell clear cut against our sunset sky,
Hedged in, shut up and hidden from the world.
As though it said, "I have no words for you;
I'm not a part of you; your ways aren't mine."
Hedged in, shut up with low log cabins built—
How snugly!—in the quaint old fashioned way;
With fields of yellow maize, so small that you
Might hide them with your palm while gazing on 10

Them from the hills around them, high and blue.
Hedged in, shut up with long forgotten ways,
And stories handed down from sire to son.
Hedged in, shut up with broad Oktaha, like
A flash of glory curled among the hills!
How it sweeps away toward the morning,
Deepened here and yonder by the beetling
Crag, the music of its dashings mingling
With the screams of eagles whirling over,
With its splendid tribute to the ocean! 20
And this spot, this nook is Tulledega;
Hedged in, shut up, I say, by walls of hills,
Like tents stretched on the borders of the day,
As blue as yonder op'ning in the clouds!

[published about 1900]

Title: Posey's name for the area where he grew up, near the Tulledega Hills (Littlefield, *Alex Posey* 23).
14 **Oktaha**: town in the Muskogee Nation.

The Arkansas River

I dread thee, mighty River! There's a flush
Of anger on thy face that will not pale.
Thou'st treach'rous, turbulent, and move
Within thy roomy bed as if unconfined.
Before thy deep cold tide, and majesty,
Man pauses, lingers, and is mute with awe.
The white dust hanging over thee, when winds
Are high, must surely be the anxious ghosts
Of all the drowned, expecting that thou wilt
Someday go dry, and disappear from Earth. 10

[written about 1900, published 2008]

Ode to Sequoyah

The names of Watie and Boudinot—
The valiant warrior and gifted sage—
And other Cherokees, may be forgot,
But thy name shall descend every age;
The mysteries enshrouding Cadmus' name
Cannot obscure thy claim to fame.

The people's language cannot perish—nay,
When from the face of this great continent

Inevitable doom hath swept away
The last memorial—the last fragment 10
Of tribes,—some scholar learned shall pore
Upon thy letters, seeking ancient lore.

Some bard shall lift a voice in praise of thee,
In moving numbers tell the world how men
Scoffed thee, hissed thee, charged thee with lunacy!
And who could not give 'nough honor when
At length, in spite of jeers, of want and need,
Thy genius shaped a dream into a deed.

By cloud-capped summit in the boundless west,
Or mighty river rolling to the sea, 20
Where'er thy footsteps led thee on that quest,
Unknown, rest thee, illustrious Cherokee!

[1899]

Title: Sequoyah (1767–1843), revered Cherokee silversmith who invented the Cherokee writing system, a syllabary rather than an alphabet. **2 Watie**: famous Cherokee Confederate Brigadier General Stand Watie. **2 Boudinot**: Elias Boudinot (Buck Watie), brother of Stand Watie, founder and editor of the *Cherokee Phoenix*, the first American Indian newspaper. The last syllable of *Boudinot* is pronounced like *knot* and thus rhymes with *forgot* in line 3. **5 Cadmus**: ancient Phoenician prince said to have brought the alphabet from Phoenicia to Greece.

An Outcast

Pursued across the waning year,
By winds that chase with lifted spear,
A leaf, blood-stained, fell spent at last
Upon my bosom. Poor outcast!

[1899]

The Decree

What does the white man say to you?
Says he, "You've got to hoe; you've got to plow;
You've got to live by the sweat of your brow—
Even as I. You've held your last powwow
And your last revelry.
The council fire whereby you hold debate
Against my stern decree
Is flickering out before the breath of fate."

What does the white man say to you?
Thus speaketh he to you: "You've got to cast 10
Your laws as relics to an empty past.
You've got to change and mend your ways at last.
I am your keeper and
Your guardian, in the judgment of mankind,
And 'tis mine to command
You in the way that leaves your savage self behind."

[1900]

On the Capture and Imprisonment of Crazy Snake, January, 1901

Down with him! chain him! bind him fast!
Slam to the iron door and turn the key!
The one true Creek, perhaps the last
To dare declare, "You have wronged me!"
Defiant, stoical, silent,
Suffers imprisonment!

Such coarse black hair! such eagle eye!
Such stately mien!—how arrow-straight!
Such will! such courage to defy
The powerful makers of his fate! 10
A traitor, outlaw,—what you will,
He is the noble red man still.

Condemn him and his kind to shame!
I bow to him, exalt his name!

[1910]

Title: Chitto Harjo (in English, Crazy Snake), the legendary and charismatic Muskogee (Creek) anti-allotment leader, formed an alternative Muskogee government in the fall of 1900 with his traditionalist followers, who in English were called Crazy Snakes or Snakes. Federal troops arrested Harjo and other Snake leaders in January, 1901. On Posey's journalism about Chitto Harjo and the Crazy Snakes, see Littlefield, *Alex Posey* (143–47).

The Fall of the Redskin

(With apologies to Edwin Markham)

Awed by the laws of Arkansas, the whims
Of Hitchcock, and the bill that Curtis sent
To him, he leans against a witness tree
And gazes on the fur-blazed section-line,
The emptiness of treaties in his face,

And on his back the burden of the squaw.
Who made him dead to raptures of the chase,
The ills of not desiring to allot,
A thing opposed to change, that never files,
Stubborn and slow, a brother to the Boer? 10
Who loosened and let down the pledge—
"As long as streams give tribute to the sea,
And grass spreads yearly banquet for the herds?
Whose breath blew out the faith within this brain?
Is this the thing the Lord God made and gave
To have dominion over sea and land;
To hunt the deer and chase the buffalo
From climes of snow to climes beneath the sun?"
Is this the dream He dreamed who shaped Tom Platt
And sent Roosevelt on his career of light? 20
Down all the stretch of Carbetbaggers to
The last man fresh from Maine or Illinois,
There shines no ray of hope for him! He sees
But darkness filled with censure of his ways—
Night filled with signs and portents that appall—
Greed fraught with menace to his grass and ore!

What gulf between him and home rule! The ward
Of Uncle Sam's high-salaried minions,
What to him are Tams Bixby, J. George Wright?
What the long reaches of the tape of red, 30
The splendors of the carpetbag regime?
Through this dread shape the Filipino looks;
The vow not kept is in that doubting stare;
Through this dread shape humanity betrayed,
Plundered, profaned and disinherited,
Cries protest to the judges of the courts,
A protest that is also made in vain.

O, Bill McKinley, Hanna, bosses in
All lands Republican beyond dispute,
How will you reckon with this Indian in 40
That hour when he unchallenged casts his vote,
When whirlwinds of Democracy blow J.
Blair Shoenfelt back north to see the folks,
And spiders weave their nets in spacious rooms
And corridors of Misrule's capital?

How will it be with towns that batten on
The wrong—with those whose bread depends upon

The shame—when Bradford's dream becomes a fact
And pies of politics are baked at home?

[1901]

Epigraph: The poem is loosely based on Edwin Markham's hugely popular 1899 poem "The Man with the Hoe." **1 laws of Arkansas**: as Indian Territory moved towards statehood, the United States made the Territory follow the laws of the neighboring state of Arkansas instead of the laws of the Territory's individual Indian nations. **2 Hitchcock**: Ethan Allan Hitchcock, U.S. Secretary of the Interior. Posey's Fus Fixico letters spoof him as Secretary It's Cocked. Posey complained, with understatement, that Hitchcock, known for imposing rules, "failed to issue 'rules and regulations' pertaining to the Indian land in the Territory for several days" (Littlefield, *Alex Posey* 162). **2 bill that Curtis sent**: see note to Posey's "O, Oblivion!" above, line 6. **4 section-line**: land boundary. **8 to allot**: to divide up communal Indian lands for individual owners. **9 files**: anti-allotment conservatives, such as the Crazy Snakes, sometimes refused to file for allotments. **10 Boer**: in 1899–1902, the Boers—white descendants of Dutch and other settlers—fought against the more powerful British in what is now South Africa. **19 Tom Platt**: Thomas Collier Platt, Republican U.S. senator from New York and state political boss. Wary of his rival, New York governor Theodore Roosevelt (see line 20), Platt promoted Roosevelt as a nominee for vice president during President McKinley's reelection campaign in 1900. After the poem was published in January, while Roosevelt was vice president elect, Roosevelt became president when McKinley was assassinated later in 1901. **27 home rule**: self-government by the Indian nations of Indian Territory. **29 Tams Bixby, J. George Wright**: Bixby was chairman of the Dawes Commission and Wright was Indian inspector for Indian Territory. In Posey's political writings, both were objects of scorn for corruption. The Fus Fixico letters dub them Tams or Dam Big Pie and J. or Jay Gouge Right. **32–33 Filipino looks; / The vow not kept**: referring to Filipino resentment that after the Spanish-American War in 1898 the United States annexed the Philippines rather than live up to the promise many believe U.S. officials had made to respect Filipino independence. **38 Bill McKinley**: William McKinley, president of the United States from 1897 to 1901. **38 Hanna**: Mark Hanna, McKinley's campaign manager in the election of 1896 and then U.S. senator from Ohio. **42–43 J. Blair Shoenfelt**: Indian agent to the Five Civilized Tribes (Cherokees, Chickasaws, Choctaws, Creeks, and Seminoles) scorned for corruption in Posey's Fus Fixico letters, which dub him J. Bear Sho' Am Fat. **48 Bradford**: Daniel F. Littlefield, Jr., suggests that this refers to Gamaliel Bradford, a banker who criticized the Republican Party in *The Lesson of Popular Government* (1899) (Littlefield cited in Sivils 190).

Saturday

To my friend Jim Cowin

Danged, if I kin be content 'round'
  Home on Saterday—gits me down.
It's a day to smoke cigyars on,
  Hear tall talk an' see airs on,
A day to gas an' whittle on,
  Maybe, take a little on!

Jes 'pears like Sunday when you stay
  'Bout home, glum like, on Saterday.
Somehow it gits me out o' hitch,
  Gives me the all-overs an' sich   10

Till I saddle old Jude an' set
  Her clean to town in a fret.

I jes can't he'p but go to town
  On Saterday, an' loaf aroun'.
It's a day to git the news on,
  To play at cards an' lose on;
It's a day for folks to meet on,
  To spark the gal you're sweet on.

It's jes in me to be in town
  On Saterday, a mozin' 'roun'. 20
It's a day to trade an' swap on,
  To soak your hoss an' crop on.
It's a day to have your fun on,
  To get your grindin' done on.

Don't keer if it pours down for weeks,
  On Saterday I'll head the creeks!
It's a day to go to town on,
  The folks you know ar' foun' on:
It's a day to git home late on,
  Have the ol' woman wait on. 30

I never missed but once to go,
  An' jacks I felt worse a week er mo'.
It's a day one ort not pick on
  To complain an' be sick on.
It's a day to get up soon on,
  An' ride to town 'fore noon on.

Ginst one Saterday passes by,
  Another's loomin' in my eye.
It's a day to Jew an' buy on—
  I mean the things they're high on— 40
To take the editor's hint on,
  Pay up an' git in print on.

My plow, when Saterday comes 'roun',
  Kin stand till Monday in the groun'.
It's a day to see the sights on,
  To drop in at Abe Kite's on;
A day to eat a tamale on.
  To be in Eufaly on!

[1901]

46 **Abe Kite**: hide dealer in Eufaula (Sivils 199). 48 **Eufaula**: town near where Posey lived.

On Hearing a Redbird Sing

Out in the howling wind;
Out in the falling snow;
Out in the blight and gloom
Of a desolate world,
I hear a lone bird sing,
"O it is sweet, sweet, sweet!"

Out in the sunless fields;
Out in the moaning woods;
Out in the dark and cold
Of a drear stricken world, 10
    I see the roses bloom
    And hear the drop of leaves!

[1903]

It's Too Hot

He hates to sweat
Does Bill Mellette.
  He'll wait till frost, no doubt;
It's too hot yet
For Bill Mellette
To turn the rascals out.

[1903]

2 **Bill Mellette:** William Mellette, U.S. attorney who at first declined to investigate illegal land deals by federal officials and other members of the Dawes Commission. Mellette explained that the weather was too hot for an investigation. Posey brings out a pun in the word *hot*, referring both to hot weather and to hot controversy (Littlefield, *Alex Posey* 176–77).

A Freedman Rhyme

Now de time fer ter file
Fer you' Freedman chile.
You bettah lef' dat watermelon 'lone
An' go look up some vacant lan'
Fer all dem chillun what you t'ink is yone.
De good lan' aint-a-gwine ter last.
Tell Gabul blow de Judgment blast.
Hits miltin' like snow
Up eroun' Bristow;
Dey'll be none lef' but rocks an' river san'. 10

De Injun filin' mighty fast;
Bettah hum Yo'se'r, nigger,
An' gin ter kin' 'o figger.

—Fus Fixico

[1905]

Note: When Muskogees filed to receive their land allotments as called for in the Dawes Act, Posey objected that Muskogee freedmen—black former slaves of Muskogees—were included. Drawing on a wide range of offensive racist stereotypes, this poem tries to make fun of a Muskogee freedman. 11 **Bristow**: town in the Muskogee Nation. **Fus Fixico**: fictional Muskogee character in series of newspaper pieces by Posey.

On Viewing the Skull and Bones of a Wolf

How savage, fierce and grim!
His bones are bleached and white;
But what is death to him?
He grins as if to bite.
He mocks the fate
That bade, "Begone."
There's fierceness stamped
In ev'ry bone.
Let silence settle from the midnight sky—
Such silence as you've broken with your cry; 10
The bleak wind howl, unto the utt'most verge
Of this mighty waste, thy fitting dirge.

[2008]

A Vision of Rest

Some day this quest
Shall cease;
Some day,
For aye,
This heart shall rest
In peace.
Sometimes—ofttimes—I almost feel
The calm upon my senses steal,
So soft, and all but hear
The dead leaves rustle near
And sigh to be
At rest with me.

Though I behold
The ashen branches tossing to and fro,
Somehow I only vaguely know
The wind is rude and cold.

[1910]

William Abbott Thompson, Cherokee, 1844?–1899

Will A. Thompson was a teacher and worked for newspapers in the Cherokee Nation. In 1888 he was business manager of the briefly lived *Telephone*, and from 1891 to 1893 he edited the *Indian Sentinel*. His only surviving poem takes a playful rather than a conventionally literary approach and holds its value as a humorous, revealingly misogynist and cynical portrait of one person's perspective on late nineteenth-century Indian Territory. At the bottom of the poem he notes its place of composition as Tahlequah, capital of the Cherokee Nation. (Littlefield and Parins, *Biobibliography*, *Supplement* 292)

You Can Always Tell

You can always tell a dude by his shape,
You can always tell a dude
Cause you know he is very rude,
And his manners they remind you of an ape!

You can tell a crooked lawyer by his cheek;
You can tell a crooked lawyer,
And although he never saw you
He is "poking" in your business with his beak.

You can tell most any printer in the land,
You can tell most any printer 10
Cause he'll work for you all winter,
Then he'll "work" some other fellow if he can.

You can tell a "smart" physician by his head,
You can tell a "smart" physician,
By the size and position
Of the graveyard where he stores away his dead!

You can tell an "office" seeker by his coat.
You can tell an office seeker,
Cause you know he's always meeker,
When he's trying to work a fellow for his vote. 20

You can tell an office-holder by his clothes—
You can tell an office-holder
'Cause his office makes him bolder
And he sometimes doesn't pay up what he owes.

You can tell an engineer by his style—
You can tell an engineer
By the way he takes his beer,
And he irrigates his "whistle" with a smile.

You can tell the "comin' woman" by her walk—
You can tell the "comin' woman" 30
'Cause they've got so common,
And they make you very tired by their talk.

You can tell a pretty widow by her smile—
You can tell a pretty widow
If you'll only just consider
That her ways are just as tender as a bile!

You can always tell a bully by his boots—
You can always tell a bully
'Till he tumbles in a gully
'Cause he tried to bluff a man "what shoots." 40

You can tell a big Reporter from the "Hub"—
You can tell a big Reporter
If you see him in Dakotah,
From the way he eats the other fellow's grub.

[1895]

Rufus Buck, Yuchi, born about 1873, died 1896

During his teens, Rufus Buck of Okmulgee in the Creek Nation in Indian Territory attended Wealaka Mission boarding school for Indians, until the school expelled him for meanness. Driven partly by resentment against the whites who were encroaching on Indian Territory, Buck led a brutal gang on a rampage of murder, robbery, and rape in 1895. The following year, he and his followers were convicted and sentenced to hang by the famous "Hanging Judge Parker." After Buck died, a picture of his mother was found in his cell. On the back of the picture, in surprisingly eloquent language possibly influenced by the hymns he and his gang sang as they waited to die, the marginally literate murderer had written a poem. (Harman 495–514; Shirley)

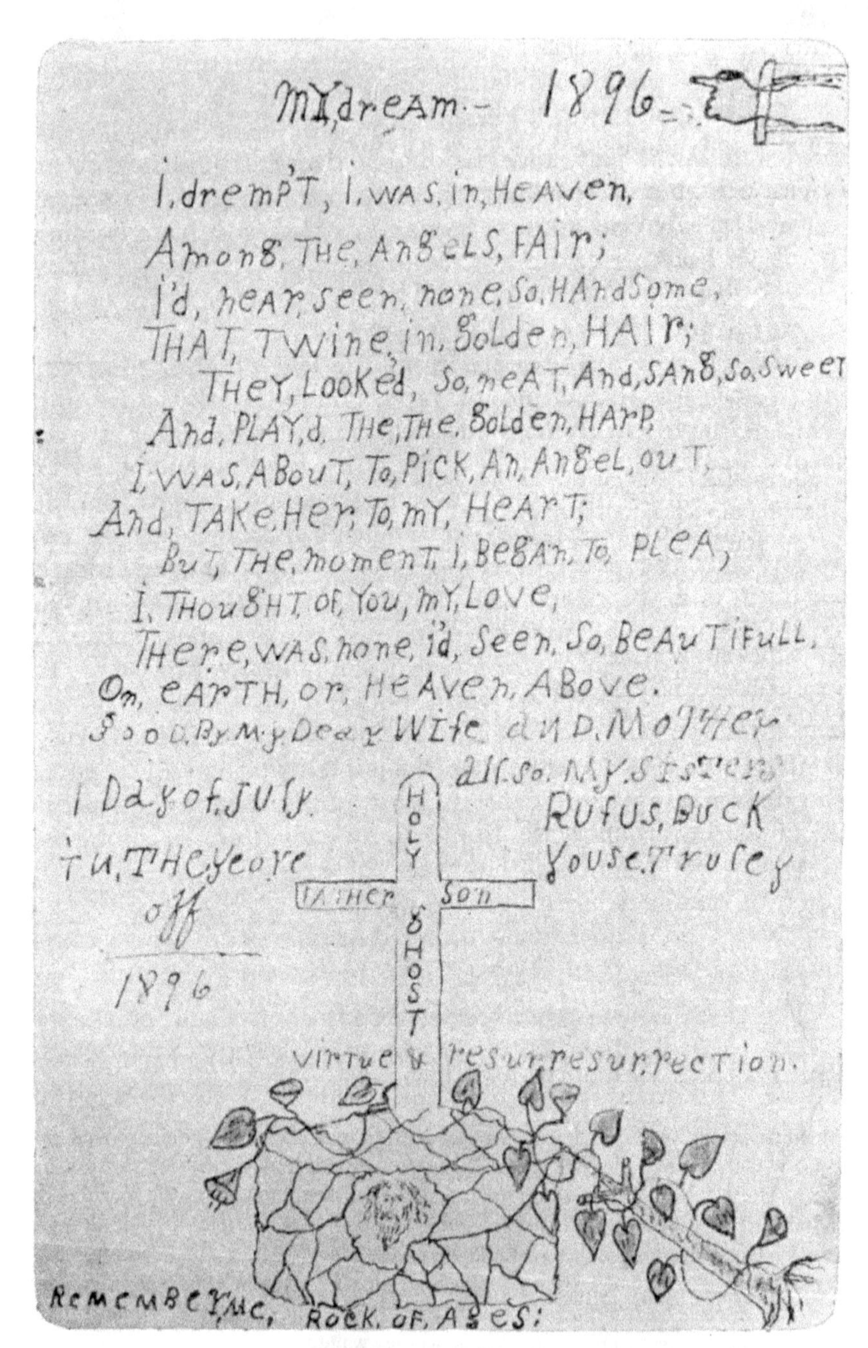

MY, dream.- 1896

I, drempT, I, WAS, in, HEAVen,
Among, THE, AnGeLS, FAir;
I'd, hear seen, none, So, HAndSome,
THAT, TWine, in, Golden, HAir;
THeY, LooKed, So, neAT, And, SAnG, So, SweeT
And, PLAY,d, THe, THe, Golden, HArP,
I, WAS, ABouT, To, PicK, An, AnGeL, ouT,
And, TAKe, Her, To, mY, HeArT;
But, THe, momenT, I, BeGAn, To, PLeA,
I, THouGHT, of, You, mY, Love,
THere, WAS, none, id, Seen, So, BeAuTiFuLL,
On, eArTH, or, HeAVen, ABove.
Good, By My Dear Wife and Mother
also My Sister

1 Day of July
in, THe year
off
1896

Rufus, Buck
Youse Truley

HOLY
FATHER SON
GHOST
virtue & resurresurrection.

REMEMBER ME, ROCK, OF, AGES;

Figure 5. Rufus Buck's semi-literate "My Dream," scrawled on the back of a photograph of his mother as he awaited his execution in 1896. S. W. Harman, *Hell on the Border: He Hanged Eighty-Eight Men* (Fort Smith, Ark.: Phoenix, 1898), 514.

My dream 1896

I drempt I was in heaven
Among the angels fair;
I'd near seen none so handsome,
That twine in golden hair;
They looked so neat and sang so sweet
And play'd the golden harp.
I was about to pick an angel out
And take her to my heart;
But the moment I began to plea
I thought of you my love. 10
There was none I'd seen so beautifull
On earth or heaven above.
Good by my dear wife and mother
all so my sisters
1 day of July H Rufus Buck
Tu, the yeore O Youse truley
off L
1896 Y
father son
G
H
O
S
T
virtue & resurressurrection

Remember me rock of ages:

[written 1896, published 1898]

My dream 1896: For ease of reading, the transcription regularizes the left margin and the capitalization, puts spaces between words, and removes superfluous commas that Buck wrote between words where we might expect spaces. It also puts periods at the ends of lines 6 and 10 and removes an extra "the" from line 6. Readers can see the poem as it looks in the original, with illustrations, in Figure 5. For a less regularized transcription, see the introduction to this volume.

James Roane Gregory, Euchee (Yuchi) and Muskogee (Creek), 1842–1912

Gregory grew up in Wagoner County, Indian Territory, attended the Tullahassee Mission school, and spent most of his adult life near Inola. Early in the Civil War, his father was killed by pro-Confederate bushwhackers. Gregory enlisted in the Union Army and was wounded while fighting with the "loyal Creeks," Muskogees who sided with the Union and were led by Opothleyahola. After the war, he studied law, practiced in the Creek courts, served several terms as an elected judge, and served as Superintendent of Creek Schools. Gregory caused a stir in 1891 when he had himself declared a legal citizen of the United States, leading some to question his citizenship in the Creek Nation ("In the Indian Country"). He supported the allotment of Creek lands, and in 1896 he was the Progressive Party's unsuccessful candidate for Principal Chief of the Creek Nation. The following year, he served the Dawes Commission as it determined which Creeks were eligible for allotments. He published a poem of more than 700 lines (far from his best work), called *A Poem, Entitled Lucy's Poney*, as a separate book in 1895. Fluent in Muskogee (Creek) and English, Gregory often served as a translator and said that he thought in Muskogee. His English prose reads clearly, but his poetry frequently resorts to awkward syntax that makes the poems difficult to follow, though even his marginally intelligible poems sometimes achieve their own brand of lyricism. ("In the Indian Country"; "Gregory, James Roane Interview"; "Obit for James Roane Gregory"; Cox)

The Promised Seal

Monopolies greedy host, Pander,
Claiming right, held justice to repeal,
Truest honor to deride and slander,
Helpless children, crushed 'neath tyrant's heel.
Boodlers and drunken Sages, meander.
While the pure, for just right, vain appeal.
On their homes, land, lone outcasts, wanderers.
Soon, heed ye well for the promised seal.

That seal will equalize, the plunder
Will be true and show each just right real. 10
Least dishonor and might asunder,
Each child shall retain humanity's weal.
The seal of next September's thunder.
Count each vote, vaunting haught' kneel.
Injuns can remember—yhu'll wonder;
They strike strong, when Injuns cast the seal.

[1895]

Title: the editor has not managed to identify the seal referred to in this poem. While it may have something to do with the Oklahoma land run, no September 1895 event fitting the description in this poem has yet been identified. See also Gregory's "Otheen, Okiyetos," below, line 5. **1**: It is hard to tell whether *host* is a noun or a verb. If it is a noun, then the line refers to monopoly's greedy host, that is, to the greedy host of monopoly. *Host* makes more sense as a verb, suggesting that greedy monopolies host and pander. **5 Boodlers**: bribers. **6 vain**: perhaps *vain* means *vainly*. **12 weal**: well-being. **14 haught'**: unclear, perhaps a printer's abbreviation for haughty (which would make *kneel* a noun), as in the original printing the word presses against the right margin without room for a *y*.

Otheen, Okiyetos

To these little ones, hast thou been true;
Wouldst thou cast thy right hand, then to save,
With heaven's breath of life, thy soul pure,
To each lawful right, just wish crave?

Or hast thou from thy high gifted seal,
Heaven's gift of speech, betrayed with a lie,
Denied thy tongue, humanity's weal;
With thy false soul, the evil one's eye?

Myriads of dangers compass the land,
Each broken promise of thine, a moan, 10
Each link of hope, prove a chain of sand,
Each promise, a viper of hell, sown.

When did the Muskogee blood kneel low?
Answer! (then ye will praise honor's grave).
Never, till they fell 'neath the death blow,
Returned glory's gift to God that gave.

How ye built love's fold; with lash and pain,
Striking against one Muskogee home,
To thee, that blow will rebound again,
When thy shield is false, swift it will come. 20

Equity of home right, is the law,
To each one extend by bonds of love,
Why with false tongue attempting to awe,
The weak, the weary, and the child dove?

Each Muskogee, come to thy trial,
A living oath of honor, each greet:
Drink the love of home, or death's vial,
Honor's guiding will, with each heart beat.

For a home to each, in full redeem,
For a name to each, on honor's roll, 30
Saved from lying monopolists' scheme,
Greet of joy, to each Muskogee's soul.

[1895]

Title, Otheen, Okiyetos: Muskogee (Creek) for "I really, really mean what I am saying" (translation by Rosemary McCombs Maxey). **5 seal**: see also Gregory's "The Promised Seal," above. **12 weal**: well-being.

Rain

Trusting hope, and yet thy heart fears.
Merciless, the dry hot wind blows,
Blasting midst the well tilled corn rows,
Shall the weak cry for bread in vain?

With each killing blast, thy hope sears,
Brave thy will, midst fearing heart throes,
Still strong in hope, midst evil woes,
Will the rain come with the moon's wane?

Sure promise, midst the bladed spears,
Tilling the earth from thorn to rose, 10
Ye will eat bread, rest and repose.
Thy duty done, thy hopes remain.

The angels sympathetic tears,
From Oceans of mercy's zeal, flows,
Many blessings of life bestows,
Sent to thee, with the rain.

[1895]

Storm Lights

Midst darkness the lightnings flash,
Heralded by deep-toned roar,
Heaven's swift sparkling fire lash,
By the darkened hill and moor,
  Glory's streaming light,
   Glory's deep-toned might,
Every echo rebounding,
Each brightened cloud resounding;
                    Glory of light.

"By darkness let there be light," 10
Commanded the mighty voice,
"Casting away death and night,
That my children may rejoice."
   Thrill lights swiftly flow,
   Cast from Heaven's bow;
Every echo commanding,
Midst darkness, light demanding,
                    Power of light.

Appalling storms of love flow,
The flashing lightnings reveal, 20
Midst the storm's loud crashing blow,
Midst the thunder's loud-toned peal,
Mines of mighty store,
Strewn upon earth's floor,
To obey the child's command,
Swift following the child's hand,
Darkness to light.

The electric wires will go
To each home in every land:
The command will swiftly flow, 30
Sent from an infant child's hand,
The wheels will then turn,
The lamps will then burn,
The mighty storm's strife power,
Will then kneel to duty's hour,
By the storm's light.

By the lightning's sparkling gift,
The world heeds a child's command,
A child the mighty reins lift
By soft cunning touch of hand; 40
The wheels are turning,
The lamps are burning,
An infant child bids them "come"
To bless and light the way home;
Blessings of light.

The hearts of the seas quiver,
The wings of lightning hasten,
The child's message deliver,
Bidding the mother "listen,"
Love and light flow, 50
Sent from Heaven's bow,
Remembering her child dove,
Guiding the fountain of love,
By Heaven's light.

[1895]

TWO ORIGINAL POEMS

Written Especially for The Record
JAMES R. GREGORY.

THE GREEN CORN DANCE.

My children are happy unto this day
He-yo-we-yoo! my mother! Hi-yo-chee!
The ashes of the fires were cold and gray,
The paths are long that lead from the blue sea;
The Southern winds breathed and the snow was gone.
The warm sun counseled with the great dark cloud,
Then He-yo-we-yoo sent down his new corn
With his lightning fire dancing, singing loud,
He-yo-we-yoo-hi-yo.

The children of the storms rejoice this day:
He-yo-we-yoo! my mother! Hi-yo-chee!
The ashes of the fires are blown away,
The rain came up straight from the deep blue sea.
The Southern winds came blowing the new corn,
The warm sun counseled with the lightning cloud;
He-yo-we-yoo sends the lightning free born.
With his lightning fire we dance singing loud.
He-yo-we-yoo-hi-yo.

NINETEENTH CENTURY FINALITY.

Nineteen hundred and it rains fire and blood,
Fast filling up hell and the grave;
A million lives trampled in gory mud,
They kill to kill—killing to save.

Great wars fought for paradise by the lost,
Hark! Widows' cries and orphans' wails!
God of Love! Pierce our hearts with cold death frost!
Crown Jesus Christ a stone, God Baal!

The love of God for man deified him,
The Gentiles glorified his name.
The Roman and the Jew crucified him,
Ssience covers His love with shame.

Figure 6. James Roane Gregory's "The Green Corn Dance" and "Nineteenth Century Finality" as they appeared in *Wagoner Record*, 9 August 1900.

The Green Corn Dance

My children are happy unto this day
He-yo-we-yoo! my mother! Hi-yo-chee!
The ashes of the fires were cold and gray,
The paths are long that lead from the blue sea;
The Southern winds breathed and the snow was gone.
The warm sun counseled with the great dark cloud,
Then He-yo-we-yoo sent down his new corn
With his lightning fire dancing, singing loud,
He-yo-we-yoo-hi-yo.

The children of the storms rejoice this day: 10
He-yo-we-yoo! my mother! He-yo-chee!
The ashes of the fires are blown away,
The rain came up straight from the deep blue sea.
The Southern winds came blowing the new corn,
The warm sun counseled with the lightning cloud;
He-yo-we-yoo sends the lightning free born,
With his lightning fire we dance singing loud.
He-yo-we-yoo-hi-yo.

[1900]

Title: The Green Corn Dance, an extended annual harvest festival and the major ceremonial event of the year, marks the renewal of the calendar and of social and spiritual life for the Muskogee (Creek) and the Yuchi peoples and for many other Southeastern American Indian peoples.

Nineteenth Century Finality

Nineteen hundred and it rains fire and blood,
Fast filling up hell and the grave;
A million lives trampled in gory mud,
They kill to kill—killing to save.

Great wars fought for paradise by the lost,
Hark! Widows' cries and orphans' wails!
God of Love! Pierce our hearts with cold death frost!
Crown Jesus Christ a stone, God Baal!

The love of God for man deified him,
The gentiles glorified his name. 10
The Roman and the Jew crucified him,
Science covers His love with shame.

[1900]

3–6 A million lives trampled . . . / Great wars: there were too many wars in 1899 and 1900 to list them all here. In 1899 The United States Senate ratified the peace treaty ending the Spanish-American War. Other wars in 1899–1900 that received extensive press coverage in the United States included the Philippine American War, the Boer War, and the Boxer Uprising. **8 Baal**: the Biblical Hebrews saw the gods of their neighbors, often called Baal, as false gods.

Kingfisher (Cherokee)

After the Curtis Bill Passes

After the Curtis bill was passed
And jurisdiction given,
Many were the cries that 'rose
"You've taken away our livin.'"

The officers, from chief to solicitor,
At Uncle Sam did howl;
But among the common farmers
I never heard a growl.

The admirers of the chief
All had a paying place; 10
No difference how the funds went
All had a smiling face.

Then the chief called the council,
From different parts they came;
And they drank Jamaica ginger
Till their heads were very lame.

The chief chose the delegates
The council clinched the nail;
Then off to Washington they went,
The U. S. Congress to assail. 20

They spent the peoples' money
For whiskey and good clothes:
They brought the evidence back
Painted on their nose.

Amongst the officers, Soggy was
The biggest—Joe Ross the smallest;

Bunk Marcum was the top man,
  Because he was the tallest.

Uncle Sam has taken us
  From our dear Sammy's arms; 30
Now thieves and politicians
  Can go to work on farms

The Curtis bill has knocked them out,
  And tribal courts don't go;
They are trying now to get d— fools
  To follow them off to Mexico.

Don't listen to a word they say,
  For in the end you'll find
The men who have gone to Mexico
  Have axes for to grind. 40

They are ready to take the lines
  And drive you if you'll go,
To desert lands and burning sands
  In the state of Mexico.

Let's remain just where we are,
  Far away Mexico has no charms;
Let's all remain and go to work
  Upon our fertile farms.

Yes; we'll go to work with plow and hoe
  This is the best for us I know; 50
Then the thieves and politicians
 Will have to go to Mexico.

As for myself, I've gone to work—
  Let politicians plan;
I'm sure we're better off right here
  In the care of Uncle Sam.

[1898]

Title: On the Curtis Bill (or Act), see note to Posey's "O, Oblivion!" above, line 6. Many traditionalist Cherokees considered moving to Mexico if the Curtis Act passed. Since the poem was published in April 1898, before the act was passed in June, the events it describes are speculative. **12 chief**: Samuel Houston Mayes, who had been accused of corruption (Hoig 256). **15 Jamaica ginger**: a popular patent medicine with a high alcohol content. **27 Bunk Marcum**: attorney Thomas Marcum.

J. C. Duncan, Cherokee, born about 1860

J. C. Duncan lived in the Sequoyah District of the Cherokee Nation. Though the little-known Duncan seems not to have been a practiced poet, and though his only known poem has survived in print so faint it cannot all be deciphered, his poem carries considerable political interest. In the transcription below, illegible words are filled out with the letter x, and uncertain words are indicated with bracketed question marks. The poem also has typographical errors. It is possible that the transcription below includes mistakes as well as uncertainties.

The Red Man's Burden

Parody on Kipling's Poem

Look at the Redman's burden
  Place in thy Christian scales,
In the hands of Dawes Commission,
  For that is what prevails.
Yes, look at the Redman's burden,
  That caused the "exiled son"
To "face the stormy waters,"
  Seeking their golden mun.

"Half devil and half child" you call
  The aborigines, 10
'Tis better far to be half child
  Than be a devil all.
No "heavy harness" need be spent,
  Nor "Christians" hide in wait,
  Just keep a radical president,
And Curtis to legislate.

Behold the white man's burden
  Of gold and silver bullion,
Of Redmen's scalps and broken vows
  By hundreds, yes by millions. 20
Yet fill their mouths of famine xxx,
  With bombshells and with grape,
For that's the way all "Christians" do
  Like Shafter did of late.

From Florida to Havana
  One stride the goddess made,
To cheer the word "expansion,"
  And in seas of blood to wade;

The xxxxxxx Philippine xxxxxx
In less than half a stride, 30
And spread the eagle's wing o'er
The world xx in style to xxxxx.

From side to side that eagle xxxxxxxxxxx
Above the "image's[?]" moan,
His beak upon the frozen beach[?],
His tail the torrid zone.
All for "Christianity's sake,"
Quoth Kipling, in his rhyme,
Perhaps he better poems make
Than truths every time. 40

Another portion yet is sought
The North Pole, so 'tis said,
The problem yet has not been wrought
But will be live or dead.
To make a plain and easy way
For the white part of creation,
Publicly though the presses say,
It's an Indian reservation.

White man, shake off thy burden,
'Tis enough thy pride to yoke, 50
Give us back our freedom,
And return to thy British yoke.
Return our land and moneys,
Then Christianity take,
Return us to our innocence,
We never burned at stakes.

[1899]

Title: The title plays off the title of Rudyard Kipling's famous poem of 1899, "The White Man's Burden: The United States and the Philippine Islands." Though Kipling's poem is often reprinted without its subtitle, it responds to the controversial American decision in 1898 to make the Philippines an American colony, a decision ratified by treaty in February 1899 as Kipling wrote his poem. J. C. Duncan may also have been responding to Too-qua-stee/DeWitt Clinton Duncan's "The White Man's Burden," originally published three days before J. C. Duncan's poem and reprinted on the same day that J. C. Duncan's appeared. Compare Too-qua-stee's poem, also in this volume. **3 Dawes Commission**: On the Dawes Act, see note to Posey's "O, Oblivion!" above, line 11. The Dawes Commission was charged with administering the Dawes Act, and in the process it produced "Dawes Rolls," official lists that codified who belonged to individual Indian nations. The rolls generated controversy, for Indian people could enroll in only one Indian nation, regardless of their ancestry, and many Indian people feared giving the federal government authority over their identity and the identity of their fellow citizens. Moreover, the Commission's criteria, based on so-called blood, poorly matched most traditional Indian criteria for determining who is Indian or who belongs to a given Indian nation. **16 Curtis**: see note to Posey's "O, Oblivion!" above, line 6. **22 grape**: grapeshot, grape-size iron balls used as cannon shot. **24 Shafter**: Major General William Rufus Shafter, who led American troops in Cuba during the Spanish-American War.

Richard C. Adams, Delaware (Lenape), 1864–1921

Richard Calmit (sometimes spelled Calmet) Adams was born in Kansas and grew up at Russell Creek in Indian Territory (now Oklahoma). His father was a Baptist minister and a founder of the Delaware Baptist Church who was active in Delaware tribal matters, and his father's two brothers were chiefs. Unable to afford law school, Adams taught himself the law by reading. He represented the Delaware Nation in Washington, D.C., from 1897 to 1921 and published five books about Delaware history and culture. A founder of the Brotherhood of the North American Indians, he was an active campaigner for Indian rights and the rights of the Delaware people, especially land and mineral rights. Disputes over land arose from the forced removal of the Delaware Nation from the Delaware River region to Ohio, and then to Indiana, and then to Missouri, then to Kansas, and then in 1867 to the Cherokee Nation in Indian Territory, leading to disputes over land rights between the Cherokees and the Delawares. (Nichols)

To the American People

With your kind permission, your attention I will claim,
I am only just an Indian, it matters not my name.
But I represent my people, their cause and interest, too;
And in their name and honor, I present myself to you.
They have your sacred promise, your pledge of friendship warm,
That you would always aid them and protect them from all harm,
And in my humble efforts, as I briefly state their case,
Will you pardon my shortcomings, and my errors all erase?

I do not come with grandeur, or boast of any fame,
Rank in politics, society, or wealth I cannot claim, 10
I never went to college, have no title of LL.D.,
As the Great Spirit made me, is all that you may see.
With the forces that oppose me, I certainly should pause,
If I were not depending on the justice of my cause.
I am only just an Indian, who here represents his band;
With this simple introduction, I extend to you my hand.

[1899]

Title: Adams uses this poem to introduce himself as the official representative of the Delaware Nation to the United States and to the American people, envisioning his readers ("you"), in this poem and his other poems, as Americans who need to be convinced about the rights of the Delaware people.

A Delaware Indian Legend

Long, long ago, my people say, as their traditions tell,
They were a happy, powerful race, loved and respected well.
To them belonged the sacred charge, the synagogue ([1]) to keep,
And every Autumn to the tribes, the Manitou's praises speak.
And all things went with them full well, the Manitou was pleased;
The Indian race was numerous then, countless as the trees;
The Manitou was kind to them, he filled the woods with game,
And in the rivers and the seas were fish of every name.

And to his children did he give the vast and broad domain;
Some the mountains and valleys took, while others chose the plain; 10
And everything to comfort them did the Manitou provide,
He gave them fish, game, herbs and maize, and other things beside.
He gave them rivers, lakes and bays, o'er which canoes did glide,
Forests dense and mountains high, great plains the other side.
The men were strong and brave and true, to them belonged the chase,
The women loving, kind and good, who filled a simpler place.

And they were taught while here on earth their spirits to prepare,
To join the Manitou himself, in the happy hunting-ground ([2])
somewhere;
That they must never lie and steal; must for each other care;
That principles are gems that pass us to that country there. 20
And even though the wars do come with aggressive tribe or band,
No warrior shall strike a fallen foe, or wrong a helpless hand;
And if your foe shall sue for peace, let not his plea be vain,
Produce the pipe, and smoke with him, smothering the wrathful
flame.

And while the smoke ascends above, breathe a prayer together,
That spirits of departed friends make peace beyond the river;
The Manitou's compassion seek, for he was sorely grieved,
Provide for the widows of the slain, ([3]) that their needs be relieved.
If a stranger enters in your lodge, give him both food and bed,
E'en if known to be your foe, no harm hangs o'er his head, 30
For now he is your honored guest, your protection he does claim;
Whate'er your source of difference be, contest it on the plain.

The voice of the Great Spirit now, is heard in every clime,
The rumblings of the thunder, the whisperings of the pine;
The works of the Great Spirit are seen on every hand,
Flowers, forests, mountains, stars, sun and even man.
The Lenape ([4]) all should gather in the Autumn there to praise
The wonders of the Manitou, the goodness of his grace;

And they to tell the Nations what to them he has unbound,
And the way for them to reach the happy hunting-ground. 40

Once many thousand moons ago, in the synagogue there came
All the tribes and warriors from the forest, hill and plain;
And while they were assembled there (5) a young man rose to say,
The Manitou had shown him in a vision on that day
From afar a huge canoe with pinions spreading wide,
Coming o'er the waters from across the sunrise side;
And in that huge canoe were people strange of dress,
All were armed as warriors, though they peacefulness professed.
They told them of their God, "who came and died for men,"
And they were messengers from Him to save them from their sin, 50
But first, they said, they must have land, and thus a home prepare,
Then they would teach them truth, and heaven with them share.
The young man to the warriors old his vision further told,
And prophesied that from that day these tempters would grow bold;
That each would have a different creed, to teach a different tribe,
And when one told another each would think the other lied.
The young man for his people lamented loud and long;
He saw the friendship broken that always had been strong,
Dissension, war, and trouble, their happiness succeed,
Tribes rise against each other, their warriors die and bleed. 60
At last, their faith all shattered, home, game and country gone,
Dejected, broken-hearted, he saw them westward roam.
The Manitou was sorrowful that they should faithless (6) be,
"And now where is the heaven the stranger promised thee?"
And some of the young warriors did live to see the day,
When across the sea from sunrise, with pinions flying gay,
Came great canoes with strangers who soon did boldly land,
And with a friendly gesture, extended the right hand.
Forgetful of the warning, they received them all as friends;
And made the sacred pledges to share with them their lands. 70
The Indians, true and faithful, their promise did fulfill,
And eager sought the teachings of the white man's God and will.
And this recalls sweet memories of at least one truthful man;
He made and kept a promise in treating for our land;
His deeds of loving-kindness strength to their teachings lend,
And sacred in our memory is the name of William Penn.
But alas! for faith and trusting, few others like him came,
The white man's promised friendship, thenceforth we found was vain.
While noble were his teachings, his practice was deceit, (7)
And thus the friends we trusted, our fondest hopes defeat. 80
And now the road is open across the stormy sea,

The strangers are invaders—our friends no longer be!
Our Manitou is angry, their God hears not our cry,
On the bloody field of battle the noble warriors die.
Again with peace and presents our friendship would be sought, (8)
Requesting that our vengeance on some other tribe be brought.
And now for this protection and their proffered friendship-hand,
The boasted Christian strangers ask to have as much more land. (9)
Now many moons have passed, the Indians are but few;
For comments on the prophecy, I'll leave that all to you. 90
Is the white man still deceiving? Is the Indian being robbed?
Will he yet share his heaven and the teachings of his God?
The Indian was just a savage, but he would not lie and steal,
The white man's highly civilized, but his conscience could not feel,
To rob poor, trusting Indians—well to him it was no sin,
And to break a solemn treaty was a very clever thing.
And when the Indian to the white man makes complaint about his
land,
He is told with solemn gestures, "Seek the Government—not the
man."
"He will be your good, great father and adopt you as his child,
He knows better what you need, and will protect you all the while." 100
But the father was forgetful (10) of his foster children's care,
So the Indian thus discouraged, finds relief not anywhere.
Will a Nation for its actions have to pass the judgment bar,
Or will God excuse the people, if the deeds the Nation's are?
He now sees the "Good, Great Father," better known as "Uncle Sam,"
Offering home, aid and protection to the poor of foreign lands;
Sees the foreigners in numbers seek his own beloved shore,
Where justice, love and liberty reign free forever more.
Sees the foreigners in Council, aid in making laws most just,
While he's no voice in legislation and his lands are held in trust. 110
Do you know a greater torture, or think his feelings can be guessed
When he sees such freedom cherished, while his own rights are
oppressed?
When on the day of judgment, their records there to see,
As God turns o'er the pages, who will the braver be?
For one is just a savage, his simple faith applies;
The other one, a white man, very highly civilized.
And should they be together long enough to treat,
Do you suppose the white man the Indian there would cheat?
Or if the chance is given, when the judgment's handed down,
Would the white man take his heaven or the Indians' Hunting-
Ground? 120

Do you think that Missionaries need be sent to foreign land,
To find fields for Christian duties and neglect the savage man?
In the land of peace and freedom can bondmen still be found?
Where every man does loudly boast class-legislation is not known!
Should neither one sit on the jury without the aid of ex-parte law,
Were the records brought from heaven, the court hear what the
  angels saw,
Have you doubts about the judgment? Would the white man pay
  the cost?
Or would the heir by birthright learn that there his case was lost?

In this the Indian's version, can he still be justified,
Or was it for his poor sake, too, that Christ was crucified? 130
Will Christians stand by idly, nor lend a helping hand,
And by their silence justify the seizure of his land?
Or will their God from heaven hear the Indian's plea
And prompt the Christian people to lend him sympathy,
And through their earnest efforts, not sympathy alone,
Redeem the Nation's credit before the Judgment Throne?

Let the Indian have some duties, treat him as a worthy man,
Give him voice in the elections, give him title to his land,
Give him place of trust and honor, let him feel this yet his home,
Let him use his mind and muscle, let his actions be his own, 140
Pay him what is justly due him, let your Government be his, too,
He will battle with each problem, just as faithfully as you.
One who proves himself a warrior and of danger knows no fear,
Surely can find ways to master each new problem that draws near.

NOTE 1. The Delaware Indians on the full moon of each October have a religious meeting in a large, long building, which lasts twelve days. Here the clans of the Delawares gather and other Indian tribes are invited. The ceremonies are conducted in the way of a dance around a fire built in the centre of the building. At these meetings any brave or chief may tell his experience in hunting or warfare, his dreams or impressions, and give his own interpretation of the same, never claiming any of the honors himself if he has been successful in any event, but thanking the Great Spirit or Manitou for his success. They believe that every person has a guardian spirit whose duty is to watch and prompt him in his daily actions, and if the individual listens to his guardian spirit he will not meet with any mishap or danger.

NOTE 2. The North American Indian, and especially the Algonquins, of whom the Delawares were the head, is perhaps the most religious being on the face of the earth. While he was warlike and always ready to assert his rights, he was always fearful of angering the Great Spirit, and careful to follow the principles of his traditional teachings, and if it had not been for this sentiment, I do not believe the Indians would ever have allowed the white man to secure a foot-hold on this continent.

NOTE 3. One of the principles of Indian warfare, when peace was made, was to send men from one tribe to the other where the most warriors had been slain, who would provide game for their widows, at least for a certain length of time.

NOTE 4. Some of the Delaware Indians still keep up the old traditionary worship, and on their reservation in the Cherokee Nation, on the forks of Caney, may be seen one of their synagogues, where each October they gather to praise the Great Spirit as their ancestors had taught.

NOTE 5. I have heard many old men of the Delaware tribe of Indians refer to this prophecy.

NOTE 6. Some of the Delawares to this day fully believe that their troubles are attributable to the fact of the Indians deserting the form of worship their ancestors had taught and taking up the white man's religion.

NOTE 7. I quote from the address delivered by Hon. Herbert Welsh before the Society of the Indian Rights Association, April 9, 1892.

The Indian version of this matter is even more pathetic than this account:

"Zeisberger's Christian Indians['] communities were the admiration of all who visited them. They shone as gleams of sunlight amid the sombre forests of Pennsylvania. Indians, who but a short time before had been wild and revengeful men, became under the preaching and indefatigable labors of Zeisberger, peaceable and industrious. They felled the great trees, cultivated the soil; built dwellings and Mission Chapels, and settled into peaceful and as they thought, permanent communities. But they were from the first regarded with envy and suspicion by the rougher elements in the rough and unrestrained colonial population. Ravaging war parties, composed of French officers and savage Indians, devastated the frontier settlements during the French and Indian war, and naturally there arose in undiscriminating and ignorant minds an intense hatred of all Indians. The Moravian Missionaries and their followers were obliged to fly for the protection of the British garrison in Philadelphia to find a shelter, which was grudgingly and timidly given. But a momentary respite was obtained. New York was asked the privilege of an asylum for the Moravian Indians, but the request was refused. A year of heart-sick wandering and exile ensued. The Indians were finally permitted to make the futile attempt of creating new homes for themselves in their native regions. When the storm of the Revolution broke, they were again subjected to the same persecutions as before, culminating in the shameful tragedy known as the Massacre of Gnadenhutten, where ninety of their men, women and children fell unresisting victims beneath the mallets and scalping knives of American Rangers. The Moravian Missions never fairly rallied from this blow. Zeisberger, one of the noblest and most Christian of men, died at Goshen, on the shores of the Tascanawas, at a great age. Strong in the testimony of a good conscience, but with the harvest of his life's work lying waste about his dying eyes, he gazed sadly on the remnant of his Indian followers who gathered to bid him farewell. From the standpoint of worldly success, his life had been in vain, but not as viewed from the higher standpoint, for he had brought hundreds not only to the conception of a noble life, but to such living of it as put the behaviour of their enemies to shame."

I also refer you to the massacre in Ohio at the Jesuit Mission in 1781 where more than one hundred Christian Indians were killed and burned, mostly women and children, by the American soldiers.

NOTE 8. The first treaty the United States ever made was made with the Delaware Indians, and the greater portion of the Delawares assisted the United States in the Revolutionary war; also in the Civil war the Delaware Indians furnished 170 soldiers out of an adult male population of 218.

NOTE 9. Immediately after the close of the Revolutionary war, the United States Government made treaties with other tribes of Indians, and secured from them the very lands they had formerly acknowledged to belong to the Delawares, and the Delaware Indians received nothing whatever for the same. The tract consisted of several million acres, located in Ohio and Indiana.

NOTE 10. See Manypenny's report of how the Army Officers of Fort Leavenworth and other prominent persons assisted the settlers in making settlements on Delaware lands in Kansas, and by their actions finally discouraged the Delawares so much that they were forced in self-defense to sell their lands in Kansas and purchase homes in the Cherokee Nation, Indian Territory, a title to which was guaranteed by the United States Government. The same treaty also guaranteed them all civil rights and a voice in the Government of the Cherokee Nation. Now the Delaware Indians are forced to sue the Cherokees for this land at great expense to themselves, after they have paid for the lands and improvements more than $1,000,000.

[1899]

5 **Manitou**: spirit. 59 **their happiness succeed**: come after their happiness. 96 **thing**: the uncharacteristic off-rhyme between *thing* and *sin* may sound awkward, but it echoes the break that it describes. 125 **ex-parte law**: *ex parte* is a Latin legal term for legal proceedings where only one side gets to present its case, thus violating due process. **Note 7 Zeisberger**: David Zeisberger (1721–1808) was a Moravian missionary. **Note 7 But a momentary**: Only a momentary. **Note 7 Massacre of Gnadenhutten**: in 1782, American militia clubbed to death 96 Christian Indians in revenge for acts of war by other Indians. None of the murderers was prosecuted. **Note 7 Goshen, on the shores of the Tascanawas**: Goshen Township, Ohio, on the Tuscarawas River. **Note 10 Manypenny's report**: George W. Manypenny (1808–1892), commissioner of Indian Affairs 1853–1857. Outraged at white settlers' treatment of the Delawares and other Indian nations in Kansas, Manypenny quotes from his several reports and summarizes the events in *Our Indian Wards* (123–29).

To the Delaware Indians

I have travelled o'er the country that once was our domain,
Seen the rivers and the mountains, the broad and fertile plain,
Where the Indian chased the buffalo, the antelope and deer,
When the smoke from Indian wigwams arose from far and near;
Seen the lovely Susquehanna, where our council fire would burn,
And all the tribes and warriors would gather there to learn
The wise teachings of our chieftains and their traditions old,
And to tell it to their children as to them it had been told.

I see, from time immemorial, by stories handed down,
We had exclusive title to our homes and hunting-ground, 10
But then there came some pilgrims from a far and distant shore,
As they said "with Christian motives," our country to explore;
For us, "a poor heathen nation," their hearts were truly sad;
And to save us from "the infernal powers" they'd be very glad.
But to provide the daily bread of those who laid the plan,
Well, of course, we'd be expected to give them plenty of land.

But for that we should not care, they would lead us on to light,
And "in heaven we'll be rewarded" they say, for doing right,
For there the Bible teaches, "our treasures we should store;"
"If our rights are there established, we need for nothing more." 20
"And Christians will gladly show us the path the pilgrims trod,
That leads unto eternal joy in paradise with God."

So we gave close attention to their actions one by one,
And this, as we have found it, is part that they have done.

They took with pious gratitude the land that was our own,
They killed the buffalo and deer and drove us from our home!
Some of our people plead with them, our country to retain,
While others did contest our rights with arms, but all in vain.
With sorrow, grief and suffering, we were forced at last to go,
From the graves of our forefathers to a land we did not know. 30
But this was now guaranteed to us, "as long as water shall run,"
Yet on they pushed us, on and on toward the setting sun!

"And this will be the last move," they tell us, if we go;
"You will hold the country this time as long as grass shall grow,
"For the good Great Father's promise is a very sacred pledge,
"And to all his children does he give the greatest privilege;"
That is to all children he adopts from every race of man,
Except the rightful owners of this broad and bounteous land!
They must in meek submission bow unto the hand of might,
To them the courts of law are barred, they can make no legal fight! 40

If the Indian seeks the Government, there his grievance to relate,
He must first obtain permission from those who rule the State!
If his rights are there denied him and an attorney he would seek,
He is sternly then reminded he has no right to speak!
"For under section so and so, which guides your legal move,
"You see no attorneys can appear for you, except if we approve;
"And if, in our opinion, your claim does not adhere
"To the interests of the public, then your cause we cannot hear."

"This is a Christian Nation," they oft with pride maintain,
And even on their money their faith they do proclaim. 50
And none can hold an office here in this Christian land,
Unless he believes in Heaven and the future state of man;
In every town are churches, God's word is everywhere,
E'en legislation, good or bad, begins each day with prayer,
"This is the home of freedom, where justice rules the land!
"And all (save Indian people) their rights may here demand!"

The foreigner from Europe's shore or the ignorant African
Has the right to sit in Congress' halls and legislation plan!
Turning the treaty records o'er, in the first that comes to view,
I see this gracious Government guaranteed these rights to you, 60
And why you're treated as children, or ruled with an iron hand,
Nor allowed to be politically free, is more than I understand,

Unless it be "in Heaven you are to find your treasures dear,"
And in your pious Christian teachers are to take "their treasures" here.

But I do not blame the Christians, if Christians true they be,
And it's not their Bible teachings that bring such grief to thee;
It is not the faith that men believe, it is the deeds they do,
That sometimes hurt their fellowmen and probe their conscience, too.
If "we are children of one God," are we not equal here?
Are not the Indian's liberties and rights, to Him as dear? 70
If we an earnest effort make, our rights here to obtain,
Then, perhaps with His assistance, that privilege we shall gain.

I believe the American people are just and kind and true,
They would fight for our protection, if our grievance they but knew.
True, some with selfish motives would keep us still suppressed,
But the great controlling public would strive to do what is best.
And none has their attention called to our sad, humiliated state,
Or quickly would they all demand that Congress reparation make.
So the fault with us has partly been, because we don't complain,
But allow ourselves thus to be robbed for selfish plotters' gain! 80

Why should we be a separate people, the target of every man?
We, who owned this country once, should be right in the van.
No one would objections raise and surely Congress can
Declare all Indians vested with the rights of every man.
And grant us prompt permission to prove our every claim,
And pay us the obligations the Government has made in vain;
Then to our oppressors will we prove, who deny our right to live,
That Indians will make good citizens, if to them a chance you give.

[1899]

5 **Susquehanna**: the Susquehanna River. 31, 34 **as long as water shall run, as long as grass shall grow**: While their general sense accurately reflects the sense of many treaties, such phrases—contrary to legend—did not appear in any treaties with the federal government (Prucha 262–63).

Too-qua-stee/DeWitt Clinton Duncan, Cherokee, 1829–1909

Born in the Cherokee Nation in Georgia, Duncan published his poetry and many of his other writings under his Cherokee name, Too-qua-stee. He survived forced removal to Indian Territory in 1839. After attending mission and Cherokee schools, he graduated Phi Beta Kappa and with honors from Dartmouth College in 1861, but the Civil War deterred him from returning to Indian Territory. He taught school in New Hampshire,

Wisconsin, and Illinois, and then in 1866 he settled in Iowa where he continued to teach and work as a school principal while practicing law and serving in local political offices. Eventually, he returned to Indian Territory where he worked as attorney for the Cherokee Nation and taught at and served as principal of the Cherokee Male Seminary. A teacher of English, Latin, and Greek, he also studied Cherokee history, wrote about the Cherokee language, and translated Cherokee laws. Duncan/Too-qua-stee wrote powerful political essays as well as powerful poetry. (Foreman, "Notes"; Littlefield and Parins, *Biobibliography* 234; Littlefield and Parins, *Native American Writing in the Southeast* 30–31)

The White Man's Burden

"Son of man," "son of man." (Ezek. 28;2.)
"Take up the white man's burden"; once again
Sing in prophetic tone the old refrain.
Go tell those white men, I myself am God,
Still hold my throne and wield the avenging rod;
'Twas I that spread the curtains of all space
And set each star to blazing in its place;
That I, it was, that formed the solid earth
And nursed the seas and mountains at their birth;
That winds were not, until I made them blow; 10
The infant rivers, too, I taught to flow;
And I, it was, that set each orb to run
Its stated journey 'round the sun;
That light and darkness ever patient stand
And move but to obey my own command.

"Son of man, "son of man."
Go tell those white men who the world propel,
The red men, doing less, are mine as well:
That naught that they can do, or say,
Can add one ounce to what they really weigh; 20
On heaven's great beam that tests the weight of all
They and their works are things exceeding small;
'Tis not what they achieve in peace, or war,
That fills the book-account; but what they are.
The red man, and the black, whom fate debars
From whited temples, see me in the stars;
With tom-tom do me more accepted praise
Than pealing organs worked on stated days.
As flowery fields, untouched by Godless art,
Spontaneous fragrance; so the contrite heart 30
Of heathen lands sends up an incense sweet
As ever rose from priestly censer's heat.

"Son of man, "son of man."
Go tell those white men not to be so proud;
'Twas I that hid the lightning in the cloud.
That twice ten thousand years, or thereabout
Should pass ere they could find the secret out,
Shows dullness quite enough to chill their pride
And make their swelling vanity subside.
Steam, too, I made; its power was nothing hid; 40
From age to age it shook the kettle's lid
Full in their view; but never could they see it,
Till chance vouchsafed from mystery to free it.
The art of printing, too, is all my own,
Lo! every foot of living thing had shown,
(I ordered so) as long as time had run.
How easily the printing job was done;
Yet time's last grain of sand had well-nigh sped
Ere their dull wit these signs correctly read;
Ere Gutenberg, by chance, could take the hint, 50
And fumbling set a thought in clumsy print;
Oft had fierce thunders, too, convulsed the earth,
And meteors flashed and perished in their birth,
Ere they could form the sulphurous grain of war,
And teach the cannon's throat to flash and roar.

"Son of man, "son of man."
Go tell those white men, I, the Lord of hosts,
Have marked their high presumption, heard their boasts.
Observe their laws; their government is might
Enthroned to rule, instead of perfect right. 60
Could I have taught them such gross heresy,
As "Greatest good to greatest number be?"
Has shipwrecked crew, with gnawing famine pressed,
A right to slaughter one to feed the rest?
Should just minorities be made to yield
That wrong majorities may be upheld?
In nature, is not this the rule that brutes
Observe in settling up their fierce disputes?
Why should the greater number have their way,
But for the power to make the less obey? 70
Again, the thing that makes a promise bind
Is that it issues from a willing mind.
But they have wrested my divine intent,
And based all right to take on the assent.
Hence starving virtue, forced to trade her bed,

Alas! with wealthy lust for needed bread,
By mere assent makes right the moral wreck
And saves the scoundrel from a broken neck.
The merchant, too, may stroll from shore to shore,
Manipulate the market, rob the poor; 80
If want o'ertake the victims of his greed,
He has his bargain, quite enough to plead.

"Son of man, "son of man."
Go tell those white men, I, who spread the plain
For homes, for grazing herds, and fields of grain,
An equal measure of the boon designed
For each of every race, or grade, or kind;
But lo! with impious disregard they break
My law; the whole, forsooth, the stronger take;
While countless millions, millions, have not where 90
To rest by night, or walk by day, nor so much air
As makes a breath, nor light to guide the eye,
Unless from some monopolist they buy,
It makes no difference how they get their pile—
By law, by force, by venal fraud, or guile—
'Tis all the same, a universal wrong,
A mode like that dumb quadrupeds among.

"Son of man, "son of man."
Go tell those white men that I look upon
Their treatment to the mother of my Son 100
With indignation. Woman was the best
Of all my works, the bloom of all the rest.
The partner of my secret counsels, she,
Pure, patient, wise, most gentle, most like me,
And yet those men, by force of muscle, rule,
And make of her a mere subservient tool,
A slave, a drudge, to common use assigned
Like some dull beast in harness—tugs confined.

"Son of man, "son of man."
Go tell those white men, I myself am God, 110
Still hold my throne, and wield the avenging rod.
Go tell them now, with culture drunk,
They're still in the barbaric gutter sunk.
That, though I use them to chastise the bad
As though no other proper wish I had,
They do not well to think that what they are
Is right, and naught that I would punish for.

They are but means selected to fulfill
The secret purpose of my sovereign will.
I send them to the world's remotest verge 120
Not to reclaim mankind but simply scourge.
The goblet from the lips of which I pour
My wrath, as often I have done before—
The glass itself, of no more value found,
Is hurled and smashed to pieces on the ground.

[1899]

Title: The title repeats the title of Kipling's "The White Man's Burden"; see notes for J. C. Duncan, "The Red Man's Burden" above. **2 "Take up the white man's burden"**: the opening line of Kipling's poem. **108 tugs confined**: like tug boats confined to harbor.

The Dead Nation

An Elegy at the tomb of the Cherokee Nation,
by one of her own sons

Alas! poor luckless nation, thou art dead
At last! and death ne'er came 'neath brighter bows
Of flattering hope; upon thine ancient head
Hath late-time treason dealt its treacherous blows.

When on the watery chaos rose the land
And built this continent thy venturous feet
Were first to tread the new-born world; a hand
Divine had given it thee thy restful seat.

Here with thy God, without such wars as tore
The entrails out of cultured Rome and Greece, 10
Thou didst abide ten thousand years or more,
Thy wants by Him supplied, in halcyon peace.

But then came Art, in rouge and ribbons dressed,
The source of woe, borne on the winged hours,
And, squat upon thine own salubrious west,
Bred pestilence and rot within thy bowers.

Smit by the blast of her contagious breath
Thy children fell in armies at thy side;
And struggling in the grip of a strange death,
Exclaimed, "O white man!" closed their eyes, and died. 20

Came also Might, the adjutant of Art,
Wrenched off the hinges from the joints of truth,

And tore its system into shreds apart—
  Repeated, in short, the moral code, forsooth.

Then first it was, that on thy peaceful plains
  The roar of onset and the saber's gleam,
Began—but hold! humanity refrains,
  And genius cannot paint a dying scream.

Thus rotting Pestilence, and Art and Might,
  In moonlight orgies o'er thy children's bones, 30
To honor civilization, hands unite
  And dance the music of their dying groans.

'Twas civilization, (said to be,) at work,
  To proselyte thy sons to ways of grace;
With savage means, the rifle, sword and dirk,
  To slaughter night, that day might have a place.

And so, indeed, they made the day to shine
  Upon thy callow brood, and with the light
Awoke those worms of greed that always twine
  In breasts exposed to suns too strangely bright. 40

Thy sons, touched by these strange transforming rays,
  Withdrew their love; to "end the strife."
They said, they aped the white man's heartless ways,
  And tore the breast that nursed them into life.

Dear Cherokee nation, with the right to live,
  Art dead and gone; thy life was meanly priced;
Thy room to civilization hadst to give,
  And so did Socrates and Jesus Christ.

[1899]

Title and subtitle: In Indian Territory, the federal Curtis Act of 1898 took power from Indian nations, including the Cherokee nation, and prepared the path for Indian Territory and Oklahoma Territory to become the state of Oklahoma in 1907. See note to Posey's "O, Oblivion!" above, line 6. Too-qua-stee also wrote many essays in response to the Curtis Act. 1 **Alas! poor**: echoing the opening words of Hamlet's famous graveyard speech to the skull of Yorick, his father's beloved jester: "Alas, poor Yorick! " (*Hamlet*, act 5, scene 1). 5 **watery chaos . . .** : While the vocabulary of water and land echoes the King James translation of Genesis in the Old Testament, here Too-qua-stee refers to the Cherokee creation story. Like most American Indian creation stories outside the Southwest, the Cherokee creation story recounts the world's beginning in an "earth-diver" story, with a small animal—for the Cherokees, Dayuni'si, the water beetle—diving into the waters and raising the earth from beneath.

A Vision of the End

I once beheld the end of time!
Its stream had ceased to be.
The drifting years, all soiled with crime,
Lay in a filthy sea.

The prospect o'er the reeking waste
Was plain from where I stood.
From shore to shore the wreckage faced
The surface of the flood.

There all that men were wont to prize
When time was flowing on, 10
Seemed here to sink and there to rise
In formless ruin blown.

In slimy undulations roiled
The glory of the brave;
The scholar's fame, the rich man's gold,
Alike were on the wave.

There government, a monstrous form,
(The sea groaned 'neath the load),
A helpless mass blown by the storm,
On grimy billows rode. 20

The bodies of great syndicates
And corporations, trusts,
Proud combinations, and e'en states,
All beasts of savage lusts,

With all the monsters ever bred
In civilization's womb,
Lay scattered, floating, dead,
Throughout that liquid tomb.

It was the reign of general death,
Wide as the sweep of eye, 30
Save two vile ghosts that still drew breath
Because they could not die.

Ambition climbed above the waves,
From wreck to wreck he strove.
And as they sunk to watery waves,
He on to glory rode.

And there was Greed—immortal Greed—
Just from the shores of time.

Of all hell's hosts he took the lead,
  A monarch of the slime. 40

He neither sank below nor rose
  Above the brewing flood;
But swam full length, down to his nose,
  And steered where'r he would.

Whatever wreckage met his snout
  He swallowed promptly down—
Or floating empire, or redoubt,
  Or floating heathen town.

And yet, it seemed in all that streaming waste
There nothing so much gratified his taste 50
As foetid oil in subterranean tanks,
And cliffs of coal untouched in nature's banks,
Or bits of land where cities might be built,
As foraging plats for vileness and guilt;
Or fields of asphalt, soft as fluent salve
Or anything the Indian asked to have.

I once beheld the end of time!
  Its stream had run away;
The years all drifted down in slime,
  In filth dishonored lay. 60

[1899]

51 **foetid**: variant spelling of *fetid*, and editor's emendation of unclear type that appears to be *foeted*. 54 **foraging**: uncertain transcription of type that is unclear before the *ging*. 55 **salve**: uncertain transcription of unclear type.

Cherokee Memories

When we survey the landscape of the past,
And strive again its pleasures to re-taste,
Awake! old memory! Chafe your drowsy eyes;
Begin and tell what charming scenes arise.

The brightest day this country ever saw,
Without a doubt, was ere the white man's law
Suppressed the conscience, and put out its light,
And made the statute the sole rule of right.
Then every man was every other's friend,
And the least call for aid made all attend. 10

Then hospitality, broad as the day,
Took in the weary traveler on his way;
Made every home a refuge from distress,
Not only one, but every man to bless.

When from our homes by the relentless toe
Of might, our tribe was kicked through seas of woe,
In this wild west to find a dismal home,
Or else perhaps a more convenient tomb,
We brushed the tear of exile from our eyes
And spread our tents beneath unwonted skies. 20

Anew the tedious march of life we sound,
And homes begin to blossom all around.
Each home became an empire in itself,
Whose wealth was useful store, not sordid pelf.

We had no money, and we needed none;
And if, in trade, a dollar durst to run,
The stray was caught, and punched and, on a string,
About the baby's neck was made to swing.

The patent man was yet unborn, and art
Went free to thrive; each farmer was in part, 30
His own artificer in iron, wood,
Or stone, or any thing that made for good.

Whilst one man made the plow, or shaped the hoe,
Another built the cart and made it go;
Another turned the sod, or pushed the plane,
And so life's toil was shared, and so the gain.

But stay, old memory, here awhile and tell
About those early homes' plain personnel.

As yet the ostrich was allowed to wear
Its own bright plumage in its native air; 40
No hand, as yet, the song-bird's wings had torn
In vain some fancied beauty to adorn.

But woman's face, just as the Maker made it,
With every tinge of grace just as He laid it—
A full-orbed beauty in its simplest trim—
Beamed ever 'neath a pasteboard bonnet's rim.
The worms of Italy, the looms of France
Were needed not her beauty to enhance.
Queen of the loom and spinning wheel, she wore
What her own hands produced and nothing more. 50

The men wore buckskin pants and elkhide shoes,
And caps of just such pelt as each might choose.
With hunting shirts all bound around with fringe,
And all made bright with beads of various tinge.
In these gay suits, it was the woman's pride
Her husband's formless altitude to hide,
And send him out, by odds, the best kept man—
The proudest brave—in all his savage clan.

Now, say, my friend, think you these much-wronged folk
To humor dead? Unskilled in mirth-proving joke? 60
Or civilization's cunning should employ
To show them how to live and to enjoy?

Ah! those were the days when peace in rivers flowed,
And plenty stalked and laughed along the road;
When the brown year, spontaneous fruitage on't,
Shed plums and nuts into the lap of want.

The jolly husking done, at close of day,
The tables, chairs, and stools are cleared away;
The puncheon floor is burnished with a broom,
And none but dancers occupy the room. 70
Impatience marks the features of each face;
Like coursers, all are prancing for the race.
The fiddler twangs the signal, "Ready all!"
A tide of music then rolls down the hall;
They cast themselves upon its lethean crest,
And in a dream of pleasure, all are blest.

The air that seemed the dreamers most to please,
Was reminiscent, and the words were these:
"The Indian gone to Arkansaw,
'Cause he couldn't stand the white man's law," etc. 80
And so, in buckskin pants and homespun gown,
We played and danced misfortune's miseries down.

But civilization once again intrudes,
And spreads disaster through our peaceful woods.
It laughs to scorn our bows and feeble arrows;
With trained artillery wars upon our sparrows;
Declares our birds and sparrows to be outlaws;
And brings them down to death without a cause;
To reap vain glory from vast agony,
Shoots down the bison just to see him die; 90
Forbids the wild goose, in the fall and spring,

Through heaven to lead his people on the wing.
The wild blue pigeon, that in millions rise,
And cast a roaring shadow o'er the skies,
It shoots, and shoots, until the glowing bore
Exclaims, "Too hot!" "Can never shoot no more!"
Then, waiting, cools the fervid barrel again;
And shoots and shoots, till the last bird is slain.

O civilization! Thy destructive hand
Of God's free bounties, hath despoiled our land; 100
Hath set starvation on the Indian's track,
And no degree of force can drive him back.

We dance, as once of yore, and slug for help;
But fail, Alas! to hush the demon's yelp.

Sweet music fails to yield its wonted pleasure,
And all our steps have lost their old time measure.

Whate'er thy mightiness may please to give,
Without a word, we thankfully receive,
As a sweet boon in this old world of evil,
And leave the rest to thee and to the ——. 110

[1900]

75 **lethean**: emendation of *leathean*; Lethe is the river of forgetfulness in ancient Greek mythology.

Truth Is Mortal

Lines suggested by the tenor of a friendly interview between the author and the editor of the Chieftain in reference to the capture and incarceration of Crazy Snake, the Muskogee patriot.

"Truth crushed to earth will rise again,"
'Tis sometimes said. False! When it dies,
Like a tall tree felled on the plain,
It never, never more can rise.

Dead beauty's buried out of sight;
'Tis gone beyond the eternal wave;
Another springs up into light,
But not the one that's in the grave.

I saw a ship once leave the shore;
Its name was "Truth;" and on its board 10
It bore a thousand souls or more:
Beneath its keel the ocean roared.

That ship went down with all its crew.
True: other ships as proud as she,
Well built, and strong, and wholly new,
Still ride upon that self-same sea.

But "Truth," and all on her embarked
Are lost in eternal sleep,
(The fatal place itself unmarked)
Far down in the abysmal deep. 20

Let fleeing Aguinaldo speak;
And Oc̆eola from his cell;
And Sitting Bull, and Crazy Snake;
Their story of experience tell.

There is no truth in all the earth
But there's a Calvary and a Cross;
We scarce have time to hail its birth,
Ere we are called to mark its loss.

The truth that lives and laughs a sneak,
That crouching licks the hand of power, 30
While that that's worth the name is weak,
And under foot dies every hour.

[1901]

Epigraph, Chieftain: the *Indian Chieftain*, the newspaper that published the poem. **Epigraph, Crazy Snake**: Chitto Harjo (1846–1909?), translated into English as Crazy Snake, the legendary Muskogee orator and chief who led resistance to federal allotment of Muskogee lands. In 1901, federal troops moved against Harjo and his expanding group of followers (Crazy Snakes, or Snakes). On 27 January the troops arrested Harjo and many other Snakes, perhaps in time to help inspire Too-qua-stee's poem published 7 February. **1 "Truth crushed to earth will rise again"**: echoing "Truth, crushed to earth, shall rise again" from William Cullen Bryant's "The Battle-Field" (1837), line 33 (Bryant 275-77). **21 Aguinaldo**: Emilio Aguinaldo (1869-1964), Philippine general, a leader of the Philippine resistance against Spanish colonialism and then against the United States' colonialism, and first president of the Philippines, 1899-1901. **22 Oc̆eola**: Osceola (1804–1838), Seminole war chief who resisted the United States' effort to remove Seminole people from their lands. **23 Sitting Bull**: Hunkpapa Lakota spiritual leader (c. 1831–1890) famous in part for his role in defeating General Custer.

A Christmas Song

There is wanted of me a Christmas song,
To me a very unusual thing;
Yet the muse that does not to Christ belong,
Has scarce a right to be glad, or to sing.

If a friend ever died, we'll say, for me,
 Because he loved me so loud, and so well,
I am sure, I could never endure to see
 His praise proclaimed with a thing like a bell.

Let me tell you then what exactly I'd do:
 I'd drive old Claus with his load of cheap goods 10
If I could, to the place he ought to go—
 To freeze to death in the cold polar woods.

To the spot where my friend so late had died,
 I'd then with tools, by myself all alone,
Go and build a tall shaft right by his side—
 I'd build it, too, of the purest of stone.

I would build it so strong, so straight and high,
 That sky and clouds would lodge for the day,
On its head, and by night the stars would fly
 Around its breast in gay laughter and play. 20

I would found it, too, deep down in the ground,
 On rocks that hold the great earth in its place,
Where its base would be safe, unmoved and sound,
 When earth and man had completed their race.

I would then when his day of birth or death
 Occurred, I'd let the cold world have its way,
In hilarious sports to waste their breath,
 'Mid song and dance, and a high holiday.

As to me, though, I'd go and look above,
 To where that shaft is o'ertopping the years, 30
And I'd kiss its cold base with lips of love,
 And pass the day there in gratitude's tears.

[1904]

Sequoyah

Great man? Or wondrous, should I say?
 For, like a comet bursting into sight,
Launched unexpected on its arctic way,
 Through boundless fields of rayless polar night,
  Eclipsing constellations in its flight—
A flaming orb thou wert, and unforetold,
 Whose distance, altitude, and awful size,

No man, no kalendar however old,
Could tell; and sweeping through the frigid skies,
In its own distance fades from human eyes. 10

So, thou Sequoyah, from thy Maker's hand,
Wast hurled prodigious through the skies of time,
Untaught, original, and strangely grand,
Thy mighty genius rose and shone sublime,
The wonder of all eyes, in every clime.
'Twas meet that, when thy day was spent, the ground
Should fall to give thy sacred ashes room;
No low-built grave for thee shall e'er be found
Beneath the sky: 'tis needless to inhume
A Sun gone out—the universe its tomb. 20

[1904]

Title: Sequoyah (1767–1843), revered Cherokee silversmith who invented the Cherokee writing system, a syllabary rather than an alphabet.

My Mother's Ring

O, memory dear! Enchantment sweet!
That lays me at my mother's feet,
In childhood sentiment and tears,
Despite the weight of hoary years!
My mother's ring! Her wedding ring!
A precious, plain, old-fashioned thing—
Not such as princely fingers wear,
Nor such as now would please the fair.
Its meager frame, by labor worn,
Still holds its radiance all unshorn. 10
It wears the same sweet smile it wore,
When sleeping in its native ore.
Like dying love, life ebbing fast,
It charms you to the very last.
Here on its arch may yet be seen
The terrace where a gem has been:
'Tis but the ruin of its throne,
The gem itself has long been gone.

O memory dear! In infant glee,
Again upon my mother's knee, 20
I count her pretty fingers o'er,
And, do my best, can count no more.
In vain I fumble and essay

To draw her cherished ring away.
"Not so, my babe," she says: "forbear;
"Your angel papa placed it there.
"I also sail for brighter shores
"Ere long, and then the ring is yours."
Yes, Thou art mine, eld jewel bright.
Back to thy casket, warm and deep; 30
And let not time's disturbing light,
Inflame thy cheek or break thy sleep.
When I have reached the lethean stream,
T' embark from all that I am now,
Thy dear familiar touch will seem
My mother's hand upon my brow.

[1904]

33 **lethean**: Lethe is the river of forgetfulness in ancient Greek mythology.

Dignity

And what, in fact, is Dignity? In those
Who have it pure, it is the soul's repose,
The base of character—no mere reserve
That springs from pride, or want of mental nerve.
The dignity that wealth, or station, breeds,
Or in the breast on base emotion feeds,
Is easy weighed, and easy to be sized—
A bastard virtue, much to be despised.
True dignity is like a summer tree.
Beneath whose shade both beast, and bird, and bee, 10
When by the heated skies oppressed, may come,
And feel, in its magnificence, at home;
Or rather like a mountain which forgets
Itself in its own greatness, and so lets
Vast armies fuss and fight upon its sides,
While high in clouds its peaceful summit hides,
And from voiceless crest of glistening snow,
Pours trickling fatness on the fields below;
Repellant force, that daunts obtrusive wrong,
And woos the timid steps of right along; 20
And hence a garb which magistrates prepare,
When called to judge, and really seem to wear.
In framing character on whate'er plan,
'Tis always needed to complete the man;

The job quite done, and Dignity without,
Is like an apple pie, the fruit left out.

[1904]

Labor

Prone to the earth, let Labor bend,
The primal curse upon his head;
With earth's unfriendly soil contend
In a precarious fight for bread.

What did I say? A "primal curse!"
I'd fain that foolish word recall.
A thousand times our lot were worse,
Had we no work to do at all.

Let thorns and thistles take the earth:
Though neither clothes, nor roof, nor food, 10
In ages past, before our birth,
In love, God sowed them for our good.

The sweat it cost to root them out
Might else stand puddling in our veins.
Till through the system microbes sprout
And vegetate in boils and blains.

Let sloth decline to pay the tax:
A wasting rot preys on his bones;
His manhood, frail as tepid wax,
At last for such a sin atones. 20

Then let me hear at break of day,
Ere comfort wakes, the cock's shrill horn.
And eager on my dewy way,
Make for the fields of growing corn.

There with my hoe I'll wage a war
On brier, thorn and pesky thistle,
(For that is what God made them for,)
And fight for honest bread, and whistle.

While speculation lays his trap,
And watches daily where he laid it, 30
Until the loaf, with wonderous snap,
He yanks quite out the hand that made it.

[1904]

Indian Territory at World's Fair

Sweet mother, all thy first-born children dead,
That once were at thy bounteous bosom fed,
Now dry thy tears, lift up thy beauteous head,
    And to the hopeful future look;
Thy charms shall be by other loves caressed;
A new-born race shall revel on thy breast,
And all thy second life be doubly blest;
    'Tis writ in Fate's unerring book.

Yes; they will toast you at their social boards,
The eyed of ladies, and the charm of lords; 10
While the best smile thy broken heart affords,
    The secret of thy woe will keep;
But when the empty form of mirth is o'er,
And self to self comes home and shuts the door,
Thy soul will then its treasured fullness pour,
    And o'er recurring memories weep.

Thy land is framed on Nature's choicest plan—
Not only feed, but to delight the man;
Thy scenery smiles beneath the rainbow's span,
    Suggesting innocence and ease. 20
Thy beauty swells from earth to bending sky,
Affording rapturous themes, in rich supply,
For poet's pen, the painter's cunning eye,
    And for the care-worn mind release.

Thy limpid streams are symbols of good health.
Thy deep-laid mines, concealed by Nature's stealth,
Are packed with varied ores, a boundless wealth,
    Enough to meet a world-wide call.
The softest suns illume thy fertile fields;
Where summer first a bounteous harvest yields, 30
And then a supplemental crop it shields,
    From frosts, by dallying with the fall.

Ah! grandest glories wait upon thy touch,
When thou becom'st a state, or something such,
('Thout Oklahoma's parasitic clutch,)
    Thou'lt dwelt sublime in an unwonted sphere;
Installed a member of that mighty group,
The banner of thy pride may never droop.

Say, Mother; wilt thou then disdain to stoop,
And give thy buried race a tear? 40

[1904]

Title: not any Indian territory, but *the* Indian Territory, in what is now the state of Oklahoma. Indian Territory had its own building at the 1904 World's Fair in St. Louis. Addressing Indian Territory as a mother, the poem laments the demise of the Territory amid the onrush of white settlement (lines 5–6) and the likelihood that the Territory will sacrifice the sovereignty of its Indian nations in favor of gaining statehood (lines 33–38).

Thanksgiving

Thanksgiving day! Thanksgiving day!
What solemn thoughts intrude?
Let us be candid while we pray:
Ourselves be understood.

Things here below seem somewhat mixed,
The good and bad together;
The end above, as we have fixed,
Is sometimes just the nether.

What we call good, and worth our lays,
Is apt to be an evil: 10
We're apt to give to God the praise,
That's only due the devil.

One cannot thunder 'round the world,
And make the nations tremble;
We march to church; with flags unfurled,
To thank God, we assemble.

But who can say the victory won,
Has come to us a blessing;
And not a wrong ourselves have done,
Good conscience sore distressing? 20

Yet, after all, there's much no doubt
To safely thank God for.
To make true gratitude—without
The doubtful fruits of war.

His suns have warmed our stubborn soil;
His clouds have sent us rain;
The year has paid our anxious toil,
And filled our barns with grain.

His hand has stayed the pestilence,
And peace pipes through the land, 30
Fair labor has its recompense;
Our commerce lines the strand.

But why stop here to specify?
The whole is one word:
Our good is not what it should be;
We've too much bad aboard.

Yet this is naught to stumble at
The blushful revelation;
We've less of this, and more of that,
Than any other nation. 40

Then let us give to God the day,
In humble gratitude,
And thank Him in our purest way,
And better if we could.

[1904]

9 lays: songs. **12–20**: Too-qua-stee expresses his skepticism about American colonialism in the Philippines and Cuba. **30 peace pipes**: *pipes* here appears to be a verb, not a noun.

Olivia Ward Bush-Banks, Montaukett, 1869–1944

Born in Sag Harbor, New York, in eastern Long Island, Bush-Banks and both her parents were Montaukett (Montauk) and African American. She identified strongly with both sides of her ancestry and was active in Montauk and African American communities and organizations. The selections below include African American-focused poems, for to exclude them would distort her work and life and distort the histories of the many people who are both African American and American Indian. Moreover, her poems about race relations often reverberate for both African Americans and American Indians. After her mother died and her father remarried, Olivia Ward was raised by her mother's sister in Providence, Rhode Island. As an adult she lived in Providence, Boston, Chicago, New Rochelle, and Harlem, working as a seamstress and drama teacher and also serving as Montauk tribal historian. Bush-Banks published two books of poetry: *Original Poems* (1899) and *Driftwood* (1914). Paul Laurence Dunbar praised her poetry and asked, in one of his poems, "Did this wood come floating thick / All along down 'Injin Crik?'" (Dunbar 277). Bush-Banks also wrote drama (including a play called *The Trail of the Montauk*), stories, and essays. For a valuable edition of her writings, see *The Collected Works of Olivia Ward Bush-Banks*, ed. Bernice F. Guillaume. Guillaume's edition provides the source for "Symbols" and "Filled with You." (*Collected Works*, ed. Guillaume; see also Guillaume and Blue)

On the Long Island Indian

How relentless, how impartial,
  Is the fleeting hand of Time,
By its stroke, great Empires vanish,
  Nations fall in swift decline.

Once resounding through these forests,
  Rang the war-whoop shrill and clear;
Once here lived a race of Red Men,
  Savage, crude, but knew no fear.

Here they fought their fiercest battles,
  Here they caused their wars to cease, 10
Sitting round their blazing camp-fires,
  Here they smoked the Pipe of Peace.

Tall and haughty were the warriors,
  Of this fierce and warlike race.
Strong and hearty were their women,
  Full of beauteous, healthy grace.

Up and down these woods they hunted,
  Shot their arrows far and near.
Then in triumph to their wigwams,
  Bore the slain and wounded deer. 20

Thus they dwelt in perfect freedom,
  Dearly loved their native shores,
Wisely chose their Chiefs or Sachems,
  Made their own peculiar laws.

But there came a paler nation
  Noted for their skill and might,
They aroused the Red Man's hatred,
  Robbed him of his native right.

Now remains a scattered remnant
  On these shores they find no home, 30
Here and there in weary exile,
  They are forced through life to roam.

Just as Time with all its changes
  Sinks beneath Oblivion's Wave,
So today a mighty people
  Sleep within the silent grave.

[1890]

Originally published as a broadside (a separate publication of a short work, usually on one page) in 1890, this poem was reprinted in *The Annual Report of the Montauk Tribe of Indians for the Year 1916.* **24 peculiar**: distinctive. **31 exile**: Bush-Banks here describes the condition of many Long Island Indians, like herself, who moved away from their ancestral communities because of the cramped conditions imposed by white settlers. See Strong, which also documents the tendency of many Montaukett Indians to merge into African American communities.

Morning on Shinnecock

The rising sun had crowned the hills,
And added beauty to the plain;
O grand and wondrous spectacle!
That only nature could explain.

I stood within a leafy grove,
And gazed around in blissful awe;
The sky appeared one mass of blue,
That seemed to spread from sea to shore.

Far as the human eye could see,
Were stretched the fields of waving corn. 10
Soft on my ear the warbling birds
Were heralding the birth of morn.

While here and there a cottage quaint
Seemed to repose in quiet ease
Amid the trees, whose leaflets waved
And fluttered in the passing breeze.

O morning hour! so dear thy joy,
And how I longed for thee to last;
But e'en thy fading into day
Brought me an echo of the past. 20

'Twas this,—how fair my life began;
How pleasant was its hour of dawn;
But, merging into sorrow's day,
Then beauty faded with the morn.

[1899]

Title: The Shinnecock Reservation, home of the Shinnecock Indian Nation. The Shinnecocks are western neighbors and close relatives of the Montauketts.

A Hero of San Juan

Among the sick and wounded ones,
This stricken soldier boy lay,

With glassy eye and shortened breath;
His life seemed slipping fast away.

My heart grew faint to see him thus,
His dark brown face so full of pain,
I wondered if the mother's eyes
Were looking for her boy in vain.

I bent to catch his feeble words:
"I am so ill and far from home. 10
I feel so strange and lonely here;
You seem a friend; I'm glad you've come.

"I want to tell you how our boys
Went charging on the enemy.
'Twas when we climbed up Juan's hill;
And there we got the victory.

"The Spaniards poured a heavy fire;
We met it with a right good will.
We saw the Seventy-first fall back,
And then our boys went up the hill. 20

"Yes, up the hill, and gained it, too;
Not one brave boy was seen to lag.
Old Glory o'er us floating free,
We'd gladly died for that old flag."

His dim eye brightened as he spoke;
He seemed unconscious of his pain;
In fancy on the battlefield
He lived that victory o'er again.

And I; I seemed to grasp it too,—
The stalwart form, the dusky face 30
Of those black heroes, climbing up
To win fair glory for their race.

The Spaniards said that phalanx seemed
To move like one black, solid wall;
They flung defiance back at Death,
And, answering to that thrilling call,

They fought for Cuban liberty.
On Juan's hill those bloody stains
Mark how these heroes won the day
And added honor to their names. 40

March on, dark sons of Afric's race,
Naught can be gained by standing still;
Retreat not, 'quit yourselves like men,
And, like these heroes, climb the hill,

Till pride and prejudice shall cease;
Till racial barriers are unknown.
Attain the heights where over all,
Equality shall sit enthroned.

[1899]

Title: African American troops took an active role in the famous charge of American troops up San Juan Hill in Cuba during the Spanish-American War in 1898. **43 'quit**: acquit.

Symbols

Time was when holly, evergreen
And bright red berry,
Were holy, age-old tokens,
Of abundant yule-tide cheer.
When carols echoed and re-echoed
The immortal message
Of "peace on earth," good-will,
To all mankind.

And now, these precious symbols,
Are shorn of sacred meaning, 10
They are but feeble gestures
Revealing man's descent
From lofty faith and purpose
From love to brother-man,
To unholy planes of selfishness,
And worthless gain.

[written after 1900, published 1991]

Filled with You

By your fireside, close to my side,
You are sitting silently,
Eyes so tender—I surrender
To their charm and mystery:
All the room is filled with you.

Tho' no word of hope you've spoken,
Still my faith remains unbroken:

All the room is filled with you, dear,
  Filled with you.

In the twilight, by your firelight, 10
I would linger yet awhile,
Waiting gladly, loving madly
You, your sweetness and your smile:
  All my world is filled with you.

Even tho' your love lies sleeping,
In the silence you are keeping:
All my world is filled with you, dear,
  Filled with you.

[written after 1900, published 1991]

Regret

I said a thoughtless word one day,
A loved one heard and went away;
I cried: "Forgive me, I was blind;
I would not wound or be unkind."
I waited long, but all in vain,
To win my loved one back again.
Too late, alas! to weep and pray,
Death came; my loved one passed away.
Then, what a bitter fate was mine;
No language could my grief define; 10
Tears of deep regret could not unsay
The thoughtless word I spoke that day.

[1905]

Heart-Throbs

We suffer and ye know it not,
  Nor yet can ever know,
What depth of bitterness is ours,
  Or why we suffer so;—

If ye would know what anguish is,
  Ask of the dark-skinned race,
Ay! ask of him who loves to know
  The color of his face.

Then plead as he has often pled
  For manhood among men, 10

And feel the pain of rights denied;
  Thou canst not know till then.

Or share with him for one brief space,
  Ambition's fond desire,
Reach out, and strive, as he has striven,
  And aim for something higher.

Let knowledge cultivate, refine,
  Let culture feed the mind,
Then fondly dream of hopes fulfilled,
  And dreaming wake to find;— 20

That merit worth or patient toil
  Does not suffice to win.
Then learn the cause of this defeat,
  The color of the skin.

The mother of the dusky babe,
  Surveys with aching heart
Bright prospects, knowing all the while,
  Her off-spring shares no part.

The child attains to manhood's years,
  Still conscious of the same, 30
While others boast of Life's success,
  He knows it but in name.

Yes, aim, reach out, aspire and strive
  And know, 'Twere all in vain,
And e'en in Freedom's name appeal,
  Then ye can sense our pain.

We suffer and ye know it not,
  Nor yet can ever know,
What depth of bitterness is ours,
  Or why we suffer so. 40

[1914]

BOARDING SCHOOL POEMS

Adin C. Gibbs, Delaware (Lenape), born about 1797

A Munsee Delaware, Adin C. Gibbs was born in Pennsylvania, where he worked as a clothier until 1818, when he left for the Cornwall Foreign Mission School in Connecticut. Gibbs's classmates at the Cornwall School came from many countries and included John Ridge (father of John Rollin Ridge, whose poetry appears in this volume) and Israel Folsom (whose poetry also appears in this volume). Gibbs's poem about the Cornwall School is his only known poem. He was a well-liked student and a powerful public speaker. After completing school in 1822, he worked among the Choctaw in Mississippi as a missionary and schoolteacher. (Foreman, Proske, and Schmidt)

The Cornwall Seminary

Now in Connecticut there stands,
On Cornwall's low and pleasant lands,
A school composed of foreign youth,
For propagating gospel truth.
And on this consecrated ground
Are those from many nations round;
But mostly of the *Cherokees*,
The *Angloes*, and the Owhyhees.
The languages are now thirteen;
Twelve nations here likewise are seen, 10
And students thirty-two are found,
From regions of remotest bound.
But charity's propitious hand,
Which traverses o'er sea and land,
To seek for good, and lend her care,
Has brought these various nations here.

[1822]

8 **Owhyhees:** Hawaiians.

Corrinne, Cherokee

Corrinne was the pen name of a student at the Cherokee Female Seminary.

Our Wreath of Rose Buds

I.

We offer you a wreath of flowers
Culled in recreation hours,
Which will not wither, droop, or die,
Even when days and months pass by.

II.

Ask you where these flowers are found?
Not on sunny slope, or mound;
Not on prairies bright and fair
Growing without thought or care.

III.

No, our simple wreath is twined
From the garden of the mind; 10
Where bright thoughts like rivers flow
And ideas like roses grow.

IV.

The tiny buds which here you see
Ask your kindly sympathy;
View them with a lenient eye,
Pass each fault, each blemish by.

V.

Warmed by the sunshine of your eyes,
Perhaps you'll find to your surprise,
Their petals fair will soon unclose,
And every bud become—a Rose. 20

VI.

Then take our wreath, and let it stand
An emblem of our happy band;
The *Seminary*, our *garden* fair,
And *we*, the *flowers* planted there.

VII.

Like roses bright we hope to grow,
And o'er our home such beauty throw

In future years—that all may see
Loveliest of lands,—the Cherokee.

[1854]

Lily Lee, Cherokee

Lily Lee was the pen name of a student at the Cherokee Female Seminary. Perhaps her poem puts a playful twist on an event at the seminary or on some other event in the Cherokee Nation.

Literary Day Among the Birds

Dark night at last had taken its flight,
Morn had come with her earliest light;
Her herald, gray dawn, had extinguished each star,
And gay banners in the east were waving afar.

That lovely goddess, Beautiful Spring,
Had fanned all the earth with her radiant wing;
"Had calmed the wild winds with fragrant breath,"
And gladden'd nature with an emerald wreath.

Within the precincts of the Bird Nation,
All was bustle and animation; 10
For that day was to witness a literary feast,
Where only Birds were invited guests.

The place of meeting was a leafy nook,
Close by the side of a sparkling brook.
Soon were assembled a merry band,
Birds from every tree in the land.

Mrs. DOVE came first, in soft colors drest;
Then Mr. CANARY, looking his best.
The family of MARTINS, dressed in brown,
And Mr. Woodpecker, with his ruby crown. 20

The exercises opened with a scientific song,
By the united voices of the feathered throng.
Then was delivered a brilliant oration,
By 'Squire RAVEN, the wisest bird of the nation.
Master WHIP-POOR-WILL next mounted the stage,
Trying to look very much like a sage.

Eight pretty green Parrots then spoke with art;
Though small, with credit they carried their part.
Again an oration by Mr. Quail,
Spoken as fast as the gallop of snail. 30
And lastly, Sir BLACKBIRD whistl'd off an address,
Of twenty odd minutes, more or less.

Then came the applause, so loud and long,
That the air echoed the joyous song.
But the sun was low, so soon they sped
To their quiet nests and their grassy beds;
And rocked by the breeze, they quietly slept,
Ere the firstling star in the blue sky crept.

[1855]

N., Cherokee

N. was the pen name of a student at the Cherokee Male Seminary.

[Farewell]

To school-mates dear, to teachers kind,
To FRIENDS I bid adieu,
And I am truly proud to think
My friends are not a few.

I used to think, a pleasant thing
'T would be—how strange to tell!—
When I, as free as air, should say
To all of you, farewell.

My feelings now are not as then—
In bidding you adieu, 10
I know I part from old friends,
To join myself with new.

'Tis not so pleasant as I thought,
Nor is it strange to tell,
For though I'm free from rules of school
Then comes that word farewell.

The future now, all mixed with doubt,
Presents itself to view,—

A happy time, I scarce expect,
  Like that I spent with you. 20

When summoned to our daily tasks,
  By ringing of the bell,
We had no time to ponder, then,
  About the word farewell.

The pleasant scenes of four years past
  Are present to my mind;
The scenes in school, and out of school,
  Yes, all of them combined.

We roamed upon the mountain top
  And wandered through the dell, 30
All heedless of the time to come,
  When we must say farewell.

As every transient breeze that blows
  May bring relations new,
So we, my friends, must surely part
  Though you be kind and true.

And now adieu to all the scenes
  That once I loved so well—
You surely will not wonder then,
  'Tis hard to say farewell. 40

[1855]

Emma Lowrey Williams, Cherokee, born about 1834

Emma Lowrey Williams graduated from the Cherokee Female Seminary in 1856 and then taught at Green Leaf School, a Cherokee public school. (Starr 228)

Life

We can not tell what happiness
We might on earth possess
If in singleness of heart
We would strive to act a proper part.
'Tis true we see the effects of sin
All without and all within.
We long may live a life in vain,

Much good possess, but still complain.
We may appear to other eyes,
To be extremely rich and wise; 10
But if our hearts are not right,
Life will not be beautiful and bright.
Oh! may our life, day by day,
In love and duty pass away;
And at last when our bodies die,
We may live in that world above the sky;
Where free from sin, death and pain,
The good will meet and love again.

[written 1855, published 1922]

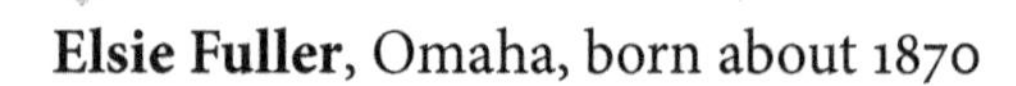

Elsie Fuller, Omaha, born about 1870

Born in Nebraska, Elsie Fuller was a student at Hampton Institute from 1885 to 1888. (Littlefield and Parins, *Biobibliography* 241)

A New Citizen

Now I am a citizen!
They've given us new laws,
Just as were made
By Senator Dawes.

We need not live on rations,
Why? there is no cause,
For "Indians are citizens,"
Said Senator Dawes.

Just give us a chance,
We never will pause. 10
Till we are good citizens
Like Senator Dawes.

Now we are citizens,
We all give him applause—
So three cheers, my friends,
For Senator Dawes!

[1887]

4 **Senator Dawes:** Senator Henry L. Dawes sponsored the General Allotment Act of 1887, better known as the Dawes Act. See note to Posey's "O, Oblivion!" above, line 11. The Dawes Act led to a massive loss of land for Indian nations. Nevertheless, the issue of *Talks and Thoughts of the Hampton Indian Students* that published Fuller's poem supported allotment enthusiastically. 5 **rations:** such as rations from the United States government agreed to in treaties.

Samuel Sixkiller, Cherokee, born 1877

Samuel Rasmus Sixkiller was born in the Cherokee Nation in Indian Territory. His great-grandfather Redbird Sixkiller was elected to the Executive Council of the Cherokee Nation (Starr 299) and elected Associate Justice of the Supreme Court of the Cherokee Nation. His grandfather Samuel Sixkiller, High Sheriff of the Cherokee Nation and Captain of the United States Indian Police, was famously murdered while on duty in 1886. Sixkiller was class poet for the class of 1895 at the Carlisle Indian School. After graduating that year, he lived in Indian Territory (later Oklahoma), working as a bookkeeper for the *Muskogee Phoenix.* Later he lived in Texas. (Starr 299, 654–55; Littlefield and Parins, *Biobibliography* 293)

To Class '95

Farewell to dear class, to friends and to strangers,
  Assembling here in our honor today,
To help Nature's children—the wildflower rangers,
  And make pure Americans from ocean to bay.

At last we have roamed from woodland and mountain;
  From the murmur of pines and the emerald sea,
To drink of the pure—that life-giving fountain,
  And bask in the sun of the noble and free.

Away from the plains where often in childhood,
  From deep slumber waked by the music of rills; 10
Away from the glory and pleasure of wildwood,
  Away from the perfume of flower-clad hills.

And still to our hearts, Nature clings as a brother;
  We dream of repose by the streams we yet love.
Can light and advancement, our thoughts of these smother?
  Of joys placed here by the Father above?

When shall the culture, the art and refinement
  Drive from our minds, roving thoughts of the past?
Shall broad education, or savage confinement,
  Conquer the Red Man now fading so fast? 20

Too soon are those features the emblems of power.
Too soon are they leaving his countenance bold.
Alas, they shall fade or to fierce foeman cower,
And die with the past as a tale that is told.

Sad be the day when the sun in his glory,
Shall shine on the last of the noble Red Man
Or set for this race whose life is a story,
The true, the only American.

And now we must part, may it not be forever!
But if on this earth we can ne'er share our love. 30
God grant that the ties we have here had to sever,
May be reunited in that kingdom above.

[1895]

[My First Winter Out of School]

Well, well, Miss Paull, forgotten you?
I don't believe it's right,
For when I think of Old Carlisle,
Come memories fresh and bright

Of the many familiar faces,
Of the many ups and downs,
Of every thing and every place,
That is upon the grounds.

I was sitting here this afternoon,
With a paper in my hand, 10
And all at once I thought of friends,
Back in that Eastern land.

I knew that you had written me,
About two months ago,
And why I never answered you,
I'm sure I do not know.

I 'spose you wonder what I'm doing,
And then would like to KNOW,
For every one who leaves Carlisle,
Of course, the mark must toe. 20

But I'll tell you just the straight, of things,
If you'll promise not to quack.
For it's very little I have done,
Since Spring, when I came back.

You know when a fellow wants to work,
And tries to find a place,
If he cannot get just what he wants,
He'll get down in the face.

Well, I'm in that position,
With nothing much to do, 30
But still with friends and kin-folks
I can most always chew.

I'm getting mighty tired, though,
With nothing 'tall to do,
If a fellow cannot get a job,
I don't blame him, do you?

This is my first winter out of school,
For quite a while, you know,
And all this thing of finding work,
With me goes pretty slow. 40

I've found out that a fellow,
If he makes a start at all,
Must have a great amount of cheek,
What most of us call "gall."

You know that is my weakest point,
But still I'm in the ring,
And I guess ere very long,
This bird will learn to sing.

I have not heard from old Carlisle,
For two or three months, I guess, 50
Surely things about the place,
Haven't got in such a mess

That you can't write a fellow,
Or tell him what's the news.
I haven't got a HELPER,
Since the gray mule lost his shoes.

Tell the printers that a brother,
Away out in the West,
Is thirsty for some knowledge,
Of the big and cosy nest. 60

Some day their wings will stronger grow,
Then they will have to fly
To some far distant Western home,

And for the nest they'll sigh.
How about the old bird (?)?
I hope he's well and strong.
And able still for many a year,
To help the cause along.

I've thanked him many and many a time,
For all that he has done. 70
The Indians had ne'er a better friend,
Beneath the shining sun.

You know now who I'm talking about;
You surely can see that.
Who in the wide world could it be,
But good old Captain Pratt?

Well seems to me it's getting late,
I guess I'll have to close,
For if I don't I'm pretty sure,
That I'll begin to doze. 80

The boys, I guess, that they're all right,
And up to all their tricks,
But now goodbye, I said I'd close,
I remain as ever,
SIX

[1896]

Title: As the poem was published without a title, the present title has been supplied by the editor. An introduction to the poem acknowledged that it was published without Sixkiller's knowledge: "We feel a little chary about publishing it without permission, but Samuel is a printer and understands how when the publisher gets hold of a good thing he always wants to give others the benefit of the same." **1 Miss Paull:** teacher at Carlisle. **55 HELPER:** *Indian Helper*, the Carlisle journal that published this poem. **65 bird (?) ?:** perhaps indicating the 1896 editor's uncertain transcription of Sixkiller's writing, or Sixkiller's or the editor's effort at humor. **76 Captain Pratt:** Richard Henry Pratt (1840–1924), famous founder and superintendent of Carlisle.

Melinda Metoxen, Oneida

Melinda Metoxen, from Wisconsin, graduated from Carlisle Indian School in 1902 and then worked at the Wisconsin Oneida School as a seamstress (Littlefield and Parins, *Biobibliography* 269). In this poem, Metoxen takes on the voice of a visitor to Carlisle from Iceland.

Iceland

I come from that northern isle,
Far off in the Arctic Sea,
Where legend and myth beguile,
And a fairy land have we.

I come from Iceland's shore,
To bring you greetings true,
To "Susans," "Standards" galore,
And brave "Invincibles" too.

Oh, a mighty land have we,
Of mountains, snow-capped and grand, 10
Rivers rushing to the sea,
Nestling lakes o'er all the land.

Great lava beds, moss adorned,
Sweet wildflowers found everywhere,
Chasing, where the wind hath mourned,
And water-falls sparkling fair.

Most glorious is our sky:
Our sunsets, pastures most rare.
When day is about to die,
Gently passes day dreams fair. 20

For a thousand years and more,
Our island, man's history
And nature's handiwork bore,
A field for rich reverie.

Norway's lordly Vikings came,
When our land was clothed in ice
To herald my country's fame,
And thither oppress'd men entice.

They gave our Isle winter's name—
Iceland, though from Southern seas 30
Mild waves to us ever come,
Fanned by many a gentle breeze.

You should e'er remember here,
Iceland's voyagers, so bold,
First discovered, in days drear,
America,—so we're told.

A simple people are we,
Living in that far off land,

Loyal to our own country,
A small, peaceful, joyous band. 40

An Arctic expedition,
Came to us at Reykjavik,
With the daring of tradition;
And rode thence to Capiervike.

Plucky leader of this band,
Was Miss Jessie Ackerman,
And Miss Shaffner,—her right hand,
With Miss Pratt comprised the clan.

Two months in our land they stayed,
Speaking Temperance far and wide, 50
Many converts for us made,
And made stronger our own side.

Come Sisters, join me in song,
Sing Iceland's Melody here.
Let Carlisle remember long,
Our visit and song so dear.

[1896]

7–8 **Susans, Standards, Invincibles**: the Susan Longstreth Society, the Standard Literary Society, and the Invincible Debating Society, student clubs at Carlisle Indian School, usually called the Susans, the Standards, and the Invincibles. Metoxen was an officer of the Susans (*Indian Helper* 31 Mar. 1899: 2). 46–47 **Miss Jessie Ackerman, Miss Shaffner, Miss Pratt**: all associated with Carlisle and the Women's Christian Temperance Union. Ackerman, president of the Australian WCTU, visited Carlisle and traveled widely as a missionary for the WCTU. Ruth Shaffner was the matron in charge of girls at Carlisle. Nana Pratt, a clerk at Carlisle and daughter of Richard Henry Pratt, Carlisle's founder and superintendent, hosted a WCTU visitor from Iceland at Carlisle the following year (*Indian Helper*, Oct. 1, 1897: n.p.). The poem indicates that Ackerman, Shaffner, and Nana Pratt traveled to Iceland on behalf of the WCTU.

J. William Ettawageshik, Ottawa, born about 1889, died 1942

As a student at the Carlisle Indian School, William Ettawageshik worked in the print shop. After graduating in 1911, he worked in northern Michigan as a newspaper editor and printer. (Littlefield and Parins, *Biobibliography, Supplement* 209)

The Glow-Worm

Shine on, Oh Glow-Worm,
    For the day is o'er;

You toil not; think not
  Of to-morrow's store;
The present only thy concern need be,
  Thy Maker knoweth what is best for thee.

Shine on, Oh Glow-Worm,
  For the day is past;
Sorrow and weariness
  Are o'er at last; 10
Twilight is falling.
  Soon will come the night,
Shine on, Oh Glow-Worm,
  With thy cheery light.

Shine on, Oh Glow-Worm,
  When the day is done
Your clear light shining
  Dissipates the gloom.
May we, when on us
  Falls the gloom of night, 20
Like thee, light up the way
  With Faith's clear light.

[1911]

Anonymous Carlisle Student

In an article titled "A Carlisle Poet Discovered," the *Carlisle Arrow* introduces this poem with the following words: "Room Eight boasts of having a poet in its class, the fact being revealed by the final tests given last week. In response to the request to write a composition on 'My Industrial Work,' the following poem was given." The poem by the anonymous poet from Room Eight gives a picture of life for a Carlisle student. By the end, the poem sounds less proud than the school administrators who chose to publish it may have realized.

My Industrial Work

At half past two in the afternoon
You can find me in twenty-eight room,
About three or four covers deep;
You turn them back and you'll find me asleep.
And there I lie and patiently wait
For the final exams we have in Room Eight.

When the whistle blows at half past five,
Once more I am up and still alive.
Then I run down and wash my face,
Then comb my hair and I'm ready for grace. 10
In fifteen minutes there's a bugle call,
The troops fall in and the roll is called.
Then out in front the troops all stand,
Saluting the flag with our hats in our hand.
While standing in the wind our hair gets wavy
But, just the same, we right face, and march to gravy.
Now this may sound like going a fishing,
But this is my only industrial position.

[1913]

Lillian Simons, Mashpee

In this, her only known poem, Simons writes playful and sometimes surprisingly frank riddles about her classmates at the Carlisle Indian School. Perhaps one of the riddles describes her.

Silhouettes—Guess

Tall, ruddy-cheeked, mind without relaxation,
Jerky, but quite proper, in both speech and action.

Hair hard to manage and always in her way,
But in logic her thoughts seldom go astray.

Just medium in looks, but not by any means a fright,
But on the football field he is just all right.

Solemn-eyed and noted for her wisdom,
With knowledge gleaned from all Christendom.

Tall, lean, and handsome, always to be seen;
A bright particular star on our football team. 10

Dresses just a little short, a dainty maid and fair;
"A Swede" some say. An Indian, of a type that is somewhat rare.

Short, bright, witty, and full of pranks,
A knightly boy who is ever ready with his "thanks."

Slight of form and fair to look upon,
"Peaches and cream" her face suggests anon.

Handsome, but quite hidden behind that big horn,
The playing of which makes him look rather worn.

With sparkling eyes and sweetly joyous mien,
The well-beloved "infant" of class '14. 20

Neither one nor 'tother, but musical indeed,
Upon kindred subjects his hungry mind doth feed.

Eyes, nose, smiling lips, and chin,
Tell the tale of loving heart within.

In all the class he is the smallest of the boys;
Who has long since put away his toys,
For he will soon be a graduate,—Oh joy!

Slender in form and a decided brunette;
Of her companions she is very select.

Slow in speech, erect, and very tall, 30
At the game of "Blind Man's Bluff" he beats them all.

Short and plump, fair and rather sweet,
With a ready smile for every one she meets.

Dignified and calm as becomes her weighty mould,
One who at the game of "wit" is very rarely sold.

[1913]

Maude Cooke, Mohawk, and **Agnes Hatch**, Chippewa

Maude Cooke was from New York, and Agnes Hatch was from Michigan. Their poem shows part of what the Carlisle Indian School expected from female students. (Littlefield and Parins, *Biobibliography, Supplement* 194, 226)

Our Cottage

'Neath the shade of the trees, in the campus breeze,
Stands our Model Home Cottage for profitable ease;
With dwellers that vary in size and in manner,
But vow to live up to our Model Home banner—

This Model Home banner which teaches so true,
The ways of plain home life and happiness, too,—
The planning and serving of different foods,
That would set grouchy people in pleasurable moods.

In this Model Home Cottage are furnishings plain—
The reason for this we shall later explain. 10
It is not with rich trappings we aim to thrive,
But toward plain economy we patiently drive.

The flickering shadows that dance on our hearth,
Delight us with joy and laughter and mirth.
The fairy tales told by our teacher, Miss Keck,
We are storing away in our hearts by the peck.

The days come and go like swift aeroplanes,
But this is no reason why one should complain;
For with each fleeting moment we all hope to gain,
A knowledge which may be both useful and sane. 20

[1917]

Francis L. Verigan, Tlingit

Frank Verigan was born and raised on Puget Sound and attended boarding schools in Washington state (perhaps Cushman Indian School) and Oregon (probably Chemawa Indian School), followed by a year of public school in Tacoma. He then "went home," as he later described it, to "my people in Alaska." There he felt not Indian enough "to be an Indian, and not enough white . . . to be a paleface. So I drifted away from my people and roamed at will, laying my hand to any occupation that offered food and shelter for the time being, figuring also to earn enough to help me on to wherever my will directed. In this way, I managed to visit thirty-six different states in the Union, three provinces in Canada, and made several trips into old Mexico." A "white clerk working in the office at the Blackfoot Agency in Montana . . . became interested in me and arranged for my shipment to the Carlisle Indian School in Pennsylvania. At this school, I was made to feel that there was something in me, but before it could be brought out, the Government had closed the school, so I was homeless again" (Brudvig). He wrote this account of himself while a student in the class of 1921 at the Hampton Institute in Virginia, an historically African American school that concentrated, for almost fifty years, on educating American Indians as well as African Americans. At Hampton Verigan won awards for writing and for public speaking. Later, he also attended Phillips Academy in Massachusetts. ("Prize-Speaking Contest"; "Adams Prize Debate" 140; Adams Essay Contest"; "Athletic Notes"; Littlefield and Parins, *Biobibliography, Supplement* 298; Brudvig)

Be a Carlisle Student

Say Chief: Just a minute of your time is all I pray,
There are a few neglected phrases that I have to say,
I hope within them flutters something helpful to us both,
Tho I know you'll scorn these verses, it is just the talk you loathe.
But take it for it's something that must come—
Be a Carlisle Student, not a reservation bum.

Did it ever dawn upon you as you lived your Carlisle life,
You were sent here for this purpose—get mental lessons for the strife.
You're not here because you're Indian—that's just a Carlisle rule.
You were sent here by your people, be to them a helpful tool. 10
Let this on your heart strings thrum—
Be a Carlisle student, and not a reservation bum.

Look your best you'll then feel better, there's noble blood in all your
veins,
You're the hope of all your people—show them something for their
pains.
Don't be helpless, hopeless, useless, getting by with old time bluff,
Strike a gait with business to it, if there's evil treat it rough.
Take a bulldog grip—make something come—
Be a Carlisle Student, not a reservation bum.

[1917]

The Martyrdom of Funny Face

(The following verses were suggested by actual events that befell the cat that lived at the first farm. Seed corn was properly hung in the attic for next season's crop. The squirrels finally located it, and so "Funny Face" was assigned the duty of stopping their onslaught. He did well in the Seed Corn War. He took prisoner after prisoner, until in one Verdun-like battle he was compelled to retreat, which he did in good order. He entrenched himself between the attic floor and downstairs ceiling and couldn't get out. There he died for the want of assistance.

It is evident that "Funny Face" was patriotic while alive, and in death he is still doing his bit. His remains were disposed of in an agricultural way. His corpse was thrown into the fertilizer can and scattered on the field, where it will add plant food and organic matter to the soil.

As his living energy saved the seed and as his dead energy made it grow, we should regard next season's corn crop as a living monument to patriotic "Funny Face." —F.L.V.)

A cat has nine lives in his earthly span,
  Which he daily lives in a cat's own way;
But for serenading the sleeping man,
  Sometimes his extra lives are used to pay.

I am going to tell of "Funny Face,"
  A good natured cat of the blackest blue,
Whose habitat was the Giffen place,
  Where all day long he sang his happy mew.

He had not a care as he lived his lives,
  But for drinking old Spot's creamy brew, 10
And to purr on the porch where the lilacs thrive,
  And dream of Miss Tabby the whole day through.

One night Ma Giffen to Pa Giffen said,
  After the evening chores were all done:
"I think 'Funny Face' should work now instead
  Of pruning himself in the springtime sun.

The seed corn we have for next season's crop,
  Double stringed and hung in the attic;
The squirrels have found, we must put a stop
  To the ruin they will bring most emphatic." 20

"Funny Face" was wise as some felines are,
  Therefore he noticed the restless world;
He knew his earth gods were under a star,
  Where enemies' shrapnel and dum-dums whirled.

When he was drafted to the attic war,
  He called on himself not to slack.
He adopted a war hymn instead of a purr
  And he rubbed the fur wrong on his back.

Of the squirrels he fought there were many,
  And the seed that he saved was a lot; 30
Yet his pension it won't be a penny,
  Though by his nine lives our corn crop he bought.

Twixt attic floor and the downstairs ceiling
  "Funny Face" was caught and couldn't get out.
We talk of his death with reverent feeling
  As he martyred nine times in the bout.

But his work on earth is not finished yet,
  On plowed up soil he was scattered and thrown

And the seed he saved will thrive you bet,
  On his crumbling flesh and his limey bone. 40

He was nothing but an old black maltese,
  Just living from day to day on the place.
Fall's golden grains will bring us memories
  Of our four-footed loyal "Funny Face."

[1918]

first farm: Carlisle Indian School had two farms. **Verdun-like**: allusion to the notoriously long and fierce Battle of Verdun in 1916 during World War I. **entrenched**: allusion to the trenches of World War I. 24 **dum-dums**: First made by the British in Dum-Dum, Bengal, dum-dum bullets cause severe wounds, and though they were banned by international agreement, there was controversy about their use in World War I.

Tyler Young, Arapaho, 1900–1924

Tyler Young, Bacone College class of 1923, was from Oklahoma. In a 1922 essay in a Baptist magazine, he eloquently decried traditional Indian life and appealed for new Indian leadership and increased assimilation into the surrounding American culture. While his poem and essay were signed Tyler Young, his gravestone (pictured online) says Tyler Youngbull. (Young; Littlefield and Parins, *Biobibliography* 313)

Just Imagine!

I say, old top,
Did you ever stop to blink and think,
How funny it would be
To look around and see
Our President shooting pool,
Brother Clouse in a jazzing school,
Kahoe leading Y. M. C. A.,
Clifford King in a cabaret,
We'uns bragging on our grub,
Freshmen eager for a rub, 10
Mrs. Perkins trying to dance,
Mr. Weeks in DeRoin's tight pants,
Jennie Smith run a mile,
Juniors studious, once in a while,
Oh! Boy! Oh! Joy!
Wouldn't it make you smile?
Of course, you see,

It will never be;
But one for fun,
Might try to picture this, 20
Even though it be amiss:
The movies closed for lack of trade,
Our debts at the Parisian paid,
Receptions given, now and then,
By Dormitory Girls for Rockefeller Boys,
Miss Ripley in a happy mood,
Mr. Dubach refusing food,
Bud Walker to come in late,
And Mr. Cass to have a date,
A prize fight in Assembly Hall, 30
Or Mrs. Mother to take a fall;
Such sights, by rights,
Would make the heavens fall.

[1920]

25 Rockefeller: in 1885, Indian University (as it was then called) moved to a new building called Rockefeller Hall, after a donation of $10,000 from oil magnate and philanthropist John D. Rockefeller.

Mabel Washbourne Anderson, Cherokee, 1863–1949

A granddaughter of the controversial Cherokee leader John Ridge and niece of Ridge's son John Rollin Ridge, whose poetry also appears in this volume, Anderson was an 1883 graduate of the Cherokee Female Seminary, one of the schools in her poem "Nowita, the Sweet Singer." She taught in public schools, including Cherokee schools in Vinita, Indian Territory. A frequent contributor to newspapers and magazines, she also published a biography of her distant cousin Stand Watie, the famous Cherokee Confederate brigadier general.

Nowita, the Sweet Singer

A Romantic Tradition of Spavinaw, Indian Territory

Spavinaw is the most beautiful stream in the Cherokee Nation. Nourished by the sparkling waters of the many springs in that locality, it winds like a shining thread of crystal through the narrow valleys between the hills which bear its name; curving its way by circuitous route, as if reluctant to leave its native hills, the murmur of whose pines chant a tuneful accompaniment to the music of its waters.

Nestled among the hills and within these valleys are the homes of many of the fullblood Cherokees, who seek the seclusion and the quiet of the forests in preference to the open prairies, dotted with farms and towns and traversed by railroads. These little Indian cabins are scarcely less difficult to locate than are the haunts of the deer. Secluded in the summer by the luxuriant foliage of the forest trees, the unfamiliar traveler might well imagine, by the whispering of the pines, that "this is the forest primeval."

In one of the most picturesque spots of this section of the country stands a lonely Indian cabin which possesses more than ordinary interest to the stranger, for all the world loves a romance, as well as a lover. Tall pines and moss-grown rocks shelter the building from the gaze of the intruder. Fate seems to have chosen this site as a fit setting for the gem of romance that has made this cabin an object of interest and curiosity. It was once the home of a young Indian girl, the heroine of a romance that had its origin in the National High Schools of the Cherokee Nation, which are located at Tahlequah, the national capital. 'Tis the pathetic story of Nowita, a sweet singing Cherokee maiden, a pupil in the Female Seminary, and a young professor from the East, who taught in the Cherokee Male Seminary.

The Male and Female Seminaries were originally situated three miles from the town of Tahlequah, and separated from each other by the same distance of lonely prairie—lonely in the winter when the unbroken landscape lay bleak and colorless, but beautiful in the summer, when you might gaze as far as eye could reach over the green billows of waving grass, brightened with the variegated hues of many wild flowers, away in the distance to the purple line of the Boston and Ozark mountains.

It was an old custom, years ago, at the Female Seminary, to give a reception to the teachers and pupils of the Male Seminary, once every quarter, and every year, on the seventh day of May, the anniversary of the founding of the two schools, was celebrated by a picnic upon the beautiful banks of the winding Illinois, three miles away. Thus it came about that Nowita, the sweet singer, sang ballads in her own native tongue to the "pale face stranger" on "reception days," and on May-day picnics they wandered side by side down the lovely stream, allured from the society of the others by the music of its waters, gathering the spring violets as they went, which they afterward made into a wreath for Nowita's dark braids, all unconsciously weaving a bleeding heart among the purple blossoms, for the little Indian maid had learned the language of love more rapidly than she had acquired English, though unusually bright and advanced for her age and environments, her broken sentences and quaint expressions amused and charmed her admirer as much as the musical cadences of her voice.

So time went by and the young man realized that he welcomed with an indefinite eagerness every opportunity that threw him in the society of the young Indian girl, and noted, too, that her dark eyes, usually so serene and melancholy, shone with a happy luster in his presence, and he found a vague and pathetic pleasure in the thought that the school days were almost over, and that their final parting was near.

But Fate, that with cruel and relentless hand, had brought together these two young people so dissimilar by environments and nationality, decreed that one of them at least, should fulfill the destiny allotted to her. So, when the summer vacation came, and Nowita returned to the primitive home of her parents among the hills, contrary to the advice of his friend and the accusing memory of a pair of blue eyes among the green mountains of New Hampshire, the young professor joined a camping party for a fortnight's recreation on the banks of the Spavinaw, ostensibly to gather "Indian lore and legends." It is needless to say that he soon sought and found the home of Nowita, the object of his thoughts.

The old story begun at the school was renewed and continued among more romantic surroundings, and with fewer obstructions, save for the grave rebuke and distrust written upon the austere faces of the girl's parents and acquaintances which found no expression in words, for whatever may be said of the refining influence of civilization upon the Indian, the dignity and native pride of a fullblood Cherokee are conceded by all who are at all familiar with their character. Cruel and revengeful they may be, when under oppression, and perhaps treacherous, but coarse or vulgar, never. This Indian romance of local celebrity is given below in parodical form:

Should you ask me whence this story,
Whence this romance and tradition
Of the sad-eyed Indian maiden,
Of Nowita, the sweet singer,
I should answer, I should tell you
Of a pale and handsome stranger
Teaching at an Indian college
In the village of Tahlequah
At the time that you shall hear of;
I should speak up, I should tell you: 10
How this fair and fickle stranger
Trifled with this child of nature,
Singing with her gay and thoughtless,
Every moment when together,
Never weary grew the maiden,

Singing with the handsome stranger,
And their voices sweetly blending,
Could be heard throughout the building,
Singing old love songs together,
Ballads old and ever lovely, 20
He pronouncing words in English
She expressing them in Indian;
And he praised her voice and beauty,
Whispering words which mean to flatter,
And Nowita, sweet and child-like,
Listened to his honeyed speeches—
Knew no word which meant deceiving,
And her heart to love unlettered
Filled with new and dreamy music,
And she called him Ska-kle-los-ky 30
Ska-kle-los-ky, the sweet speaker.

Listening in the halls below them
Stood the friend of Ska-kle-los-ky,
With a cynic's face, he listened
To their voices softly singing,
Threw his shadow dark and chilling
Like an evil spirit near them,
As a thorn upon a rose stem,
So his presence stung the maiden,
For she felt his disapproval 40
Of the friendship they were forming,
And she called him Oo-naw-whee-hee—
Oo-naw-whee-hee, cold and cruel.
When the sultry days of summer
Came with all their brilliant splendor,
And upon the green prairie
Danced the vexing "Lazy Lawrence;"
When her school mates all departed
To their homes and to their parents,
None were half so heavy-hearted 50
As this gentle Indian maiden,
As Nowita, the sweet singer;
All the wild birds of the forest,
All the singing brooks and rivers.
All the breath of bursting blossoms
From the sweet wild honey suckle[6]
And the calling of the pine trees
From her home among the mountains,

Failed to interest their comrade
Or her homeward steps to hasten. 60
Sad at heart, this forest maiden
Left the village of Tahlequah,
Went back to her home and people,
To her home among the pine trees.
And she fancied she was dreaming,
Dreaming of the vanished hours,
When, one evening in the twilight
Came her pale and handsome hero;
"'Tis his spirit that appeareth,
"And my love is dead," she murmured. 70

Then he told her all the story,
How his friend and other comrades
Had encamped within the valley
Seeking rest and recreation,
How with eagerness he joined them
That again he might be near her,
Saying, "Won't you give me welcome
To the shelter of your pine trees?
I have come to know your people,
Learn your language, customs, habits, 80
Learn your legends and traditions;
Will you be my skillful teacher?
I will help you with your English,
With your books of prose and verses,
And we'll while away the hours
Helping, teaching one another."
And he quickly read his answer
In the lovelight on her features.
He abandoned all the future
To the pleasures of the present. 90
Thus, the days they spent together,
Like the ancient days of Eden,
Passed in guileless, blissful pleasure
With no shadow to disturb them,
Save the stolid disapproval
Of her own suspicious people,
For her parents and grandparents
Looked with stern disapprobation,
Looked with distrust at the stranger—
With a jealous eye they watched them. 100
Then she told him all their story,

Why against the "pale-faced nation"
All this prejudice had arisen,
Of their former home in Georgia,
On the banks of the Osternarly;
Further westward they'd been driven
Like the hunted deer and bison,
And their home was now uncertain—
Soon it would be taken from them.

She must pour him con-noh-ha-neh,[1] 110
She must make him sweet con-nutch-chee,[2]
He must smoke the pipe taloneh;[3]
And a magic chain of wampum[4]
From her ancient beads she gave him;
He must dive with Ooch-a-latah—[5]
He must friendly be among them,
So they might begin to trust him,
And her people be his people.
So she made him buckskin slippers—
"Moccasins all brightly beaded," 120
And a hunting shirt of homespun[8]
From her mother's loom she made him;
"Taught him to flint and feather arrows"
"How to shoot them when completed."

Down the river in the moonlight
In her own canoe they glided,
While she sang him songs so dreamy
That the great rocks caught the echo
And in phonographic measure
Still repeats them to the forest. 130
Thus the days of summer glided
Onward toward the coming autumn,
And the day of his departing
Dawned with its foreboding shadows.

But he vowed unto his sweetheart:
"I'll be true to thee, my song-bird,
Never love another maiden,
Never sing with any other,
Soon will come the happy springtime
When I will return to wed thee, 140
And we'll live and sing together,
And will nevermore be parted."
So with many vows he left her,

Standing lonely in the twilight
"Looking back as he departed"—
With her solemn faith unshaken.
Each day waited fond Nowita;
Happy was the little singer,
Looking forward to the springtime.
Thus the long and weary winter 150
Passed away with leaden footsteps,
And again the hills and valleys
Wakened from their chilly slumbers,
And the laughter of the waters
Called to her with happy voices;
And she answered with her singing
Till the song birds in the forest
Caught and mocked the happy echo,
But the voice she loved and longed for,
And the step for which she listened, 160
And the man for whom she waited,
Never would come again to greet her.
And the maiden, sadly singing
In the starlight in the morning,
Seemed to draw him near in spirit
From his distant home and people.

But the grand dame of the maiden
Looked with sorrow on her grandchild,
Looked with sadness at her fading
Looked with anguish at her pining. 170
She who had been so light-hearted
Till she met the pale-face stranger,
Till she met the handsome Yankee—
Till she met with "Ska-kle-los-ky."
"My dear daughter," said the grand dame,
"Choose a young man of your tribe
Do not waste your youth in pining,
Wait not for the fickle stranger,
Weep not for your fair-faced lover—
Awful queer folks are the white folks." 180

Many springs and many winters
Passed away in swift rotation,
And the gentle Indian Maiden
Grew into a sad-faced woman.
No more twilight found her singing,
Silent was her voice forever.

Said the men among her people,
"Let him come once more among us
To deceive us with his friendship;
When he comes again he'll tarry, 190
Tarry in these hills forever."

All the powers of the magician,
All the pleading of her people,
Failed to change the silent singer,
Or arouse her admiration,
For the tall and handsome suitors—
Chiefs from far and distant nations—
Who had learned her hapless story
And had traveled far to woo her,
But she heeded not nor heard them, 200
For her thoughts were with the stranger,
And the echo of his whispers
Silenced all the other voices.

Thus in melancholy sadness,
With her mind to mem'ry wedded,
And in patient resignation,
So her days alike were numbered;
Thus she passed away in silence
To the land of the hereafter.

Still her sad, unhappy story 210
Is repeated to the traveler,
And her home among the mountains
To this day is sought by strangers.
If you go alone at twilight
To the cave beside the river[7]
Where the lovers in the evening
Rowed together in the gloaming,
You may hear the repetition
Of the songs as they were uttered,
By this charming Indian maiden, 220
By Nowita, the sweet singer.

Explanatory Notes [These notes are in the original, including the irregular sequence of numbers and the variable spelling between the notes and the text.]

The figures below correspond with the figures in the poem, explaining the meaning of the Cherokee words used:

1 "Connoh-ha-neh," the national drink of the Cherokees, made from the pounded grits of the new Indian corn. An old adage says, Drink Connoh-ha-neh with a Cherokee, and you will be ever among them.

Figure 7. Under the watchful eyes of an interested Uncle Sam, concerns about gender evoke concerns about colonialism as Miss Indian Territory looks doubtfully at the advances of Mr. Oklahoma. This drawing from the cover of *Sturm's Statehood Magazine* in October 1905 suggests how supporters of separate statehood for Indian Territory looked on with apprehension as they watched the federal government pressure Indian Territory into merging with Oklahoma Territory to form what is now the state of Oklahoma, established in 1907.

2 "Con-nutch-chee," a Cherokee dish prepared from the beaten meat of the hickory nut, including both the kernel and the shell.

3 "Ta-lo-neh," a mixture of tobacco and dried leaves of the red sumach. Another old adage, current among the Cherokees says, Smoke Ta-lo-neh from the same pipe with a Cherokee and you will be friends forever.

4 "Wampum Beads," beads made by the Cherokees many years ago from the bones of the squirrel and colored different shades. They were supposed to possess the magic power of preserving the wearer from the evil one and of keeping him in health.

5 "Ooch-a-la-tah," the last full blood Chief of the Cherokee Nation.

6 "Wild Honeysuckle," a lovely species of the honeysuckle found in the Cherokee Nation only among the rocks of the Spavinaw.

7 A cave on the shores of Spavinaw, where a low sound as of singing may be heard, borne on the waters of the interior of the cave, called by the natives De-cu-na-gus-ky-skilly, or, Singing Spirit.

8 "Hunting Shirt," an ornamental article of apparel used in olden times by the Cherokees, which took the place of a coat. Now in disuse.

[1900, 1903, 1906]

Subtitle: A Romantic Tradition of The Spavinaw Hills (1900). *Prose introduction.* **this is the forest primeval**: These words begin each of the first two stanzas of Henry Wadsworth Longfellow's famous poem *Evangeline* (1847; Longfellow 57). **Illinois**: the Illinois River in the Cherokee Nation (now in Oklahoma), not the Illinois River in the state of Illinois. **parodical form**: The poem uses the famous meter (trochaic tetrameter) of Longfellow's most famous poem, *The Song of Hiawatha* (1855), though since the poem is not comic, the metrical form comes across more as an imitation than as a parody. **1–10**: These lines echo the opening ten lines of *The Song of Hiawatha*: "Should you ask me, whence these stories? / Whence these legends and traditions, / . . . / I should answer, I should tell you . . ." (Longfellow 141). **101–9 Then she told him . . .** : Nowita tells how the United States forced the Cherokee people from their homes in the Southeast to Indian Territory in what is now Oklahoma, leaving the Cherokees fearful that even the land granted them in Indian Territory would soon be taken away. **105 Osternarly**: the Oostanaula River in the Cherokee Nation in northwest Georgia. **145 "Looking back as he departed"**: a line from *The Song of Hiawatha*, part X (Longfellow 201). **187–91 Said the men . . .** : This stanza is not in the 1900 version.

Henry B. Sarcoxie, Delaware (Lenape), died 1901

Henry B. Sarcoxie attended Bacone Indian University in Indian Territory in the early 1890s. His friend and classmate Alex Posey wrote that they "used to scribble doggerel verses to each other during study hours." Sarcoxie suffered from tuberculosis and traveled west for his health. The two poems included here come from his four "Rhymes Written at Las Vegas." (Littlefield, *Alex Posey* 58–59, 285)

In the Desert

Far as the searching eye can see,
Space, emptiness and vacancy—
A cloudless sky, low-arched and blue—
A mirage yonder—just a mile or two!

[1900]

Up the Washita

The crook'dest road I ever saw
Was that road up the Washita,
Where grapes and plum and cherries,
Wild currants and gooseberries
Grew thick on every hand, and luscious,
And people dreamed of metal precious.

[1900]

Evalyn Callahan Shaw, Creek (Muskogee), born about 1861

Evalyn (sometimes listed as Eva, Evelyn, or Jane Evylin) Callahan Shaw lived in Wagoner, Indian Territory. She probably grew up in Sulphur Springs, Texas, though with strong ties to Indian Territory, where her father owned a large ranch. Samuel Benton Callahan, her father, was a leading figure in Creek politics. An advocate for states' rights who owned many slaves and yet opposed slavery, he was a captain in the Confederacy and represented the Creek and Seminole Nations in the Confederate Congress. Later, he worked as a newspaper editor and served as Clerk of the House of Kings in the Creek National Council, Clerk and then Justice of the Supreme Court of the Creek Nation, and executive secretary to several principal chiefs. He also often served as a Creek delegate to Washington, D.C. Evalyn Callahan Shaw's younger sister, S. Alice Callahan, wrote *Wynema: A Child of the Forest* (1891), a short novel and one of the first Indian-written novels. (Editorial note to "October"; Foreman and M.H.W. [Muriel H. Wright], "S. Alice Callahan"; Ruoff xiv–xv, xliv–xlv)

October

October is the month that seems
All woven with midsummer dreams;
She brings for us the golden days
That fill the air with smoky haze,
She brings for us the lisping breeze
And wakes the gossips in the trees,
Who whisper near the vacant nest
Forsaken by its feathered guest.
Now half the birds forget to sing,
And half of them have taken wing, 10
Before their pathway shall be lost
Beneath the gossamer of frost.
Zigzag across the yellow sky,
They rustle here and flutter there,
Until the boughs hang chill and bare,
What joy for us—what happiness
Shall cheer the day the night shall bless?
'Tis hallowe'en, the very last
Shall keep for us remembrance fast,
When every child shall duck the head 20
To find the precious pippin red.

[1900]

Laura M. Cornelius, Oneida, born 1880, died about 1949

Laura Minnie Cornelius (later Laura Minnie Cornelius Kellogg) was born and raised on the Oneida Reservation in Wisconsin and studied law and other topics at Barnard College, Cornell University, the New York School of Philanthropy, Stanford University, and the University of Wisconsin (without completing a degree). Fluent in Oneida and Mohawk, she was a founding member of the Society of American Indians in 1911, although she eventually separated from the SAI. At the time she published "A Tribute to the Future of My Race," her only known surviving poem, she was an instructor at the Sherman Institute, a boarding school for Indian students in Riverside, California. A dynamic orator and organizer, an advocate of Indian self-government and economic independence, a critic of the Office of Indian Affairs education policies, and a controversial Iroquois land-claims activist (she was accused—but not convicted—of taking funds she raised for land claims cases), she also wrote stories, plays, and political essays as well as *Our Democracy and the American Indian: A Comprehensive Presentation of the American Indian Situation as It Is Today* (1920) and other books and pamphlets that have not survived in any known copy. (Hauptman)

A Tribute to the Future of My Race

Not a song of golden "Greek,"
Wafted from Aegean shores,
Not from an Olympian height
Come my simple syllables:
But from the northern of Wisconsin,
From the land of the Oneidas,
From the chieftain clan Cornelius,
From the friendly Iroquois
Comes the greeting of the wampum
And a tribute, humble, simple, 10
From the pines' soft, lingering murmurs,
From the "pleasant water courses,"
From the morn-kissed, mighty highlands,
From the breezes and the flowers
Nodding secrets to each other,
From the din of metropolitans,
From the wisdom of their sages,
I have caught this sage's epic.
Ye who love the haunts of nature,
Love the sunshine of the meadow, 20
Love the shadow of the forest,
Love the wind among the branches
And the rushing of great rivers
Thro' their palisades of pine trees,

Ye whose hearts are kind and simple,
Who have faith in God and nature,
Who believe that in all ages
Every human heart is human,
That in even savage bosoms
There are longings, yearnings, strivings, 30
For the good they comprehend not.
That the feeble hands and helpless,
Groping blindly in that darkness
Touch God's right hand in that darkness
And are lifted up and strengthened.
Ye, who sometimes in your rambles
Thro' the green lanes of the country
Pause by some neglected graveyard
For awhile to muse and ponder
On a half-effaced inscription, 40
Writ with little skill of song-craft,
Homely phrases, yet each letter,
Full of hope, and yet of heart-break,
Full of all the tender pathos
Of the here and the hereafter—
Stay ye, hear this rude-put story
Of the future of a nation.
Many moons have waxed and waned
Since their chieftain clans were numbered,
Since from seas of rising sun 50
To the far coast of her setting,
From the white bear's colder regions
To the high-noon of their borders
Roamed an infant, warrior people,
A whole continent their own!
Ah, who were they? All barbarians? Were they men?
Without legend or tradition,
Without heroes, gods, religion,
Without thought of the hereafter?
Did they enter nature's gardens— 60
In her temples of the forest
With their warriors' hearts unmelted?
Did they tread her wreathed pathways
Without learning tenderness?
Did they see the roses' dew-drop
And not wonder whence it came from?
And traced savage eyes the hemlock
Without learning majesty?

Is it nature's law to teach not?
Ah, too often do we think not 70
That the human race for ages
Suffer countless throes, upheavals,
Ere they blossom beauteous.
But to day my epic telleth
Not the lore of idle camp-fire,
Not the past so buried deeply
'Neath the mound of gracious kindness,
But of beauteous enlightenment.
Who has made it? Who will make it?
That the golden sun of freedom 80
May shine brighter and still further
Till our glorious America
Be the world's salvation—haven.
Ah, I've seen her high-born heroes
Who've attained life's highest summits,
Stretch their hands to weary climbers
Without thought of race or color,
That a man may yet be saved!
And among the foot-sore climbers
I've beheld a stoic brother 90
Climbing silently and slowly,
All unnoticed, all alone?
Till perchance, he puts his step where
In a moment he has lost it.
Then the world's quick recognition!
"He has fallen! He has fallen!"
Hark! a voice from yonder summit—
He is up, and tries again.
And—I can't tell how I know it—
But two guardian angels' trumpets 100
Blow against the gate of heaven,
And their descending volumes turn
To earth's bright gladness and her flowers.
Then another rises onward
With chieftain fire in his eyes.
I see him mount unmindful
Of the rocks and sounds of way
Till at length I see him reach it,
And he, too, stand among
The heroes of that band! 110
So for him who mounts through
All the hardships of the mountainside.

I pray, to him give patience,
For, what the future holds
In the imperial sway of Time
No man can tell. No sentence
Without first indubious conviction
And, ere conviction, just chances, give.
And, oh, ye sons of Tonner hall
And all ye daughters, true, 120
Ye have it in your power to say
Of what, and when a race shall be;
Ye spring from noble warrior blood,
As brave as Saxon, Roman, Greek,
And the age that waits upon you all
Has begot a race of kingly men.
May your careers be as complete
As the arches of your mater halls,
And when the noon of mankind comes
May it find you all more nearly 130
With the noblest offspring
Of our dear, great land,
Such as Smiley, Pratt and Garrett,
Such as—oh, a thousand more
Along your young paths daily known!
Ah, they've taught us, we'll remember
Beauteous enlightenment,
Then to each with one accord
We will extend the wampum strand
Made of friendships, purest pearl, 140
Made of gratitude, deep-rooted,
Made to last eternal summers.
Yea, the hearts' right hand we give them,
Blue-eyed Royalty American,
Theirs, our native land forever,
Ours their presence and their teachings.
Ours the noblest and the best.

[1903]

8 Iroquois: The Oneida Nation is one of the nations in the Iroquois Confederacy, known now as the Haudenosaunee (People of the Long House) or the Six Nations. **12 "pleasant water courses"**: quoting from the introduction to Henry Wadsworth Longfellow's famous *The Song of Hiawatha* (Longfellow 142). **19–46 Ye who love the haunts of nature / . . . / Stay ye, hear this rude-put story"**: These lines come almost word-for-word from the introduction to *The Song of Hiawatha*, skipping the lines from Longfellow's poem that would not make sense in a poem that is not about Hiawatha. This means, for example, that the word "savage" (line 29) comes from Longfellow, though Cornelius chose to repeat it. Perhaps Cornelius expected readers to recognize the source; she would certainly expect them to recognize that most of her poem follows the famous trochaic tetrameter meter of *Hiawatha.* **119 Tonner hall:** a building at the Sherman Institute, named after A. C. Tonner, an acting Superintendent of Indian Affairs. **128 mater:** Latin for mother. **133 Smiley, Pratt and Garrett:** Richard Henry Pratt founded the Carlisle Indian School; Albert K. Smiley and Philip C. Garrett were prominent white philanthropists and "friends of the Indian."

Hen-toh/Bertrand N. O. Walker, Wyandot, born about 1870, died 1927

Bertrand N. O. Walker published his poems under his Wyandot name, Hen-toh (sometimes spelled Hen-to or Hento). In 1843 his parents were removed from Ohio to Kansas, where he was born. He came from a distinguished Wyandot family and was related to William Walker, who has poems in this volume. In 1874 Bertrand Walker joined the Wyandots who were removed to the Quapaw Agency in northeastern Indian Territory. He attended the Friends' Mission School in Wyandotte, Indian Territory, followed briefly by public school in nearby Seneca, Missouri and then by four years of study with someone he described as "an old College Professor" (Walker 90–91). Beginning in 1890 he worked for the Office of Indian Affairs in Indian Territory as well as in Kansas, western Oklahoma, California, and New Mexico. He spent ten years teaching in reservation schools and then worked as a clerk, mostly at the Quapaw Agency, where at his death he was Chief Clerk. He was proud that over the years he kept his home on his allotment where his parents moved in 1874. A wide reader, he built a large library and a collection of traditional Wyandot wampum belts. From 1918 to 1923, he worked full-time at writing. He published a book of Wyandot animal stories, *Tales of the Bark Lodges*, in 1919 as well as a book of poems, *Yon-Doo-Shah-We-Ah (Nubbins)*, in 1924. Many of his later poems work with dialect in the manner of some of the poems of Alex Posey (whose work appears in this volume) and of Posey's renowned Fus Fixico letters. In those poems, Hen-toh adopted the patterns of speech he heard among Wyandot speakers whose English sometimes drew on Wyandot grammar. Most of the poems included here appeared in *Yon-Doo-Shah-We-Ah*, and they follow the versions in that book. Other versions have slight differences in wording as well as differences, large or small, in lineation or stanza form, which might sometimes come from editors or typographers. Variants are not noted here unless they notably affect the meaning. (Walker; Littlefield and Parins, "Introduction")

A Mojave Lullaby

Sleep, my little man-child,
Dream-time to you has come.

In the closely matted branches
Of the mesquite tree,
The mother-bird has nestled
Her little ones; see

From the ghost-hills of your fathers,
Purpling shadows eastward crawl,
While beyond the western sky-tints pale,
As twilight spreads its pall. 10
The eastern hills are lighted,
See their sharp peaks burn and glow,
With the colors the Great Sky-Chief
Gave your father for his bow.
Hush my man-child; be not frighted,
'Tis the father's step draws nigh.
O'er the trail along the river,
Where the arrow-weeds reach high
Above his dark head, see
He parts them with his strong hands, 20
As he steps forth into view.
He is coming home to mother,
Home to mother and to you.

Sleep my little man-child,
Daylight has gone.
There's no twitter in the branches,
Dream-time has come.

[1903, 1905, 1924]

Pontiac

Patriot, seer, proud product of Nature
In a triumphant hour, wert thou Pontiac,
   Though ill-starred thy destiny!
Yet, the motives which inspired thee to act
Must aye be held in honor'd veneration
By scattered remnants of thy valiant race.

Born of the wilds, yet with a mind endued
With latent power to grasp, to view, to know
The import of the ever-changing hour,
He saw the hapless fate of his people. 10
Brave, proud and free they had ever been
Unfettered by any law save custom,
Wherein is found the origin of good;
Their own arts, primitive as they were,
Supplied their every want and humble need.

Sadly he noted changes brought about
By the advent of the subtle stranger;

The bow and spear, pride of their fore-fathers
Disdain-ed for the gun of the pale-face;
And spear and arrow-head for ages wrought 20
With skill by their own hands, were neglected;
While knives, hatchets and steel of the whiteman
Were the pride of the young men and warriors.
E'en rich robes of buckskin and of beaver,
Adorned and fashioned by their women's craft
Were exchanged for the gay and gaudy blankets,
Or for draughts of potent fire-water
That maddened and enfeebled the young men.
Often too, did the trustful owner
Give fine furs for only tawdry tinsel; 30
The cunning traders being only govern'd
By the unwritten, ne'er repeal-ed law:
"Tis no great crime to fleece an Indian."

Must their forests be wantonly stripped
Of the game within its endless reaches;
All the young men become weak and worthless,
On their prowess as great hunters not dependent;
Their lands given them by the Great Spirit
Bartered be for hawks-bells, gauds and trinkets
To sate this greed termed civilization! 40

Deep within the heavy heart of Pontiac,
Thoughts like these burn'd fiercely there and rankled.
Untaught as he was, yet much he pondered
And beheld the menace to his people.
Though un-versed in all the wisdom of his
Brother, yet Great Nature unto him had
Given much of all her hidden lore;
And life, and men as he observed them
Had added something to his eager mind.
His keen and clear foresight brought to his view 50
The doom not of his tribe alone, but that
Of all the tribes of their far-reaching lands;
Sadly he thought on their waning glory.
That they should calmly wait and accept
Whatever fate might offer them, was folly;
This, his fierce, proud spirit could not brood.
His must be the self-imposed duty
To arrest and quell this dreadful peril.

He was by nature a leader of men,
Even as was he, who led his people 60
Out of bondage to the grim wilderness;
And nobly he proposed and planned the course
To be pursued.

Naught of selfish gain or vain ambition,
Naught of hope that greatness would accrue
To the name of Pontiac, none of these
Moved him to still and earnest effort
To bring forth his warriors' strength and forefend
Threatened danger to their homes and children;
Boundless love of country and its lodge-fires 70
Urged him to the task as given to him.

Courage, valor, steadfastness of purpose
Are shown in his brief, laconic answer
To the intrepid commander, who so
Candidly termed him an Emperor;
Like speech of famed Spartans 'twas uttered:
"I stand in the path."

As vain as was the trial of that King
Of old, to stem the ocean's restless tide,
So was Pontiac's to thwart the tide of 80
Progress and the whiteman's civilization;
Yet if the man we calmly, justly scan
By his aims, his efforts and desires,
His name deserves rank among great heroes.

Most tragic and pitiable was his death;
And over his lost grave that same progress,
Which he so vainly strove to turn aside
As monument has raised a splendid city,
On the site where the great chieftain fell.

[1906]

Title: Pontiac, the famed Odawa (Ottawa) war chief who fought against the British in what is known as Pontiac's Rebellion, 1763–1766. **74 commander**: Major Robert Rogers, commander of the famous Rogers' Rangers, who wrote a not necessarily reliable account of Pontiac in his 1765 A Concise Account of North America (239–44). **78-79 King / Of old, to stem the ocean's restless tide**: Canute (c. 995–1035), King of Denmark, Norway, part of Sweden, and England. According to an apocryphal story, he commanded the tide to halt. When it failed to obey him, he proclaimed the power of kings worthless next to the power of God. **88 city**: Pontiac was murdered in 1769 near St. Louis, Missouri.

A Desert Memory

Lonely, open, vast and free,
The dark'ning desert lies;
The wind sweeps o'er it fiercely,
And the yellow sand flies.
The tortuous trail is hidden,
Ere the sand-storm has passed
With all its wild, mad shriekings,
Borne shrilly on its blast.

Are they fiends or are they demons
That wail weirdly as they go, 10
Those hoarse and dismal cadences,
From out their depths of woe?
Will they linger and enfold
The lone trav'ler in their spell,
Weave 'round him incantations,
Brewed and bro't forth from their hell?
Bewilder him and turn him
From the rugged, hidden trail,
Make him wander far and falter,
And tremblingly quail 20
At the desert and the loneliness
So fearful and so grim,
That to his fervid fancy,
Wraps in darkness only him?

The wind has spent its fierce wild wail,
  The dark storm-pall has shifted,
Forth on his sight the stars gleam pale
  In the purpling haze uplifted.
And down the steep trail, as he lists,
    He hears soft music stealing; 30
It trembling falls through filmy mists,
    From rock-walls faint echoes pealing.

Whence comes this mystic night-song
With its rhythm wild and free,
With its pleading and entreaty
Pouring forth upon the sea
Of darkness, vast and silent,
Like a tiny ray of hope
That oft-times comes to comfort
When in sorrow's depths we grope? 40

'Tis the An-gu, the Kat-ci-na,
'Tis the Hopi's song of prayer,
That in darkness wards off danger,
When 'tis breathed in the air;
Over desert, butte, and mesa,
It is borne out on the night,
Dispelling fear and danger,
Driving evil swift a-flight.

[1906, 1924]

A Song of a Navajo Weaver

For ages long, my people have been
  Dwellers in this land;
For ages viewed these mountains,
  Loved these mesas and these sands,
That stretch afar and glisten,
  Glimmering in the sun
As it lights the mighty canons
  Ere the weary day is done.
Shall I, a patient dweller in this
  Land of fair blue skies, 10
Tell something of their story while
  My shuttle swiftly flies?
As I weave I'll trace their journey,
  Devious, rough and wandering,
Ere they reached the silent region
  Where the night stars seem to sing.
When the myriads of them glitter
  Over peak and desert waste,
Crossing which the silent runner and
  The gaunt co-yo-tees haste. 20
Shall I weave the zig-zag pathway
  Whence the sacred fire was born;
And interweave the symbol of the God
  Who brought the corn—
Of the Rain-god whose fierce anger
  Was appeased by sacred meal,
And the trust that my brave people
  In him evermore shall feel?
All this perhaps I might weave
  As the woof goes to and fro, 30

Wafting as my shuttle passes,
Humble hopes, and joys and care,
Weaving closely, weaving slowly,
While I watch the pattern grow;
Showing something of my life:
To the Spirit God a prayer.
Grateful that he brought my people
To the land of silence vast;
Taught them arts of peace and ended
All their wanderings of the past. 40
Deftly now I trace the figures,
This of joy and that of woe;
And I leave an open gate-way
For the Dau to come and go.

There is an irregularity in every design woven into a Navajo blanket, thus leaving a place for the "Dau" or spirit of the blanket to go out and in.

[1906, 1924]

A Wyandot Cradle Song

Hush thee and sleep, little one,
The feathers on thy board sway to and fro;
The shadows reach far downward in the water
The great old owl is waking, day will go.

Rest thee and fear not, little one,
Flitting fireflies come to light you on your way
To the fair land of dreams, while in the grasses
The happy cricket chirps his merry lay.

Tsa-du-meh watches always o'er her little one,
The great owl cannot harm you, slumber on 10
'Till the pale light comes shooting from the eastward,
And the twitter of the birds says night has gone.

Hi-a-stah, Wynadot for father.
Tsa-du-meh, Wynadot for Mother.

[1910, 1916, 1924]

Title: "A Wyandot Lullaby" in the 1916 version. The earlier versions have another stanza between the 1924 version's first and second stanzas: "Sleep thee and dream, little one, / The gentle branches swing thee [or in 1910 *you* rather than *thee*] high and low; / Thy father far away among the hunters / Has loosed his bow, is thinking of us now." Hen-toh's note about the Wyandot word for father suggests that the removed stanza at some point appeared in a draft for the 1924 version. 7 **fair**: *fairy*- 1910. 9 **Tsa-du-meh**: *Mother* in the earlier versions.

Arrow-Heads

Bit by bit with tireless effort,
Was the hard flint flaked to form
Tip for shaft and spear-head
Long ago.

Time was counted naught in those days,
And the end sufficed the needs
Of the patient worker
For his bow.

Skilled in craft of plain and mountain,
He must ever be alert, 10
In the haunts of bison,
Or of deer.

On the shores of lake and river,
Trod his moccasin'd foot,
As he sought shy quarry
For his spear.

Lithe of limb with might of muscle,
Swiftly wends he o'er the portage,
Shoulders bearing lightly
His canoe. 20

Should he meet a wily foeman,
As he treads the darksome glades
His the need to dare then
And to do.
Thoughts like these come as we wander
O'er the fallowed fields and find
In our path an old
Arrow-head.
And we form in fervid fancy,
As we scan th' enduring flint, 30
A measure of those brave
Warriors dead.

[1915, 1924]

25–31 we: *I* in earlier versions.

The Warrior's Plume

On the plains and in the vales of Oklahoma,
Grew a flower of the Tyrian hue,

The color that is loved by the Redman,
That tells him light and life,
And love are true.

Long ago it flamed in beauty on the prairies,
Lighting reaching vistas with its glow;
Ere advent of the whiteman and his fences,
Told the care-free, roving hunter
He must go. 10

The throng, the herd, and greed have madly trampled
Prairie, woodland, valley, and the height;
Crushed the feath'ry flower and rudely blighted
Its pride and life and beauty,
And its light.

Today 'tis found in silent glades and meadows
Where by twos and threes it greets the May.
Like the scattered braves who loved its color,
It has passed, been trodden out
Along the way. 20

As the oriflamme it flaunted through past ages
Went to gladden the fairness of the earth;
So the greatness of the Indian will linger
In the land that loves them both
And gave them birth.

The Scarlet Painted Cup was called by the Wynadots, the Warrior's Plume.

[1915, 1924]

21 **oriflamme**: flag or inspiring symbol.

A Strand of Wampum

With what almost infinite patience and skill,
Was each shapely bead so dextrously wrought;
By hands trained to deftness through uncoerced will,
To fashion with beauty the shred of a thought
From the fragments of shells brought from ocean's far shore.

The sheen of the shell, perchance, prompted the striving
To form of the bauble a trinket so rare;
And the yearning for beauty, content, in deriving
The recompense: pleasure, for patience and care
In task rudely essayed and fitly achieved. 10

Of what might you tell, whether barter or glory,
Of compact or revels in ages long past?
The heart of the Redman will e'er hold in story,
Thy lore and thy legends while mem'ry shall last;
And thy shim'ring beauty shall e'er be undimmed.

[1915]

Title: Though European settlers treated wampum as money, it was originally designed as a record of or memory-prompt for events and ceremonies.

The Calumet

Sent from the white lands of the North,
Emblem of peace and brotherhood,
Its first fruits ever are offered
To The Great Spirit, then to the Sun;
To our Mother, the Earth; and the Waters;
To the North, to the South, the East, the West;
  Then to each other.

A prayer goes to the One Great Spirit, thus;
Oh that the whole wide World could now
Accept the Redman's ancient symbol, 10
Off'ring its incense to the Universe;
And blot out fierce, wild war's red stain,
Bringing Good-will to earth again
  With Peace, white Peace.
1918

[1919, 1924]

Title: "The Calumet or Peace-Pipe" in the 1919 version. **1918**: The year at the bottom of the 1924 version underlines the poem's connection to World War I, which ended in November 1918.

My Fren'

To J. W. C.
On his leaving for the Army during the great war.

You my fren', no diff'ence what say, anyone,
If I seen you now, or don' see fo' years.
You know reason, t'aint what I done,
You could look my eye, don' seen it tears,
  When you sed it: 'Good-bye'.

You my pardner, you sed it one time,
It's l-o-n-g 'go, but me, I don' fo'get;

If you go flat bust, an' I got one dime,
I know wha' you could fin' nickel, I bet,
Or mebbe ten cent. 10

It's jus' that way all time, me an' you,
We bin know'd each otha' how you say, well.
I don' care fo' hundred snakes what you do;
Even you tell it me: "You go to hell,"
I could do it, e-a-s-y.

You come back war-trail, it's be jus' same,
Kin' a smile and sed it: "You my pardner yet?"
I jus' look at you an' sed it you name,
Mebbe so wink it, then sed it: "You bet!"
I don' fo'gotten nothin'. 20

[1924]

Injun Summa'

You seen it that smoky, hazy, my frien',
It's hangin' all 'roun' on edges of sky?
In moon of fallin' leaves, 'at's when
It's always come, an' jus' floatin' by.

You know, my fren', what's make it that kin'?
It's spirits o' home-sick warriors come;
An' somewha's his lodge fires all in line.
Jus' near as could get it to his ol' home.

I think he's like it, Happy Huntin' Groun',
It's mus' ta be a nice, eva'thin' ova' tha'; 10
But, mebbe so, fo' little' bit, jus' kin' a look 'roun'
When year it's get ol', an' days an sky it's fair,

He's kin' a like to wanda' back ol' huntin' groun'.
But don't want a stay, No, cause it's all gone,
Beaver, Bear, Buffalo, all; it's can't be foun';
Anyhow, makes good dream fo' him, 'bout eva' one.

So he's come back an' make it his lodge fire,
All 'roun' ova' tha' on edges of sky;
An' it's nice wa'm sun, an' you don't get tire,
Cause it's Ol' Injun Summa'-time, 'at's why. 20

[1924]

Title: Though the poem relies on familiar images of so-called Indian summer, it might also draw on "Injun Summer," a famous illustrated narrative by John T. McCutcheon, published in the *Chicago Tribune* in 1907 and often reprinted.

The Seasons

What sed it Ol' Injuns 'bout a spring-time?
Oh it's pritty girl, it's comin' from a south,
All dress' up in fine white buckskins.
He don' walk, he's jus' dance,
He don' look, he's jus' glance,
Roun' at eva'body, pleasant,
Jus' like happy;
An' he's bring it nice bowl o' strawberry,
An' jus' scatta' eva'wha'.

What sed it Ol' Injuns 'bout a summa-time? 10
Oh it's good woman followed that girl,
An' it's dress like a nice, jus' all kin' a green.
He don' dance, jus' kin' a float,
Like on wata', seen it, boat,
An' jus' smile 'roun' eva-wha' goes,
Jus' like good;
An' he's bring it string o' squaw-corn,
An' jus' pile up eva'wha'.

What sed it Ol' Injuns 'bout a fall-time?
Oh it's young man comes from kin' o' west, 20
Huntin' shirt an' leggin' kin' o' color brown.
He's straight jus' like an arrow,
An' his fringes color, 'yarrow'.
He's got laugh in eye an' it's a keen,
Jus' like brave;
An' he's bring it bunch o' wil' grape an' acorn,
An' jus' hang up eva' wha'.

What sed it Ol' Injuns 'bout a winta-time?
Wooh! It's o-l' man, he's comin' from a north,
From lan' of Great White Rabbit, 'at's his home. 30
His long robe it's shine an' glis'en,
You could heard it clink, you lis'en,
When he's walk kin' o' slow
Jus' like tired.

He's bring lots o' ice an' plenty snow,
An jus' drift up eva'wha'.

[1924]

Fishin'

Eva' fishin' much? It's good.
Sunshine in sky, shake in a wood,
Down on riva' bank jus' wait an' wish
I could ketch 'im hurry, that dam fish;
Take 'im home, cook 'im, an' eat 'im.

Sometimes it's ketch 'im right now,
Sometimes don' ketch 'im all day;
But Injun he's sure know how
He could ketch 'im a'right, 'notha way.

Long 'go 'fore whiteman, he's come here, 10
Ol' Injun use to fishin' with spear.
That kin' o' spear it's made o' stone;
He's got hook too, made o' bone;
But he could ketch 'em plenty fish—sometime.

Sometime he's fishin' on a shore,
Sometime he's fishin' in canoe;
Some day he's ketch 'em plenty more,
Some day it's jus' nothin' do.

Now-days he's got littl' stick, green an' red,
L-o-n-g line, he's wind it up, 'at's how he sed. 20
It's tie on end littl' fish made o' wood,
Lot's o' hook, seems to me it's no good;
But he's sure ketch 'im b-i-g one, bass.

That bass he's like Injun, mebbe so,
Whiteman's fool 'im easy, since long 'go.
Spec' so, dam fool, bofe of it,
Cause you can't fool 'im, whiteman, littl' bit.

[1924]

Fire

I think Injun like it betta' 'an anythin', fire,
But I don' jus' know why.

Mebbe so it's cause 'at smokes go high,
Way up towa'ds a sky,
An' could carried it message, higher an' higher,
'Til He's got it, Great Spirit.

When he's smoke it, Peace Pipe, anywha'
Council, or in lodge,
Smokes curl roun' 'jus' kin' a like it's dodge
An' gatha' up eva'body's message 10
An' carried it off, jus' way up tha',
'Til He's heard it, Great Spirit.

Long 'go sometime, he's want it sen' word
His frens way off, 'notha' wha.
He's fin' it high place, an' tha'
Make it smokes go straight in air,
An' his frens, it's like they heard,
What he's ask Him, Great Spirit.

An' Injuns, his folks, time come when he die,
He's bury him somewha', not far, 20
An' on grave, 'bout time it's shine star,
He's make it littl' fire. What for?
It's make it light fo' soul on road, 'at's why,
To place wha' He's call 'im, Great Spirit.

[1924]

Smokin'

Say, he don' smokin', jus' to smokin',
Ol' Injun, long 'go,
Like he's do eva'body, eva'wha' now days,
Jus' puff, puffin' so.

Long 'go, Injun', he's thinkin' an' thinkin'
'Bout word he's want to sent,
To Great Spirit, somethin' it's good one
To help 'im, what it's meant;
Then he's smokin' plenty.

He don' sed nothin', jus' smokin' an' think 10
Jus' 'bout that what he's want.
He's do this way long time, himse'f,
'Til he's sure it's that way.

Don' tole nobody 'bout it but jus' hese'f,
'Cause too much talk no good.
Whiteman he's smart, but not foun' that out yet,
'Spec' so no b'lieve it, if he could.

"Put it in you pipe an' smoke it",
I hear 'im, whiteman say.
It's jus' how he's do, Ol' Injun, 20
Meb' so, 'at's how he pray.

Cause he don' like it to talk to Great Spirit,
An' tole 'IM it, what mus' do,
So he's think it, an' smoke carry thinkin'
Eva'wha', up wha' looks blue.

[1924]

Big Tree's Horse

Ol' Big Tree, he's bin down this way,
He's tole me 'bout it, his horse.
It's kin' a "baw-ky", how you say?
Jus' stan'in', won't go, of course.

He say it's all a time makes 'im mad,
That horse, 'cause it's don' want go;
Sometime he's want a work prit' bad,
An' that horse he's stan' jus' so.

Otha' day, he's plow in squaw-corn patch,
'Long side big road, down tha'. 10
That horse jus' stan', don' move one scratch;
Big Tree, he's cuss 'im but horse don' ca'.

By um by it's comin' down a road
That place, Big Tree, he's plow,
Big noise, it's what you call 'im, Foad,
Lots a rattle, it's ol' one, now.

It's come right wha' he's stan', that horse.
He's jump, Big Tree heap holla' whoa;
That horse he's plenty scare of course,
Don' lis'n to Big Tree, jus' keep on go. 20

Big Tree he's go prit' hurry up too,
'Cause it's lines tie togetha, roun' back.
He's pull on lines, but that don' do,
He's jus' got to folla' in track.

He's tell it, Big Tree, an' he's say:
"Horse heap dam' fool, that's the one;
Sometime he's go, sometime he's stay,
He's jus' too 'nuff or too none."

[1924]

15 **Foad**: Ford car.

A Borrowed Tale

Say, you know that time that Ol' Otta'
He's slide down that mount'in from th' sky?
Well, he's wored it jus' all a fur off his tail,
Jus' smoof, an' skin looks ugly an' a' dry.

He's sure feel sorrow, 'cause it's always bin,
He's kin' o' proud o' that tail jus' all a time,
'Cause it's always bin cova' jus' nice sof' fur,
An' it's looks good draggin' long behin'.

Don' got none, nobody, 'at looks so fine,
'Less it's Mus'rat, his jus' 'bout nex' best; 10
He's sure feelin' prit' bad, 'at Ol' Otta',
'Cause now his tail it's look bad, 'mongst th' rest.

He's jus' stay at home, don' went no-wha'
'Cause he's shame how it's spoil it, 'at tail;
It's look so bad, he's think eva'body laughin',
If they seen 'im comin' down a trail.

But it's "Rah-shu" come 'long an tole 'im,
'Bout big council, down a lake, he's haf to go;
He don' sed it nothin', jus' like thinkin',
Then he's start it, like he's know what's goin' to do. 20

Mus'rat, he's not b'long to that big council,
Sol Ol' Otta' he's go to Mus'rat, his lodge.
That fella' he's sittin' outside singin'
But when he's see Ol' Otta', he's dodge,
  In a wata'.

Ol' Otta' couldn' seen 'im nowha', Mus'rat,
So he's holla': "Ho' my fren', I like spoke to you now;
I like to borrow'd you' tail, to wear big council;
We could swap 'til I come back, I tole you how."

Mus'rat, he's good fella', so he's sed it, "A'right!" 30
An' he's swap with him his tail, that Ol' Otta'
By um by he's look behin' 'im, see that tail
An' he's so scare,
He's jus' hurry tumble ova' in a wata'
To hide it that tail.

Ol' Otta' he's go down a road, kin' a chuckle, feelin' good;
It's look good, that Mus'rat tail, draggin' tha' behin'.
So he's go to that big council, jus' feelin' kin' o' proud;
But he neva' did gif back to him, his tail, that Mus'rat,
An' he's eva' since stay in a wata' Mus'rat. 40

[1924]

Coyote

Yo-ho, Little Medicine Brother in gray,
Yo-ho, I am list'ning to your call
As it comes from the edge of th' chapparral,
And I wonder, what is that you say.

Now your voice is faint, it sounds far away.
Are you telling of the coming of friends?
Or do you say that the bison-herd wends
Hitherward, is distant but a day?

Now your notes are broken, sharp, and clear,
Warning of the coming of the foe; 10
Of their warriors and their spears I must know,
And must reckon by your yelps if they're near.

When your tones quaver low like a child,
I know that gaunt famine cometh nigh;
And you shiver on your hummock closely by,
As you scent the grim, gray norther wild.

[1924]

An Indian Love Song

Light o' the lodge, how I love thee,
Light o' the lodge, how I love thee,
Mianza, my wild-wood fawn!
To wait and to watch for thy passing.
On hill-top I linger at dawn.

Glimmer of morn, how I love thee,
Glimmer of morn, how I love thee!
My flute to the ground now I fling,
As you tread the steep trail to the spring,
For thy coming has silenced my song.

Shimmer of moon on the river, 10
Sheen of soft star on the lake!
Moonlight and starlight are naught;
Their gleam and their glow is ne'er fraught
With such love-light as falls from thine eyes.

[1924]

Wyandot Names

"O-he-zhuh"! 'Ats how sed it, Wyandots;
"O-hee-oh"! 'At's how say, Frenchman;
"O-hi-o'!" At's how sed it, Long Knives;
'An' it's mean, beautiful riva'.

"To-roon-toh"! 'At's what say, ol' Wyandots;
"To-ron-toh"! 'At's what call it, French;
"To-ron-to"! 'At's what say, British;
An' it's mean, great rock standing.

"Sci-non-to"! It's that way in Wyandot;
"Sci-yun-toh"! 'At's what sed, French; 10
"Sci-o-to"! 'At's how sed Long Knives;
'An' it's mean, plenty deer.

[1924]

Huntin'

Win' it's in a south,
Kin' a cloudy in a sky,
Good time to huntin'
Spec' I go by um by.

Looks kin' a smoky
All 'roun a edge,
Spec' could fin' it, rabbit,
Down tha' 'long a hedge.

'Way down a Sycamo',
Wha' that ridge look blue, 10

You could fin' it buck o' doe,
Oh, fifty years 'go.

An' 'way cross that valley,
Wha' that timba thicken,
Early in a mornin'
Lots a pra'rie chicken.

Ova' that long ridge,
Wha' sky seem kin' a murky,
You could hear 'em callin'
Plenty big wil' turkey. 20

Duck, down on Gran' Riva'
Flyin' looks like cloud,
Sometime you could heard 'im,
He's quack plenty loud.

Sometime come wil' pige'un,
He's fly two three day,
Must a be fo' milli'un
'Fo he's all gon 'way.

Oh, lots a games them days,
You could prit' nea' grab it. 30
Now, can jus' go down a road
An' mebbe so fin' rabbit.

[1924]

Triplets

It's in Ohio, Shawnee town, all same time they born:
    Te-cum-tha, La-lee-wah-see-ka, an' littl' 'notha one.
He's die that 'notha one, jus' when he's born,
    That las' one, poo'h littl' boy.
That fatha' that motha', both Sha-wah-no-ro-noh,
    They b'long that band what come from fa' south,
Come back to ol' huntin' grounds an' they own peoples,
    Cause Injun always like do that way;
    But got none huntin' grounds, now.

Great mans them two, Te-cum-tha, La-lee-wah-see-ka, 10
    Great chief, warriors, leader of all they peoples.
That las' one, he's Shawnee Prophet,
    An' he's see what's goin' do whitemans.

Te-cum-tha he's great warrior; La-lee-wah-see-ka,
He's big leader, always think of many things;
But shucks! It's too many whitemans.
Two mouse can't eat it big cornfield,
An' it's too many whitemans, yet.

Mebbe so he's live otha' one, poo'h littl' fella',
Three of it could done mo' betta' 'an jus' two; 20
But leva, min', I guess no use, cause whitemans,
He's jus' want what Injuns got yet;
An' he ain' got it much, eitha'.

Tecumtha (ordinary English form Tecumseh) and the Shawnee Prophet, were two of triplets, the third dying at birth.

[1924]

2 **Te-cum-tha**: Tecumseh (1768–1813), the famous Shawnee leader who organized a confederacy of Indians that fought against the Americans from 1811 to 1813. 2 **La-lee-wah-see-ka**: Lalawethika, who took the name Tenskwatawa and was also known as The Prophet or The Shawnee Prophet (1775–1836), brother of Tecumseh and religious and political leader of Tecumseh's Confederacy.

Sleep It Summa' Time

Eva' sleep it out a' doors, you,
Just on the groun'? It's you' motha'.
Could look up at sky, it's kinda' blue,
Little sta's look at each otha,
And wink 'em little bit,
Ain't it?

Wonda' what made it, all them sta'?
'Spec' it's little bits of sun broke it off;
'Cause he's run fas', and he's go fa',
And 'spec' sometimes the road's mighty rough. 10
Might be that kin',
Aint it?

Sometimes little breeze, he's blow cool,
Feel good, make it f-i-n-e sleep it.
I like that kin', I don't fool;
Fella' got sof' bed could keep it.
Don't want that kin', me,
Aint it?

Them fella's bug what a singin'
Up in a tree, go siz-z-z, 20

Soun's like a nice, that ringin';
Make it good sleep; gee whizz!
I could sleep it summa' time,
Aint it?

[1924]

August

'Bout come daylight, it's sky kin' a blue,
An' all 'roun' edges, mo' blue an' smokey;
It's kin' a chilly col', and' it's shiva', you
When you jus' move 'roun' kin' a pokey.

Hills 'way off, it's look kin' a nice,
An' you jus' like to stan' an' look
Once fa' as you could, an' mebbe so, twice,
Seems jus' like picture in a book .

Only picture, it couldn' make it that good,
'Cause Great Spirit, He's make it that one; 10
You could see wha's riva', valley, an a wood,
Ova', tha' wha' he's comin' up, son.

By um by, when sun, he's get up straight,
It's a h-o-t, you don' shiva', jus' want a laid
On a nice sof' grasses down tha' by th' gate,
Unda' big black-jack trees, in a shade, 'aint it?

[1924]

"Weengk"

"Weengk," he's lit'l fella' make you sleep it,
You can't seen 'im, you eye too big.
He's hidin' eva' wha' an he's keep it
Dance all a time, what you call it,—jig.

He's carry lit'l war-club, hit 'em on head,
Eva'body, anywha', make 'em sleepy come,
You can't stayed wake'em, go jus' like dead,
An' Weengk fin' 'notha' fella', hit him some.

He's you fren', that Weengk, 'at's a fac',
Eva'body got to sleep it, now an' then; 10
But mebbe so, he's jump it on you back,
When you hunt it, an' jus' got to shoot 'gen.

It's bad lucks that one, deer run 'way,
Cause can't shoot it good if make feel lazy,
But that fella, he's come, jus' any time a day,
An' you sure want sleep it like you crazy.

Note: "Weengk" is the Odjibwa Spirit of Sleep.

[1924]

Title: Hen-toh's note explains the title. His source may be the account of "Weeng" by Henry Rowe Schoolcraft, husband of Jane Johnston Schoolcraft, whose poetry is included in this volume. Henry Schoolcraft's source was probably Jane Johnston Schoolcraft or her family.

Agency Police

I
Big-Knife

Joe Bigknife he's liv'd ova' on a Spring Riva'
He's had ferry at th' Ol' Jim Charley Ford.
Joe, he's tallest one of them Injun Police,
An' if he's sed it somethin' he's mean it eva' word,
Tho' he don' talk it all a time eitha'.

His house it's a jus' 'bout half a mile 'way
From ferry an' the ford, it's by th' hill.
If riva's up, he's at th' house, could seen it comin' team;
Comin' otha' way, they holla', an jus' wait until
Joe, he's come took 'em ova' on th' ferry. 10

It's summa' time, evenin', it's a fella' comin' south,
He's comin down to riva', stop, an' give a shout.
Joe, he's answa' from th' house, but he's kin' a slow,
Man, he's got big hurry, try th' ford, an' jus' pull out,
When Joe, he's comin' down to th' riva'.

Joe sed it: "Whiteman, you too hurry. Don' I sed it
I come all a time if you holla'? I mean it what I say."
An' he's pull it out his gun, then sed it 'notha' 'gen:
Now turn it 'roun' you wagon, you go back 'gen otha' way,
It's kin' a deep, but 'spec' you make it, anyhow. 20

"I come ova in a boat, prit' soon, an' brought you back."
'At's what he's it, Joe, an' fella' sed: "How much?"
Joe sed it: "Keep it you' money, whiteman; nex' time
Don' hollered, you don' want a me come, cause such
Kin' a way, I don't like it that kin'.

"Dam' fool, sometimes drowned you wagon, eva'thing,
Tryin' cross a riva, when it's wata' it's too deep.
Now betta' pull it out, you got so hurry.
Betta' drive it on quick, cause mebbe I can't keep
From sayin' somethin' 'fo' you go." 30

[1924]

1 **Joe Bigknife . . . Spring Riva'**: A Seneca, Bigknife was a police officer at the Quapaw Agency in Indian Territory. As the poem indicates, Bigknife also had a ferry on Spring River in the northeast of what is now Oklahoma ("Allotments of Lands" 25; Annual Report of the Commissioner 560).

Agency Police

II
High Waters

Bearskin, he's live down on Grand Riva',
Gilstrap Ferry, on ol' Military Road,
Goin' south, down to Ol' Fort Gibson.
It's been lots a rainin', 'bout one week.
Bearskin, he's in Seneca, he's tradin',
Talkin' 'bout a weather with Murdock,
Bearskin, he's sed it:
"Oh, rain just' like a hell;
Fall down jus' like pour out a bucket.
Riva' it's a high like a tree." 10

[1924]

1 **Bearskin**: a familiar name at the Quapaw Agency. 5 **Seneca**: Seneca, Missouri, just east of Indian Territory and the present Oklahoma.

Agency Police

III
Winney

It's Winney, he's one a them Injun Poleez,
Sometimes he's got kin' a braggin' way.
It's a bunch a fellas stanin' out by a trees,
An' Winney he's tole 'em one day:
"I neva' did cock it whiteman on my pistol, yet."
Notha' 'Gen.
It's issue day at Agency, an' all them fellas on hand,
Winney, jus' kin' a braggin', he's talkn' 'bout Splitlog Band:

"Y' oughta' heard it, maybe pooty moosics,
Me, I play it secon' alto, jus' easy to blow. 10

Whitetree, he's got it, that b-i-g drum,
He's hit 'im, 'bout bust 'im, it's go bum, bum, bum.
We got it lit'l book, lots a tune, Nellie Gray,
An' Red an' White an' Blue,
An' tha' Gran'fatha Clocks, he's a dandy.
Bes' one of all of it tho', le's see, it's lumba' eight,
It's a p-o-o-t-y one, you bet'cha:
Yankey Dooley; sweet as fo' honey, ain't it, Whitetree?"

Note: He intended to say, "I never did cock my pistol on a white man yet." To understand, insert pause after "on."

[1924]

Winney: possibly James Winney, who died in 1897, but probably one of his sons, Isaac, born 1854, or Thomas, born 1875 (*Indian Territory* 282, 669–70). **8 Splitlog Band**: a musical band. **13–15**: popular songs. "Nellie Gray" is an abolitionist song by Benjamin Hanby. "Red an' White an' Blue" perhaps refers to "Red, White, and Blue" from the song "Green Grow the Lilacs." "Gran'fatha Clocks" refers to "Grandfather's Clock," a once-popular song by Henry Clay Work, which gave the name to the clocks now called grandfather's clocks.

Joseph M. La Hay, Cherokee, 1865–1911

A prominent Cherokee politician and attorney, Joseph M. La Hay was born in the Choctaw Nation but attended Cherokee schools. He served in many political offices, including mayor of Claremore, senator in the Cherokee legislature, delegate to Washington, and Treasurer of the Cherokee Nation. He was a delegate to the Democratic National Convention in1896. In 1905, the year of this poem, he was an influential member of the Sequoyah Convention, which prepared a plan for the proposed state of Sequoyah. But federal officials chose to combine Oklahoma Territory and Indian Territory into one new state, Oklahoma, which modeled its constitution on the constitution proposed by the Sequoyah Convention. (*Indian Territory* 313–14; Littlefield and Parins, *Biobibliography* 241; Maxwell)

The rampant land speculation as Indian Territory moved towards statehood included speculation over Cherokee freedmen's lands—that is, the lands of former slaves owned by Cherokees and the lands of descendants of those slaves. La Hay's poem says that John H. Pitchford expected to buy the land of a freedman named Jesse Rowe, but Rowe sold his land to someone named Charles T. Boggs. Pitchford was a prominent white attorney.

Consolation

[Those who have speculated in Freedman land in the Cherokee nation will no doubt appreciate the following verses written by Joe M. LaHay of Claremore to his friend, John H. Pitchford, of Tahlequah:]

'Tis sad indeed to have a friend
  Who wants some information;
Who calls on you in time of need
  And asks your confirmation.

Dear John, I know you're very kind—
  A dispenser of human kindness,
But for the coon by the name of Rowe
  No doubt you'll lose your fondness.

The records of this district show
  That Charles T. Boggs has beat you— 10
On August fifth in nineteen four
  The records show again yer.

In the big record book number two,
  On page four thirty-seven,
'Tis very plain that Jess did wrong
  And lessened his chance for heaven.

No doubt, dear John, your heart will throb,
  And you'll think your friends are few,
To learn that Jesse sold to Boggs,
  And thus he grafted you. 20

[1905]

8 **coon**: offensive, derogatory term for an African American. 8 **Rowe**: Two Jesse Rowes were listed as Cherokee freedmen on the 1907 Dawes Roll (no. 1746, 20 years old, and no. 2021, 37 years old [United States 483–84]). Both are also listed on the 1906 Guion Miller Roll (no. 22331 and no. 22293 [Miller]).

William D. Hodjkiss, Cheyenne, born 1845?

Immediately below William D. Hodjkiss's "Song of the Storm-Swept Plain" appeared the following note: "Mr. Wm. D. Hodjkiss, a genuine Dakota of the Cheyenne River Agency, for many years a clerk at Cheyenne and Arapahoe and Quapaw Agencies, is the author of the above poem. It is based upon the fate that this winter befell a South Dakota Shepherd attending his flock in one of the terrific storms that so frequently sweep over that country unheralded." In 1897, the annual report of the federal Quapaw agent referred to Hodjkiss as "a very bright, intelligent Sioux Indian employed at this agency" (Doane 133).

Song of the Storm-Swept Plain

The wind shrills forth
From the white cold North
Where the gates of the Storm-god are;
And ragged clouds,
Like mantling shrouds,
Engulf the last, dim star.

Through naked trees,
In low coulees,
The night-voice moans and sighs;
And sings of deep, 10
Warm cradled sleep,
With wind-crooned lullabies.

He stands alone
Where the storm's weird tone
In mocking swells;
And the snow-sharp breath
Of cruel Death
The tales of its coming tells.

The frightened plaint
Of his sheep sound faint 20
Then the choking wall of white—
Then is heard no more
In the deep-toned roar,
Of the blinding, pathless night.

No light nor guide,
Save a mighty tide
Of mad fear drives him on;
'Till his cold-numbed form
Grows strangely warm;
And the strength of his limbs is gone. 30

Through storm and night
A strange, soft light
O'er the sleeping shepherd gleams;

And he hears the word
Of the Shepherd Lord,
Called out from the bourne of dreams.

Come, leave the strife
Of your weary life;
Come unto Me and rest
From the night and cold, 40
To the sheltered fold,
By the hand of love caressed.

The storm shrieks on,
But its work is done—
A soul to its God has fled;
And the wild refrain
Of the wind-swept plain,
Sings requiem for the dead.

[1913]

Arthur Caswell Parker, Seneca, 1881–1955

Arthur C. Parker was a leading anthropologist, historian, museum administrator, and political organizer. He was born and raised on the Cattaraugus Reservation in New York state. As his father's mother and his own mother were not Seneca, and Seneca are matrilineal, he was not officially Seneca, though he was raised in Seneca culture as well as in the culture of the English-speaking world. His grandfather was an influential Seneca leader who played a key role in his upbringing, and his grandfather's brother was the famous Ely Parker, the engineer who served in the Civil War with General U. S. Grant, rose to the rank of Brevet Brigadier General, and then served as Commissioner of Indian Affairs. In 1892 Parker moved with his family to White Plains, New York. He studied for three years at Dickinson Seminary (now Lycoming College) in Pennsylvania. Parker took an interest in archeological work, attracting the support of archeologists and museum administrators. In 1903 he was formally made a Seneca and inducted into a medicine society. Parker wrote extensively, publishing many books on Seneca and Iroquois history, culture, archeology, and religion. In 1911 he was one of the founders of the Society of American Indians, which he eventually served as secretary and president. From 1915-1920 he edited the SAI journal, *American Indian Magazine*. Parker was the first president of the Society for American Archeology. From 1925 until he retired in 1946, he worked as director of the Rochester Museum (later called the Rochester Museum & Science Center). As museum director, he built a large collection of Iroquois materials and was influential in the movement to support Native artists and crafts people and develop museums as centers of education for the public. In 1944, Parker was a founder of the National Congress of American Indians. (Porter)

Parker published his poems and some of his other writings under his Seneca name Gawasa Wanneh or the pseudonym Alnoba Wabunaki. (Spellings of both names varied.)

My Race Shall Live Anew

My race yet lives,—it shall not die,
It has a mission to all earth
And will the conq'ror only heed
My race shall prove its sterling worth.

Unchain the red man, make him free
To struggle and to claim his own!
The world shall find beneath his skin
Staunch human flesh, good blood and bone.

Give freedom to the red man's mind,
Provide the tools with which to hew,— 10
To carve his way as other men;
And then my race shall live anew!

[1914]

Faith

There is a faith that weakly dies
When overcast by clouds of doubt,
That like a blazing wisp of straw
A vagrant breeze will flicker out.

Be mine the faith whose living flame
Shall pierce the clouds and banish night,
Whose glow the hurricanes increase
To match the gleams of heaven's night.

[1916]

Irene C. Beaulieu, Mdwakanton Sioux, born 1881

Irene Campbell Beaulieu lived in Pawhuska, Oklahoma and coedited *Tributes to a Vanishing Race* (1916), which included "Poor Lo." She is listed on the 1934 roll of the Lower Sioux Indian Community of Minnesota. With its rough rhythms and its list of dispossessions and abuses, her poem shows how even an unpracticed writer might seek out poetry as a way to express blunt historical and political anger. Beaulieu signed the poem Wenotah, apparently her pen name.

Poor Lo

Poor Lo's sun is setting in the west,
  Where once he roamed free at his best.
The buffalo he hunted on the plain,—
  His life was intended to sustain,—
Driven are now away forever,
  By white man's avarice, as ever.

Red plumed warriors of the plain
  Ne'er sought game just for the gain.
By his need for clothes and food
  He hunted with intentions good. 10
Gone now is his hunting ground—
  *Wa-si-cun has it all around.

Corralled oft in high stockades,
  Wigwams burned, he has no aid,
For a higher government
  His lands to gather in has meant.
Sad has been his suffering,
  Death would be sweet offering.

All he held dear has been taken,
  Graves been looted then forsaken; 20
Driv'n like wild beasts o'er the land,
  Submission won by schemers bland;
Brave hearted once, now sad and sore,
  A nobly courageous people no more.

America's dealings with her wards
  Have oft been sung by many bards.
Injustice could have been averted,
  But treaties made have been diverted
With motives low, unjust, and base
  To benefit only the alien race. 30

No more the circling camp fires burn!
  No more they counsel in grave concern,
Our fathers, who fought so valiantly
  To keep their lands indefinitely.
Red sons, red daughters onward bound
  Have peace at last in Happy Hunting Ground.

**Wasicun* is *white man* in Sioux.

[1916]

Title: refers to a famous passage in Alexander Pope's *An Essay on Man* (1733–34): "Lo! the poor Indian, whose untutor'd mind / Sees God in clouds or hears him in the wind" (Epistle 1, line 99, p. 508). In response to Pope, the expression "lo" and sometimes "poor lo" became common ways of referring to Indian people in the nineteenth-century United States. **25 wards**: Indian people were often classified legally as wards of the state, allowing unscrupulous whites to be appointed as their legal guardians with control of a ward's finances, including mineral rights.

Carlos Montezuma, Yavapai, 1866?–1923

A physician, Carlos Montezuma is famous for his unusual life story and for his political activism on behalf of Indians, but he is not previously known as a poet. Most of his poems, including all his published poems, are part of his political activism.

Montezuma's name was originally Wassaja. In 1871, he was captured by Pimas who sold him to an Italian photographer named Carlos Gentile. Gentile renamed him Carlos Montezuma, took him to Chicago and New York, and eventually gave him to the care of a Baptist minister in Illinois. The precocious Montezuma then graduated from the University of Illinois with a degree in chemistry in 1884 and completed an M.D. in Chicago in 1889. He soon moved from private practice to work for the Office of Indian Affairs (the OIA, now known as the Bureau of Indian Affairs) at the Fort Stevenson Indian School in North Dakota, the Western Shoshone Agency in Nevada, and the Colville Agency in Washington state. From 1893 to 1896 he worked for the Carlisle Indian School. He then returned to private practice in Chicago. Over the years, he made a series of trips to reconnect with relatives at the Fort McDowell Reservation in Arizona. He joined with other Yavapai to resist efforts to force the Yavapai at Fort McDowell to leave their reservation. Montezuma was highly critical of the OIA and federal policy towards Indians. Together with other Indian leaders, he founded the Society of American Indians in 1911, though as the years went on Montezuma was sometimes highly critical of the SAI's moderate positions. In 1916, he formed his own journal on Indian politics, called *Wassaja*, where he scathingly criticized the OIA and the U.S. attitude and policies toward Indians. His published poems appeared in *Wassaja*. In his final illness, Montezuma returned to Fort McDowell, where he died among relatives. (Iverson)

The long lines of Montezuma's fiercely political published poetry show the influence of Walt Whitman. "An Evening's Reverie" is one of two poems as well as notes for poems, probably all earlier work, that survive in manuscript and follow a more traditional form.

An Evening's Reverie

I sit in thought at my window
And I look far over the town,
To the distant sky in the westward
Where the sun has just gone down.

I see its tinted reflections
On the clouds in the far off west,
That it left in the downward progress
As it silently sank to rest.

Though tired and weary from labor,
Yet the thoughts come flitting by 10
That resemble the brilliant reflections
That are left on the far off sky.

And like the sun before me
Who has gone his weary way,
So I leave behind in the darkness
The cares and thoughts of the day.

I turn like him in his progress
To another inviting clime,
To another field of labor
To the field of the muse and rhyme. 20

But this thought crowds upon me,
Oh! how like life is a day
With its first sweet glow of the morning,
Then it silently steals away.

The hopes, the longings, the fancies,
They come and they go so fast,
That a life's work is scarcely founded
'Til the noon of life is past.

Then help us oh! our Father
For the work that we are to do, 30
To be both earnest and faithful
To work for the good and true.

[Not previously published.]

Changing Is Not Vanishing

Who says the Indian race is vanishing?
The Indians will not vanish.
The feathers, paint and moccasin will vanish, but the Indians,—never!
Just as long as there is a drop of human blood in America, the Indians
will not vanish.
His spirit is everywhere; the American Indian will not vanish.
He has changed externally but he has not vanished.

He is an industrial and commercial man, competing with the world;
he has not vanished.
Wherever you see an Indian upholding the standard of his race, there
you see the Indian man he has not vanished.
The man part of the Indian is here, there and everywhere.
The Indian race vanishing? No, never! The race will live on and prosper
forever. 10

[1916]

Indian Office

If the Indian Office is in existence for the best interest of the Indians,
why does it not work FOR THE BEST INTEREST OF THE
INDIANS?
Is working on the Indians as Indians, FOR THE BEST INTEREST
OF THE INDIANS?
Keeping the Indians as Wards, is that FOR THE BEST INTEREST
OF THE INDIANS?
Is caging the Indians on reservations FOR THE BEST INTEREST
OF THE INDIANS?
Does opening the Indian lands for settlers work FOR THE BEST
INTEREST OF THE INDIANS?
Are the Reimbursement Funds (Government Mortgage) FOR THE
BEST INTEREST OF THE INDIANS?
Are dams built on reservations FOR THE BEST INTEREST OF THE
INDIANS?
Giving five or ten acres of irrigation land to the Indian and taking
the rest of his land away for land-grabbers, is that FOR THE
BEST INTEREST OF THE INDIANS?
Is selling the Indians' surplus (?) land FOR THE BEST INTEREST
OF THE INDIANS?
To dispose of the Indians' mineral lands, is that FOR THE BEST
INTEREST OF THE INDIANS? 10
Selling the timber land of the Indians, is that FOR THE BEST
INTEREST OF THE INDIANS?
To discriminate and keep back the Indian race from other races,
is that FOR THE BEST INTEREST OF THE INDIANS?
Are Indian schools for the papooses FOR THE BEST INTEREST
OF THE INDIANS?
Is keeping the Indians from opportunities FOR THE BEST
INTEREST OF THE INDIANS?
Is doing everything for the Indians, without their consent, FOR
THE BEST INTEREST OF THE INDIANS?

Keeping the Indians from freedom and citizenship, is that FOR THE BEST INTEREST OF THE INDIANS?
Is keeping six thousand employees in the Indian Service FOR THE BEST INTEREST OF THE INDIANS?
For you to have sole power over the Indians, is that FOR THE BEST INTEREST OF THE INDIANS?
Speak as we may, there is not one redeeming feature in the Indian Bureau FOR THE BEST INTEREST OF THE INDIANS. WASSAJA is emphatic in claiming the Indian Office has done all the harm that has come to the Indians; it is now doing great harm to the Indians, and it will suck the life-blood out of the Indians and that is not FOR THE BEST INTEREST OF THE INDIANS.

[1916]

Civilization

Savagery! Oh, say!
Indians? You say?
High up in the air you see,
Almost reach to God—civilization!

To the heathen they carried God.
They say God no fight. God is peace.
Civilization called Indians Savages;
Indians love to scalp and fight.

Talk about Indians behind trees,
They did not dig trenches and live there. 10
Indians used bows and arrows, spears and stones,
Play-toys to modern weapons for fighting brother against brother.

Now, where is the worst savagery?
Blush! No blush in civilization today.

Civilization, thou art great, thou canst raise millions to slaughter,
Tear to pieces thy brother in the air;
Blow up cargoes to feed whales and little fishes,
And if need be kill and call it square.

Civilization, thou art using God as front.
Behind, thou art playing the cunningness of human nature. 20

You furled your flag and call it patriotism.
You say that you are fighting for this and that.
You do not know what you are fighting for.
You think it is for righteousness.

In the crucible, you will find it to be greed.
Pretension is the worst kind of patriotism.

Patriotic jealousy lurks in every move you make.
It has you bound hand and foot.
In your greatness you are acting like a child,
Peevish and snarling at everybody. 30

You may talk about honor, Kings, Kaisers and Czars (as though they
were the cause of your patriotism.)
Ah! they are nothing;
It is the Almighty dollar
That is might and not right.

Age has made civilization gruesome, hard as stone.
"Business is business,"
And growlingly he says,
"What have I to do with thee?"
And hurries on to war.

Civilization! Civilization! 40
Thou has been a light on a hill,
Spreading thy rays far and wide.
God has permitted thee to reign.
What is thy stewardship?

Thy knowledge and wisdom thou hast turned into greed.
Thou wantest the land, thou wantest the sea;
Thou forgettest God, thou forgettest thy brother.
Civilization, thou hast lost thy soul,
While carrying the cross to the heathen.
The temptations to satisfy thy greed have been too great. 50
Thy greed has blinded thy vision for the right.

Your soul is stupid, goaded with greed.
You are intoxicated for more and more.
You are not fighting for righteousness,
You are fighting on high seas,
To see who can outdo trading here and there.
It is but commercialism, and nothing more.

O God of Righteousness, stay the tide
That is rushing madly into the abyss of war.
Help us to see the right. 60
O Lord God Almighty, teach us to know,
Names we may have, but we are the same.

Teach us to look up to Thee and learn of Thee
What is right, justice and peace.

[1917]

Civilization: published in Montezuma's journal *Wassaja* with "Steady, Indians, Steady" and preceded by the following "Explanation": "The Editor wishes to say that 'Steady, Indians, Steady,' and 'Civilization' in this issue are not written for the purpose of antagonizing the war sentiment, but WASSAJA sees the opportune moment to throw the same limelight that has placed the Indian before the world as cruel and savage. And to imprint on the minds of the public the real and unjust status of the Indians in the United States." The editor and WASSAJA both refer to Montezuma himself. While the explanation could be clearer and understates the intensity of the poems' attack on World War I, the gist of it is clear enough: Montezuma sees American supporters of the war as acting with a savagery that echoes but far exceeds the savagery that many Americans wrongly imagine in American Indians. The poems appeared the same month that the United States declared war on Germany. **6 God no fight**: imitating the way that non-Indians sometimes imagine Indians speak English. **9 Indians behind trees**: shooting from behind the protection of trees. **12 to modern weapons**: compared to modern weapons.

Steady, Indians, Steady!

The Ghost Craze has come and gone,
The War Craze is on.
If you want to fight—fight—
But let no one force you in.
Steady, Indians, Steady!

In the excitement of war fury,
It requires a level head
Not to get dizzy.
Steady, Indians, Steady!

This is civilization fight. 10
You are tagged that verges on "seeking for blood."
Will it pay to prove it? Then fight.
Steady, Indians, Steady!

"Fight for your country and flag" is noble and grand,
But have you a country? Is that your flag?
With a sober mind, think on it, and do the right.
Steady, Indians, Steady!

Pause, with calm mind, think on it.
But let no one push you in it.
If you do not know what you are fighting for, stay at home. 20
Steady, Indians, Steady!

They have taken your country,
They have taken your manhood,

They have imprisoned you,
They have made you wards,
They have stunted your faculties.
  Steady, Indians, Steady!

You are not entitled to the rights of man,
You are not an American citizen—
You are an Indian; 30
You are nothing and that is all.
  Steady, Indians, Steady!

Redskins, *true Americans*, you have a fight with those whom
    you wish to fight for,
It is your birthright—*Freedom*;
Let them make good;
With better heart you will fight,
Side by side under the same flag.
  Steady, Indians, Steady!

[1917]

1 **Ghost Craze**: probably the Ghost Dance, a religious movement among Indians in the American west in 1889-90.

I Have Stood Up for You

Being of your blood,
Through thick and thin,
    I have stood up for you.
When the world's most devilish
Intrigue of humanity was set
And was coiling around you tighter and tighter—
    I have stood up for you.
When public sentiment was against you
And sent you to oblivion,
    I have stood up for you. 10
When the country was hysterically enraged
For defending your loved ones
And your birthright of priority—
    I have stood up for you.
When you were tagged as "Indians"
And outlawed creatures—
    I have stood up for you.
Haunted and hunted on thy domain,
With no chance of redress

But doomed, as though thy fate— 20
    I have stood up for you.
When you were described and pictured
And cartooned as cruel and savage—
    I have stood up for you.
When prejudice, hate and scorn
Sounded the keynote against you—
    I have stood up for you.
When starving and naked,
At the verge of your annihilation
By swords in the hands of criminals— 30
    I have stood up for you.
When the palefaces said
There was no hope for you—
    I have stood up for you.
When you were condemned and relegated
To the reservation system of hell—
    I have stood up for you.
When in prison and in bondage,
When you could neither speak nor see—
    I have stood up for you. 40
When decreed by the people across the sea
That you could neither learn nor be taught,
    I have stood up for you.
When it was put down black and white
That you could neither work nor support yourselves,
And that you were lazy and worthless—
    I have stood up for you.
When politics and greed were working you
For all that you were worth—
    I have stood up for you. 50
When everything you possessed was disappearing,
And your personal rights ignored—
    I have stood up for you.
As the Indian Bureau, like an octopus,
Sucked your very life blood,
    I have stood up for you.
For your freedom and citizenship,
By the abolishment of the Indian Bureau,
    I have stood up for you.
When the Indian Bureau says "Were you freed 60
You would starve and be cheated"—
Only to feed its 7000 employees—
    I have stood up for you.

When you were judged "incompetent"
For freedom and citizenship by the Indian Bureau—
  I have stood up for you.
God knows that I am with thee day and night;
That is why I have stood up for you.
It might have been self-sacrifice.
It might have been the hand of God leading me. 70
Whatever it was, you have proven yourselves to be
What I have stood up for you to be.

[1919]

William J. Kershaw, Menominee, 1865–1956

William J. Kershaw taught himself law and passed the bar at the age of 20. He attended St. Lawrence College and St. Francis Seminary. A prominent Milwaukee attorney, he was a First Vice-President of the Society of American Indians. His mother was Menominee, and he was formally adopted by the Menominee tribe in 1912. A Democrat, he ran for Congress unsuccessfully in 1916 and was appointed an Assistant Attorney General of Wisconsin in 1933. Though published fourteen years apart, both of Kershaw's poems included here address the land as a mother. According to *American Indian Magazine*, published by the Society of American Indians, "'The Indian's Salute to His Country' was memorized and recited by thousands of school children on American Indian Day. Yet Mr. Kershaw modestly writes us, 'It is not a poem—. Why can we not produce a real poet?'" ("News Notes" 184). (Gridley; Usher 1313–15)

The Indian's Salute to His Country

All hail to thee, Columbia,
  Dear motherland of mine!
In forests, mountain, stream, and vale
  What majesty is thine!
And we, thy children, love thee so,
  Sweet motherland of mine.

From out thy generous bosom flows
  Fair motherland of mine,
Our sustenance and happiness,
  Like ever-living wine; 10
And all we have we owe to thee,
  Kind motherland of mine.

The white man and the red man,
Brave motherland of mine,
Alike thy royal offspring are,
Like rooted oak and pine,
And firmly do they stand for thee,
Staunch motherland of mine.

What though the Indian life be gone,
Good motherland of mine? 20
Each hill and stream remains for aye
An ever holy shrine,
Where he met face to face his God,
Proud motherland of mine.

He was thy primal offspring,
Oh, motherland of mine;
And thou cans't ne'er deny thy seed,
This Indian child of thine,
While he is groping toward the goal
Old motherland of mine. 30

[1915]

Joseph Fights No More

We have fought our last fight, my brave hearted warriors,
The land we defended is ours no more,
To a stranger we yield the home of our sires,
And our vanished hopes like a dream that is o'er.
No more shall we thrill to the passion of combat,
Nor plunge to its shock on the mountain or plain,
Unconquered, but broken, our war chant is silent,
And we swear by the sun to ne'er sing it again.
Then guard Thee, Great Spirit, this land of our fathers,
Who died as they wished to die, fighting to hold, 10
This mother of Red Men against all the others,
Who plundered her bosom of silver and gold.
Her mountains look down on her valleys still smiling,
Her streams rolling on, laugh their way to the sea,
We ask Thee, Great Spirit, to keep her and bless her,
And make her forever the home of the free.

[1929]

Title: Nez Perce Chief Joseph (1840–1904) won fame for his skilled resistance to the U.S. army before surrendering in 1877.

Thomas Dewey Slinker, Choctaw, born 1898

Thomas Dewey Slinker was born in the Choctaw Nation. The editor's note introducing his only surviving poem says that it "has been received from Thomas D. Slinker, Company D, 28th Infantry, a Carlisle boy now serving in France with the American Expeditionary Forces," the forces that fought in World War I.

Our Side of It

We're not ashamed of the uniform,
  And if you are a friend
You will never say a word against it—
  Any word that will offend.
It has covered honored bodies,
  And by heroes has been worn
Since the days of the Republic
  When the Stars and Stripes were born.

Uniforms have many patterns,
  Some are khaki, some are blue, 10
And the men who choose to wear them
  Are of many patterns, too.
Some are sons of wealthy parents,
  Some are college graduates,
Some have many manly virtues,
  Some are simply reprobates.

We have many skilled mechanics,
  Men of brains and letters, who
Loyally have served their country
  That they are a credit to. 20
No, indeed, all are not angels—
  Blackguards, yes, we've some of those,
But when they came into the service
  They all wore civilian clothes.

If you meet us out in public,
  On the street or anywhere,
We don't merit sneering glances
  Nor a patronizing stare;
For we have an honored calling,
  As our garments plainly show. 30
You may be a thief, or parson—
  How on earth are we to know?

I don't care for your profession,
  Occupation, what you do.
When you are looking at a soldier
  And he is looking back at you,
Who is there to judge between you
  As you stand there man to man?
Only one, the Great Almighty.
  Name another, if you can. 40
Drop your proud and haughty bearing
  And your egotistic pride.
Get acquainted with the soldier
  And the heart and soul inside.
Test and try to analyze him,
  Criticize him through and through,
And you'll very likely find him
  Just as good a man as you.

[1918]

17 **mechanics:** skilled laborers, an older sense of the term.

James E. Waters/Wild Pigeon, Montaukett and Matinnecock, born about 1876, died 1927

A controversial figure who worked for the Post Office in Manhattan, James E. Waters was elected to the Montauk (Montaukett) Tribal Council in 1914. In a disputed election, he was chosen as chief in 1919. He led efforts to write a constitution, organize annual meetings, and prepare a tribal roll, working to include Montauketts who lived away from the traditional Montaukett lands at the eastern tip of Long Island. He lobbied strenuously for the recovery of Montaukett lands, recruiting the Dakota physician and writer Charles Eastman to represent the Montauketts in Washington, D.C. He also supported the Society of American Indians. After his efforts to recover tribal lands failed, he was defeated in the Montauk election for chief of 1923, and he sued in response. Waters—also known as Wild Pigeon—lived in Little Neck where, in his last years, as a Matinnecock chief he opposed a project to widen a road at the site of a Matinnecock cemetery. (He saw the Mattinecocks as descendants of the Narragansetts, so that some sources list him as a Narragansett chief. His *New York Times* obituary says that he was also a Shinnecock chief. The Mattinecocks, Shinnecocks, and Montauketts all live on Long Island.) ("Chief Wild Pigeon Dead," Strong)

The poems here were published in the 1919 "Report of the Annual Meeting of the Montauk Tribe of Indians." The text comes from a 1993 reprint of the 1919 report.

Montauk

The wooded hills no longer hear
The warrior's tread, the flight of deer,
Gone are the warriors, true and old,
Of kingly mien, yet fierce and bold.
Old Ocean surges on thy breast,
Lo! all these years without a rest.
Midst all the changes, waste, decay,
Custodian Thou, of Ancient Days.

The bird's sweet song, that once did fill,
The wooded heights is hushed and still. 10
Old Ocean with its ceaseless roar
Can never, never days restore.
And ling'ring by the pond or streams
Can only bring life hazy dreams,
Sweet mem'ries, deeds of men and tales,
Ere Pauguk clasped them on life's trails.

Gone are the days, and things of old,
Bro't to an end, as tales once told.
Still o'er old Ocean's fitful mood
The sea bird seeks the same for food. 20
The woods remain, still zephyrs sigh,
The fleecy clouds float in the sky,
The waters blue, thy mighty cliffs remain,
Still sinks the sun, a jewel flame.

Gone are the days, and things of old,
Dear to our life, as precious bits of gold.
As Thou, old Ocean, did forever keep
Guard o'er our warriors, as they softly sleep.
May Montauk's children, scattered tho' they be
Learn from thy lesson, ever changeless sea 30
The watch to keep, and bound in heart and hand
While life blood flows, to love their Native Land.

[1919]

16 **Pauguk**: a terrifying, skeletal death spirit. 29 **Montauk's children, scattered tho' they be**: These words address Waters' concern to include the Montauk diaspora in tribal membership and activities.

King Philip (Pometacom)

The Patrick Henry of his times,
The cruel chance of war, to try

The world-wide cry, of patriots all,
In Freedom's cause to live or die.
Around the many Council fires,
He called his warriors by their name,
He sought them on his native hills
And cried and sought, but sought in vain.
Their blood called out on every side,
He heard their whispers on his trails, 10
From grim old Pauguk, oft had come
Thro' leafy woods and flowery dales.
Their spirits called thro' forest haunts,
The whisp'ring winds so soft and mild
Bro't messages from spirit land
And sang the death chants, weird and wild.
Torn from his hands, the kingly want
By weakling once, now strong for fight,
Which mighty souled, Great Massasoit,
Had kindly nourished into life. 20
His blow was struck for Freedom's cause,
And Freedom ever it must be.
For Patriots all, this Truth will tell
There is no life, save "It is Free."

[1919]

Title: Pometacom (c. 1639–1676), often shortened to Metacom and known in English as King Philip, (c. 1639–1676) was the Wampanoag sachem during the so-called King Philip's War in 1675–1676. His forces were defeated by British colonists and their Indian allies. **1–4 Patrick Henry . . . live or die**: Henry (1737–1799), radical Virginia patriot in the American Revolution, famous for the words attributed to him urging the Virginia legislature to commit troops to defend Virginia from the British: "Give me liberty, or give me death!" **11 Pauguk**: a terrifying, skeletal death spirit. **19 Massasoit**: (c. 1581–1661), father of Metacom.

The First American Alliance

The tom-a-hawk of the great prince of the Pequots, fierce Sassacus, was against every hut and wigwam. He had never been known to bury the hatchet until now, in 1636, he sought alliance with the Narragansetts in order to wipe out the Europeans. The aborigines had a custom of burning the underbrush and clearing away the saplings of the forests, which hindered the red deer from roaming.

Scorch, we now K'har-we* mine
The tangled underbrush of years,
Apply the torch, ye hunters brave
And call again the bounding deer.

No deer can roam or freely sport,
Within this net-work of the wood,
"Come, clear away the underbrush,
And do it for the Nation's good."

Thus spake the Philip, Indian brave,
Before the pale face feet had trod 10
His native hills, his native land,
The kingly gift of the Red Man's God.

Scorch, we now, K'har-we mine
The pale face sapling that has come
To take our royal hunting-ground
And drive us from our forest home.
Thick as the underbrush that keeps,
The bounding deer from roaming free,
The pale face, like the kingly oak
"Will root themselves from sea to sea." 20

Thus, fiercely spake the Pequot brave,
Like deep that calleth unto deep
The call of blood in the Red Man's veins
A call that made the life-blood leap,
And Sassacus, with Philip bold
Had pledged his soul and heart and hand,
As free men, God had made them so,
As free men, thus to hold the land.

***K'har-we: Indian word for brother.**

[1919]

Sassacus: Pequot sachem (c. 1560–1637) during the so-called Pequot War of 1636–1637, when British colonists massacred large numbers of Pequots in southern New England and sold many survivors into slavery. The British destroyed the Pequots as a major political force in the region until the Pequot revival in the late twentieth century. Because the Narragansetts allied with the British, it is not clear what alliance Waters refers to. In no sense could it have been the first alliance among Indian peoples, though it would have been among the early alliances of Indian peoples against the British colonists. **9 Philip**: possibly King Philip (Metacom), though the history seems garbled, as Philip was born after Sassacus died. **22 deep that calleth unto deep**: echoing Psalm 42.7, "Deep calleth unto deep at the noise of thy waterspouts."

Wanda Short

While the editor has found no information about Wanda Short, the publication of "On Straight to Freedom" in Carlos Montezuma's journal, together with the poem's first-person references to Indian people, indicate that Short likely was Indian.

On Straight to Freedom

On to freedom my dear brothers,
 Freedom in your native land—
Let us stand and fight for freedom—
 And let us conquer e'er we drop it
This great fight for the red man.
 Let us see that we're victorious
For the freedom of our land,
 For our fathers here before us,
Free men in our native land,
 We're a mighty race of people 10
Owning every foot on which we stand.
 On to freedom, oh my brothers,
This was once our fathers' land—
 Let us fight till we have conquered
Freedom for the Indian man;
 Let us work and let us struggle
Till we win throughout the land,
 All that we have asked is freedom
And equal rights on which to stand—
 Freedom in a free man's land, 20
Absolutely free from the Cato gang.
Let us struggle on, my brothers,
 We know this fight is justified,
Let us think of our own fathers,
 How they fought and bled and died,
Fighting for their native country,
 And the honor of their tribe,
And we know the cause was just
 For they fought and bled for us,
Then let us see what we are doing 30
 All they'd expect of us to do,
And keep up the shout of freedom,
 Till we are rid of that Bureau crew.
Let us uphold our native rights,
 On the highways and in the dells,

And use our wits to "bust" the office
Of that great "joker," Cato Sells.
Let us go right on, my brothers,
We can win our battle now,
If we but "pull" together, 40
Now is the time to "push" the plow.
We should be free in our own country
And not held by any plan.
Our walks of life should be our own—
Not handed out by a Bureau gang.
This is but a struggle, brothers,
For our rights as men on earth,
We're only asking for our freedom,
In this great country of our birth.
Let us see that we are doing 50
Everything that we can do
To put to rout that greedy crowd,
Rightly named the Bureau crew.
Cato Sells, the prince of masters,
In his so-called human scheme,
Tells the public how he loves us—
Just another "heap pipe dream."
Let us win our battle, brothers,
With the power we have in hand,
Rid the country now and ever 60
Of that accursed Bureau gang;
Now, Mr. Cato don't you think,
Your Indian schemes are on the brink
Of utter ruin and fast decay,
When Indian freedom wins the day?
It will win, you bet.

[1920]

21 Cato: Cato Sells, Commissioner of Indian Affairs, 1913–1921. **33 Bureau:** Office of Indian Affairs, often called—and later renamed—the Bureau of Indian Affairs.

Sunhair

Sunhair published several poems in the Minnesota Chippewa journal *Tomahawk*. It is possible that Sunhair was white. While a manuscript poem by Sunhair in *The Papers of Carlos Montezuma* implies that Sunhair was white ("My presence, it seemed as I entered in / Was one more trespass—the white man's sin"; reel 9), those lines may refer to a mixed-race heritage, for Sunhair's other poems speak of being Indian in the first person. It is also possible that one or the other perspective is a poetic effort to see from the perspective of other people's eyes. Given the multiple poems that speak in an Indian voice, their appearance in *Tomahawk*, and the presence of a manuscript in Montezuma's papers, it seems reasonable to suppose, however tentatively, that Sunhair was probably Indian.

One Spirit—One Race

We see in that great disk, the sun,
An emblem of the Mighty One.
His shining face in light arrayed
Will cast all shadows from the page
Of this fair form of His.
Let not any single band
Claim the light in this great land.
But Brothers,—one in hope we stand,—
One in race,—the Indian.
We stand as one without a fear, 10
Those of tribes both far and near:
The Osage and the Pottawatamie,
Winnebago and Pawnee,
The Chippewa and mighty Sioux,
The Ottawa and Blackfeet, too.
Different tribes, but Brothers one,
All descendants from the sun,
Whose symbol sheds His Light on all,—
All we stand, or all we fall.

[1920]

A Song of Hope

The gates of day are open, a herald to the night
Proclaims Wakonda spoken to His children of the light.
We waited long in sorrow, our council fires were low,
But a ray of hope He sends us to make the embers glow.
Oh keep the fires burning, while the Spirit we invoke,—
To cleanse us all from hatred, His messenger has spoke.

Our hopes were swiftly dying, and the night was coming on.
We dared not hope for morning and the rising of the sun;
But Wakonda ever watchful, bent His ear to hear our cry,
And he whispered, 'Children, patience, the Spirit broodeth nigh' 10

And out we sent our runners swift as the waters flow,—
Wakonda, Oh Wakonda, has heard His children's woe!

As the sun is to the darkness, His messenger has come
To lift our heavy burdens, and hearten hopeless men.
Oh lift your weary heads high to greet the morning star!
Our race is not a dying race, but a mighty one in power;
So make our people ready, the hour is drawing near.
Wakonda, Tierowa has heard His children's prayer.

[1920]

2 **Wakonda:** Omaha for the creator, Great Spirit. 18 **Tierowa:** perhaps an attempt to transcribe Tirawa, the Pawnee equivalent of Wakonda, personified as the blue vault of the heavens (DeMallie).

Our Contributor, Anishinaabe?

This anonymous poem, presumably by an Anishinaabe, appeared in the *Tomahawk*, a Minnesota Chippewa (Anishinaabe) newspaper from the White Earth Reservation, under the headline "**Tries Her Hand at Poetry.** Our contributor tries her hand at rhyme this time." The poem dramatizes the sense of excitement and controversy that sometimes surrounded the Society of American Indians.

The Ne'er Digressing Quartette

Ever since the S.A.I.
Had its birth in 1911
There have been four Indian men
Who have traveled the same road, even when others turned aside for
their own glory and forgot their tribesmen's pitiful story.
Caring not the hatred they incurred,
Or the sometimes untruthful word;
Caring not, and fearing not
To send the Commissioner and his gang a fatal shot when they
digressed.
Sometimes, true, they may have been mad at each other: 10
But not once did they forget to work for their brother.
Why, this Omaha, Apache, Snohomish and Chippewa, are the
grandest men you ever saw!
Never throwing up the white flag,
Never letting their interest lag,
Never forgetting that Freedom and Justice we want,—
Even when the Commissioner says we "cawn't."

And you must all be sure to remember
That you can meet this quartette
At the conference in November.

[1920]

1 **S.A.I.**: Society of American Indians. 9 **Commissioner**: of the Office of Indian Affairs. 12 **this Omaha, Apache, Snohomish and Chippewa**: probably Thomas L. Sloan, Omaha; Carlos Montezuma, Yavapai though often thought to be Apache; Thomas Bishop, Snohomish; and perhaps Theodore E. Beaulieu, Chippewa (Anishinaabe), founder of the *Tomahawk,* which published this poem (Littlefield and Parins, *Biobibliography* 211).

Leta V. Meyers Smart, Omaha

Born in Missouri, Leta V. Meyers (sometimes spelled Myers) Smart was a student at Hampton Institute in Virginia, an historically African American school that concentrated, for almost fifty years, on educating American Indians as well as African Americans. In 1915, Meyers (who took the name Smart after marriage) began teaching at Zuni Boarding School in New Mexico, under the Office of Indian Affairs, which she criticizes in her poems. Later, she lived in Washington, D.C., and in California, where she was active in Indian political organizations, including work as one of the organizers of the Los Angeles branch of the National Congress of American Indians. (Littlefield and Parins, *Biobibliography* 294; Lindsey 204; Philp 106)

W-H-O?

Who will be the new Commissioner,
  Who, who, who?
And will he be a true Commissioner,
A wise Commissioner and a prize Commissioner,
  Who, who, who?

Who will be the Assistant man,
  Who, who, who?
And will he be a persistent man,
An Arkansas man or a "Saw-an-ark" man,
  Who, who, who? 10
And what will these two men both do,
  Do, do, do?
Will they play the same game,—
Try to make the Indian cause lame?
  Boo hoo hoo!

[1921]

"W-h-o" was published anonymously, but Meyers can be identified as its author because she sent a copy of the typescript to Carlos Montezuma, inscribing it "With the com *plea'* ments of the author—" (Meyers, Letter). 1 **Commissioner**: Commissioner of Indian Affairs. Cato Sells was Commissioner in 1913–1921 and Charles H. Burke in 1921–1929.

On a Nickel

The other day as I stood
Waiting at the telephone
For my number
With my nickel in my hand,
And toying with it,
I noticed for the first time
That directly in front
Of the Indian face
Was imprinted in small letters
The word "Liberty". 10
Liberty,—
And the Indian
Was looking toward it,
With hopeful expression me thought
Upon his face.
Liberty,—
And the Indian
Has not known it
Since he became a ward,
A subject 20
Or a prisoner of war
Of the Government,—
Or a supposed part of it,—
The Indian Bureau.
Liberty,—
And the Indian
Must have it.
It is his God right,
And he will have it!

[1921]

Title: The profile of an Indian man with the word "liberty" next to his brow appeared on one side of the Indian head nickel, 1913–1938. On the other side was a bison. 24 **Indian Bureau**: Office of Indian Affairs.

A Picture

In a certain Indian room I know
There is a picture of a
Picturesque Indian man
With his long bobbed hair,
His dark skin and eyes,
And turban of a coiled bandanna.
A half profile the picture is
Which shows the strength in his jaw,
The wisdom in his brow,
And gentleness in his mouth. 10
But in the eyes of the man
There is something so sad and pathetic
Which he tries to smile away,—
Just as though he had been struck
But was holding out the other Cheek,
And smiling to make you give him
A caress instead of a blow.
And the more I gazed upon it,
The more I thought
That here was also a picture 20
Of the Indian race
And its wonderful spirit.
For though we have been struck in the face,
And it has been painful
And hard to bear,
We are ready to forgive;
And if need be,
To hold out the other cheek,—
But for your caress.

[1921]

A Young Man's Adventure with Opportunity

In writing the following the author had in mind a certain young Indian man from the Bad (River) Reservation, the name of which place she doesn't think is the least bit misapplied and, where the situation is the best example she knows of what there OUGHT NOT TO BE.

One day not long ago a young Indian man
Jumped down from the fence where he had been sitting
With a lot of his fellows
  Who, like himself, had been waiting

For the evening train to come in,—
(Most important event of the day),
For sometimes, and indeed quite often,
It meant the coming of moonshine and "good" time;
Sometimes, however, just the coming of gossip,—
As had been their wont to spend their evenings 10
In no more meaningful way
Than this worse than idle habit of theirs!
But this one young man on this particular evening
Got tired of it all and walked away.
Alone he went, with his hands in his pockets,
Walking slowly and meditating,
In the direction of the setting sun.
Until he finally found himself
Quite some distance from the Indian village.
As he continued on his way he approached a lowland, 20
On the other side of which rose a hill, high and stately,
That the sun was setting behind.
Bright and beautiful lights were all around its summit,
And in the sky there was more glory!
The young man looked up, beheld, and enjoyed it,
But wondered a moment at the figure he saw against the skyline.
A stranger, it seemed, not known in these parts.
Like one from afar returning home after long absence,
And resting himself on his journey and viewing again some old
familiar spots,
And wondering if there wasn't someone he could meet e're
he went on his way again. 30
Finally the young man, in a voice full of courage and friendship,
Called, "Ho! there, my friend!"
And "Ho!" came back again, and more, if it pleases you to know;
"Come on up, young man.
I am surprised you do not know me,
For I am Opportunity;
With other names applied, of course, such as:
'Death to the Indians,' or,
'Reason for Putting the Indian Office Out,'—
But meaning more, I take it, of the latter than the former. 40
But come up, just the same;
I would like to meet you.
Surely you must have heard of me, though perhaps it was long ago,
In your grandfather's time, and before you were

Placed on your prairie reservation."
And the young Indian man DID remember that long ago he HAD
heard
His grandfather speak of Opportunity,
Who was so willing to come and be a friend for half a chance.
So he started up to meet him.
When lo! as if from the underworld there suddenly sprang a fence, 50
So high and unsurmountable,
That the young Indian man was dazed and awe-struck!
But the cheery voice of Opportunity still rang in his ears.
And when his amazement had left him he started to climb one of the
posts of this dreadful fence,
But lo! again—it became alive,
With hands stretched out defiantly,
And a voice that fairly screamed:
"Go back, young Indian, to your prairie reservation.
I am the Commissioner, and I am paid to keep you fastened to your
reservation.
Go back, I say, and stay there!" 60
But the young Indian man, still wanting to meet Opportunity,
Ran on to the next post that he would have climbed had not the
same thing happened, only in a smaller way,
And a voice that whined and hypnotised, like a sickly woman's
Bound to make you do her bidding,
And with hands just as defiant and eager to stay his ascent (some
think more so):
"I am the Assistant Commissioner, and I, too,
Must make believe that you are no good,
Or worthy enough to meet so great a personage as Opportunity.
You will have to go back!"
And all the other posts that made up the fence repeated the cry: 70
"Go back to your reservation!"
The outside world is much too big and far too fine for you!
For the debt we owed your people we have LET YOU HAVE (not
GIVEN),
Your prairie reservation!
And although we bargained for your full dress suit we gave you back
for it
Merely the price of a pair of sheepskin moccasins."
And the poor young Indian, only one voice against so many,
Fell back into the darkness,
With an ache in his throbbing bosom.

And a sigh in his stifled cry 80
All on account of this terrible fence
That must have sprung from hell!

[1922]

39 Indian Office: Office of Indian Affairs. **59 Commissioner:** of Indian Affairs. **75 we gave you:** editorial emendation of *we you.*

Wa Wa Chaw, Payomkowishum, Luiseño, 1888–1972

Wa Wa Chaw is a mysterious and mostly unknown story. The main source of information about her life, *Spirit Woman: The Diaries and Paintings of Bonita Wa Wa Calachaw Nuñez* (1980), edited by Stan Steiner, does not provide her story in a clear or fulsome way. Most of its few details cannot be corroborated. According to Steiner, Wa Wa Chaw was born in 1888 in southern California. She was probably Payomkowishum, born at Valley Center in the Rincon band of Luiseño Indians. The Payomkowishum or Luiseño are the Indians whom Spanish colonizers forced to work for the San Luis Rey Mission, beginning in 1798. Wa Wa Chaw believed that she was stolen or sold to the woman who adopted and raised her, Mary Duggan, a wealthy white New Yorker. Duggan dressed her adopted child in buckskin and beads and raised her in upper crust New York City. From a young age, Wa Wa Chaw loved to draw and paint. Duggan saw the girl as an artistic prodigy and provided her private tutors instead of sending her to school. Duggan's brother, Dr. Cornelius Duggan, supposedly used her anatomical, laboratory drawings for his medical research and his research on radium and radioactivity. At some point, through what was apparently a brief and unhappy marriage, she took the name Benita Wa Wa Calachaw Nuñez, but the name that appeared with her published poems (possibly before her marriage) is Wa Wa Chaw (or sometimes Wa-Wa Chaw). For awhile she sold "Indian Liniment" made with "Secret Herbs." Later, she made her living selling her paintings at outdoor art shows in Greenwich Village. She spent her last years as a recluse, living in East Harlem on welfare.

In many ways, Wa Wa Chaw is unrepresentative of other Indians and other Indian writers. She was never able to recover her lost tribal or family connections. On the other hand, while Wa Wa Chaw remains an idiosyncratic personality, many Indian children have been adopted out of their families and communities. She spent her life identifying as and being identified as an Indian. She published in Indian journals and saw herself as a lifelong activist for Indian causes. Apart from her personal idiosyncrasy, her story includes echoes of the story of a more famous adoptee, her friend Carlos Montezuma, whose poetry also appears in this volume. Wa Wa Chaw's diaries and her poem about Montezuma, "My Psyche and Wassaja," included in this volume, indicate that she saw the similarity.

Wa Wa Chaw's poems can be difficult to follow because of the combination of personal idiosyncrasy with what sometimes appears to be a desire to write in a dialect or rough English that she apparently associates, in a clichéd way, with Indian speakers. While the poems she published can be dated, the posthumously published poems in

Spirit Woman come without dates of composition. The decision to include some of them in this volume of poems from 1930 and before depends on the editor's uncertain sense that they probably were written during those years. (Nuñez; Fitzgerald)

The Trial of the Mission Indian

It was many years ago when this great story was told,
　　And the Spaniards were seeking gold;
The story was repeated by father, when I was a
　　Papoose, a few years old—
Father saw that the blood in his veins was flowing cold,
When the trial of the Mission Indian was being told,
　　And the fearless Spaniards were seeking for gold.

The Mission Indians were not for war
　　Therefore the hunt of gold never bore
The hole within the Mission soul, 10
　　But Mission Indians were forced to hunt for gold,
That the Spaniards brought forth so bold,
　　To force the Mission Indian to find the hidden gold;
And the Mission Indians were forced to leave,
　　And try to live on the food weed.

It was the trial of the Mission Indian,
　　When the seed of acorn was dry,
Indian made cakes to help the need,
　　The acorn being the only seed;
So bread was made to help give strength 20
　　And there was joy to help him see
When Indians found help from the acorn seed.

The cloud was gathering in yonder land,
　　All Indians knew they would be moved from said mast of land,
And they knew it was their trial when
　　Indian would be driven for many more miles.
The clouds grew dark and the clouds were like while dog's bark,
　　For the Missions knew it was a cry in the dark.

The cloud had broken, and the travel had begun—
　　They found they were off again, 30
Walking miles and miles on no man's land,
　　But were forced to stand!
The trial of the Mission Indian had begun.
　　Squaws and papoose were not able to move very far—
One little Indian Cry: And they saw Him,
　　Big Eastern Star;

And in one breath all Indians came
From near and far!

They see and hear great truth of the Eastern Star;
Great cries of the Chief's were heard 40
And their cattle seemed to understand their words;
It was the trial of the Mission Indian.
For good message from Him, great bird brought news
That the Spaniards had lost,
And Washington was the boss!

The star was good news, and the trials were through;
Washington builded Indian schools,
And the Indian take the great rule,
To read and write,
For Indian has good sight. 50

Mission Indian gather round and thank Him Spirit for school ground,
Where many Mission Indians can be found,
On Washington, Sherman school ground.
As much to tell, how the Indian fell,
And got up to tell how Indian fought and fell
To win him help that would stop his trial,
From trying to walk so many miles!

[1922]

Title: appears to refer not to a court trial but rather to *trial* in the more general sense of *ordeal*. Mission Indians were Indians at the Franciscan missions in California. Beginning in 1769, the Spanish colonizers brought them Christianity and forced them to work as virtual slaves under wretched conditions. From 1834 to 1838, when California was part of Mexico, the Mexican government confiscated and sold the missions, which may contribute to what the poem refers to when it describes the mission Indians as forcibly "moved," though the larger context refers to events later in the nineteenth century. As huge numbers of Americans came to California in the Gold Rush and California became part of the United States, American treatment of California Indians was notoriously brutal, not matching the poem's sometimes idealized picture of the United States. Indeed, in the late nineteenth century, Mission Indians were forcibly evicted ("moved") from their remaining lands. 27 **while**: perhaps a typo for *white*. 45 **Washington**: the United States. 53 **Sherman**: Sherman Institute, a federal boarding school for Indians in Riverside, California.

The Indian Cry

To the Great Spirit Indian sigh
With his head lifted toward the sky.
Indian thinking it will come by and by,
Great Spirit, why let me cry?

Indian think white bird great,
    Greeted him welcome at his gate;
White bird opened Indian gate.

Indian think white bird love,
    Great Spirit sent him from above.
White bird take Indian for Hate; 10
    White bird stamp on Indian gate.
White bird take Indian mind;
    Indian think too late.
When white bird gives Indian bead
    Indian think that he's in need.

When white bird discovers the seed
    Indian know no spirit on land;
Indian shake the white bird hand.
    White bird thinks of Indian land,
Indian take white bird to his teepee; 20
    White bird see squaw is free,
White bird see papoose at liberty.

White bird thinks it is great
    To be inside of the Indian gate.
I will call the chiefs to come
    To discuss their income.
We will have a little sweets
    That will make them use their feet,
And lose their heads with sweets;
    And by the land in which they have 30
White bird think Indian forget.

Indian no forget.
    Indian think we will get there yet
Although it is wet;
    Indian no forget.
White bird send Indian to school;
    Indian no fool.
White bird takes Indian.

Indian take white bird.
    White bird says you will come, 40
White bird says you will help to beat the hun.
    Indian goes to beat the war drum;
Indian walk upon the hun.

Fearless Indian stood and cried,
    White bird, White bird, we're at your side.

You are called the white Americans,
We are the red Americans;
We will be there when you cry
Just to make the hun die.
It is great when you think we are in the Indian gate. 50

Friendly Spirit,
Wa Wa Chaw

[1922]

27 **sweets:** possibly referring to alcohol that whites used to entice Indians into signing treaties that gave up Indian lands. 30 **by the land in which they have:** possibly a garbled passage meant to suggest buying or selling. 41 **hun:** Germany. Many Indians fought with the American troops in World War I.

The Indians' Spirits

Down in the deep my spirit will creep
Out of the window into the air
No one knows where.
Deathless and lifeless, sleepless of fears
Indians will keep their spirits near—
Creeping about in the open air
No one knows where.

Down in the deep my spirit will creep,
Fearless of sorrow and fearless of time,
Indian will seek a spirit to help his creed. 10
Out of the window into the air
No one knows where.
Indian spirit shall share
Deathless and lifeless, sleepless of fear
The noise of my spirit shall speak very clear.

Out of the windows into the air
No one knows where
When far into the darkened night a change in the air
The Indian spirit shall creep out of no where.

[1922]

The Indian Game

Bronze-yellowish Red Indian
The game of human likes are the same
The only difference is the Indian name
The tireless Indian umpire are always the same
The Indian Headmen and Chieftains control the game.

The Indian chiefs dare not limp,
For the Pale-face will take a glimpses.
Into the game that help him Indian to his feet
To learn to walk down the city streets.
Heap-Big-Hearts gave him Indian big treats. 10

Big-heap-heart has Pale-face chief,
The Indian game is without grief.
Heap-chiefs share the Pale-face leaf,
Friendship is the guiding game.
Indian love spirit likes are the same.
The only difference is the Indian name.

Buffaloes has left the pastures.
The eagles are without a nest.
The human Buffalo knows the Indian rest,
Chief-Buffalo-Heart knows what game is best. 20
The Indian Game.

[1922]

13 **leaf**: money.

Haunted Brains

Far into the stillness of the night,
Creeps the unknown life—Haunted Brains
Indians, No sleep, Dead no rest
Haunted Brains—Makes test
On the plain of birth
An unknown star
Indian Earth Mysteries are afar
No sleep—Dead no rest
Haunted Brains make earthly test
Tears of sheer mingle with fear 10
Justice will lead in a few years.
Death has no fear
Indian no sleep—Dead no rest.
Haunted Brains make test.
I come to lead my people,
Over rocky roads and hills,
No sleep—Dead no rest.
Arise and walk, I will guide thee.
Indians no sleep—Dead no rest
Haunted Brains make yearly test. 20

The mysteries of unknown lands.
Indian Dead—No sleep—Dead, no rest.
With their unknown plans,
If there is no death,
We will help you in your fight.
Haunted Brains will visit during the night.
Indians, No sleep—Dead, no rest.
Great Indians spirits are making earthly test.
No sleep—Dead, no rest.

[1922]

Gone Are the Days

Gone are the days when Father Junipero Serra
Instructed Indians to build these ways
And to forget their ill treatment of gone days,
When treaties were made for Indians that had no say.
Father Junipero said, "Indians, the sun shall shine some day."
The words were molded in the Mission Indian soul.
There Father Junipero was worth more than the pale face gold.
Gone are the days when the Mission Dolores
Was Indian and always thought to help and bind
And to gather all Indians within the Mission boundary line. 10
When words were sent by the pale face birds
A new treaty was signed on an open line.
Cho-o-po-, Tu-Trop, Joaquin,
The land was for a few brass rings.
No-chow-we, Ya-wil-chi-ne, Mariano,
A seal was placed to end the race.
Gone are the days when Father Junipero
Said, "Indians, be thou Indians
Tried and build your ways,
For gone are the days. 20
I cannot always live and say,
Build, my Indians,
Build your high-minded ways."

[1922]

1 **Junipero Serra**: the founding Father of the California missions in the eighteenth century. 6 **Mission Indian**: see "The Trial of the Mission Indian," above. 8 **Mission Dolores**: nickname for the Mission San Francisco de Asís, founded in San Francisco in 1776. 13–15 **Cho-o-po . . . Mariano**: these are the names of six of the twenty-eight Indians who signed the 30 May, 1851 "Treaty with the Ko-ya-te, Wo-a-si, etc." in southern California, one of eighteen treaties made in quick succession in southern California and never ratified by the United States Senate, thus depriving the southern California Indian population of agreed-to protections, with devastating results (Prucha 243–46).

The Present Indian Slave

The stillness of Death tells *voiceless Tales*
The Indian Mind *can not* fail.
Nor can the power of Man produce him a Slave
The stillness of the mystery of Death
Controls the Red Mans ways
The *Indian Slave*
May be the darken Walls *of* the Indian grave
Has strengthen the spirit that Has payed
The value of the Indian Grave
Forget not *America* the Indian 10
Help to save the homes of the brave.
The present Indian Slave.
What if freedom Voice was heard
Would its be the voiceless Words
That can be heard with in
Our mind where live the spirit of truth & knowledge
The only value of the Indian Grave
That freedom can Save
Is the Indian slave.
Oh the lips are dry 20
The minds are *shy*
Waiting for America Reply
The present Indian *slave*
Voiceless words return
Humanity will reach the Indian By & By.
Will Humanity Save
The Indian Slave
And place the value on his Grave
The voiceless words will come by & by
Altho our lips are dry 30
And our minds are shy.
The present Indian Slave.
The only value of the Indian Grave
Death has stories
Life has many.
Will humanity save
The value of the Indian Grave

[not previously published]

7 **darken:** though this word ends in *rken*, the earlier letters are not clearly legible.

My Psyche and Wassaja

My psyche is precious time. It is a Consciousness of Mind.
I traveled by night into the forest, and I walked by still Water.
Last night I visited the grave of My beloved.
My psyche whispers, Wassaja, in toneful glee, you are Free, Wassaja.
Talk to Me Indian. No dead and I no sleep.
I walk with you, Wa Wa.
I roam unseen and ramble with you far from home.
I seek your dreams. I guide your Will. I am never wrong. Nor am I
 bound. I can Laugh and frown.
Wassaja, your psychic aura.
I can run. I can stand and fight. 10
Above all I am time, Wassaja. My psyche can turn you round.
I have the Power to listen, whether you are White, Black, Brown,
 Yellow, or Red.
I can see you. Blend with an Art your thoughts into [My] thinking.
I was born when you were conceived, Wassaja.
You cannot separate Me from the others.
The psychic test of Wassaja—Indian no sleep; Dead no rest.
Montezuma, if there be goodness, then the White Man's evil is a Reality.
I lived in the flames of Rights.
My psyche listened day and night.
The plight of the cry of the Indian. 20
Don't give up the fight. Wassaja no sleep; Dead no rest.

In Memoir. Dr. Carlos Montezuma. Old timer. Passed away, Jan. 31, 1923.

[written probably about 1923, published 1980]

Title: Wassaja was the Indian name of the Indian-rights activist also called Carlos Montezuma, whose poems appear in this volume. 13 [**My**]: the bracketed interjection, probably not provided by Wa Wa Chaw, appears in the published poem.

And So All Things of the Earth

Lo the Man who Knew the Woman
 I call Mother.
Mother who Knew the Man I call
 Father.
They were dear to each other.
 Born I was.
Not of the unseen, unknown Vapor
 They call God.
They Knew colors of each other's
 Eyes. 10

They felt the desire of wanting.
Their Mind said, Yes, or
Could Express itself and say, No.
I was Born.
Neither a Doctor. Nor a Nurse.
I was Born.
The feeling of Life was theirs.
I was Born.
And so all things of the earth.

[published 1980]

In Memory of My Homosexual Friend: Imaginary Love. . . .

What mystery is the seat of personality
Whose beautiful form has neither Love
Nor the sentiment of a rose.
Whence and whither and why I have come to Thee.
Do I not travel the path of existence.
Has not My pure body a soul.
Does not My imagination cry for Love.
Do not imprison My immodest Spirit.
Is there not an ear that can hear Thy Voice.
Has not Nature linked My Manly form 10
With a Womanly passion.
Ah, the sound of Thy Voice is growing weak.
Is there not an ear that can hear the
brave tones of My soul speak,
Crying from beneath My hidden thoughts
are memories.
Lo, though I walk through the valley of Life
I Fear only the things of the Mind.
Love smothers the Womanly passion
which was conquered by time. 20
Maybe I am but a Man in form.
My Womanly passion is admitted
to feast on the open spaces.
Thy being craves and raves.
Thy Manly form refuses to respond.
Am I not the Victim of imaginary Love.

[published 1980]

17–18 **Lo, though I walk through the valley of Life / I fear only**: echoing Psalm 23: "Yea, though I walk through the valley of the shadow of death, I will fear no evil: for thou art with me."

My Secret World

My secret World is in My Mind.
My thoughts Question Love.
My thoughts ask if Hate is a Science.
My secret World says, I doubt.
My thoughts answer, Yes.
My secret World says, No.
They called Me Injun this morning.
    Ugh, Injun, they said: Ugh!
    Injun why do you live in City!
    Reservation belong to Injun!

[published 1980]

Ruth Margaret Muskrat, Cherokee, 1897–1982

Ruth Margaret Muskrat is remembered for her work as a leader in Indian education and as an activist for Indian rights. Until now her poetry has been forgotten, but before she graduated from college in 1925, she devoted herself to writing poetry. Then, just as she was coming into her own as a poet, apparently under the growing influence of a Modernism that no longer required rhyme and meter, she stopped writing poetry and concentrated on her work as an educator and activist. When she married in 1928, she took the name Ruth Muskrat Bronson.

Born and raised in the Cherokee Nation in northeastern Indian Territory (later Oklahoma), Muskrat struggled to pay for her education and thus attended a long series of schools, interrupted by two years of teaching to earn money for her studies. She attended the Oklahoma School of Technology, Henry Kendall Academy, Northeastern State Teachers College (the former Cherokee Seminary), the University of Oklahoma, the University of Kansas, and Mount Holyoke College, where she majored in English. In the summer of 1921 she worked for the YWCA as an organizer on the Mescalero Apache Reservation in New Mexico. Her report on her summer's work earned her a scholarship to the University of Kansas. In 1922 she attracted national press coverage as a delegate to the World Student Christian Federation conference in Beijing. The trip also took her to Hawaii, Manchuria, Japan, Korea, and Hong Kong, and Muskrat believed that it awakened her awareness of race and her belief in racial equality. Recognized as a leader early on, she met with President Calvin Coolidge in 1923. Impressed, he asked her to dinner at the White House.

After graduating from Mount Holyoke in 1925, Muskrat taught English at Northeastern State Teachers College and then at Haskell Indian Institute. From 1930-1944 she worked in the Education Division of the Office of Indian Affairs, and in 1944 she published her only book, *Indians Are People Too.* Drawing on her administrative experience, she was a central leader in the National Congress of American Indians in Washington, D.C., where she served in many capacities, including as executive director. Then in 1957 she moved from national politics to local activism for education on the San Carlos Apache Reservation in Arizona, working as a health education specialist for the Indian Health Service and focusing on adult education and leadership. She retired in 1962 and moved to Tucson, where she continued to work for Indian rights. (Harvey)

Songs of the Spavinaw

I am the river of Spavinaw,
  I am the river of pain;
Sadness and gladness must answer my law;
Measure for measure I give, and withdraw
Back through the hills of the Spavinaw,
  Hiding away from the plain.

I am the river of Spavinaw;
  I sing the songs of the world;
Dashing and whirling, swishing and swirling,
Delicate, mystical, silvery spray hurling, 10
  Sing I the songs of the world,
  The passionate songs of the world.

I sing of laughter and mirth,
  And I laugh in a gurgle of glee
As the myriad joys of the earth
  Trip through the light with me.
Gay shallows dimple, sparkle and ripple.
  Like songs that a lover would sing,
    Skipping in moonlight,
    Tripping in moonlight, 20
  Whispering echoes of spring.

And again
  I move with the slow sadness of pain.
In my dark blue deep, where the shadows creep,
  I catch up life's sorrows and mirror them back again.
And my song is a throbbing, pitiful sobbing,
  Choked by an agonized pain.

And then
  I move forth toward the beckoning north,
    And I sing of the power of men. 30
      As I dash down my falls,
      As I beat at my walls
Frantically fighting, running and righting,

All through the flood, through the snarling and biting,
I sing of the power of men,
Of the hurry and power of men.

I am the river of Spavinaw,
I am the giver of pain;
Sadness and gladness must answer my law;
Measure for measure I give, and withdraw 40
Back through the hills of the Spavinaw,
Hiding away from the plain.

[1920]

Sentenced

(A Dirge)

They have come, they have come,
Out of the unknown they have come;
Out of the great sea they have come;
Dazzling and conquering the white man has come
To make this land his home.

We must die, we must die,
The white man has sentenced that we must die,
Without great forests must we die,
Broken and conquered the red man must die,
He cannot claim his own. 10

They have gone, they have gone,
Our sky-blue waters, they have gone,
Our wild free prairies they have gone,
To be the white man's own.

They have won, they have won,
Thru fraud and thru warfare they have won,
Our council and burial grounds they have won,
Our birthright for pottage the white man has won,
And the red man must perish alone.

[1921]

When It's Dark

When the old clock's strikin' 'leven
An' the lights are all put out,
An' the stars up in the heaven
Chase the shadders all about,

Then's when I start feelin' shaky,
An' wishin' I'd been good,
That I hadn't teased the baby
An' had carrid in the wood.

When the hous is dark an' still-like
An' the clock ticks right out loud, 10
An' it's sorter cold an' chill-like
An' the moon's hid by a cloud;
Then's when a feller's wishin'
That he hadn't been so bad;
Hadn't run away a-fishin'
Ner had sasst-back at his dad.

When the old screech owl's a cryin'
By the winder on the south,
Then there comes a lump a-pryin'
Right up in a feller's mouth; 20
An' the dark gits full o' goblins
Where the door-post allus stood,
Then a feller 'gins resolvin'
That from this on, he'll be *good.*

[1921]

The Hunter's Wooing

Come roam the wild hills, my Cherokee Rose,
Come roam the wild hills with me.
We'll follow the path where the Spavinaw flows,
Dashing wild on its way to the sea,
On its wearisome way to the sea.
We'll chase the fleet deer from its lair in the woods;
We'll follow the wolf to his den.

When the sun hides his face, we'll rest in the woods,
Hid away from the worry of men.
Hid away from the bother of men. 10

And then we'll go home, my Cherokee Rose,
Where the Senecas live in the heart of the hills
By the rippling Cowskin, where the Saulchana grows,
We'll go home to the Coyauga hills,
To the sheltering Coyauga hills.

[1921]

13 **Cowskin**: Cowskin Creek in northeastern Oklahoma, where Muskrat grew up. 14–15 **Coyauga**: Cayuga.

An Indian Lullaby

'Cross the sky-blue water
Glides a light canoe,
'Tis thy warrior father
Coming back to you.
O'er the towering tree tops,
Where the gay stars peep,
Fall the timid dew drops.
Sleep, my papoose, sleep.

Sleep, my papoose, sleep,
Close your weary eyes; 10
While the shadows creep
And the pine tree sighs;
While the winds are blowing
And the camp fires leap,
Father's homeward rowing,
Sleep, my papoose, sleep.

Sleep, my wee papoose
In the evening breeze,
I will guard you close 20
'Neath the sheltering trees;
While the coyote's wails
Cross the lone hills sweep,
Sleep while daylight fails,
Sleep, my papoose, sleep.

[1921]

Nunih Waiyah

Take her away and lay her gently down to rest
Beneath the cool grey willows that she loved to hold.
And lay this starry flower on her breast
In her slim brown hands, so icy cold.

Lay her where the rippling of the Spavinaw
Can lull her dreamless sleep with its incessant song,
Out where the sunshine, slanting through the leaves can draw
The flowers from the earth to make her hours less long.

Take her now, my hours of tryst are over,
There's nothing else for pain to feast upon, 10
I gave her all, and, to her cold grave yonder,
All light and life for me have gone.

What difference now that I was born a paleface,
And she was Nunih Waiyah, a Redman's child?
She waits my coming out in that eternal space,
Her love by Death's cold withering blackness undefiled.

And when I go through worlds to meet her
Out in the twilight realm of dreams,
Our love will then be but the sweeter
For the crossing of Death's sullied streams. 20

[1922]

Title: Choctaw name of a revered mound in what is now Mississippi.

from Sonnets from the Cherokee

(May Mrs. Browning Pardon Me)

What is this nameless something that I want,
Forever groping blindly, without light,—
A ghost of pain that does forever haunt
My days, and make my heart eternal night?
I think it is your face I so long for,
Your eyes that read my soul at one warm glance;
Your lips that I may touch with mine no more
Have left me in their stead a thrusting lance
Of fire that burns my lips and sears my heart
As all the dreary wanton years wear through 10
Their hopeless dragging days. No lover's art
Can lift full, heavy sorrow from my view
Or still my restless longing, purge my hate,
Because I learned I loved you, dear, too late.

[1922]

Title: This poem is the third of four love sonnets gathered under the title "Sonnets from the Cherokee." The subtitle refers to the title's echo of Elizabeth Barrett Browning's famous *Sonnets from the Portuguese* (1850).

The Warriors' Dance

With the droning hum
Of the low tom-tom,
And the steady beat of the many feet;
With the wild weird cry
Of the owl near by,
Came the night of the warriors' dance.

With dark bronze faces
And gorgeous laces,
With bodies straight and stately gait;
With black hair streaming 10
With black eyes gleaming,
Came the warriors to the dance.

The moonlight beams
The campfire gleams,
The tall trees sigh as the wind rushes by;
The squaws smile in pride
At their slow solemn stride,
As the warriors march in the dance.

There is happiness there
And joys fill the air, 20
They have forgot their hopeless lot;
They are kings once more
As in days of yore,
As they swing to the warriors' dance.

[1922]

The Apache Reservation

Up in the mountains of New Mexico,
Away from the dreary brown desert below,
Out of the reach of the thorny mesquite,
Leaving the glare and the dry, stinging heat
That scorches the desert plain;
Where the breezes blow full of invigoration,
There lies an Indian reservation,
Here is the agency of the Apache,
Home of the Kenoi, Kannseah, Ballache,
Here is the Indian's domain. 10

Far to the North, and South, and West,
Towers of high peaked mountains crest;

Green as the valley's emerald green,
Touched with the fairies' glistening sheen;
When the blue of the dusk creeps in:
Lit with the light of a thousand fires
From the stars that come, as the day expires,
And hang in festoons o'er the mountain's rim
As the pine trees murmur their evening hymn
To the Maker of mountains and men. 20

Out of the deepest and darkest ravine
Spirals of white, curling smoke can be seen,
Tepees are standing in grey somber rows,
Tent casings flap when the slightest wind blows,
And papooses shout at their play:
Dressed in her blanket of purple or red,
Wearing a gay colored shawl on her head,
The old squaw is bending over her beads
Or making her basket of grasses and reeds
All through the wearisome day. 30

Town of Mescalero, all painted in yellow,
Tint of the sunset, soft-toned and mellow,
Nestled so snug in this queen of all valleys,
As the wild lily nestles the bee in its chalice
And holds it in loving delight,
You hold in your heart a tragedy old,
And throbbingly yearn for the tale to be told
Of a race that is dying, to whom any chance
Is pregnant with love, and with life and romance,
And a future of promises bright. 40

[1922]

The Trail of Tears

In the night they shriek and moan,
In the dark the tall pines moan
As they guard the dismal trail.
The Cherokees say it is the groan,
Every shriek an echoed groan
Of their forefathers that fell
With broken hopes and bitter fears
On that weary trail of tears.

Broken hopes and broken hearts,
A quivering mass of broken hearts 10

Were driven over the trail.
Stifling back the groan that starts,
Smothering back the moan that starts,
Full four thousand fell;
But still the Great Spirit his people bears
As they travel the trail of tears.

From the homes their fathers made,
From the graves the tall trees shade
For the sake of greed and gold,
The Cherokees were forced to go 20
To a land they did not know;
And Father Time or wisdom old
Cannot erase, through endless years,
The memory of the trail of tears.

[1922]

If You Knew

If you could know the empty ache of loneliness,
Masked well behind the calm indifferent face
Of us who pass you by in studied hurriedness,
Intent upon our way, lest in the little space
Of one forgetful moment hungry eyes implore
You to be kind, to open up your heart a little more,
I'm sure you'd smile a little kindlier, sometimes,
To those of us you've never seen before.

If you could know the eagerness we'd grasp
The hand you'd give to us in friendliness; 10
What vast, potential friendship in that clasp
We'd press, and love you for your gentleness;
If you could know the wide, wide reach
Of love that simple friendliness could teach,
I'm sure you'd say "Hello, my friend," sometimes,
And now and then extend a hand in friendliness to each.

[1923]

In Class

And it was so. She said I dreamed in class.
Who would not dream? From some chance word she said—
I have forgotten what,—the color red

Perhaps, or just a prism through the glass:
Enough to free my soul and let it pass
From those four walls, stripped of the dead
Dull commonplace. Singing through space it sped
Above cold seas of azure and topaz
To lands whose ships lay gleaming in the sun
Laden to sail for ports of mystery; 10
Past gardens fair, where Dido waits for one
Who does not come, and Pan laughs secretly.
Poor cheated class that heard but chemistry
And missed the evening bells of Arcady!

[1924]

11 **Dido**: founder and queen of ancient Carthage in present-day Tunisia. In Virgil's *Aeneid*, Dido kills herself after Aeneas deserts her. 12 **Pan**: lustful Greek god of pastures, forests, shepherds, and flocks, a symbol of fertility. 14 **Arcady**: Arcadia, the home of Pan, a mythical realm of shepherds, simplicity, and harmony.

To an Indian Lover

So slight a thing it may seem
That way you stand;
And yet it marks the difference
Between yourself and me.
Only an Indian whose heritage
Is older than the Painted Desert, or the peaks
Of Kish-li-pi, could stand
So straight, so still, so staring into nothingness.
Sometimes, I think, so have I seen great Kish-li-pi
Standing thus in the gloom 10
Of a darkening hour,
Remote; immovable;
Too far away for me to follow.
O I would fly to you and tear
Those folded arms apart!
—Would fire those calm, far-seeing eyes
And feel those cold, sad, contemplative lips
Grow fervent—

Do you remember, yesterday
I came upon you, laughing, from the wind 20
And found you standing thus
And turned away
With sobs instead of laughter—?

O Love, where is it
That I cannot follow?

[1924]

Broken Wing Bird

Given Broken Wing Bird's name and publishing in Indian magazines, it seems likely that he or she was Indian, though the name could be an affectation by a non-Indian.

Why? Why? Why?

Ever since I was a child
I've been wondering meek—but not mild—
Why an Indian is looked upon
As a thing of the far beyond—
An irresponsible, inhuman being,
Who had eyes, but not for seeing;
Who had feet, but not for walking,
Who had a tongue, but not for talking—
Except to say a thing not true!
And now for my wondering, 10
DO YOU WONDER WHY I DO?
Why is someone always to watch and suspect?
And from whom no good you could ever expect?
Has God gone from the hearts of men,
And isn't He ever coming back again?

[1921]

Come Back, Indians of Yesterday

Oh, where is the Indian of yesterday?
Isn't he ever coming back again?
He, who wasn't afraid to do the right,
And went ahead and did it.
And wasn't afraid to speak the truth,
And then spoke nothing but it;
And who, when he said he'd do a thing
Was always sure to do it!
Did I hear you say that he was dead?
Oh, tell me that I didn't! 10

But tell me that he's just forgot
The ways his father taught him;
Or, that he's only lost for a time,
To later find himself again,
And be himself, and keep himself,
And show there's something to him.

[1921]

Blue Feather

This poem appeared in Carlos Montezuma's journal *Wassaja*, attributed to Princess Blue Feather. The term "princess" fits a common stereotype of American Indian women, beginning with the Pocahontas story. Indeed, more than one person has taken the title and name "Princess Blue Feather." The poem's appearance in *Wassaja* indicates that the Princess Blue Feather who wrote this poem was Indian and not a pretend Indian taking on an Indian-sounding name. She may be the same "Princess Blue Feather, Aztec of Mexico," who in 1934 self-published a booklet called *Indian Mother's Lullaby*, with a photo of her in an eastern woodlands dress. One copy is inscribed "Princess Blue Feather / Saa Hahn—qua Han Doli" (R & A Petrilla).

The Lone Tee-Pee

Hark, what is it that the wild winds are saying,
As they moan around this lonely home
Telling of people slaughtered and who now are gone:
Dark clouds are scurrying onward as if angry at the sight.
They have seen the awful carnage and the deeds of fright.
White and lonely it stands, a sentinel overlooking the land.
Theirs by right, but taken by might from this brave band.

In amongst the fir trees stands another hidden there,
Wide open is the door, inside the home is bare.
Gone is the brave, his squaw and papoose of his teepee, 10
Farewell, he has said to bloody strife, and he
Rests in peace on Memloose Isle; his bones washed by sea,
It will be handed down in history's page,
He died for justice and liberty at an early age.

Ah, sad are the hearts of the remaining few,
Who wait in silence, stoical and brave for their last call,
Learning to read and pray, as their white brothers do;
Even to drink "fire-water"—hush, is it to forget their fall,

Or does it recall those days gone by
When they lived in happiness and were brave to die? 20
Where justice reigned in all this land,
The red men were a peaceful and contented band.

When they roamed at will over all this land,
Hunting the wild buffalo, band after band;
Happy and free, just children of nature alone,
God grant you, for this lone tee-pee have not to atone;
So be just to the few left and fast disappearing.
Their days are numbered and their end is nearing,
Free the few who are left—let them mingle together,
Is the plea and the prayer of Princess Blue Feather. 30

[1921]

12 **Memloose Isle**: probably the best known of several Memaloose Islands (in current spelling), also called Lower Memaloose Island, in the Columbia River near present-day The Dalles, Oregon. Traditionally, Indians in the region often lay their dead on Memaloose Island. The U.S. government removed most of the island's graves in 1957, flooding the area for Bonneville Dam.

Mrs. Minot Carter, Dakota, born about 1878

Mrs. Minot Carter lived in Los Molinos, California when an acquaintance sent two of her poems to the *Indian Leader* for publication. The acquaintance described her as proudly Indian and 44 years old, and as an avid gardener with twelve children.

Raindrops

Have you heard the raindrops
  On a field of corn,
Pattering ov'r the green leaves
  Dusty and forlorn?
Did you ever fancy
  They were little feet
Hurrying out with water
  Thirsty ones to meet?

Have you seen the raindrops
  Falling on the lake?
How they flash and sparkle
  Tiny splashes make.

Did you ever fancy 10
 They were diamonds rare
Scattered by an aeroplane
 Sailing through the air?

[1922]

Fancies

If we could return from our last long rest
And seek out the ones we loved the best,
Though not in a form to cause them fear,
Just gently to let them feel us near,

Would we come in the scent of the evening flowers
Bringing to mind past happy hours?
Would we come in the song of the mourning dove
Recalling to them our endless love?

Would we come in the sound of the falling rain
Telling them gladly "We shall meet again"? 10
Would we come in the silently falling snow
With memories of rosy cheeks long ago?

Would we come in the rainbow or sunset's hue
Repeating to them "Be true, be true"?
Would we speak in some sad sweet song's refrain
Bidding them wait in gladness, not pain?

These are but fancies, faint and dim;
For dare we question the wisdom of Him
Who gave us through death the victory sweet
To be with our loved ones in joy complete? 20

[1922]

Alfred C. Gillis, Winnemem Wintu

Alfred C. Gillis worked with the Indian Board of Co-operation, a California Indian rights organization. Their journal, the *California Indian Herald*, published his poems and referred to Gillis as "highly educated" and as singing traditional Indian songs. ("Members of Indian Board"; "Mewuk Indian Tribe"; "Mr. Collett's Reply")

The Bird with the Wounded Wing

A Wintune Indian Legend Put into Verse
High in the hills in the drifted snow,
On an Indian trail in the long ago,
A lovely bird that had missed its way,
Down in the snow exhausted lay.
Far from the North it had winged its way
To the snowy vales that Southward lay.
Spent and weary, with injured wing,
It fell to earth, a helpless thing.
A Wintune trod that lonely way,
And saw the bird that wounded lay. 10
With tenderness his heart was filled,
He warmed the bird the cold had chilled,
And placed it in his warm black hair.
In calm content it nestled there.

On Saunchululi* wild and high,
Near where the rugged trail goes by,
Where leaps the dashing Trinity
In scenes of great sublimity,
He sat and gently bathed that wing
Until, relieved, the bird did sing. 20
It sang and sang its sweetest lay.
Then, in the darkness, flew away.
But never sweeter song was heard
Than was caroled by that grateful bird.

The years passed on, yea, rolled away.
Helpless, alone, the Indian lay.
A bird flew in his wigwam door,
And sang and sang as ne'er before,
Yes, sweetly sang as if to say,
A debt of love I come to pay. 30
The aged Indian raised his head,
And to the bird he softly said:
"O Messenger of good to me,
The Spirit Great now speaks through thee.
O sing again—my heart is sad,
O sing again—and make me glad.
Relieve me of my aches and pains
Restore me unto health again."

As though he understood each word,
Such song ne'er came from throat of bird, 40
He sang as though his song should say,
I've come my precious debt to pay.
He sang away the Indian's pain,
And brought new life and health again.

This is the tale the Shaman told.
This is the tale the mountain told.

This treasure in these words I find,
The greatest good is to be kind.

*Saunchululi—"black rock mountain," a sacred mountain in Trinity County.

[1923]

17 **the dashing Trinity**: the Trinity River in northwestern California, a swift river that winds through canyons, mountains, and meadows.

An Indian Cradle Song

Sleep, my little one, sleep away!
Above thee watching angels stray.
No harm can come to thee by day,
Sleep, my little one, sleep away!

Out of the heav'nly pools of space,
The stars look down upon thy face;
Child of beauty, charm and grace,
Sleep, my little one, sleep away!

Upon thy brow the pale moonlight,
Steals its kisses with delight. 10
No harm can come to thee by night,
Sleep, my little one, sleep away!

Soon the morn will dawn for thee,
Brighter days and joys to see;
Love's young dream will come to thee,
Sleep, my little one, sleep away!

Growing on from day to day,
Leaving childhood far away;
On to manhood's fuller day,
Sleep, my little one, sleep away! 20

Soon the birds will call to thee,
And thou, too, shall mated be;

Where the wild rose blooms for thee
Sleep, my little one, sleep away!

[1923]

The Shasta Lily

*Den-Hu-Luly

Fragrant, perfumed, rich and rare,
Wondrous sweet beyond compare,
I fain would pluck thee from thy stem,
O, thou priceless mountain gem.

When I beheld thee smiling there,
Filled with perfume was the air,
Borne on the night wind o'er the glade,
Where Shasta casts her mighty shade.

There blooms no fairer, sweeter flower
In all wild Nature's wondrous bower. 10
I fain would pluck thee from thy stem,
O, thou priceless mountain gem.

*A much admired flower by the early Wintoone. It grows in the high regions of the Sierras, in the environs of Mount Shasta. The Shasta Lily is also found in high altitudes of the Sierras. When President Harding passed through Dunsmuir he was presented by the citizens with a special bouquet of Shasta Lilies.

[1923]

To the Wenem Mame River

Once again my footsteps stray
Where the mountain waters play,
I hear again the river's roar
That breaks upon its rocky shore.

Through silent canyons wild and deep,
Its raging waters plunge and sleep,
Above the ancient mountains rise,
And point their columns to the skies.

O, land where lilies bloom and fade,
The spotted lilies in the glade, 10
Here water ferns in beauty grow,
Green mosses in the melting snow.

Of all fair rivers I have known,
No fairer waters than thine own.
O, topy mame,[1] we love thy name,
Famous waters Wenem Mame.[2]

On thy banks what combat raged,
What duels, what brave acts were staged,
Here ancient tribes in battle stood
In yon fair glade by yonder wood. 20

Here Modoc and the Wintoons fell,
Their spears lie broken in the dell,
Here arrow heads lie broken round
In scattered heaps upon the ground.

Here, too, the warlike Shastas came
To test the Wintoons' Warrior's claim,
And looked with eager longing eyes,
Yea, fought to win their long sought prize.

Their strong yew bows were sinews strung
And loaded well their quivers hung, 30
And close within their long black hair,
A long bone knife lay hidden there.

Elk hide cloaks each warrior wore,
And fought and bled upon thy shore,
In mortal combat, fierce and fast,
Till crimson ran thy tide at last.

All is over now and done,
Peaceful now thy waters run,
Side by side the warriors sleep,
In thy canyon wild and deep. 40

Above eternal Shasta's[3] snow
Gazes o'er the scene below,
And west the Yolla Bulley's[4] keep
Vigil o'er their slumber deep.

And Saun-chu-luli[5] wild and high
Where the shawmn's trail went by
Hears no more the wild war song
Floating on the breeze along.

Here Indian youth and maiden strayed
And nature's children laughing played 50

And near yon tall piney wood,
Once the War Chief's village stood.

Where chants from a thousand throats
Rose unto Heaven in sweetest notes,
Here Norail-poot-as[6] lived and died
And now lies sleeping by thy tide.

O, white man, take this land of ours,
Guard well its hills, streams and bowers,
Guard well the Mounds where Wintoons sleep,
Guard well these canyons wild and deep. 60

NOTES

1 The McCloud was known to all surrounding tribes as Topy Mame, meaning the valuable and coveted river.
2 Wenem Mame: Middle River. Wintoons' name for the McCloud River.
3 Sacred mountain of the Wintoons.
4 Snow mountain. A sacred mountain.
5 Black Rock Mountain, in Trinity County. A sacred mountain.
6 South Indian Summer. The last great Chief of the Wintoons.

[1924]

21 **Modoc**: neighbors of the Wintoon (Wintun or Wintu). 25 **Shastas**: neighbors of the Wintoon.
46 **shawmn's**: shaman's.

The Sacramento River

Flow on, O winding river, flow,
Through the canyon deep below,
Where the willows bend and lean
In graceful beauty to the stream,
And thy soft sweet waters flow
To the sunny vale below,
Where the grasses fringe thy side
And whisper softly to thy tide.

I love to watch thy waters sweep
In majestic beauty to the deep; 10
To hear thy soft and gentle song
As thy waters steal along.
From the mountains crowned with snow,
She cuts her rocky way below,
While from her banks the stately pine
Bravely guards the stream divine.

Here the wild deer come to drink
On the green and grassy brink,
And the tall firs bend and lean
And cast their shadows on the stream. 20
The canoe long has left thy shore,
Left thy tide for evermore,
Where once in stillness it did glide
On thy deep and moving tide.

Onward through the valley free,
Surging toward the singing sea,
Whispering softly to the strand,
Rolling o'er its golden sand.
Alas, the bay, extended wide,
Anxious to embrace thy tide, 30
Where at last, thy waters lost,
On the ocean to be tossed.

[1924]

Where Sleep the Wintoon Dead

Here by these Indian rivers,*
Far from the white man's tread,
Kind hands have secretly laid them,
And they sleep the sleep of the dead.

Here the winding trails go by,
The ancient Indian mound,
Where a thousand Wintoon warriors lie
Wrapped in sleep profound.

Here Nature grows her wild bouquets,
And mountain lilies love to bloom, 10
And soft winds whisper through the pines,
In dirges o'er their mountain tomb.

*The Sacramento and McCloud Rivers.

[1924]

The Klamath Girl

Far to the west where the Klamath rolls,
In my sunny youth I chanced to stroll;
A maiden fair, with flowing hair
And wondrous eyes beyond compare,

Stood by that river rolling free
And cast a loving glance on me.

Softly the wavelets kissed the strand
As it silently washed its golden sand,
While near and far the bird of love
Sang sweet and low, the turtle dove. 10
O, wondrous was that night in June,
We loved beneath that summer moon.

Sweet were the promises we made,
Like dreams of youth too soon to fade.
Too soon! Too soon! our ways did part,
And O, the anguish of the heart.
Tho years have sped I can't forget
That sweet girl face, I see it yet.

Those days are gone, yea, turned to years,
And broken now my heart with tears, 20
I still look back across the way,
That long gone youthful summer day.
Too soon! Too soon! our youth is fled,
O, what is life when love is dead?

[1924]

Title: the Klamath are neighbors of the Wintoon. 1 **the Klamath**: here referring to the Klamath River.

My Prayer

God pity us all, for our hands are red,
With the wars we've made, the blood we've shed,
As we battle to death, for greed and gain,
Red are our hands, with the thousands slain.
Redeem us from our wild passion's flame,
The consuming fire of our hate and shame.
And lead us from the blood-stained way,
O, teach our hardened hearts to pray,
The Angels of God, o'er a world proclaim,
"Peace on earth, good will to men." 10

[1924]

Arsenius Chaleco, Yuma, born about 1889

Arsenius Chaleco was born in Arizona and worked as a stock tender (U.S. Census). Someone who wrote so skillful and powerful a poem as "The Indian Requiem" probably wrote other poems as well, but the editor of this volume has not found more poems by Chaleco. A 1928 California Indian Census lists Chaleco at the Yuma Agency ("California Indians"). Beneath the poem's original publication in *Indian Teepee* appears the following note from William Tomkins, a non-Indian adopted by Sioux who in 1926 would publish a book about Indian sign language and pictographs: "In my humble opinion it [Chaleco's poem] ranks with the greatest of sorrow songs of any race, and I am happy to give it to the Teepee, and welcome any Indian poems."

The Indian Requiem

In the loose sand is thrown
The warrior's frame, now mouldering bone.

Ah, little thought the strong and brave
Who bore the lifeless chieftain forth,
Or the young wife who, weeping gave
Her first born, (years wasted now)
That through their graves would cut the plow.

Before the fields were sown and tilled,
Full to the brim our rivers plowed.
The melody of waters filled 10
The fresh and boundless wood.

Torrents dashed and rivulets played,
And fountains spouted in the shade.

These grateful sounds are heard no more.
The springs are silent in the sun,
And rivers, through their blackened shores,
With lessening currents run.

They waste us—ah, like April snow
In the warm noon, we shrink away,
And fast they follow as we go 20
Towards the setting day.

But I behold a fearful sign
To which the white man's eyes are blind,
Their race may vanish hence like mine
And leave no trace behind,

Save ruins o'er the region spread,
And tall white stones above the dead.
And realms our tribes were crushed to get
May be our barren desert yet.

[1924]

Lynn Riggs, Cherokee, 1899–1954

Lynn Riggs (sometimes R. Lynn, Rolla Lynn, or Rollie Lynn Riggs) is known mostly as a playwright, but he was also devoted to writing poetry. He was born in Indian Territory, in the present Oklahoma. Growing up, he played guitar and sang and was a skilled horseman. After graduating from high school in 1917, Riggs worked a variety of jobs from cowpuncher to proofreader for the *Wall Street Journal* to extra in cowboy movies, and he traveled widely, including to Chicago, New York, and Los Angeles. In 1920, he enrolled at the University of Oklahoma to study music and drama, drawing in part on funds from mortgaging his allotment. There he taught freshman English in 1922–1923, wrote poems and plays, joined literary groups and began to publish, and joined a singing quartet. But then, suffering from tuberculosis and depression, he left school in 1923 and moved to Santa Fe, New Mexico where he soon recovered and found an encouraging community of writers and artists as well as the setting for some of his poems. In the late 1920s he lived in Chicago, New York, and France. His best known play, *Green Grow the Lilacs,* staged in 1931 and nominated for a Pulitzer Prize, was the model for the hit Broadway musical *Oklahoma!* (1943). Later, Riggs lived in Los Angeles, Santa Fe, and New York, writing plays and screenplays. He died from stomach cancer. (Braunlich)

With one small exception acknowledged in the notes, the texts below come from the only book of poems Riggs published while he lived, *The Iron Dish* (1930), which collects his best poetry. For his published poetry up to 1930, see the bibliography in this volume, but because he published widely, that bibliography is likely incomplete. A collection of his later poems was published in 1982 under the title *This Book, This Hill, These People: Poems by Lynn Riggs*, ed. Phyllis Cole Braunlich. The sequence of poems below follows the sequence in *The Iron Dish*, though some of them, as indicated, were also published earlier.

Charger

And now the little chargers split the street—
Black and dappled, iron rusty, gray—
Rolling their velvet eyes toward spurring feet,
Beating the cobbles to a creamy spray.
All in their dazzling mail the riders sit
Secure and roweled, exquisites on leather.

Their hands are learning from the silver bit,
Their lips are speaking of the chiseled weather.

Who will unlock the stable in the alley
Where gaunt limbs flex, and sandy eyes are peering 10
Past the bright cavalcade; who loose the sally
Of whip on flank? Those nimble feet uprearing
Claw at the board; the brittle bit is banging.
By one red bolt the stable door is hanging.

[1928, 1930]

Song of the Unholy Oracle

Be that placated
Monastic one—
Chill fingered, gated
From the sun!

Shrubs may be tended
With the shrunk wrist,
Oaks grow splendid
Unsunkissed.

Furrows long fattened
May turn from sleep 10
Sprouting, flattened
Worms shorten and creep,

Feverish earth—
Field, thicket, plain—
Come to birth
Without pain.

In the beginning,
This was your wish:
To feed unsinning
At the iron dish. 20

Be that lone diner
On the grubby root—
You who want no finer
Disastrous fruit!

[1930]

Spring Morning—Santa Fe

The first hour was a word the color of dawn.
The second came, and gorgeous poppies stood,
Backs to a wall. The yellow sun rode on.
A mocking bird sang shrilly from a nest of wood.

The water in the acequia came down
At the stroke of nine, and watery clouds were lifting
Their velvet shadows from the little town.
Gold fired the pavement where the leaves were shifting.

At ten, black shawls of women bowed along
The Alameda. Sleepy burros lay 10
In the heat and lifted up their ears. A song
Wavered upon the wind and died away.

And the great bells rang out a golden tune.
Words grew in the heart and clanged, the color of noon.

[1930]

5 **acequia:** communal irrigation ditch. 10 **Alameda:** tree-lined street.

The Wolves

Puzzled and challenging
At our fear,
They have wavered, waiting to spring
Ear by ear.

Circuitous their path
Through rivers of mud,
Avoiding our spilt wrath
Like blood.

Laughter may suffice
To avert the pack— 10
Fanged, snapping, twice
Turned, but never turned back.

[1928, 1930]

Santo Domingo Corn Dance

The Chorus
"Bring rain,
As we bring now

Our gift of dance and song
To You—who dance not, nor sing—
Bring rain!"

The Dancers

Bodies
Reddened, and gourds,
Rain girdles, ornaments, 10
The skins of foxes—what should please
You more?

Portent

But look!
Where the line whips
Like rain in corn, like clouds
Wind beaten, or like the frown
Upon His brow!

Song of the Bodies

"I am 20
Naked before
You, High One—look! Hear me!
As I stamp this ground worn smooth
By feet.

"Not as
A supplicant
I shake the doors of earth—
Let the green corn spring to meet
My tread!"

The Clouds 30

Just now
Across the line
Of these red men there swept—
Like wings of thunder at the sun—
Shadows!

The Koshari

As if
Their feet were stuck
With scorn, their hands with pride—
Koshari glide, halt, grimace, grin, 40
And turn.

The Child Dancer

"But that
I am a child,
I should not notice the branch
Of spruce tied on his arm
In my eyes."

The Orchard

Beyond
The baking roofs, 50
A barren mountain points
Still higher, though its feet are white
With bloom.

Rain

One drum—
Note more, one voice,
One slant of bodies,
And my tears will fall like rain
Upon this ground.

[1926, 1930, 1934]

Title: Santo Domingo Pueblo in New Mexico. **19** ***Song of the Bodies***: this heading, which appears in the 1926 and 1934 versions but not in the 1930 version, is restored here by emendation, supposing that it was left out by accident. Other differences between versions are too minor to note. **36 Koshari**: sacred clowns.

A Letter

I don't know why I should be writing to you,
I don't know why I should be writing to anyone;
Nella has brought me yellow calendulas,
In my neighbor's garden is sun.

In my neighbor's garden chickens, like snow,
Drift in the alfalfa. Bees are humming;
A pink dress, a blue wagon play in the road;
Guitars are strumming.

Guitars are saying the same things
They said last night—in a different key. 10
What they have said I know—so their strumming
Means nothing to me.

Nothing to me is the pale pride of Lucinda
Washing her hair—nothing to anyone:

Here in a black bowl are calendulas,
In my neighbor's garden, sun.

[1930]

Bird Cry

There is tall crying in the willow reeds
From the kinless bird on that water
Which is a mirror depthless and deceitful,
Silvered by the wind and set with tiny seeds.

What great eye, benevolent and curious,
Its look clean as a released blade,
May wound the water sailed by a crying bird,
Lay bare the source of that hurt cry mysterious?

Many an ear has heard—the snake's, the otter's—
Curl at the bank. In motion sinuous 10
And still, they are waiting, waiting the voice in the reeds
From the bird stirring those waters.

[1930]

Wonder

This is the wonder of wonders:
To be assailed
By this sharp incredible beauty,
To be nailed
By such arrowy barbs to a cross
Of my own making,
While the chants rise from the harsh hills,
And from under
The near crags dawn is breaking!
This is the wonder . . . 10

[1930]

The Deer

It is a pool of shadow close and blue;
The slant ray
Of the sun is a golden javelin to run it through
But not to slay.

Three tan deer are nimbly at the cool
Grass nibbling. Their sides are thin,
Each liquid eye a little pool
For javelin.

[1930]

The Hollow

It is quiet here. Tree shade
Is a cool place. I will rest
Easily in the shadow. I will lie
On the earth's breast,
And look at what sky I can see
Through leaves, or perhaps look
At dandelions bowing gravely
To themselves in the brook.

Not thinking of this thing or of that thing,
I will lie 10
And forget the road I have traveled over
To look at the sky.

Perhaps I shall forget the brown bluff
Over the brook I must climb
As high as the trees are high.
Perhaps I shall forget time
And lie here forever, forgetting
How soon it will be
Before I must leave this hollow
Reluctantly. 20

[1930]

The Golden Bee

A bumblebee with a back of golden plush
And black lace wings upon his lacquered length,
Having flown too long in the sun from bush to bush,
Once clung to the oaken door with failing strength.
And when I pushed the door into the sun,
With a whir of wings he spiraled out of sight,
And left me marveling at the wise one,
Who most had wanted shade, accepting light
Without a flutter at a choice not free.
He was gone—gold, lace, and all—for the flowers' yield, 10

Leaving me sadder than I wished to be
For one gold bug gone flowering to the field.

[1930]

Angry Sea

"Now I shall be at peace," I said,
Accepting you,
"For after love there is a calm place."
I thought I knew.

But now, in this noisy dawn, through my window
The hot sun leaps, and I have not been sleeping;
But tossing and crying out in my pain I have had
Not even the peace of weeping.

Love is no wave, but a crested and angry sea
To be taken and taken forever, billow on billow, 10
Though the mind break with the body's senseless breaking.
This I know, on my pillow.

[1930]

The Golden Cockerel

That weathercock, compassion,
Veering on his pole,
Has made a crested virtue
Of his unanchored soul.

His gilded feathers sparkle
And lift in any wind,
And the harsh croak of his pity
Falls without end.

Summer storm, lightning
And the crack of thunder 10
Cannot rend his throat
Or his sides asunder.

[1928, 1930]

Skulls Like These

Skulls like these
Inhabiting

Gardens given over
To Spring
Can never flower
Again, or be
In their death
Sap for a tree.

Wide browed
But uncelestial, 10
They must keep
Their bestial
And undisintegrate
Identity
In a garden
Eternally.

[1930]

For a Silent Poet

How can she be so quiet, she
Whose voice has never been subdued
At the shut door? No misery
Cries from her grave's quietude.

No slurring crumb is cast to her,
Nor cloak of wool. How should
She sleep so well, who knows the whir
Of tiny wings in a wood,

Who long in ecstasy has lain
Under the oak, the ghostly beech— 10
By a white star and a cloud's disdain
Troubled into speech?

[1930]

Moon

What I had waited for in the silken wind
Came over me at last. Radiant I stood
In silver. Silver the pavement's end.
Chaste every poplar, every cottonwood.

A light in the *portales* of the hill
Opened the earth. A cricket shook the air.

On Monte Sol guitars of gold, too still
For music, said a silver prayer.

[1930]

5 *portales*: Spanish for portals. 7 **Monte Sol**: Spanish for Sun Mountain, near Santa Fe, New Mexico.

Those Who Speak in Whispers

They must be taut, hard, sibilant—
They who speak
In whispers, they must form words for reluctant ears only
And not soft sounds, as two cheek to cheek.

Knowing no ease, they know too
They are the quarried things
Fingers will crook at slightly, at which eyebrows are always lifted
Because of their whisperings.

See them—their white faces, their frenzy—
And how they scurry 10
Down the unfriendly alleys
On feet not furry.

[1930]

The Perfect Tree

And thus no farther than the perfect tree
By the sweet earth and the moment made,
They came to rest where the robins hungrily
Nicked a green ring around the oval shade.

Two that will never know a stranger thing
Than singing birds alive to ring them round
Bend to each other in the shade and cling
In the uneven circle of that sound.

Their minds rebel at the concentric rings
That hold them captive to this age and breast; 10
To wider air and timeless worshipings
Of gods they knew, they thrust their futile quest.

Nor will they find upon that pliant shell
Of body they enfold the crystal wing
Dimly remembered glittering as it fell
Arc-like from shoulders gold and quivering.

And yet, in velvet palm or flick of sun
Across the hair, some likeness to those spears
Of light on wing may cause the heart to run
Choking, and the eye to cloak with tears. 20

The robin song has left its dark and passed,
The cottonwood released a silver wool.
And the heart, enamored, finds itself at last
Undesiring and more beautiful.

[1930]

The Vandals

When those who scraped the granite hill,
Harried, confused its flowing line,
Blasted its edge, its summit till
Boulders were crystals sharp and fine—
They had gone up, breathing the rare
Ethereal vapor, quick and winy.

Flurried wings hammered the air;
A horn of gold, remote and tiny,
Ruffled the quiet at their ears
Like protestation shrunk to song. 10

Yet all that horde were without tears
Or cognizance of any wrong.

[1930]

The Corrosive Season

We will need even these stumps of cedar,
The harsh fruit of the land.
Our thirst will have to be slaked, if at all, by this thin
Water on the sand.

If we have demanded this corrosive season
Of drought, if we have bent
Backward from the plow, asking
Even less than is sent,

Surely we may be no bitterer
Than the shrunk grape 10
Clinging to the wasted stem
It cannot escape.

[1927, 1930]

Endless Legend

. . . And the well-stone polished and the rounded cobbles
With the cool green grass
Lifting over them. There is an arch of iron
To frame the sky, that hushed and holy space,

And one to come forever with the jar
Of jade and silver, of amethyst or clay,
Stooping to draw the sky-dissolving water
That will not shrink away . . .

[1930]

Before Spring

When the day comes
Before a stalk
Of grass opens the earth
And the birds talk,
What of him who knows
Beyond Spring
Swales of the crisp grass
And gray birds shivering?

[1930]

The Cross

This burden burdened him:
To love the sapless limb
Because he hated those
Which blossomed while he froze.

This burden weighed him down,
So he became a clown
With tatters of a joy
He fashioned when a boy.

The tatters were like wings
Grown from the wooden things; 10
And the cross he had to bear
Was feathery in air.

[1930]

Shadow on Snow

I, a shadow, thinking as I go,
Feel the need of a mimicry
To say this in music: how the moon is one
With the snow, and the snow warmer than I shall ever be—
I, a shadow, moving across the snow.

There shall be no more shadows after mine shall go
Hissing over ice, cracking the black river glass.
There shall be still a moon, but never a sun,
Never an earth again with its triumphing grass—
Only the moon and the snow. 10

[1930]

The Impenitent

They, the impenitent, discordant
Of voice, with their high scorn,
Fail in the land of willows, fail
In the broad wood, in the country of corn.

In the groaning hill, the desert that is stricken
And barren of fruit,
Or in crawling sand under water,
Let them strike root.

[1930]

Change

This is the way of things in this mad world:
Blue lights in children's eyes are overcast;
Summer is wrenched at its bright root and whirled
Out of the mind with all its locks aghast;
Cones bleed and fall; dusk comes again; a shiver
Stirs the slim beech; October noons are white
And blistering with sun; the tawny river
Breaks from its bed to scar the sand by night.

And the great copper elms grow gray; the worm
Munches the leaves; dew thins to air; the wheat, 10
Bundled in sheaves, is smoky with decay;
Age stiffs the knees of horses—and all form

Crumbles like stones of cities in the heat
And cold of day that follows day on day.

[1930]

Footprints

Over the gold-leafed road, the drenched willow
Leans. The flayed track, smooth as stone,
Will be printed with our feet passing over,
And we shall be gone.

You will not find trace of us after the fall of rain
Sweeps again. You will not find
Trace of us in the orchard or the pasture
Or in the mind.

Only these prints of feet—and ephemeral!—
In the sand and clay, 10
And you will forget why it is we have gone
And which way.

[1930]

Hour After Dawn

Hour after dawn,
Burst, and stain
The rigid basin
Of the brain.

In that wan shell
Compose your luster
Till it become
A molten cluster.

Burning to wash
At every beach 10
Up and down
The body's reach.

[1928, 1930]

D'Arcy McNickle [D'Arcy Dahlberg], Confederated Salish and Kootenai, 1904–1977

D'Arcy McNickle is widely acclaimed as a fiction writer, political activist, government official, anthropologist, and historian. But early in his life he was also an accomplished poet.

McNickle was born on the Flathead Reservation in Montana. His mother's parents—including his grandfather Isidore, the topic of one of his poems—were Canadian Métis (Cree, Anishinaabe, and French) who fled to Montana in 1885 after joining the Métis rebellion in Canada. McNickle was enrolled in the Confederated Salish and Kootenai Tribes in 1905. He attended the mission school on the Flathead reservation before federal officials took him away from his mother and sent him to the Salem Indian Training School, later known as the Chemawa Indian School, in Oregon. After he returned to the Flathead he took his stepfather's name, Dahlberg, and he published his poems (except the last poem, "Sweet Is the Prairie") under that name before resuming the name McNickle. He majored in English at the University of Montana and worked on a university-based magazine that published all his published poems except "Old Isidore." As a senior in 1925, before graduating, he sold his land allotment to fund study at Oxford University. In 1926 he moved to New York City, where he worked at a variety of jobs while writing a novel, which after many revisions was published as *The Surrounded* in 1936. After working for the Federal Writers Project in 1935, McNickle joined the Office (later Bureau) of Indian Affairs in 1936 to work with reformist Commissioner John Collier. He traveled to reservations across the United States, trying to improve the dialogue between Indian communities and OIA officials. In 1944, he was one of the founders of the National Congress of American Indians. Later, he worked as a development organizer for Indian communities and began a program of workshops for young Indian leaders. In 1966, he founded and directed the Anthropology Department at the University of Saskatchewan, and then in 1971 he founded the Newberry Library's Center for the History of the American Indian (now called the D'Arcy McNickle Center for American Indian History) in Chicago. (D. R. Parker)

Besides *The Surrounded*, a powerful, understated novel set on the Flathead Reservation, McNickle published *Runner in the Sun: A Story of Indian Maize* (1954), a young adult novel set in the American Southwest long before 1492, and *Wind from an Enemy Sky* (1978), which dramatizes conflicts between federal officials and Indian people on a fictionalized version of the Flathead Reservation. His nonfiction books include *They Came Here First: The Epic of the American Indian* (1949, 1975); *Indians and Other Americans* (with Howard E. Fey, 1959, 1970); *Indian Tribes of the United States: Ethnic and Cultural Survival* (1962, revised as *Native American Tribalism*, 1973); and *Indian Man: A Life of Oliver La Farge* (1971). His stories are collected in *The Hawk Is Hungry and Other Stories* (1992).

McNickle's poems match the mountain and farm world of his fiction. "Sweet Is the Prairie," from 1934, extends beyond this volume's 1930 boundary, but flexibility about the date seems appropriate, given that it is McNickle's last known poem and one of his best, and that his poems—which have not even been listed in bibliographies before, let alone commented on—are one of the major contributions of this volume.

Plowing

Oh, the joy of the touch of the turning sod,
The spraying dust and the crumbling clod!
The greatest boon that life may give is not to die
while yet you live!

[1924]

Cycle

The night slips to its ending,
A new day shall come—
There shall be new roads wending,
A new beating of the drum—

Men's eyes shall have fresh seeing,
Grey lives reprise their span—
But under the new sun's being,
Completing what night began,

There'll be the same backs bending,
The same sad feet shall drum— 10
When this night finds its ending
And day shall have come. . . . .

[1924]

Today

What did we talk about today?
Oh little things—little things—
The thin smiles that come to men
And why a child sings.

And what all did we do today?
Oh little things—little things—
Walked easily, arms brushing,
Watched a bird's wings.

And know? What did we know today?
A little thing—a simple thing— 10
Because of winter's long sitting by
The roadside . . . . . we have spring.

[1925]

Minuet in G

Exquisite song of the little grey-days,
And of the night-time—
Poignantly side by side
In faded, faded tapestry . . .

Exquisite sadness of men who walk,
When somewhere—
The swing of an endless dance . . .
Gracefulness that, somehow, never comes,
Only as a shadow through the singing summer-air . . .
But oh, the long, long hope! 10

[1925]

The Mountains

There is snow, now—
A thing of silent creeping—
And day is strange half-night . . .
And the mountains have gone, softly murmuring something . . .

And I remember pale days,
Pale as the half-night . . . and as strange and sad.

I remember times in this room
When but to glance thru an opened window
Was to be filled with an ageless crying wonder:
The grand slope of the meadows, 10
The green rising of the hills,
And then far-away slumbering mountains—
Dark, fearful, old—
Older than old, rusted, crumbling rock,
Those mountains . . .
But sometimes came a strange thing
And theirs was the youth of a cloudlet flying,
Sunwise, flashing . . .

And such is the wisdom of mountains! 20
Knowing it nothing to be old,
And nothing to be young!

There is snow, now—
A silent creeping . . .

And I have walked into the mountains,
Into canyons that gave back my laughter,

And the lover-girl's laughter . . .
And at dark,
When our skin twinged to the night-wind,
Built us a great marvelous fire 30
And sat in quiet,
Carefully sipping at scorching coffee . . .

But when a coyote gave to the night
A wail of all the bleeding sorrow,
All the dismal, grey-eyed pain
That those slumbering mountains had ever known—
Crept close to each other
And close to the fire—
Listening—
Then hastily doused the fire 40
And fled (giving many excuses)
With tightly-clasping hands.

Snow, snow, snow—
A thing of silent creeping

And once,
On a night of screaming chill,
I went to climb a mountain's cold, cold body
With a boy whose eyes had the ancient look of the mountains,
And whose heart the swinging dance of a laughter-child . . .
Our thighs ached 50
And lungs were fired with frost and heaving breath—
The long, long slope—
A wind mad and raging . . .
Then—the top!

> There should have been . . . something . . .
> But there was silence, only—
> Quiet after the wind's frenzy,
> Quiet after all frenzy—
> And more mountains,
> Endlessly into the night . . . 60
>
> And such is the wisdom of mountains!
> Knowing how great is silence,
> How nothing is greater than silence!

And so they are gone, now,
And they murmured something as they went—
Something in the strange half-night . . .

[1925]

Old Isidore

Lord God! Give him rest,
Out in those far obscure hills,
Where for him was peace—
And where his heart wandered sadly . . .

I.

I have wondered how it is that you are here,
O Montana,
For I have come to you many a time,
Dumb with the wonder of you;

I have come to you in the dawn-time
When all a Universe seemed sleeping in your forests, 10
And your great mountains boomed tremendously—
And know that you were mystery . . .

I have come to you in July hay-fields,
Walked at evening through your shadowed hay-cocks,
Walked in the fragrance of your youthful meadows—
And this was mystery . . .

I have come to you at quiet stream-sides,
Dropped and drunk of the crystal water,
Laughed and flipped pebbles at timorous minnows—
Knowing how there was mystery . . . 20

On sunset prairies I have come to you,
And seen you flash from a dreary cabin window
The fire and song of all effort and hope—
Poignant, ageless beauty . . .

And so these many times I have come to you,
O Montana,
And I have wondered—
Wondered . . .

II.

But I had not known,
Until that day in a shabby dead-man's parlor, 30
How much was answered in Old Isidore—
Old Isidore strangely dead.

You do not know Old Isidore,
You, men of the toiling Now,

You, men who will toil in the Future's hundred years—
Nor do you need to know Old Isidore.

For as I stood in the house of death
I looked long . . .
And into my ears came singing,
And into my heart, mystery— 40
And an answer for mystery.

I knew, that as he alone had not given voice to you,
O Montana,
That he alone had given this much—
This unalterable, deathless bit . . .

And how many hundred others,
Coming at last to a shabby house of death,
Giving you a voice,
O Montana!

But where they came from, or why, 50
That you do not know,
Men of the Now, and of the Future—
Nor do you need to know!

III.

But into my ears came singing,
The singing of Old Isidore—
And it was this that he sang,
That he shall sing to me down through the days of my living—

High and clear,
Singing as the waters of the mountains,
On the wind, winging high and clear: 60

"In starlight,
In ancient faded starlight,
I have talked with One who is my God;
And know that life is small,
For He has shown me how it is so
And the ageless lapping of water,
In the timeless throat of the songbird,
In the endless dream of the mountain . . .

"In starlight,
In ancient splendid starlight, 70
I have known life to be bitter

For my God has shown me
Tears—
Tears from all Beginning to all Ending,
Tears for the living, and
Tears for the dead.
"And so . . . and so—
I have lived,
And some things have been good . . .

"And I die, 80
Here in a far dim corner;
I do not even go upon the wind
To tell man that I die;
It is well that none should care,
For I have but come with a song for singing.
I have chopped at trees for a pathway,
I have held the plow to the earth-breast,
I have tamed the wildness of horses—
Now,
Others may come with their songs for singing, 90
And their singing shall be but life.

"And so . . . and so—
I have lived . . .
And I die . . . "

IV.

No, you do not know Old Isidore,
But I have come from him,
I have come from his side
Where I have touched his lips
And know his heart to be chill
With the strange chill of the silent heart. 100
And because of touching him
I know that there is still the mystery,
And it is the mystery of breath and blood.

V.

O, there is need of many fathers to give birthright to a state,
And many fathers shall be but thin grey men,
With their hearts still in the forests
And on the prairies
Where before had been the whisper of their quickened tread.

And because of them you are here,
O Montana— 110
And there is no mystery
That is not the mystery of breath and blood . . .

You have taken Old Isidore away, now,—
Let there be warmth in the young breast of you,—
Bring the silence out of your dim hills,—
And shroud him . . .

[1925]

Old Isidore: McNickle's grandfather, Isidore Parenteau. "Old Isidore" won first prize out of "four hundred and twenty-odd" entrants in a contest sponsored by the *Sunday Missoulian*, which published the poem on its front page under a banner headline, with an article about the poem by the judges and a photograph of the poet. In the article, H. G. Merriam—one of McNickle's teachers—wrote that he chose "Old Isidore" because it "best reports the quality of Montana life, the fibrous spirit of it, in moving form and rhythm and powerful and haunting phrases. . . . Here, in this poem, is no transient view of Montana life, no superficial observation of its picturesque features. Here is no 'booster's' flattering catalogue of its virtues. Here is no reportorial account of its happenings. Here is order outpouring of a Montana-grained nature, springing from sustained love of association with the state. Here is penetrative vision of its heart of hearts, yesterday, today, and forever. The poem has magnificent interpretive power. In it Montana is made not only unique but of life, not only yesterday's or today's, but time's." The other judge, Lucy H. Carson, wrote that she "ranked 'Old Isidore' highest because of its insight and appeal. The poet and his reader stand with uncovered heads in the presence of the mystery of Montana, sense its past in its present, and pay their reverent tribute to the partial solution of the mystery in the person of Old Isidore."

Man Hesitates but Life Urges

There is this shifting, endless film
And I have followed it down the valleys
And over the hills,—
Pointing with wavering finger
When it disappeared in purple forest-patches
With its ruffle and wave to the slightest-breathing wind-God.

There is this film
Seen suddenly, far off,
When the sun, walking to his setting,
Turns back for a last look, 10
And out there on the far, far prairie
A lonely drowsing cabin catches and holds a glint,
For one how endless moment,
In a staring window the fire and song of the martyrs!

There is this film
That has passed to my fingers

And I have trembled,
Afraid to touch.

And in the eyes of one
Who had wanted to give what I had asked 20
But hesitated—tried—and then
Came with a weary, aged, "Not quite,"
I could but see that single realmless point of time,
All that is sad, and tired, and old—
And endless, shifting film.

And I went again
Down the valleys and over the hills,
Pointing with wavering finger;
Ever reaching to touch, trembling,
Ever fearful to touch. 30

[1926]

Sweet Is the Prairie

Re-creations, by one who does not remember the original words, of four French-Canadian songs.

VISIONS OF GOLD

Whenever I walk upon this land I seem to see
Visions of gold . . .
Whatever the hand that laid these hills would surely be
Cunning and bold,
He walks upon the prairie
And never grows old.

MY LOVER WILL COME

Sweet is the prairie when bright flowers blow,
Sweet is the warm wind after the snow;
Spring with the bird deep into the sky,
My lover will come when summer is nigh. 10

Darkling the river that bore him away,
Bore him to northward one bleak autumn day;
His traps in his boat, his fiddle put by,
My lover will come when summer is nigh.

Winter is longer than soul can withstand,
Endless the wind that blows 'cross the land;

Spring brings the thaw and brant cleave the sky,
My lover will come when summer is nigh.

Rich be the cargo he brings from the north,
Beaver and fox skins, a king's ransom's worth; 20
Then we will wed, my lover and I,—
I pray he returns when summer is nigh!

MOURNING SONG

I walk the prairie floor
And hollow falls the sound,
My step rings hollow on the ground
My heart is hollow more.
Night comes, I stand alone,
Gone is my lover, gone
Into dust and my heart to stone.

ROVING SONG

The mountains around me 30
The blue sky over,
The prairie before me—
My heart is a rover!
I'll have earth for bed,
Make dew my bread
And walk till my hunger is fed.

[1934]

Ben D. Locke, Choctaw, 1882–1928

Captain Ben Davis Locke was part of a prominent family in the Choctaw Nation. He served as private secretary to his brother, Victor M. Locke, Jr., who was Principal Chief from 1910 to 1917. His mother-in-law, Alice Brown Davis, was Chief of the Oklahoma Seminoles from 1922 to 1935. At the age of nineteen, Ben Locke became a deputy United States Marshal. He then joined the Oklahoma National Guard and led a mostly Indian battalion that backed up the Army during the fighting on the Mexican border in 1916–1917. During World War I he commanded a mostly Indian unit of field artillery. He spent his last four years ill in a hospital in Muskogee, Oklahoma where he edited *Trench 90*, a hospital newsletter that included his own humorous dialect stories and poems. His writing appeared in other publications as well, though the only poems that have been found are the two included here. ("Capt. Ben Locke"; Littlefield and Parins, eds., *Native American Writing in the Southeast* 232; Thoburn 1378, 1427; White, Ch. 1)

The Doughboy

Handed down from generation to generation
Is the blood of the noble chiefs
Who ascended to glory and victory
By will of their powerful beliefs.

Thus the son of his fathers,
The Indian brave of today,
Forged to the front in battle,
In Khaki his war debt to pay.

The Doughboy, an emblem of courage,
Who gave his all in the fight, 10
Stands as a hero undaunted
To a race fast fading from sight.

To The Doughboy his people have given
A reverence, great and sublime,
A pride in his wondrous achievements
Dimmed not by the passage of time.

To you on the brink of the abyss,
Whose morale and courage run low,
Remember the Spirit of the Doughboy!
The Indian, the Arrow, the Bow. 20

[1925, 1928]

Squaw-lls

by Zoe A. Tilghman

Good morning, Katie Fixico,
Who's your guardian to-day?
And where's the latest law suit brought,
And what judge has the say?

And have you married number three,
—Or is he number two?—
And does he for the license pay
Or is that up to you?

Excuse me! It is Wosey Deere
Who's marrying number four. 10
And have they yet found Maude Lee Mudd
Whose millions pile up more?

And how about that old divorce
Seven lawyers got for Exie Fife?
She paid them well; but now, it seems,
A dire conspiracy was rife.

Injunctions, kidnapping and suits,
Hearings, appeals galore;
Investigations, federal, state,
And probes of probes before; 20

Lawyers and guardians and courts,
Fights open, or by stealth,
The battle rages, "ins" and "outs"
Which gets the Indian's wealth.

Note: Zoe A. Tilghman was a widely published writer who often wrote about Oklahoma topics. Locke's "Hobachi (Echo)" (below) responds to—echoes—Tilghman's poem. Tilghman edited *Harlow's Weekly*, which published this poem on 2 April 1927. Locke's poem appeared the same month. In *Harlow's Weekly* that April, Tilghman also published Genoa Morris's "Oklahoma," a poem that addresses Indians in a derogatory way, which may have contributed to Locke's resentment. In Morris's poem, an Oklahoma Indian says "The laggard's way is the way I know." **Title:** a contraction of "squaw ills," evoking the sound of colloquial speech and punning on *squalls*. The women mentioned in the poem, Katie Fixico (Creek), Wosey Deere (Creek), Maude Lee Mudd (Osage and Seneca), and Exie Fife (Creek), were each at the center of notorious legal squabbles (squalls about "squaws," from Tilghman's perspective) as abusive whites concocted shady legal shenanigans to steal wealth that the women gained through mineral rights, especially oil. **2 guardian:** Indians in eastern Oklahoma were frequently ruled legally incompetent and forced to have a white guardian run their finances, a process widely abused for the profit of guardians, especially when oil income made some Indians in eastern Oklahoma wealthy. Such abuses were eventually investigated by a variety of official commissions, as noted later in the poem.

Hobachi (Echo)

He say "Good mornin' Katie Fixico,"
(I say it—'Hello Miss Vanderbilt)
Where you learn it 'bout divorce,
How much you pay for lawyer-tilt?

How come you marry Number Three,
And do like white woman do;
Which one grafter find yo' man
An' how long befo' you sue?

Why say "Scuse me Wosey Deere?"
White woman marry heap much too; 10
Why say "Where Maude Lee Mudd?"
Crook lawyer know what she do!

She get 'em "old divorce" alright
  That girl you name Exie Fife;
Yes, she pay "seven lawyers" good—
  Bob Williams no use his knife.

You shame it whole United States
  When you tell world "Indian tale,"
He was ward of Uncle Sam
  No live now on "open trail." 20

Indian was like his simple life
  But when he got "rich monies"
White man spoil the happy homes
  When he talk that grafter "honies."

But jus' same we got left
  Blood of Redman, noble, brave—
Come from chief of long generation
  What "fool Indian" shame to grave.

[1927]

2 **Vanderbilt**: name of a famously wealthy American family.

Molly Spotted Elk (Molly Alice Nelson), Penobscot, 1903–1977

Molly Alice Nelson, who took the performance name Molly Spotted Elk, grew up on the Penobscot Reservation in Old Town on Indian Island in Maine. She went to school on the reservation and then to junior high and high school on the mainland. Her father served as the Penobscot representative in the Maine State Legislature in 1921–1922 and as governor of the Penobscot Nation in 1939–1940. A talented dancer and a devoted reader and writer, Nelson interrupted her studies to earn money for school by dancing for traveling vaudeville acts. Then, sponsored by University of Pennsylvania anthropologist Frank Speck, she went to Swarthmore Preparatory School and audited classes in anthropology and English at the University of Pennsylvania, while also supporting herself by dancing in clubs and theaters. She left Pennsylvania to dance in a Wild West show and save for more schooling and then went to New York, where she joined some of the best known nationally traveling dance revues and also danced in a wide variety of clubs and revues, from the seedy to the swank.

Meanwhile, Nelson read widely, including Flaubert, Baudelaire, H. G. Wells, Proust, and Joyce, and she wrote poetry and fiction, including literary and adventure stories and traditional Penobscot stories. She carried her typewriter into dressing rooms and wrote between shows. She published stories and poems, probably at least some of the time under pseudonyms, though none of her published poems has been found. She also starred in the acclaimed 1930 film *The Silent Enemy.*

In 1931, Nelson left for Paris to dance with the United States Indian Band, and when the band returned home, she stayed. Parisian and European audiences let her dance more as she wanted to dance and less according to the clichés that Americans expected. From Paris, she traveled and danced across France as well as in Belgium, Italy, and Spain. Continuing her intellectual interests, she worked with French anthropologists, including Marcel Griaule and Michel Leiris, and went to Marcel Mauss's lectures at the Sorbonne. She often blended performances with lectures, including at museums and at the Sorbonne. Meanwhile, she worked on but never finished a novel set on Indian Island. In the late thirties, she came back to the United States for four years, where she danced and found bit parts in movies. After she returned to France in 1938, a French publisher was about to bring out her Penobscot stories when World War II intervened. Caught in the war and desperate to escape, Nelson fled across the Pyrenees carrying her daughter, much of the way on foot. Scarred by the trying escape and the death of her French husband during the war, and perhaps cornered by the decreasing opportunities for dancers of her age, she worked lesser and lesser jobs, especially in New York, and floated between work and her home on Indian Island, deteriorating mentally and spending part of her time institutionalized. She spent her last years at home, often unclear in her mind and often pounding away at her typewriter late into the night, writing works that she rarely finished and never published. (McBride)

Molly Spotted Elk's beautifully written traditional Penobscot stories were published at last in 2003 in a book that also includes her notes on language: *Katahdin: Wigwam's Tales of the Abnaki Tribe and a Dictionary of Penobscot and Passamaquoddy Words with French and English Translations.* Nelson wrote the poems below, published here for the first time, in 1926–1927, when she joined a dance troupe at the Aztec Theater in San Antonio (McBride 76–80). As they come from her manuscripts, they have a few quirks from their status as less-than-final drafts, but they appear to be nearly complete.

["Down in the land of roses"]

Down in the land of roses
Near the dreamy Rio Grande
I met and loved a maiden
In the shadow of the Alamo
Night-eyed virgin; Rosa
A jewel from old Mexico.
There, 'neath the spell of twilight
And the beauty of her being
My heart and love I gave her.
The palms above us   10
Whispered softly to the breezes
While myriads of stars
Cast lingering spells
On two lone souls at peace.

["I never knew of such a place"]

I never knew of such a place
Of clear blue skies and billowy clouds
Of soft/gray dawns and silvery nights
Of sunshine smiling everywhere
That lasts thru out the whole year too—
Where birds go sailing in the air
And sing while on the wing—
Where the river, like a snake
Curls in and out and all about,
With the city in its tiny grip— 10
In its quaint and narrow edges
Old stone walls and dobi huts
Stately date palms and eucaluptus
Wide leaved banana trees and cactus—
And man made bridges hug
The shores of San Antonio.

I never knew of such a place
Of historic, picturesque beauty
As the sacred, age worn Alamo
Nestling in the Plaza, lost in sight. 20
Amid the modern buildings round it—
Lost not the value, nor the story
That thru the crumbling walls do tell
Where Texas glory and its manhood—
Might live again immortal
And in its silent walls, once more
The thoughts prayers of sacrifice remains—
—Of hidden and scattered Missions
Whose crumbling walls, bear scars
Of plunder, time and warfare 30
Where neath the ravages of weather
Gleams the artistry of Spain
And the brilliant hues of sainted painters—
—Of the Governor's Palace
Once the flower of a grandee
Now in obscurity, a forgotten hut
That bears no sight on strange eyes.

I never saw such a place
Where narrow streets were thronged
With crowds of different folks— 40
~~There were~~ Where the swaggering cowboys

In for a holiday, from near-by ranches
Saunter in their riding boots
And tell-tale gallon hats
Of swarthy, shifting Mexicanos
And coal hued Ethiopians
So many boys imprisoned
in uniforms of Uncle Sam
Of movie chaps from Hollywood
In wool and sport galore 50
Of oldtimers, gray and bent
Ruddy faced and beaming eye—
of brand new millionaires
Veneered in sudden wealth—
Of tourists with the cow muhs
Of many climes and countries—
Go jostling each other
Most every day, in San Antone.

3 **soft/gray**: *gray* is written above *soft*. 12 **dobi**: adobe. 41 **~~There were~~ Where**: *There were* is crossed out and *Where* written above it. 55 **cow muhs**: the editor's best effort to transcribe an uncertain phrase: *cow* and *hs* seem more likely accurate transcriptions than *mu*. Perhaps the word or words were not written as Nelson intended.

["Twas only a bunch of roses"]

Twas only a bunch of roses
Sweet, yellow Spanish roses
That bloomed in the courtyard
Of your distant and lovely hacienda
You sent her, kind friend,
In admiration as you said
Of the grace and savagery
That spoke to you and thrilled
The watchers of her dances.

They gave her joy, she smiled 10
For a stranger in the audience
Whose kindness was a pleasure
Each Sunday afternoon—
While he, the giver of the roses
Sat amid the many there
And drank in the vision of her
Filled with strange emotions.

Each week, they came, the roses
Sweet, yellow Spanish roses

Pinned to a little note. 20
Until one day, the sender met
The maiden of the dance—
A pleasant chat, a wholesome laugh
Two newfound friends at last.

Back to the lovely hacienda
Near the famous Bandera Road
There lives within the gray stone wall
He, who gave of all, his dearest
Of his roses, heart and love
And a memory of her. 30

We're In the Chorus Now

Aztec Days—
We are the famous Aztec Girls
You've heard so much about
We're noted for our happy smiles
And for our dancing too
Most everybody likes us
We hope you'll like us too.

As we go dancing
And old Kirk begins to play
You can hear them saying 10
The Aztec Girls are surely
Just the thing!

A Russian Mystery
She was the lily, fair and white
With golden curls and wistful eyes
She was a fairy in the light
A mystery, enshrouded in lies.

Lilyan, whose lovely face
A thing of beauty
Led the line, to grace 20
In loveliness and duty.

The Rascal
Audrey, whose petite being
And twinkling orbs
Childish outbursts
And supple back
Was the kid and acrobat.

The Singing Deceiver
Mabelle, who was like a chameleon
And whose tongue mellowed 30
With bitter and sweet words.

The Gold Digger
Ruth, whose shapely figure
And superstitious nature
Red haired vamp we called her
Had beaus from the smart set
And friends from the ranches.

Her Pardner
Jean, from old St. Louis
A champ Charlestoner 40
And St. Louis demonstrator
A typical show girl who knew
All stage language and tricks
And rivaled a parrot for swearing.

An English Heather Bloom—
Violet; the teaser and vivacious
Whose personality beamed
And feet that could tap
Their size didn't stop
Any pep for a Tiller step— 50
One of the Hipp Girls
Who has fallen in love
With that bright-haired Jackson
That witty newsman in front.

A Bit of Sweetness
Mabel, a lovely flower from New York
Her friendships and smiles
Are like haunting fragrance
That linger long, after she has gone.

Untold Charm 60
Charlotte, there's beauty in her
soul
And love shines from her
eyes—
Who still can blush and
graceful be
To those who know her well,

We Moderns

Betty, a damsel from San Antonio
Who can pet, and smoke and drink 70
And gain more jolly pounds
Than any one I've ever known
Yet who loves her Billy so
She doesn't know just what to do.

—A Rare Book—
Orcella, is like a rare book
Bound in all that is worthwhile
By the leather of Intelligence
On whose pages one can find
Understanding, love and trust— 80
A ballerina, who some day
Will take her name to fame
Because its ballet, true she likes
And art to her is work and strife.

50 **Tiller step**: Named after the influential choreographer John Tiller, whose Tiller Girls were famous for linking arms and kicking in precise unison. 76 **Orcella**: In her journal, Spotted Elk wrote of her roommate Orcella, "I like her immensely—she is a real, intellectual and refined girl, there is no effectiveness [affectation, falsity] in her make-up."

Winnie Lewis Gravitt, Choctaw, 1895–1974

Gravitt worked as a public librarian in McAlester, Oklahoma. She attended the University of California at Berkeley and graduated from the University of Oklahoma. In addition to the poem included here, from April through July of 1935 Gravitt published poems in a short-lived journal, the *Tushkahomman*, published by (among others) her brother Grady Lewis. (Gravitt 326; "Dr. Anna Lewis, Choctaw Historian")

Sippokni Sia

(I am old or I am a Grandmother, in Choctaw)

I am old, Sippokni sia.
Before my eyes run many years,
Like panting runners in a race.
Like a weary runner the years lag;
Eyes grow dim, blind with wood smoke;
A handkerchief binds my head,
For I am old. Sippokni sia.

Hands, once quick to weave and spin;
Strong to fan the tanchi;
Fingers patient to shape dirt bowls; 10
Loving to sew hunting shirt;
Now, like oak twigs twisted.
I am old. Sippokni sia.

Feet swift as wind o'er young cane shoots;
Like stirring leaves in ta falla dance;
Slim like rabbits in leather shoes;
Now moves like winter snows,
Like melting snows on Cavanaugh.
In the door I sit, my feet in spring water.
I am old. Sippokni sia. 20

Black like crow's feather, my hair;
Long and straight like hanging rope;
My people proud and young.
Now like hickory ashes in my hair,
Like ashes of old camp fire in rain.
Much civilization bow my people;
Sorrow, grief and trouble sit like blackbirds on fence.
I am old. Sa Sippokni hoke.*

*For I am old, indeed

[1927]

9 **tanchi**: corn. 18 **Cavanaugh**: Cavanaugh or Cavanal Mountain or Hill, in Poteau, Oklahoma.

Sunshine Rider, Cherokee

Sunshine Rider was one version of the stage name of a New York City concert singer and Indian arts activist whose legal name was variously reported in press accounts as Eva, Iva, and Ida Rider and who usually went by the name Princess Atalie Unkalunt or Princess Atalie Unkalunt Rider. She was born in Indian Territory, and her father, Thomas L. Rider, served in the Oklahoma legislature. Rider studied at the Northeast Conservatory of Music in Boston. During World War I, she sang with the YMCA to entertain the troops and won a British citation for valor under fire. In 1920 she founded the First Sons and Daughters of America, an organization to support Indian arts. She reported 2,900 members of the organization in 1933 ("Indian Maid Sings"). She published *The Earth Speaks* in 1940, a collection of stories based on traditional Cherokee tales and accompanied by her own illustrations. By referring to herself as a princess and claiming descent from a chief, Rider took advantage of stereotyped expectations for Indian women. ("Ainslie 'Princess' Repudiates Title"; "Indian Maid Sings")

The Conquered Race

"I am sad!" mourned an aged chieftain
As the sunset sank to rest;
"Because our pathways have been taken,
Our bows unstrung—our homes forsaken,
Our braves—the White Man's ways have fled;
They tolerate their slurs—Lo, the Poor Red."

But the Paleface spoke with sympathy
As he watched the chieftain old.
"Your young will learn and prosperous be,
And all will say, 'A mighty citizen is he!' 10
Now the gloom which wraps your heart must break,
For the modern Redman—is wide awake!"

But the chieftain's eyes were flashed to flame,
As he stood with folded arms;
For the stranger had kindled a fire of old
That leaped to life, from a warrior bold;
But he fell foremost on the earth-beaten sod,
And left the rest to the White Man's God!

[1927]

6 **Lo, the Poor Red**: refers to a famous passage in Alexander Pope's *An Essay on Man* (1733–34): "Lo! the poor Indian, whose untutor'd mind / Sees God in clouds or hears him in the wind" (Epistle 1, line 99, p. 508).

Mary Cornelia Hartshorne, Choctaw, born about 1910

Mary Cornelia Hartshorne published poems in *The American Indian* and eventually joined the magazine as Contributing Editor of its "Poetry Page." *American Indian* often featured young Indian women on its cover and profiled them in the magazine. Hartshorne appeared on the cover for July 1928, and the profile of her notes that she was "descended from two of the most influential families of the Choctaw tribe, the Fulsoms and the McCurtains" and that Choctaw District Chief Cornelius McCurtain was her grandfather. "She declares, however, that she is *not* a 'princess,' and that the title was unknown among the Choctaw Indians" ("Introducing Miss Hartshorne"). (If she was descended from Cornelius McCurtain, she was probably something more like his great-great grandchild.) Hartshorne was so good a student that she completed elementary and high school in only six years. She published poetry in school magazines and then went to the University of Oklahoma, where she was active in the Indian, Spanish, and Poetry Clubs. After time away for illness, she resumed her studies at the University of Tulsa. In 1929, she won a *Tulsa Tribune* contest for essays about the new "talkie movies." She and twenty-three other winners from across the country won a trip to Hollywood where they met with Mary Pickford, the famous movie star. *American Indian* published Hartshorne's winning essay with an essay she wrote about her trip to Hollywood, along with a cover photo of her arm in arm with (and towering over) Pickford (February 1929). But nothing has yet turned up about Hartshorne later in her life.

More than any poet in this collection, more even than Lynn Riggs, Hartshorne's sophisticated sense of the poetic line, with its flexible length and its flexible array of enjambments and caesuras, anticipates the style of later poetry.

The Poet

Sunlight was something more than that to him.
It was a halo when it formed a rim
Around some far-off mountain peak. He called
It thin-beat leaf of gold, and stood enthralled
When it lay still on some half-sheltered spot
In gilt mosaics where the trees forgot
To hide the grasses carpeting the spot.

The sky to him was not just the blue sky,
But a deep, painted bowl with clouds piled high;
And when these clouds were tinted burning red, 10
Or gold and bacchic purple, then he said:
"The too-full goblets of the gods had over-run,
Nor give the credit to the disappearing sun
Who flames before he leaves the world in dun."

Between his eyes and life fate seemed to hold
A magic tissue of transparent gold,
That freed his vision from the dull, drab, hopeless part,
And kept alive a fresh, unsaddened heart.
And all unselfishly he tried to share
His gift with us who see the harsh and bare; 20
But we refused. We did not know nor care.

[1927]

14 **dun**: darkness.

Fallen Leaves

(An Indian Grandmother's Parable)

Many times in my life I have heard the white sages,
Who are learned in the knowledge and lore of past ages,
Speak of my people with pity, say, "Gone is their hour
Of dominion. By the strong wind of progress their power,
Like a rose past its brief time of blooming, lies shattered;
Like the leaves of the oak tree its people are scattered."
This is the eighty-first autumn since I can remember.
Again fall the leaves, born in April and dead by December;
Riding the whimsied breeze, zigzagging and whirling,
Coming to earth at last and slowly upcurling, 10
Withered and sapless and brown, into discarded fragments
Of what once was life; dry, chattering parchments
That crackle and rustle like old women's laughter
When the merciless wind with swift feet coming after
Will drive them before him with unsparing lashes
'Til they are crumbled and crushed into forgotten ashes;
Crumbled and crushed, and piled deep in the gulches and hollows,
Soft bed for the yet softer snow that in winter fast follows
But when in the spring the light falling
Patter of raindrops persuading, insistently calling, 20
Wakens to life again forces that long months have slumbered,
There will come whispering movement, and green things
unnumbered
Will pierce through the mould with their yellow-green, sun-
searching fingers,
Fingers—or spear-tips, grown tall, will bud at another year's
breaking,
One day when the brooks, manumitted by sunshine, are making
Music like gold in the spring of some far generation.
And up from the long-withered leaves, from the musty stagnation,
Life will climb high to the furthermost leaflets.
The bursting of catkins asunder with greed for the sunlight; the
thirsting
Of twisted brown roots for earth-water; the gradual unfolding 30
Of brilliance and strength in the future, earth's bosom is holding
Today in those scurrying leaves, soon to be crumpled and broken.
Let those who have ears hear my word and be still. I have spoken.

[1927]

Three Poems of Christmas Eve

LAST NIGHT
Flooded with silver from a star-studded sky
Bethlehem lies in quiet sleep.
In a field nearby
Shepherds keep vigilance under the staring moon.
They watch the restless sheep
And sing perhaps some ancient peasant tune
Of men and flocks;
When suddenly dazzles a great light,
And the star glorified night
Is thrice glorified. The wonder shocks 10
The shepherds mute.
As sweetly as the sound of lute
Played in a forest at the birth of day,
An angel voice tells of the Miracle.
From far away
Is heard the singing of a heavenly throng.
The winds of earth carry the sacred song.

TONIGHT
The clink of ice against thin rounded glass
Mingled with laughter from wide lips that pass
From each to each some hollow senseless quip,
Voices that stammer, and ill-used tongues that trip
Through muddled phrases. So the night wears on
To meet at last the desecrated dawn.

And far across the town a mother kneels
Beside a bed. With tender hands she feels
A flickering pulse, and has no time for tears,
But saves her strength to fight the thing she fears. 10
(The gas burns very low; the heater is so small
That one might safely say it makes no heat at all.)
She need not grieve. Someone will "help the poor."
Tomorrow she will find a basket at the door.

CHRIST
You walk abroad tonight as you walked then:
In spirit, Lover of All Men.
Your wounded hands have only love to give;
Your wounded heart may only bid us live.
You throw no copper pennies in the dust
For wretched ones to grovel for. You thrust

No souls into the mire that you may throw a rope
For them to climb out by. But blazing hope
Burns on your forehead, and within your eyes
The tender mercy of your Father lies. 10

[1927]

Hills of Doon

When I beheld the squatted Hills of Doon,
Blistered and bald and bare,
Sketched in a ragged semi-circle on the air
That quivered up from the parched earth at noon;
When I beheld the stately pale-green spears
Of cottonwood arrayed against the sky,
Sternly aloof and high,
My heart grew heavy, but there were no tears.
And when I felt the lonely quietness that crept
Down from the brooding hills at dusk, 10
On breezes tinctured with faint woodland musk
That lulled my brain, like poppies, 'til I slept,
I pictured the low house near the great bay,
The down-plunging cliffs of rock
Battling the waves' recurrent shock,
The stretch of pebbled beach where, day by day,
I used to stand and watch the sea birds swerve
On sunlit wings swift and alive and free,
And fancied that the unleashed soul of me
Raced with them there above the ocean's curve. 20

The Hills of Doon were huge and strange and old,
I had seen great liners slowly pass.
There were long blades of lightly stirring grass;
I had played with whitecaps salt and cold.
I had seen mad waters lashed to foam;
I had heard sea-voices' friendly taunt;
These inland hills and trees, indifferent and gaunt,
Filled my sick soul with longing for my home.

But that was years ago. Today the sound
Of leaves, whirled by some hurried breeze, 30
Dancing a silver dance in the prim trees,
Quenches the scrape of fishing boats coming aground.
And there is golden magic under a golden moon;
Magic of bird-song and small, shrill-mouthed things at play:

The boom of waters fainter grows each day.
I am at home again—here in my Hills of Doon.

[1928]

Title: probably in Ireland.

April Will Come

April will come, and with it April rain
Singing among young oak leaves; the refrain
Of it will lie upon the opalescent mist
Like bells of Angelus. Green bugle vine will twist
And coil itself around the trunks of trees long dead;
And moistened grasses, crushed beneath one's tread,
Will fill the hazy air with pungent scents,
Stirring the dream-fraught earth from somnolence.

But for me there can be no glory either night or day
In April—it was April when you went away. 10

[1928]

Wind in Mexico

Purple and white, the water-flowers are resting
On a pool of ink-blackness. So they had rested
When she had come to them. So they had lain quiet, quiet,
While the wind played in the tall bordering grasses.

White sunlight falls through the ebony branches,
The sunlight is old; she once dipped her brown hands in it.
The silence is old; she loved the great stillness
Two thousand years away from this thundering greed.

Her feet were small: they pressed lightly among the rushes;
They did not disturb the turtles asleep in the mud. 10
Her hands were like moths skimming over the glowing blossoms.
Her eyes were a-dream with the beauty of high-noon in Mexico.

The coolness of sheltering shadows engulfed her;
A breeze, sweet with the breath of the forest, brushed by her;
She heard a lute's voice and a drum's throb afar in the village,
Warp and woof of a skillfully woven old dream-telling pattern.

Her own fingers sought after music and found it
On thin harp-strings when the heat of the day was asleep;
And night was awake and she sat in the house of her father

And the song of frogs floated up from the pool of white flowers. 20
Harp-strings a-quiver flung silver afar in the starlight,
And her silver singing went surging around and above it;
The wind bore it outward, caressing the land of the Aztecs,
Spilling it into the hearts of the Children of Freedom.

But the wind that wearily ripples the palm-leaves,
That glides through the pool-margining grasses here in the sun's glare,
Bending them low like swords bent low in subjection,
Has been robbed of its treasure. It moans in the ebony branches.

For the ages have muffled the music of her who once walked here,
Have choked out the echoes of laughter, have stifled the flute notes, 30
And the wind is filled with the weeping of Mexico's daughters.
The Children of Freedom are slaves in the home of their fathers.

[1928]

Sonnet

The whirling stars that shower swift-winged light,
The headstrong rivers running to the seas,
The rushing, random wind among the trees,
The clouds pushed onward in an enforced flight,
Season crowding on season, day on night,
Echoes of sound flooding the earth—all these
Move, and will move through coming centuries
In the divine pageant of Eternal Might.

But the plan itself remains immutable.
Rooted in that stability man's soul 10
Finds time to grow; from that deep calm
Draws sanity; meets the inscrutable
With this great truth deciphered from life's scroll:
The universe lies tranquil in God's Palm.

[1928]

Julia Carter Welch, Chickasaw

Julia Carter Welch published a number of yet unfound poems in local newspapers in Richmond, Virginia and in church magazines as well as poems in *American Indian*, the source for the poems included here. Her father, Charles David Carter, served in many offices for the Chickasaw Nation and then, after Oklahoma became a state, in the U.S.

Congress for twenty years, including as Chairman of the Committee on Indian Affairs. Her husband was Gus Welch, a famous Carlisle quarterback and track athlete, a teammate and friend of Jim Thorpe who worked as a coach and athletic director at many schools, colleges, and universities. Her sister, Stella LeFlore Carter, also has a poem in this volume.

Fall

Fall's a little Indian witch,
With wild grapes twined in dusky hair,
Eyes as deep as purple twilight—
Moccasined feet as light as air,
Dancing o'er deep forest trails
Touching them with red and gold,
Making all the world forget

How soon comes winter's cold.
Painting asters by the brook
With rainbow colors from the sky, 10
Pausing long enough to watch
The wild geese honking high.
Bursting burs on nuts so brown
And hiding them deep in the grass,
Knowing well they will be found
By happy children as they pass.

Kissing apples till they blush
On fruit trees bending low—
Setting sumac hedge aflame
To guide us as we go, 20
Through the misty twilight
Where the moon comes up like gold,
Blue wood-smoke her incense fires,
Harvest thank offerings of old.

[1929]

The Weaver

Pakali sits before her blanket loom,
And softly sings of love, the while she weaves.
Her dark eyes, filled with dreams, can scarce keep pace
With her tiny hands, as bronze as autumn leaves—
She weaves with crimson thread, and all may see—
Her lover comes today, the Cherokee.

Life swiftly moves. A wife and mother now,
She marks upon her loom the fleeting moons—
A gray-eyed papoose wakes with lusty cry,
She rocks him gently to and fro, and croons, 10
"Toni, Toni, Tuka Toni"—
The old, old Indian lullaby.

Moons wax and wane. A withered squaw, alone,
She weaves upon her loom with somber shade—
Life, Love, and Death are woven all in one,
With colors true that ne'er shall dim or fade.
'Tis done! She breaks the thread with trembling hand—
Gray eyes are beckoning from the Spirit Land.

[1930]

Indian Lament

Wife he die,
I so sad.
My ol' hoss
Done gone bad.

Buy ol' Ford,
No good too—
Ride and push
No can do.

White man banker
No can trust, 10
Take it monies—
Bank go bust.

Republican,
Stock-market hogs,
Run it country
To the dogs.

Democrat,
He Hoover man—
Hoover man,
Republican. 20

No more Democrat,
By damn—
Guess me vote
For Uncle Sam.

[1930]

1 **he**: she, following the grammar of some Indian languages that leads speakers of those languages to use masculine pronouns in English where other English speakers use feminine pronouns. 18 **Hoover**: Republican Herbert Hoover, president of the United States from 1929-1933, during the stock market crash and the early years of the Great Depression. The sense of the passage seems to be that things have gotten so bad that even Democrats have become Republicans.

Redman

The council-fires are blackened,
In ruins the teepees lie—
Where once the plaintive flute called
The lonely coyotes cry.

The mystic throbs of tom-tom
Will never pulse again—
Death and desolation
Followed by greed and gain.

"As long as ever grass grows
As long as waters run"— 10
The White Man's promise given—
Broken 'ere set of sun.

Brave patient, trusting Redman—
Robbed, starved, crucified.
Before the Great Spirit's Tribunal
Surely justice will not be denied!

[1930]

10–11 **"As long as ever grass grows / As long as waters run"**: While their general sense accurately reflects the sense of many treaties, such phrases—contrary to legend—did not appear in any treaties with the federal government (Prucha 262–63).

Gust-ah-yah-she, Menominee

The Indian's Plea

The "Indian's Plea" was written by a Menominee friend—Gust-ah-yah-she. The Menominee reservation is one of the most beautiful in the country. The Wolf River runs through the reserve, and is unsurpassed for the wildness and beauty of its scenery. Every few miles there is a lovely water-fall, and a movement is on foot to dam up certain of the falls and use the water power. There has been a difference about it—the majority of the Indians do not want this beautiful country of theirs destroyed, and that was the reason for the writing of this poem. It expresses the opinion of the Menominees very well indeed.

As the Indian sat in his little canoe
Paddling away o'er the water so blue,
He thought of the time when the land was his own
Before those white men ever were known.

When those white men came and lodged on our soil,
We lived in our huts, without sorrow or toil,
We hunted the otter, the beaver and deer,

We knew in those woods there was nothing to fear.
When those white men came to visit our land,
We used them like brothers, we gave them our hand, 10
We saw they were weary, we gave them repose
Never dreaming those men would ever turn foes.

But soon they began to intrude on our own,
Which caused us poor Indians in sorrow to roam.
Now driven away from our own native shore
And the light of our wigwams we never see more.

It's on our rich prairie their farm house is found
They own all the country from Texas to Maine,
It's on our rich prairie they build their large town.
And the red deer is driven out over the plain. 20

It's a fight for the forest—the red deer is gone
The tall pine and cedar the axman cut down,
The otter, the beaver, the huntsmen have slain
And we can hunt through our forest in vain.

They took all our timberland, animals, fish;
And now for our waters to take is their wish,
To change them and take all their beauty away
It seems such a wrong thing to do it I say.

Why can't we have something that we can enjoy,
Oh! Leave it as God made it—do not destroy, 30
The light from our wigwams has passed as the day,
Now please do not take our waters away.

[1929]

Note beneath title: appears in the original publication in *American Indian* and was apparently written by the editor, Anne E. Ford. For the dispute over dams on the Wolf River, see Beck 114–19. **25 fish**: the lake sturgeon holds a central place in Menominee history and belief, but dams had already driven the lake sturgeon from the Wolf River.

Stella LeFlore Carter, Chickasaw, born 1892

Stella LeFlore Carter's father, Charles David Carter, served many years as a representative in the U.S. Congress. Her sister, Julia Carter Welch, also has poems in this volume.

Inauguration Day

The cowboy and the farmer, in chaps and Sunday clothes,
Indian and country lawyer, and folks nobody knows,
Oil magnates, women in Paris gowns, a motley, strange array,
The high and low, the rich and poor, are in "The City" today.

All proudly pay their tribute to Oklahoma's son,
"Alfalfa Bill," they call him, in half-admiring fun.
His roughened, weather-beaten face and careless dress proclaim
That he's a real pioneer and worthy of his name.

Here is no man that men can rule; his virile, homely face
Shows scars of many battles—but of weakness not a trace. 10
Here is the poor man's sponsor—he has known poverty.
His rugged, fearless honesty a child could plainly see.

They say he lacks in culture—yet an eager scholar he,
Of history and jurisprudence and lore of the tepee;
A typical Oklahoman—here's to a native son!
God give him strength and wisdom to run well his race begun.

[1930–1931]

Title: In 1930, William Henry David Murray was elected governor of Oklahoma. A longtime Oklahoma politician who married into a prominent Chickasaw family and often supported Chickasaw and Indian causes, Murray was dubbed Alfalfa Bill because he called for crop rotation with alfalfa. He often advocated progressive policies, and so he might be thought to deserve Carter's praise as "the poor man's sponsor" (11), but he was not a sponsor for all the poor, for he enthusiastically supported Jim Crow (anti-African American) legislation.

Elise Seaton, Cherokee and Chickasaw

Born in Oklahoma, Elise Seaton and her sister Elisebeth were dancers who studied dance and drama in New York City before returning to Bartlesville, Oklahoma. They danced in vaudeville and traveled widely as extras for a magician. Because they looked alike, the magician could hide one sister and then seem to make her magically reappear when the other sister came on stage from another direction. The sisters ran a dancing school in Bartlesville. ("Introducing"; Wallis 206)

Orientale

Rhythm-color
Splotches duller than the
Sounding of the cymbals and the
Thumping of the tom-tom.

Swaying, bending,
Colors blending
With the whirling and the twirling
Of the dancer—
Nadja.

Sands are burning; 10
In my heart they
Leave a yearning,
For I long to be an
Orientale.

[1930]

9 **Nadja**: either a specific dancer, such as a dancer from the Ballets Russes, the famous modernist Russian ballet company, or simply a Russian name to indicate a generic Russian dancer. 14 **Orientale**: modernist dance, such as the exoticizing orientalist ballets performed by the Ballets Russes, including one called *Les Orientales*.

Riverside

Have you ever been on Riverside
When the moon is beaming bright
And the lights across on Jersey shore
Are winking in the night?

There you see the sign of "Linit"
Read the merits of its starch,
For it flashes time each minute
As you stand by Grant's tomb arch.

If you stroll on up the river
Next you'll see Mazola's praise; 20
You'll be healthy and have vigor
If you use their mayonnaise.

Then sometimes on the river
Uncle Sam's fleet lies once more
And her wireless blinks a message
As it winks at Jersey's shore.

Now I see again that river,
See the signs at night once more;
In my mind I stand there looking
At those lights on Jersey's shore. 30

[1930]

Title: Designed by landscape architect Frederick Law Olmsted, Riverside Drive is the scenic road that runs along the west side of northern Manhattan across the Hudson River from New Jersey, passing by the advertising signs and other sights described in the poem.

Notable False Attributions

This appendix lists items identified as poems by American Indians that are not actually poems by American Indians. In their invaluable biobibliography (1981, 1985, and online at the American Native Press Archive) Daniel F. Littlefield and James W. Parins choose to list songs as poems, a legitimate choice, though not a choice adopted for this volume, because this volume serves a more poetry-specific purpose. In this list of notable false attributions, songs are not included when the word "song" appears in the title, for the appearance of "song" in the title already explains why such items are not always included in this volume's bibliography of poems. Sources of false attributions are not listed unless they are especially relevant.

"A."

"The Two Ships." *Cherokee Advocate* 5, 41 (9 February 1881). While this poem may have been written by a Cherokee, the only evidence that it was written by a Cherokee is that it was published by the *Cherokee Advocate*, which often published poems by non-Indians.

Anderson, Mabel Washbourne (Cherokee)

"To Auld Lang Syne." *Indian Chieftain*, 2 July 1896. This is a song, not a poem.

"Father of His Country." *Vinita Weekly Chieftain*, 23 February 1905. This poem is by Amanda Waldron, not by Anderson. It appears under Waldron's name in *Washington Day Entertainments*, ed. Jos. C. Sindelar (Chicago: A. Flanagan, 1910).

Anonymous

A poem "written on the death of Catharine Brown" was sent, apparently separately, to the *Cherokee Phoenix, and Indians' Advocate* and to the *Western Intelligencer, Religious, Literary and Political* by "the Philadelphian" (the newspaper of that name, or its editor, or some other person from Philadelphia). The Philadelphian reported that the poem came from a lady who said it was "written by an Indian and sent in a private letter to a minister." Both papers published the poem, but the *Phoenix* explained why its editors did not believe the poem was written by an Indian.

"Indian Poetry" ("written on the death of Catharine Brown, the first convert to the Christian faith at Creek-path, Cherokee Nation") *Western Intelligencer, Religious, Literary and Political* (Hudson, Ohio), 7 February 1829, 3.

"Written on the death of Catharine Brown, the first convert to the Christian faith at Creek-path, Cherokee Nation." *Cherokee Phoenix, and Indians' Advocate* 1, 52 (11 March 1829). Elsewhere in the same issue the editors of the *Cherokee Phoenix* explain that they believe the poem was written not by an Indian but "years ago . . . by a lady in Charleston. Mr. [David] Brown, the brother of the subject of the poetry, probably communicated the name of the Supreme Being to the writer, who, mistaking the letter *c* for *e* wrote galvlatichi, instead of galvlatiehi."

Apes, William (Pequot)

"Indian Hymn." This poem or hymn appears at the end of Apes's (Apess's) *A Son of the Forest* (1829) and is reprinted in *On Our Own Ground: The Complete Writings of William Apess, A Pequot*, ed. Barry O'Connell (Amherst: University of Massachusetts Press), 1992, 96–97. O'Connell points out that Apes took the poem—or hymn—from Elias Boudinot, *A Star in the West; or A Humble Attempt to Discover the Long Lost Ten Tribes of Israel . . .*, 1816 (O'Connell xli–xlii, 97). (This Elias Boudinot is not the famous Cherokee Elias Boudinot, previously named Buck Watie; it is the white mentor whose name Buck Watie took.)

Boudinot, Elias Cornelius (Cherokee)

"The Rose, the Bird and the Bride." This poem was published in *Southern Workman* 16 (Dec. 1887): 128, which described it as a poem and attributed it to Boudinot, whom it called "A Cherokee Poet." But rather than a poem by Boudinot, it is a previously published and, so far as I have found, anonymous British poem. Boudinot was the son of the famous Elias Boudinot, editor of the *Cherokee Phoenix*, brother of William Penn Boudinot, whose poems appear in this volume, and uncle of another Elias Cornelius Boudinot, with whom he was often confused.

Bow, Claude (Sioux)

"A Fairy Tale." *Southern Workman* 17 (July 1888): 80. This is prose, not poetry.

Chapman, Arthur

So far as I can see, the only reason these poems by Arthur Chapman have been said to be by an Arthur Chapman who was a White Earth Chippewa is that they appeared in *Tomahawk*, a journal from the White Earth Chippewa Reservation in Minnesota, and in Carlos Montezuma's *Wassaja* (which might have reprinted its poem from *Tomahawk*, if the dates of publication are not precise). They are interesting poems, but I suspect they were written by the then famous "cowboy poet" Arthur Chapman, though they do not appear in any of his books. I have not found records of any White Earth Chippewas or Minnesota Chippewas named Chapman.

"Indians in Khaki." *Tomahawk*, 11 September 1919.

Reprint: "Indians in Khaki." *Southern Workman* 49 (November 1919): 607. Reprinted from *American Indian Magazine.*

"The White Man's Road." *Wassaja* 5, 4 (July 1920): 4.

Reprint: "The White Man's Road." *Tomahawk*, 4 August 1921.

Gillis, Alfred C. (Wintu)

"The California Indians." *California Indian Herald* 2 (January 1924): 13–14. This is prose, not poetry.

Hen-toh / Walker, Bertrand N. O. (Wyandot)

These poems are not clearly attributed in *Sturm's Oklahoma Magazine*, leading to the mistaken impression that they were written by Hen-toh, but they are both by Alex Posey.

"Bob White." *Sturm's Oklahoma Magazine* 1 (October 1905): 85.

"Evening Star." *Sturm's Oklahoma Magazine* 1 (October 1905): 84.

Hughes, Eula (Chickasaw) Actually Martha, not Eula.
"Bread Making." *Native American*, 16 May 1914. This is a song, not a poem.

J. W. Ivey
"My Wife Lottie." *Cherokee Advocate*, 3 October 1884. James Washington Ivey married a Cherokee (his second wife Charlotte—his first wife was also named Charlotte) and lived part of his life in Indian Territory but apparently was not Cherokee himself. See "Children of Robert Ivey Jr. & Elizabeth West" and O'Beirne, H. F., and E. S. Beirne (440).

Johnston, George (Chippewa, Anishinaabe)
"Algonac, a Chippewa Lament on Hearing the Revellie at the Post of St. Mary's" from Henry Rowe Schoolcraft's handwritten magazine *The Muzzeniegun or Literary Voyager*, 1827; first published in 1962 (Mason 87–89). According to Philip P. Mason, "The author of this poem is not known. It was probably one of the Johnstons, perhaps George" (178). The Johnstons are Jane Johnston Schoolcraft, one of the poets in this volume, her father, and her siblings. As it turns out, however, this poem was written by her non-Indian husband, Henry Rowe Schoolcraft. It appears in manuscript in Henry's papers and in Henry's handwriting, and it was published in one of his books of poems. Moreover, George Johnston was too far away to submit the poem at the time it appeared in the *Literary Voyager*. For more details, see Jane Johnston Schoolcraft (258).
The Bayliss Public Library in Sault Ste. Marie, Michigan, has a collection of papers from George Johnston. The papers include poems that have been attributed to George Johnston, though they are actually his copies of poems by other writers.

Marmon, Kenneth A. (Laguna Pueblo)
"El Jaboli y la Zorra (The Wild Boar and the Fox)." *Sherman Bulletin*, 28 May 1913. This is a translation from the eighteenth-century Spanish poet Félix María de Samaniego.

McKenzie, Minnie (Cherokee)
"Valedictory—'Service.'" *Indian School Journal* 19 (June 1919): 41–42. This is prose, not poetry.

McKinney, William H. (Choctaw)
"It Hishi Yvmma Hisht Ch'thaiyana-li Hoke" / "A Leaf that Reminds Me of Thee." Choctaw and English versions. This has been described as a poem written by McKinney in Choctaw in 1878 and translated into English. Actually, it is his translation into Choctaw of a poem in English by Samuel Lover, included in Lover's *Songs and Ballads* (Montreal: D. & J. Sadlier, 1853), 154–55.

Red Eagle, Leroy (Quapaw)
"The Spring." *Carlisle Arrow*, 11 April 1911. This is prose, not poetry.

Ridge, John (Cherokee)
In the Payne Papers at the Newberry Library there survive a number of poems in the hand of John Ridge, the father of John Rollin Ridge, from John Ridge's days at the Cornwall School in Connecticut. In 1819, John Ridge wrote his name and the date at the bottom of some of these poems. Nevertheless, he did not write the poems and probably did not mean for anyone to suppose that he wrote them. All the poems were previously

published, some anonymously and some by well-known poets such as Edward Young. While it may seem obvious to a literary scholar that a fifteen-year-old would not have written the sophisticated lines of these poems, historians have taken for granted that Ridge wrote them, even though historians are accustomed to looking at nonliterary documents with a skeptical eye.

Schoolcraft, Janee and John Johnston (Chippewa, Anishinaabe)
Henry Rowe Schoolcraft: A Register of His Papers in the Library of Congress; Washington, D.C.: Manuscript Division, Library of Congress, 2004 and earlier versions, printed and electronic for Box 70 (reel 56) lists among its contents "Poems of Schoolcraft's Children, ca. 1841–1873," meaning poems by the children of Henry Schoolcraft. Henry's children, Janee Schoolcraft and Johnston Schoolcraft, were also the children of the Ojibwe writer Jane Johnston Schoolcraft (included in this volume), Ojibwe children who grew up speaking Ojibwe. But having compared the handwriting of these poems to the letters of Janee and Johnston, also in the Library of Congress Schoolcraft Papers, the present editor can say with confidence that Janee and Johnston did not write any of these poems.

Traversee, Edna
"From fair Dakota's fertile plains." *Southern Workman* 17 (July 1888): 80. The attribution of this poem to Edna Traversee, a student at Hampton Institute, appears uncertain at best. She is said to have recited the poem, not to have written it. While the poem seems written for her to recite, it does not look like the work of a student.

"U-na-kuh"
"School Episode." *Cherokee Advocate*, 13 Oct. 1880. According to Daniel Littlefield, U-na-kuh was probably a white person (personal communication). U-na-kuh (variously spelled in other, prose publications in the *Cherokee Advocate*) is "perhaps a corruption of the Cherokee *yonega*, or white person" (in Posey, *Fus Fixico Letters* 24).

Walker, William (Wyandot)
In William Elsey Connelley, *The Provisional Government of Nebraska Territory and the Journals of William Walker Provisional Governor of Nebraska Territory* (Lincoln: State Journal, 1899, 14–15), Connelley could be taken to imply that a certain poem and an additional set of lines were written by William Walker. Connelley quotes "Oft in the Stilly Night" as a "favorite . . . with all the Wyandots" and provides a Wyandot translation of one stanza. But "Oft in the Stilly Night" is a poem and song by the famous Irish poet and songwriter Thomas Moore. Then Connelley quotes four lines from Walker's journal, beginning "Sweet vale of Wyandott, how calm could I rest." These lines are from Moore's "The Vale of Avoca," with a few words misremembered and with Avoca adapted to read Wyandott.

War Bow, Blanket Indian
"War Bow Heap Farm." *Carlisle Arrow* 10, 37 (22 May 1913).
Reprint: *Chronicles of Oklahoma* 14, 2 (June 1936): 224. This looks like a non-Indian's effort at a supposedly humorous, fictional version of what an Indian might write.

White Eagle
A pamphlet of five poems attributed to "White Eagle" appeared in 1918 under three different titles (*The Dog Supper and Other Poems*; *The Dog Supper and Other Poems of Cowboy and Indian Life: A Curious Strange Little Book. All Its Own*; and *Poems of Indian*

Life). Apart from the titles, the versions of the pamphlet are the same. One of the poems refers to "White Eagle" as "Old Chief Moore." Many web sites offering to sell rare copies of the pamphlet include the following description, without citing a source: "White Eagle was a Sioux chief from Wyoming, who was an expert horseman—winning medals for his skill—and who also prided himself as a poet." One of the poems, called "Indian Maid Up-to-Date," was reprinted in *American Indian Advocate* in 1925. Beneath the reprinted poem, a note describes White Eagle as "an old Indian Sioux—a cowboy of the old school from the Dakota country. He is alone in life and has lost both his speech and hearing. We have opened our Indian Home at Mountain Grove for him, and he will do light work about the place. This is not Reverend Chief White Eagle." (Reverend Chief White Eagle presumably refers to "Big Chief White Horse Eagle," who is also on this list of "Notable False Attributions.") While there is thus testimony that White Eagle was Indian, the poems sound to me like the work of a fraud, a fake Indian. They occasionally have a crude interest and humor, if we read generously, but they are disrespectful of Indian people in general and of Indian women in particular. They seem to me deeply reliant on clichéd language ("heap big," etc.) and on trivializing ideas about Indians that are common among non-Indians writing about Indians but extremely unlikely among Indians, even Indians who have absorbed anti-Indian prejudices from the surrounding culture. Consulting with others who know the ostensibly Sioux context of these poems better than I do has given me no reason to doubt the impression that they are fraudulent.

Big Chief White Horse Eagle

"The Indian's Lament." *American Indian* 2, 3 (Dec. 1927): 5. Big Chief White Horse Eagle, a professional Indian who traveled widely, claimed to be Osage. He published an as-told-to autobiography in German. He was clearly a fraud, was probably not Indian, and surely was not so Indian as he claimed.

Bibliography of Poems by American Indians to 1930

This bibliography includes all known poems by American Indians through 1930. Poems not included in this volume are marked with a diamond (◊), except in the case of the collections of poems by Bush-Banks, Hen-toh, Posey, Ridge, Riggs, and Schoolcraft. This volume provides only a selection of the poems from those collections. For each poet, poems are listed in chronological order, except that reprints are listed after the original publication. Recent or relatively recent reprints are not listed. An "S" before a listing indicates a poem from a boarding school. An asterisk after a listing indicates an item I have not seen personally. While this bibliography is as complete (through 1930) as I have been able to make it, there are no doubt poems that I have missed.

Adair, John Lynch (Cherokee)
"Hec Dies: An Imitation." *Cherokee Advocate*, 13 June 1877.
Reprint: "Hec Dies." In H. F. O'Beirne and E. S. O'Beirne. *The Indian Territory: Its Chiefs, Legislators and Leading Men.* St. Louis: C.B. Woodward, 1892. 267–68.*
"Joy Returneth with the Morning." *Indian Chieftain*, 14 February 1889.
Reprint: "Joy Returneth with the Morning." In H. F. O'Beirne and E. S. O'Beirne, *The Indian Territory: Its Chiefs, Legislators and Leading Men.* St. Louis: C.B. Woodward, 1892. 266–67.*
Reprint: "Joy Returneth with the Morning." *Indian Chieftain*, 29 October 1896.

Adair, Lena Harnage (Cherokee)
"Tahlequah." *Tahlequah Arrow*, 19 February 1916.◊
Reprint: Emmet Starr. *History of the Cherokee Indians and Their Legends and Folk Lore.* Oklahoma City: Warden, 1921. 333.

Adams, Emmett (Delaware)
"A Tribesman's Departure." 1921. Reprint Deborah Nichols, "Richard C. Adams: 'Representing the Delaware Indians,'" in Richard C. Adams, *Legends of the Delaware Indians and Picture Writing* (1905; rpt. Syracuse, N.Y.: Syracuse University Press, 1997). xliv–xlv.◊

Adams, Richard Calmit (Delaware)
"Addenda." Adams, *A Delaware Indian Legend and the Story of Their Troubles.* Washington, D.C., 1899. 65.◊
"A Delaware Indian Legend." Adams, *A Delaware Indian Legend and the Story of Their Troubles.* Washington, D.C., 1899. 7.
"To the American People." Adams, *A Delaware Indian Legend and the Story of Their Troubles.* Washington, D.C., 1899. 5.

"To the Delaware Indians." Adams, *A Delaware Indian Legend and the Story of Their Troubles.* Washington, D.C., 1899. 73–75.
To the Delaware Indians. 1899. 2nd ed. Washington, D.C., 1904.

Anderson, Hellen Rebecca (Cherokee)
"The Unruly Pigs." *Twin Territories* 5 (April 1903) 136.◊

Anderson, Mabel Washbourne (Cherokee)
"Nowita, Sweet Singer" [sic]. *Indian Chieftain*, 23 August 1900.
Reprint: "Nowita, the Sweet Singer." *Twin Territories* 5 (January 1903): 1–2.
Reprint: "Nowita, the Sweet Singer, a Romantic Tradition of Spavinaw, Indian Territory." *Sturm's Statehood Magazine* 1 (1906): 86.

Anonymous Carlisle student
S "My Industrial Work." *Carlisle Arrow*, 27 March 1913, 1. From Carlisle Indian School.

Beaulieu, Irene Campbell (Sioux)
"Poor Lo." *Tributes to a Vanishing Race*, ed. Irene C. Beaulieu and Kathleen Woodward. Chicago: privately printed, 1916. 55.

Benoist, Laura L. (Sioux)
S "Class Poem." *Indian News* 13 (May–June 1911): 1–2. From Genoa Indian School, Nebraska.◊

Bishop, William C. (Cayuga)
S "Senior Class Song." *Carlisle Arrow*, 19 April 1912. From Carlisle Indian School.◊

Blue Feather
"The Lone Tee-Pee." *Wassaja* 7, 12 (December 1921): 2.

Boudinot, William Penn (Cherokee)
"Life's Phantom." *Arkansian*, 2 April 1859.
Reprint: "The Spectre." *Indian Missionary* (April 1889): 1.*
Reprint: "The Spectre." *Red Man* 9 (May 1889): 1.
Reprint: "The Spectre." H. F. O'Beirne and E. S. O'Beirne, *The Indian Territory: Its Chiefs, Legislators and Leading Men.* St. Louis: C.B. Woodward, 1892. 266–68.
Reprint: "The Spectre." *Muskogee Phoenix*, 14 February. 1899.
Reprint: "The Spectre." *Twin Territories* 1 (July 1899): 166.
Reprint: "The Spectre." *Vinita Leader*, 29 June 1899: 4.
Reprint: ["There is a spectre ever haunting."] *Cherokee Advocate*, 25 March 1851. Signed "Cherokee."

Broken Wing Bird
"Come Back, Indians of Yesterday." *Tomahawk*, 17 November 1921.
"Why? Why? Why?" *Wassaja* 7, 9 (September 1921): 4.

Brown, David J. (Cherokee)
"Kee-Too-Whah." *Telephone*, 26 July 1889.◊
"Sequoyah." *Cherokee Advocate*, 26 February 1879.
Reprint: "Sequoyah." *Indian Chieftain*, 25 March 1886.
Reprint: "Sequoyah." *Twin Territories* 2 (June 1900): 113.*

Buck, Rufus (Yuchi)
"MY dream." S. W. Harman, *Hell on the Border: He Hanged Eighty-Eight Men.* Fort Smith, Ark.: Phoenix, 1898. 514.

Bush-Banks, Olivia Ward (Montauk/Montaukett)
Poems that appear only in *The Collected Works of Olivia Ward Bush-Banks* or the two volumes of poetry that *The Collected Works* reprint are not listed separately.
Banks, Olivia Ward Bush. "Morning on Shinnecock." In *Annual Report of the Montauk Tribe of Indians for the Year 1916.**
Reprint: *The History & Archaeology of the Montauk*, ed. Gaynell Stone. 2nd ed. Readings in Long Island Archaeology & Ethnohistory 3. Stony Brook, N.Y.: Suffolk County Archaeological Association, Nassau County Archaeological Committee, 1993. 470.
Bush, Olivia B. "On the Long Island Indian." Providence, R.I., 1890. Broadside.
Reprint: Banks, Olivia Ward Bush. In *Annual Report of the Montauk Tribe of Indians for the Year 1916.**
Reprint: *The History & Archaeology of the Montauk*, ed. Gaynell Stone. 2nd ed. Readings in Long Island Archaeology & Ethnohistory 3. Stony Brook, N.Y.: Suffolk County Archaeological Association, Nassau County Archaeological Committee, 1993. 471–72.
Bush, Olivia Ward. "Regret." *Voice of the Negro* 2, 6 (June 1905): 400.
———. "Voices." *Voice of the Negro* 2, 12 (December 1905): 866.◊
The Collected Works of Olivia Ward Bush-Banks. Ed. Bernice F. Guillaume. New York: Oxford University Press, 1991. Includes reprints of all Bush-Banks's known separately published poems.

Campbell, C. H. (Cherokee)
["Our tribe could once of many *warriors* boast."] *The Wreath of Cherokee Rose Buds* 1 (August 1855): 4.

Carter, Caleb W. (Nez Perce)
S "Class Poem." *Carlisle Arrow*, 19 April 1912. From Carlisle Indian School.◊

Carter, Mrs. Minot (Sioux)
"Fancies." *Indian Leader*, 10 November 1922.
"Raindrops." *Indian Leader*, 10 November 1922.

Carter, Stella LeFlore (Chickasaw)
"Inauguration Day." *American Indian* 5, 3 (December 1930–January 1931): 6.

Chaleco, Arsenius (Yuma)
"The Indian Requiem." *Indian Teepee* 9, 4 (September 1924): 12.

"Cherokee" (Cherokee)
["Faster and fiercer rolls the tide."] *Cherokee Advocate*, 8 July 1871.

Comingdeer, John (Cherokee)
"A Vacant Chair at Home." *Tahlequah Arrow*, 12 January 1901.◊

Cooke, Maude (Mohawk)
S With Agnes Hatch. "Our Cottage." *Carlisle 1917.* Carlisle, Pa.: U.S. Indian School, 1917. 40. From Carlisle Indian School.

Cornelius, Laura M. (Oneida)
"A Tribute to the Future of My Race." *Red Man and Helper*, 13 March 1903. Reprinted from *Riverside Daily Press*.

Corrinne (Cherokee); pseudonym
S "Our Wreath of Rose Buds." *Cherokee Rose Buds*, 2 August 1854: 1. From Cherokee Female Seminary.
Reprint: "Our Wreath of Rose Buds." *Youth's Companion*, 7 September 1854: 80.

Daugherty, Matthew (Cherokee)
"To Elza." *Muskogee Morning Times*, 12 February 1897.◊

De Grasse, Alfred (Mashpee)
S "Our Trees. *Carlisle Arrow*, 11 April 1911. From Carlisle Indian School.◊

Dorman, Ellen (Ukie [Yuki])
S "1910 Class Poem." *Sherman Bulletin*, 12 May 1909. From Sherman Institute.◊

Downing, Louis (Cherokee)
S "Senior Class." *Indian School Journal* 18 (June 1918): 59. From Chilocco Indian School, Oklahoma.◊

Doxon, Charles (Onondaga)
S "Hampton." *Talks and Thoughts of the Hampton Indian Students* 19 (February 1906): 1. From Hampton Institute.◊

Duncan, De Witt Clinton. See Too-qua-stee.

Duncan, J. C. (Cherokee)
"The Red Man's Burden: Parody on Kipling's Poem." *Indian Sentinel*, 30 March 1899.

Dutton, Eugene (Ojibwe, Odawa, Potawatomi?)
S "Playing and Haying." *Red Man* (December 1910): 146. From Mt. Pleasant Indian School, Michigan.◊

Eleazar
"In obitum Viri verè Reverendi D. Thomae Thacheri, Qui Ad Dom. ex hâc Vitâ migravit, 18.8.1678." In Cotton Mather, *Magnalia Christi Americana*, Book 3. London: Thomas Parkhurst, 1702. 152–53.

Ettawageshik, William (Ottawa)
S "The Glow-Worm." *Carlisle Arrow*, 27 January 1911. From Carlisle Indian School.

Fielding, Jeanette (Mohegan)
"Welcome to the Wigwam." Mimeograph, 1910. Reprint in Melissa Jayne Fawcett, *Medicine Trail: The Life and Lessons of Gladys Tantaquidgeon*. Tucson: University of Arizona Press, 2000. 56–59.◊

Fifth Grade (Shawnee?)
S "The fields look gray and sober." *Indian Scout: A Pathfinder for Indians* 4, 2 (October 1918): 12. Fifth Grade of the Indian School, Shawnee, Oklahoma.◊

Fish, Frank (Peoria)
S "Haskell Song." *Indian Leader*, 8 December 1905. From Haskell Institute in Kansas.◊

Folsom, Israel (Choctaw)
"Lo! The Poor Indian's Hope." *Vindicator*, 1 May 1875.

A Former Student of the Male Seminary (Cherokee)
"The Rose of Cherokee." *Sequoyah Memorial* 1, 1 (2 August 1855): 3.

Fox, Finis (Chickasaw)
"The Kentuckian's Lament." *Daily Oklahoman*, 24 June 1906: 5.◊

Fuller, Elsie (Omaha)
S "A New Citizen." *Talks and Thoughts of the Hampton Indian Students* 2 (April 1887): 1. From Hampton Institute.
Reprint: "I'm a Citizen." *Southern Workman* 16 (May 1887): 56.

Gansworth, Leander (Tuscarora)
S ["Come now thou bright and sunny spring."] *Red Man* 12 (May 1895): 5. From Carlisle Indian School.◊

Garvie, James William (Sioux)
S "The Broad Highway." *Carlisle Arrow*, 4 June 1915. From Carlisle Indian School.◊

Gibbs, Adin C. (Delaware)
S "The Cornwall Seminary." In "A Journey in New England." *Evangelical and Literary Magazine* 5, 9 (September 1822): 463–73 (poem 465).
Reprint: "The Cornwall Seminary." *Evangelical Monitor* 2, 13 (12 October 1822): 104.
Reprint: "The Cornwall Seminary." *Indian Chieftain*, 6 May 1886.

Gillis, Alfred C. (Wintu)
"The Bird with the Wounded Wing." *California Indian Herald* 1 (April 1923): 10.
"An Indian Cradle Song." *California Indian Herald* 1 (July 1923): 10.
"The Klamath Girl." *California Indian Herald* 2 (July 1924): 14.
"My Prayer." *California Indian Herald* 2 (August 1924): 3.
"The Sacramento River." *California Indian Herald* 2 (April 1924): 3.
"The Shasta Lily, Den-Hu-Luly." *California Indian Herald* 1 (December 1923): 3.
"To the Wenem Mame River." *California Indian Herald* 2 (February 1924): 10.
"Where Sleep the Wintoon Dead." *California Indian Herald* 2 (June 1924): 8.

Gravitt, Winnie Lewis (Choctaw)
"Sippokni Sia." *American Indian* 1, 7 (April 1927): 9. Apparently reprinted from *Harlow's Weekly.*

Gregory, James Roane (Euchee, now Yuchi)
"The Green Corn Dance." *Wagoner Record*, 9 August 1900.
"Home's Chief." *Wagoner Record*, 12 July 1895.◊
"Life." *Wagoner Record*, 16 August 1900.◊
"Nineteenth Century Finality." *Wagoner Record*, 9 August 1900.
"Otheen, Okiyetos." *Wagoner Record*, 21 June 1895.
A Poem, Entitled Lucy's-Poney. Wagoner, Indian Territory: Record Print, 1895.◊
"The Promised Seal." *Wagoner Record*, 29 March 1895: 2.
"Rain." *Wagoner Record*, 21 June 1895.
"Spring Sparks." *Wagoner Record*, 5 April 1895.◊
"Storm Lights." *Wagoner Record*, 6 December 1895: 6.

Gust-ah-yah-she (Menominee)
"The Indian's Plea." *American Indian* 3, 6 (March 1929): 5.

Guy, James Harris (Chickasaw)
"Fort Arbuckle." H. F. O'Beirne, *Leaders and Leading Men of the Indian Territory. With Interesting Biographical Sketches.* Vol. 1, *Choctaws and Chickasaws: With a Brief History of Each Tribe: Its Laws, Customs, Superstitions and Religious Beliefs.* Chicago: American Publishers Association, 1891. 213.
Reprint: "Fort Arbuckle." *Daily Ardmorite*, 18 August 1907.
Reprint: "Fort Arbuckle." *American Indian* 4, 9 (June 1930): 5.
"The Lament of Tishomingo." *Council Fire* 2(January 1879): 15.
"Old Boggy Depot." *American Indian* 1, 8 (May 1927): 4.
["The white man wants the Indian's home."] *Council Fire* 1 (July 1878): 110.

Hare, De Witt (Sioux)
"The mighty rivers. . . ." *American Indian Magazine* 7, 3 (Fall 1919): 137.◊

Hartshorne, Mary Cornelia (Choctaw)
"April Will Come." *American Indian* 2, 5 (February 1928): 4.
"Fallen Leaves." *American Indian* 2, 2 (November 1927): 5.
"Hills of Doon." *American Indian* 2, 4 (January 1928): 5.
"The Poet." *American Indian* 1, 5 (February 1927): 11.
"Sonnet." *American Indian* 2, 10 (July 1928): 5.
"Three Poems of Christmas Eve." *American Indian* 2, 3 (December 1927): 12.
"Wind in Mexico." *American Indian* 2, 9 (June 1928): 5.

Hatch, Agnes (Chippewa)
S With Maude Cooke. "Our Cottage." *Carlisle 1917.* Carlisle, Pa.: U.S. Indian School, 1917. 40. From Carlisle Indian School.

Hawkins, Edna (Cheyenne)
S "Class Song: To Beethoven's Minuet in G, No. 2." *Chilocco Senior Class Annual.* Chilocco, Okla.: Chilocco Indian School, 1920. 40.◊

Hen-toh/Walker, Bertrand N. O. (Wyandot)
Poems reprinted in *Yon-doo-shah-we-ah (Nubbins)*, 1924, are indicated with a *Y.* Poems that appear only in *Yon-doo-shah-we-ah* are not listed separately.
"Arrow-Heads." *Indian School Journal* 15, 6 (February 1915): 291. *Y.*
Reprint: "Arrow-Heads." In *Tributes to a Vanishing Race*, comp. Irene C. Beaulieu and Kathleen Woodward. Chicago: privately printed, 1916. 29.
"The Calumet or Peace-Pipe." *Southern Workman* 48, 1 (January 1919): 30. *Y.*
"A Desert Memory." *Sturm's Oklahoma Magazine* 3, 3 (November 1906): 88. *Y.*
Reprint: "A Desert Memory." *Indian School Journal* 7, 4 (February 1907): 64.
"A Mojave Lullaby." *Twin Territories* 5 (May 1903) 165. *Y.*
Reprint: "A Mojave Lullaby." *Sturm's Oklahoma Magazine* 1 (October 1905): 84.
Reprint: "A Mojave Lullaby." *Indian School Journal* 7, 4 (January 1907): 31.
"Pontiac." *Indian School Journal* 6, 6 (April 1906): 49–50.
"The Song of a Navajo Weaver." *Indian School Journal* 6, 9 (July 1906): 9. *Y.*
Reprint: "The Song of a Navajo Weaver." *Indian Leader*, April 30 1909.*
Reprint: "Song of the Navajo Weaver." *Oglala Light* 12 (November 1911): 393.*

"A Strand of Wampum." *Indian School Journal* 15, 8 (April 1915): 112.
Reprint: "A Strand of Wampum." *Indian's Friend* 27 (July 1915): 8.
"Sunset in the Colorado Desert." *Sturm's Statehood Magazine* 1 (January 1906): 94.◊
Reprint: "Sunset in Mojave Land." *Indian School Journal* 7, 7 (May 1907): 24
"The Warriors' Plume." *Indian School Journal* 15 (May 1915): 474. *Y.*
"A Wyandot Cradle Song." *Red Man* 2, 7 (March 1910): 25. *Y.*
Reprint: "A Wyandotte Cradle Song." *Oglala Light* 12 (June 1911): 34.*
Reprint: "A Wyandot Lullaby." In *Tributes to a Vanishing Race*, comp. Irene C. Beaulieu and Kathleen Woodward. Chicago: privately printed, 1916. 45.
Yon-doo-shah-we-ah (*Nubbins*). Oklahoma City: Harlow, 1924.

Hill, Mina (Klamath)
S "Class Poem." *Sherman Bulletin*, 10 June 1908. From Sherman Institute.◊

Hitchcock, Raymond (Hupa)
S "The Webs of Life." *Carlisle Arrow*, 8 April 1910. From Carlisle Indian School.◊

Hodjkiss, William D. (Dakota)
"Song of the Storm-Swept Plain." *Indian School Journal* 13, 7 (March 1913): 332.
Reprint: "Song of the Storm-Swept Plain." *Indian's Friend* 25, 8 (May 1913): 10.

Hors de Combat (Cherokee); pseudonym
["I've returned to home and scanty lunch."] *Indian Chieftain*, 14 April 1887. (This poem has been listed under the title "This Ends the Poetry," but that is an editorial note in the form of a headline. The poem itself was published without a title.)

Hudson, Frank (Pueblo)
S ["'Tis not strong in limb as yonder oak."] *Red Man* 12 (May 1895): 5. From Carlisle Indian School.◊

An Indian [Jesse Bushyhead?] (Cherokee)
"The Indian's Farewell." *Indian Advocate* 3 (November 1848): 3.

Jessan, Lillian W. (Eastern Band Cherokee)
S "Junior College Class Poem." *Indian Leader*, 6 June 1930, 6. From Hampton Institute.◊

Johnson, Victor H. (Dalles)
Reprint: "The Brook." *Arrow*, 12 July 1907. Reprinted from *Dartmouth Magazine*.*◊
Reprint: "The Brook." *Indian's Friend* 20 (September 1907): 7.*
Reprint: "The Brook." *Indian Craftsman* (May 1909): 55.
Reprint: "The Brook." *Southern Workman* 39 (December 1910): 649.

Kellog, Laura Minnie Cornelius (Oneida)
See Cornelius, Laura M.

Kershaw, William J. (Menominee)
"American Indian Day." *Indian Teepee* 9, 4 (September 1924): 2.◊
"The Indian's Salute to His Country." *Indian Leader* 19, 5 ([8] October1915): 9. As part of report "Conference of the Society of American Indians," 3–11.
Reprint: "The Indian's Salute to His Country." *American Indian Magazine* 4, 1 (January–March 1916): 66.

"Joseph Fights No More." *American Indian* 3, 5 (February 1929): 5.
"A National Anthem by a Native American." *American Indian* 3, 9 (June 1929): 5.◊

Kingfisher (Cherokee)
"After the Curtis Bill Passes." *Tahlequah Arrow*, 9 April 1898.

La Hay, Joseph M. (Cherokee)
"Consolation." *Tahlequah Arrow*, 26 August 1905.

Lashen, Dan M. (Oto)
"A Poem." *Indian's Friend* 13, 9 (May 1901): 12.◊

Lee, Lily (Cherokee); pseudonym
S "Literary Day Among the Birds." *Cherokee Rose Buds*, 1 August 1855. From Cherokee Female Seminary.

Lelia (Cherokee); pseudonym
S "We have faults . . ." *Cherokee Rose Buds*, 1 August 1855 (in article called "Critics and Criticism"). From Cherokee Female Seminary.◊

Lipe, John Gunter (Cherokee)
"To Miss Vic." In Emmet Starr, *History of the Cherokee Indians and Their Legends and Folk Lore*. Oklahoma City: Warden, 1921. 144, 571.

Locke, Ben D. (Choctaw)
"The Doughboy." *American Indian* 2, 4 (January 1928): 6.
"Hobachi (Echo)." *American Indian* 1, 7 (April 1927): 9.

Lowry, Maude (Washoe)
S "The Purple and the White." *Chemawa American* 15, 9 (June 1913): 27. From Chemawa Indian School, Oregon.◊

Martin, Edna I. (Citizen's Band Potawatomi)
S "Class of '18." *Indian School Journal* 18 (June 1918): 58. From Chilocco Indian School, Oklahoma.◊

Martin, Joseph Lynch (Cherokee)
"A Dream." *Cherokee Advocate*, 9 February 1881.
"Stanzas by Uncle Joe." *Cherokee Advocate*, 1 April 1891.

McKenzie, Minnie (Cherokee)
S "Doings at Chilocco." *Indian School Journal* 18 (June 1918): 61. From Chilocco Indian School, Oklahoma.◊
S "Nineteen." *Indian School Journal* 19 (June 1919) 47. From Chilocco Indian School, Oklahoma.◊
S "An Ode to the Juniors." *Indian School Journal* 18 (June 1918): 56. From Chilocco Indian School, Oklahoma.◊
S "To Our Teachers." *Indian School Journal* 19 (June 1919): 27. From Chilocco Indian School, Oklahoma.◊
S "What's in a Name." *Indian School Journal* 19 (June 1919): 48. From Chilocco Indian School, Oklahoma.◊

McNickle, D'Arcy [D'Arcy Dahlberg] (Confederated Salish and Kootenai)
"Cycle." *The Frontier: A Literary Magazine* 5, 1 (November 1924): 3.
"Man Hesitates but Life Urges." *The Frontier: A Magazine of the Northwest* 6, 2 (March 1926): 16.
"Minuet in G." *The Frontier: A Literary Magazine* 5, 2 (March 1925): 11.
"The Mountains." *The Frontier: A Literary Magazine* 5, 3 (May 1925): 10–11.
"Old Isidore." *Sunday Missoulian*, 21 June 1925: 1.
"Plowing." *The Frontier: A Literary Magazine* 4, 2 (March 1924): 23.
"Sweet Is the Prairie." *Frontier and Midland: A Magazine of the West* 15 (Autumn 1934): 8.
"Today." *The Frontier: A Literary Magazine* 5, 1 (November 1924): 24.
Reprint in Henry Thomas Schnittkind, *The Poets of the Future: A College Anthology for 1924–25*. Boston: Stratford, 1925. 5.

Metoxen, Melinda (Oneida) 30
S "Iceland." *Red Man* 13 (January 1896): 6. From Carlisle Indian School.

Montezuma, Carlos (Yavapai)
It appears that the poems in Montezuma's journal *Wassaja* are written by him except when otherwise indicated. For some works in *Wassaja* it is not self-evident whether they are poems, as some of his prose comes in short paragraphs that can look like the long lines of what I am calling poems. In accord with standard practice, I have supposed that short paragraphs (beginning with the indenting that signals a new paragraph) are prose, whereas long lines indented not at the beginning of the line but instead where the line cannot fit and runs over, as is typical in the poetry of Walt Whitman, are poetry. As if that were not tricky enough, some runover works come in one line and one sentence, and I have not included those. Perhaps Montezuma was not fastidious about distinguishing between poetry and prose, and indeed such distinctions can depend on a degree of arbitrariness. Montezuma's manuscripts include two unpublished poems (one selected for this volume), copies of at least one song by someone else, and fragments, drafts, and notes for several more poems. One short, fragmentary, and not always legible draft begins "O you she-devil." Another begins "There was once an Indian Buck who / rode on a Cayuse from Sagebrush state," and another "There is a chance of singing Indian song."
"Changing Is Not Vanishing." *Wassaja* 1, 3 (June 1916): 4.
"Civilization." *Wassaja* 1 (April 1917): 2–3.
"An Evening's Reverie." Manuscript. *The Papers of Carlos Montezuma, M.D.*, ed. John William Larner, Jr. Microfilm. Wilmington, Del.: Scholarly Resources, 1983. Reel 7.
"I Have Stood Up for You." *Wassaja* 4 (May 1919): 3.
"Indian Office." *Wassaja* 1, 9 (December 1916): 2.
"Indians, Playing the Game!" *Wassaja* 5, 6 (September 1920): 4.◊
"The Sparkle of Her Eye." Manuscript. *The Papers of Carlos Montezuma, M.D.*, ed. John William Larner, Jr. Microfilm. Wilmington, Del.: Scholarly Resources, 1983. Reel 7.◊
"Steady, Indians, Steady." *Wassaja* 2 (April 1917): 3.

Moore, Thomas E. (Muskogee)
"A Spring Shower." *Indian School Journal* 28, 30 (May–Jun. 1929). [Published under the name Chinnubbie.]◊

Morris, L. Pearl (Cherokee)
S "A Reverie." *Sherman Bulletin*, 2 February 1910. From Sherman Institute.◊

Mumblehead, James W. (Eastern Band Cherokee)
S "Class Poem." *Carlisle Arrow*, 21 April 1911. From Carlisle Indian School.◊

Muskrat, Ruth Margaret (Cherokee)
This list probably includes the vast majority but not all of Muskrat's poems. It concludes with several poems reported to have been in clippings in Muskrat's scrapbook with no indication of the source of publication.
"The Apache Reservation." *University of Oklahoma Magazine* 10 (February 1922): 15.
"Come and Bide a Wee." *University of Oklahoma Bulletin: University Anthology*, ed. Joseph Francis Paxton. Norman: University of Oklahoma, 1921. 42.◊
"Heaven's Law."*◊
"The House by the Ferry." *University of Oklahoma Magazine* 9 (November 1920): 10.◊
"The Hunter's Wooing." *University of Oklahoma Magazine* 10 (October 1921): 4.
"If You Knew." *University of Oklahoma Magazine* 11 (April 1923): 4.
"In Class." *Mount Holyoke Monthly* 32, 4 (February 1924): 182.
"An Indian Lullaby." *University of Oklahoma Magazine* 10 (December 1921): 13.
"The Jar Flies." *University of Oklahoma Magazine* 9 (February 1921): 16.◊
"My House of Dreams." *University of Oklahoma Magazine* 10 (November 1921): 4.◊
"My Warrior." *University of Oklahoma Magazine* 8 (April 1920): 4.◊
"Ni-wah-nee." *Mount Holyoke Monthly* 33, 5 (February 1925): 128.◊
"Nunih Waiyah." *University of Oklahoma Magazine* 10 (January 1922): 5.
"On a Christmas Eve." (January 1922).*◊
"Only a Dream."*◊
"The Road to Arden." *University of Oklahoma Magazine* 9 (December 1920): 17.◊
"Sentenced *(A Dirge)*." *University of Oklahoma Bulletin: University Anthology*, ed. Joseph Francis Paxton. Norman: University of Oklahoma, 1921. 9.
"The Shady Deeps." *University of Oklahoma Magazine* 9 (April 1921): 4.◊
"Songs of the Spavinaw." *University of Oklahoma Magazine* 8 (February 1920): 4.
"Sonnets from the Cherokee (May Mrs. Browning Pardon Me)." *University of Oklahoma Magazine* 10 (January 1922): 11.◊ [One of the four "Sonnets from the Cherokee" is included in this volume.]
"A Spirit of the Past."*◊
"To an Indian Lover." *Mount Holyoke Monthly* 32, 7 (May 1924): 323.
"The Trail of Tears." *University of Oklahoma Magazine* 10 (February 1922): 14.
"Walleah." "Sentenced *(A Dirge)*." *University of Oklahoma Bulletin. University Anthology*, ed. Joseph Francis Paxton. [Norman: University of Oklahoma, 1921]. 43.◊
Reprint: *University of Oklahoma Magazine* 10 (December 1921): 12.
"The Warriors' Dance." *University of Oklahoma Magazine* 10 (January 1922): 23.
"A Welcome to the New Year." *University of Oklahoma Magazine* 10 (January 1922): 4.◊
"When It's Dark." *University of Oklahoma Bulletin. University Anthology*, ed. Joseph Francis Paxton. Norman: University of Oklahoma, 1921. 41.

N. (Cherokee), pseudonym
S [Farewell.] "To school-mates dear, to teachers kind." *Sequoyah Memorial*, 1, 1 (2 August 1855): 1. From Cherokee Male Seminary.

Natoni, Pauline (Navajo)
S "Class Prophecy." *Purple and Gold.* Riverside, Calif.: Sherman Institute, 1923. 29. From Sherman Institute.◊

Newashe, Emma M. (Sac and Fox)
S "Limericks." *Carlisle Arrow*, 19 April 1912. From Carlisle Indian School.◊

Nichols, Roland A. (Potawatomi)
"Pay Your Freight." *American Indian Magazine* 5, 3 (July–September 1917): 136.◊

O'Field, Ina (Cherokee)
S "A Sonnet: In the Month of May." *Bacone Chief.* Bacone, Okla.: Bacone College, 1923. 76.◊

Oshkosh, Alice C. (Menominee)
"Joy and Sorrow." *American Indian* 4, 4 (January 1930): 5.◊

Our Contributor (Anishinaabe?)
"The Ne'er Digressing Quartette." *Tomahawk*, 9 September 1920.

Owen, Narcissa (Cherokee)
"Now." In *Memoirs of Narcissa Owen, 1831–1907.* 1907. Reprint as *A Cherokee Woman's America: Memoirs of Narcissa Owen, 1831–1907*, ed. Karen L. Kilcup. Gainesville: University Press of Florida, 2005. 46.◊

Palmer, John (Skokomish)
[I Remember You.] ("Yes, Sister, I Do Always Remember You.") *Council Fire* 3 (March 1880): 48.

Parker, Arthur Caswell (Seneca)
"Faith." (As Gawasa Wanneh.) *American Indian Magazine* 4, 2 (October–December 1916): 317.
"My Race Shall Live Anew." (As Alnoba Wabunaki.) *Quarterly Journal of the Society of American Indians* 2 (April–June 1914): 90.
"The Robin's Song." (As Alnoba Waubunaki.) *Quarterly Journal of the Society of American Indians* 2 (July–September 1914): 125.◊

Peters, Bert (Pawnee)
S "1924 Class Poem." *Bacone Chief.* Bacone, Okla: Bacone College, 1924. 106.◊

Pitchlynn, Peter (Choctaw)
"Song of the Choctaw Girl." Peter Pitchlynn Papers. Gilcrease Museum, Tulsa, Oklahoma. Typescript.
["Will you go with me."] Peter Pitchlynn Papers. Gilcrease Museum, Tulsa, Oklahoma. Manuscript.

Posey, Alexander Lawrence (Creek [Muskogee])
Song of the Oktahuche: Collected Poems. Ed. Matthew Wynn Sivils. Lincoln: University of Nebraska Press, 2008. Posey published too widely to make it practical to list all his known published and reprinted poems here. *Song of the Oktahuche* collects all Posey's known poems, including poems not previously published.

Rice, Samuel J. (Mission)
"Courage." *The Indian*, March 1922: 11.◊
Reprint: "Courage." *The Indian*, October 1922: front cover.

Rider, Sunshine [Atalie Unkalunt] (Cherokee)
"The Conquered Race." *American Indian* 1, 4 (January 1927): 8.

Ridge, John Rollin/Yellow Bird
Poems reprinted in *Poems*, 1868, are indicated with a *P.* Poems that appear only in *Poems* are not listed separately. Some poems not listed as reprinted may have been reprinted under an alternate title.
"The Arkansas Root Doctor." *Weekly California Express*, 28 November 1857.* *P.*◊
"A Bright Summery Morning on the Sea Coast." *Hesperian* 7 (November 1861): 451.* Probably one of the poems in *P*, possibly "California."◊
"California." *Daily Alta California*, September 10, 1859. *P.*◊
Reprint: "California." *Hesperian* 3 (October 1859): 345–47.*◊
"The Dark One to His Love." *Arkansas State Democrat*, 14 September 1849.
"The Douglas Star." *Daily National Democrat*, 12 February 1859.*◊
"Erinna." *Arkansas State Democrat*, 27 October 1848. *P.*
Reprint: "Erinna." *Golden Era*, 16 March 1862.*
"Eyes." *Daily Evening Herald*, 12 August 1853.* *P.*
Reprint: "Eyes." *Hesperian* 6 (June 1861): 209–10.*
Reprint: "Eyes." *Owyhee Avalanche* (Ruby City, Idaho), 22 May 1869.
"False but Beautiful." *Golden Era*, 24 November 1861.* *P.*
"Far in a Lonely Wood." *Arkansas Gazette*, 20 July 1941.◊
"The Gold Seekers." *Weekly California Express*, 23 January 1858.*◊
"The Hills." *Poetry of the Pacific*, ed. May Wentworth. San Francisco: Pacific, 1867. 88–89. *P* as "October Hills."
"The Humboldt Desert." *Hutchings' California Magazine* 3 (1858): 448.* *P.*
Reprint: "The Humboldt Desert." In *Poetry of the Pacific*, ed. May Wentworth. San Francisco: Pacific, 1867. 90–93.
"Humboldt River." *Shasta Courier.** *P.*
Reprint: "Humboldt River." *Hesperian* 4 (March 1860): 21–22.*
Reprint: "Humboldt River." *Hesperian* 4 (April 1860): 82–83. Correcting March 1860 version.*
Reprint: "Humboldt River." *Arkansian*, 1 June 1860.*
Reprint: "Humboldt River." *Arkansas True Democrat*, 11 August 1860.*
"An Indian's Grave." *Arkansas State Democrat*, 6 August 1847. Probably a version of "Far in a Lonely Wood."
"Maid of the Mountains." *Golden Era*, 11 [or 14, sources differ] August, 1861.* *P.*◊
"The Man of Memory." *Arkansas State Democrat*, 4 August 1848.
"The man twenty feet high, having the features of the Indian race, said to have been recently discovered in a cave somewhere in the Rocky Mountains." *Arkansas State Democrat*, 15 December 1848.
"Mount Shasta." In Ridge, *The Life and Adventures of Joaquín Murieta, the Celebrated California Bandit.* San Francisco: W.B. Cooke, 1854. *P.*
Reprint: "On Mount Shasta, Seen from a Distance." *Weekly California Express*, 22 May 1858.*

Reprint: "Mount Shasta." *Daily Alta California*, 7 May 1863.
"My Harp." *Arkansas State Democrat*, 31 March 1848. Probably a version of "The Harp of Broken Strings" in *P.*
"My Lost Love." *Poetry of the Pacific*, ed. May Wentworth. San Francisco: Pacific, 1867. 94–96. Reprinted from *P.*◊
"An October Morn." [Mentioned in Parins 54.]*◊
"Ode to the National Flag." *Daily Appeal* [Marysville, Calif.], 29 September 1861: 4. *P.*◊
"On the Laying of the Atlantic Telegraph Cable. In *The California Scrap-Book: A Repository of Useful Information and Select Reading*, ed. Oscar T. Shuck. San Francisco: H.H. Bancroft, 1869. 483–85. *P*, as "The Atlantic Cable."
"A Pleasant Morn in June." *Fort Smith Herald*, 23 August 1848.* *P.*◊
Reprint: "A June Morning." *Southwest Independent.**
Reprint: "A June Morning." *Daily Bee*, 5 June 1857.*
"Poem." In Willard B. Farwell, *Oration Delivered Before the Society of California Pioneers, at Their Celebration of the Eighth Anniversary of the Admission of the State of California to the Union.* San Francisco: Alta Job Office, 1859. Probably one of the poems in *P.*◊?
"Poem." *Arkansian*, 9 November 1860.* Probably one of the poems in *P.*◊?
"Poem Delivered at Marysville Fair." *Daily Union*, 6 [or 8? sources differ] September, 1860.* Probably one of the poems in *P.*◊?
"Poem Written for Fourth of July Celebration, 1861." *Daily Alta California*, 6 July 1861. *P* as "Poem" ("All hail, the fairest, greatest, best of days!").
Reprint: "Poem Delivered at Metropolitan Theater, San Francisco, 4 July 1861." *Golden Era*, 7 July 1861.*
Reprint: "Poem." In J. D. Whitney, *Address Delivered to the Celebration of the Sixth Anniversary of the College of California*, 1861. N.p. [51]–54.
Poems. San Francisco: H. Payot, 1868.
"The Rainy Season in California." *Hesperian* 4 (May 1860): 103–4.* *P.*
"Reflections Irregular." *Arkansas State Democrat*, 28 January 1848.
"The Robber's Song to His Mistress." *Arkansas State Democrat*, 17 September 1847.◊
"Rosa Dunn." *Golden Era*, 22 December 1861.* *P.*◊
"A Scene—The Feather River Sloughs." *Pacific Monthly* 11 (April 1864): 544–46.*◊
"Song" ("Come to the river's side, my love"). *Arkansas State Democrat*, 28 July 1848.
Reprint: "Song—Sweet Indian Maid." *Hutchings' California Magazine* 3 (April 1859): 494.*
"Song" ("I saw her once—her eye's deep light"). *Arkansas State Democrat*, 13 October 1848.
"The Still Small Voice" ("Alas, how every thing will borrow"). *Arkansas State Democrat*, 3 November 1848. *P.*
"The Still Small Voice" ("There is a voice more dear to me"). *Marysville Herald*, 29 March 1851.*
"Sunday in the Woods: Impromptu, Addressed to L——." *Daily Bee*, 15 June 1857.* Probably a version of "Far in a Lonely Wood" and possibly a version of "The Woods."◊
"To — —." *Golden Era*, September 29, 1861.* Possibly one of the poems in *Poems.*◊?
"To A*****." *Marysville Herald*, 15 April 1851.*◊
"To a Mocking Bird." *Arkansas Intelligencer*, 29 May 1847.* *P.*

Reprint: "To a Mockingbird Singing in a Tree." *Hutchings' California Magazine* 4 (August 1859): 65.*

"To a Star Seen at Twilight." *Arkansas State Democrat*, 13 July 11849. *P.*

"To Mrs. C. of Mo." *Arkansas State Democrat*, 2 Jun. 1848.◊

"The Unknown Lover." *Hutchings' California Magazine* 4 (November 1859): 227.* Possibly one of the poems in *Poems.*◊?

"The Waves that Murmur at Our Feet." *Pamphlets on the College of California.* San Francisco: Whitton, Waters, 1861. 51–54. *P* as "Poem" (The waves that murmur at our feet").

"The Woods." *Sacramento Union*, 27 May 1853.* Probably a version of "Far in a Lonely Wood" and possibly a version of "Sunday in the Woods."◊

"Yuba City." *Marysville Herald*, 1850.* *P* as "On Yuba City."◊

Riggs, Lynn (Cherokee)

Poems reprinted in *The Iron Dish*, 1930, are indicated with *ID.* Poems that appear only in *The Iron Dish* are not listed separately. Because Riggs published widely, this bibliography is likely incomplete. Riggs continued to publish poetry after 1930. His later poems are collected in *This Book, This Hill, These People: Poems by Lynn Riggs*, ed. Phyllis Cole Braunlich (Tulsa: Lynn Chase, 1982). Some of Riggs's poems are published under other forms of his name, such as R. Lynn Riggs.

"Advice to a Mendicant." *The Nation* 125 (2 November 1927): 472. *ID.* ◊

"The Arid Land." *Laughing Horse* 14 (Autumn 1927): 7.◊

"Beauty Has Gone." *University of Oklahoma Magazine* 12 (Fall 1923): 2.*◊

"Before Winter." *The Nation* 125 (14 December 1927): 686. *ID.* ◊

"Bird Cry." *New York Herald Tribune*, 15 March 1927.*◊

"Bootheels." *Laughing Horse* 11 (September 1924): n.p.◊

"The Choice." *Laughing Horse* 10 (May 1924): n.p.◊

"The Corrosive Season." *The Nation* 134 (23 March 1928): 319. *ID.*

"Dawn—Late Summer." *Poetry: A Magazine of Verse* 26 (August 1925): 255.◊

"The Deacon." *Smart Set* 70, 2 (February 1923): 122.◊

"Endless Legend." *New York Herald Tribune*, 11 December 1927*◊

"Epitaph." *Bookman* 65 (August 1927): 633.◊

"Footprints." *New York Herald Sun*, 26 December 1928.*◊

"Gilded Cavern." *Poetry: A Magazine of Verse* (August 1928): 260–64. This poem consists of "Charger" (260–61), "Bastinado" (261),◊ "Wolves" (262), "Portrait of a Peer" (263),◊ and "The Fountain" (264),◊ which each appear separately in *ID.*

"The High Words." *Bookman* 64 (September 1926): 93. *ID.* ◊

"I Have Grown Dull." *Smart Set* 70, 2 (February 1923): 48.◊

"I Have Not Looked on Beauty." *Contemporary Verse* 16 (December 1923): 93.◊

"The Impenitent." *New York Herald Tribune*, 11 December 1927*◊

The Iron Dish. Garden City, N.Y.: Doubleday, Doran, 1930.

"The Mermaid—A Fantasy." *Overland Monthly* 77, 2 (January–February 1921): 74.◊

"One Who Never Died." *New York Herald Tribune*, 29 April 1928.◊

["The orchard here is near and homelike—"] In Phyllis Cole Braunlich, *Haunted by Home: The Life and Letters of Lynn Riggs.* Norman: University of Oklahoma Press, 1988. 39.

"The Patrician." *Reviewer* 3 (October 1922): 622.◊

"Rhythm of Rain." *Poetry: A Magazine of Verse* 22 (August 1923): 252–53.◊

"Santa Fe Sonnets." *Laughing Horse* 12 (August 1925): 18.◊
"Santo Domingo Corn Dance." *The Nation* 122 (April 14, 1926): 407. *ID.*
Reprint: *New Voices of the Southwest,* ed. Hilton Ross Greer and Florence Elberta Barns. Dallas: Tardy, 1934. 172-74.
"Sonnet Tetrad." *University of Oklahoma Bulletin: University Anthology*, ed. Joseph Francis Paxton. Norman: University of Oklahoma, 1921. 106–7.◊
"Spring Day." *Contemporary Verse* 17 (April 1924): 54.◊
"Still Season." *New Republic* 54 (25 April 1928): 296. *ID.* ◊
"Threnody for the Slain." *New York Herald Tribune*, 4 March 1928.◊
"To Vachel Lindsay." *University of Oklahoma Magazine* 10 (February 1922): cover.◊
"The Vandals." *New York Herald Tribune*, 18 March 1928. *ID.*

Riley, Agnes. (Cheyenne)
S "'Dear School.'" *Indian School Journal* 18 (June 1918): 59. From Chilocco Indian School, Oklahoma.◊

Ross, A. Frank (Choctaw)
"Our Paper." *Indian Missionary* 6 (November 1890): 5.◊

Ross, Joshua ["The Wanderer"] (Cherokee)
"My Ruling Star." *South West Independent*, 10 February 1855.
"On a Lady's Eyes." *Arkansian*, 12 March 1859.
"Sequoyah." *Sequoyah Memorial*, 31 July 1856.
"The Wanderer." *Sequoyah Memorial*, 31 July 1856.

Ross, Lucinda M. (Cherokee)
"Cousin Vic." Emmet Starr, *History of the Cherokee Indians and Their Legends and Folk Lore.* Oklahoma City: Warden, 1921. 233.◊

Sarcoxie, Henry B. (Delaware)
"Rhymes Written at Las Vegas." Includes "In Mexico," "In the Desert," "In the Mountains," and "Up the Washita." *Twin Territories* 2 (September 1900): 193.

Schoolcraft, Jane Johnston (Ojibwe)
For all Schoolcraft's known surviving poems, see *The Sound the Stars Make Rushing Through the Sky: The Writings of Jane Johnston Schoolcraft*, ed. Robert Dale Parker. Philadelphia: University of Pennsylvania Press, 2007.

Seaton, Elise (Cherokee)
"Orientale." *American Indian* 4, 12 (September–October 1930): 5.
"Riverside." *American Indian* 4, 12 (September–October 1930): 5.

Shaw, Evalyn Callahan (Creek)
"October." *Muskogee Phoenix*, 1 November 1900. Reprinted from *Wagoner Sayings.*

Short, Wanda (unidentified)
"On Straight to Freedom." *Wassaja* 4, 10 (January 1920): 4.

Simons, Lillian (Mashpee)
S "Silhouettes—Guess." *Carlisle Arrow* , 22 May 1913. From Carlisle Indian School.

Sisson, Henry (Cherokee)
"Cookee." *Cherokee Advocate*, 12 March 1879.◊

Si-tu-a-kee, Jr. (Cherokee)
"To the Talehquah Gals." *Cherokee Advocate*, 5 November 1850.

Sixkiller, Samuel (Cherokee)
S [My First Winter Out of School.] "Well, well, Miss Paull, forgotten you?" *Indian Helper*, 10 January 1896. From Carlisle Indian School.
S "To Class '95." *Red Man* 12 (February 1895): 6. From Carlisle Indian School.

Skiuhushu (Red Fox, Red Fox Skiuhushu, Francis St. James) (Blackfoot)
"My Creed." *American Indian Advocate* 4 (Winter 1922): 8.◊
"Spirit of Cooperation." *The Indian*, January 1922: 1.◊

Slinker, Thomas Dewey (Choctaw)
S "Help a Fellow Forward." *Carlisle Arrow*, 27 October 1916. From Carlisle Indian School.◊
"Our Side of It." *Carlisle Arrow and Red Man*, 22 March 1918.

Smart, Leta V. Meyers (Omaha)
"On a Nickel." *Tomahawk*, 10 March 1921.
"A Picture." *Tomahawk*, 17 March 1 1921.
"Who." In *Supplement to the Papers of Carlos Montezuma, M.D.* Ed. John W. Larner, Jr. Microfilm. Wilmington, Del.: Scholarly Resources, 2001. 10 December 1920.
"W-H-O?" Anonymous. *Tomahawk* 6 (January 1921).
"A Young Man's Adventure with Opportunity." *Tomahawk*, 28 September 1922.

Snyder, Cora (Seneca)
S "The Frequent Showers of April." *Red Man* 12 (May 1895): 5. From Carlisle Indian School.◊

Spotted Elk, Molly [Molly Alice or Molly Dellis Nelson] (Penobscot)
Molly Spotted Elk Collection. Maine Folk Life Center. University of Maine, Orono.

Sunhair
["I stood in a hallowed place today—"] Manuscript. In *The Papers of Carlos Montezuma, M.D.* Ed. John William Larner, Jr. Microfilm. Wilmington, Del.: Scholarly Resources, 1983. Reel 9.◊
"One Spirit—One Race." *Tomahawk*, 4 November 1920.
"A Poem" ("Sweet Messenger of Light!"). *Tomahawk*, 14 October 1920.◊
"A Song of Hope." *Tomahawk*, 30 December 1920.

Te-con-ees-kee (Cherokee)
"Suggested by the Report, in the Advocate, of the Laying of the Cornerstone of the Pocahontas Female Seminary, Cherokee Nation." *Cherokee Advocate*, 15 May 1848.
["Though Far from Thee Georgia in Exile I Roam."] *Cherokee Advocate*, 3 July 1848.

Thompson, Martha (Tuscarora)
"The Red Cross Christmas Roll Call." *Indian Leader* 22 (December 1918): 15.◊

Thompson, William Abbott (Cherokee)
"You Can Always Tell." *Arrow*, July 5, 1895.

Too-qua-stee/Duncan, De Witt Clinton (Cherokee)
"The Angel of Hope." *Indian Chieftain*, 11 October 1900.◊

"Cherokee Memories." *Indian Chieftain*, 4 October 1900.
"A Christmas Song." *Vinita Weekly Chieftain*, 19 May 1904.
"The Dead Nation." *Indian Chieftain*, 24 April 1899.
"Dignity." *Vinita Weekly Chieftain*, 11 August 1904.
"Good Manners." *Vinita Weekly Chieftain*, 6 May 1904.◊
"Indian Territory at World's Fair." *Vinita Weekly Chieftain*, 29 September 1904.
Reprint: "Indian Territory at World's Fair." *Muscogee Democrat*, 1 October 1904.
"Labor." *Vinita Weekly Chieftain*, 8 September 1904.
"My Mother's Ring." *Vinita Weekly Chieftain*, 7 July 1904.
"Sequoyah." *Vinita Weekly Chieftain*, 2 June 1904.
"Sitting Bull's Address to His Braves upon the Eve of the Battle of the Little Big Horn." Mentioned in Foreman, "Notes" (307), but no copy has been found.*◊
"Thanksgiving." *Vinita Weekly Chieftain*, 24 November 1904.
"Truth Is Mortal." *Indian Chieftain*, 7 February 1901.
"A Vision of the End." *Indian Chieftain*, 3 August 1899.
"The White Man's Burden." *Daily Chieftain*, 27 March 1899.
Reprint: "The White Man's Burden." *Indian Chieftain*, 30 March 1899.
Reprint: "The White Man's Burden." *American Indian*, 2, 9 (June 1928): 17.

Tsoo-le-oh-woh (Cherokee)
"A Red Man's Thoughts." *Cherokee Advocate*, 25 May 1853.
"What an Indian Thought When He Saw the Comet." *Cherokee Advocate*, 28 September 1853.

Valley of Mountains (Klamath)
"Indian Memory." *American Indian Advocate* 3 (Grass Moon 1922): 1.◊

Verigan, Francis L. (Tlingit)
S "Be a Carlisle Student." *Carlisle Arrow and Red Man*, 2 November 1917. From Carlisle Indian School.
S "The Martyrdom of Funny Face." *Carlisle Arrow and Red Man*, 22 March 1918. From Carlisle Indian School.
S "Stick: After General Pratt's Address." *Carlisle Arrow and Red Man*, 9 November 1917. From Carlisle Indian School.◊
S "To Our Service Men." *Carlisle Arrow and Red Man*, 21 December 1917. From Carlisle Indian School.◊
S "To the 'Mysterious Stranger.'" *Carlisle Arrow and Red Man*, 25 January 1918. From Carlisle Indian School.◊

Walker, Bertrand N. O. See Hen-toh.

Walker, William (Wyandot)
["Oh, give me back my bended bow."] In Homer Everett, *History of Sandusky County, Ohio*. Cleveland,: H.Z. Williams, 1882. 17.
"The Wyandot's Farewell." In Homer Everett, *History of Sandusky County, Ohio*. Cleveland: H.Z. Williams, 1882. 17.

Waterman, Leila (Seneca)
S "Farewell to Carlisle." *Carlisle Arrow*, 16 May 1913. From Carlisle Indian School.◊

Waters, James E. (Chief Wild Pigeon) (Montauk/Montaukett)

"The First American Alliance." In *Report of the Annual Meeting of the Montauk Tribe of Indians. Sag Harbor, L. I. August 29th, 1919.* Reprint in *The History & Archaeology of the Montauk*, ed. Gaynell Stone. 2nd ed. Readings in Long Island Archaeology & Ethnohistory 3. Stony Brook, N.Y.: Suffolk County Archaeological Association, Nassau County Archaeological Committee, 1993. 486–87.

"King Philip (Pometacom)." *Report of the Annual Meeting of the Montauk Tribe of Indians. Sag Harbor, L. I. August 29th, 1919.* Reprint in *The History & Archaeology of the Montauk*, ed. Gaynell Stone. 2nd ed. Readings in Long Island Archaeology & Ethnohistory 3. Stony Brook, N.Y.: Suffolk County Archaeological Association, Nassau County Archaeological Committee, 199. 481.

"Montauk." *Report of the Annual Meeting of the Montauk Tribe of Indians. Sag Harbor, L. I. August 29th, 1919.* Reprint in *The History & Archaeology of the Montauk*, ed. Gaynell Stone. 2nd ed. Readings in Long Island Archaeology & Ethnohistory 3. Stony Brook, N.Y.: Suffolk County Archaeological Association, Nassau County Archaeological Committee, 199. 473.

Wa Wa Chaw (Payomkowishum, Luiseño)

"And So All Things of the Earth." In *Spirit Woman: The Diaries and Paintings of Benita Wa Wa Calachaw Nuñez*, ed. Stan Steiner. San Francisco: Harper & Row, 1980.xix.

"Gone Are the Days." *The Indian*, March 1922: 19.

"Haunted Brains." *The Indian*, September 1922: 1.

"The Indian Cry." *The Indian*, February 1922: 9.

"The Indian Game." *The Indian*, August 1922: 1.

"The Indians' Spirits." *The Indian*, May 1922: 8.

"The Kiss." In *Spirit Woman: The Diaries and Paintings of Benita Wa Wa Calachaw Nuñez*, ed. Stan Steiner. San Francisco: Harper & Row, 1980. 56–57.◊

"In Memory of My Homosexual Friend: Imaginary Love. . ." In *Spirit Woman: The Diaries and Paintings of Benita Wa Wa Calachaw Nuñez*, ed. Stan Steiner. San Francisco: Harper & Row, 1980. 57–58.

"My Psyche and Wassaja." In *Spirit Woman: The Diaries and Paintings of Benita Wa Wa Calachaw Nuñez*, ed. Stan Steiner. San Francisco: Harper & Row, 1980. 224.

"My Secret World." In *Spirit Woman: The Diaries and Paintings of Benita Wa Wa Calachaw Nuñez*, ed. Stan Steiner. San Francisco: Harper & Row, 1980.212.

"The Trial of the Mission Indian." *The Indian*, January 1922: 1, 14.

Welch, Julia Carter (Chickasaw)

"Fall." *American Indian* 3, 12 (September 1929): 5.

"Indian Lament." *American Indian* 5, 3 (December 1930–January): 5.

"Life and Death." *American Indian* 4, 3 (December 1929): 5.◊

"Redman." *American Indian* 5, 3 (December 1930–January): 5.

"The Weaver." *American Indian* 4, 6 (March 1930): 5.

Wenonah (Cherokee)

"Thanksgiving." *Indian Chieftain*, 25 November 1886.

Wheelock, James (Oneida)

S ["The long dreary winter weather."] *Red Man* 12 (May 1895): 5. From Carlisle Indian School.◊

Whipper, Rose (Sioux)
S "Pride of Our Nation." *Carlisle Arrow*, 22 May 1913. From Carlisle Indian School.◊

Williams, Emma Lowrey (Cherokee)
S "Life." Emmet Starr, *History of the Cherokee Indians and Their Legends and Folk Lore.* Oklahoma City: Warden, 1921. 234. From Cherokee Female Seminary.

Wolf, Flora A. (Crow)
S "Academic Class Poem." *Sherman Bulletin*, 19 May 1909, supplement. From Sherman Institute.◊

Y. (Cherokee)
S "To the Caged Parrot." *Sequoyah Memorial* 1, 1 (August 2, 1855): 4. From Cherokee Male Seminary.◊

Young[bull], Tyler (Arapaho)
S "Just Imagine!" *Bacone Chief.* Bacone, Okla.: Bacone College, 1920. 110.

Yellow Bird. See John Rollin Ridge.

Z. (Cherokee)
"My Little Knife." *Sequoyah Memorial* 1, 1 (August 2 1855): 3. From Cherokee Male Seminary.◊

Zitkala-Sa/Bonnin, Gertrude Simmons (Sioux)
"Ballad." *The Earlhamite* 3, 7 (9 January 1897): 97–98.◊
"The Indian's Awakening." *American Indian Magazine* 4 (1916): 57–59.◊
"Iris of Life." *The Earlhamite* 5 (1 November 1898): 31.◊
"The Red Man's America." *American Indian Magazine* 5 (1917): 64.◊
"A Sioux Woman's Love for Her Grandchild." *American Indian Magazine* 5 (1917): 230–31.◊
Zitkala-Sa's poems are reprinted in *Dreams and Thunder: Stories, Poems, and the Sun Dance Opera*, ed. P. Jane Hafen. Lincoln: University of Nebraska Press, 2001.

Textual Notes

Unless otherwise indicated, all poems come from the earliest source listed in the bibliography. Titles are frequently regularized, such as by left-justifying titles that are centered in the original or by removing periods that, at the time these poems were written, often followed titles. Emendations (editorial changes) are by the editor and are recorded in the textual notes. Many of the poems lack possessive apostrophes where they might be expected. These are supplied (and recorded in the textual notes) where their absence seems accidental and not supplied where their absence seems representative of the poet's choices, though such decisions are judgments and are not always self-evident. Minor variants of punctuation are common in reprinted versions of a poem, and minor variants of words are not unusual. Such variants in reprinted poems are not recorded in the textual notes.

John Lynch Adair

- "Hec Dies: An Imitation." **Title, Imitation**: emendation of *Imitatin.* **25 we've**: emendation of *we're.*
- "Joy Returneth with the Morning." 7 **Galilee**: emendation of *Galllee.*

Mabel Washbourne Anderson

- "Nowita, the Sweet Singer." "Nowita, the Sweet Singer" was reprinted at least three times during Anderson's life, in 1903, 1906, and 1911. The three later versions have only minor differences but differ in many small and several not-so-small ways from the first version, suggesting that the 1903 version includes Anderson's corrections to the 1900 version. Because the 1911 version introduces minor but irregular changes in capitalization that imply it was not overseen by Anderson, I have chosen the 1906 version for reprinting here.

  The notes here do not record differences in stanza breaks between the first and later versions, because the pattern of stanza breaks in the 1900 version sometimes appears arbitrary, suggesting a casual approach by the printer. **Title**: There is no "the" in the 1900 title, presumably by mistake. *Prose introduction.* **dark braids**: dusky braids *1900, 1903.* 3: This line is not in the 1900 version.

Anonymous Carlisle Student

- "My Industrial Work." **Title**: The present editor has supplied the title, based on the assignment that provoked the poem.

Anonymous Cherokee

- ["Faster and fiercer rolls the tide."] 17 **Its**: emendation of *It's.* 19 **comma**: emendation of period. 23 **pled**: emendation of *plead.* **28: hearth**: emendation of *heart.* **26 man's**: emendation of *mans.* 39 **tradition's**: emendation of *traditions.*

Irene C. Beaulieu

- "Poor Lo." 21 **comma**: added by emendation. 34 **period**: added by emendation.

Blue Feather

- "The Lone Tee-Pee." 15 **comma at end of line**: emendation of what appears to be a period.

William Penn Boudinot

- ["There is a spectre ever haunting."] 8 **turns**: emendation of *terns*, following later reprintings. 32 **its**: emendation of *it's*, following later reprintings. 34 **Stir**: emendation of *Stirs*, following later reprintings.

Olivia Ward Bush-Banks

- "On the Long Island Indian." The text reproduced here is the 1890 version, because Bush (later Bush-Banks) would have seen that through the press herself. Except as noted, the 1890 version is the same as the 1916 version, except that it has slight variations in punctuation and capitalization and has no indented lines.
  29 **remains**: emendation of *remain* in accord with 1916.
- "Morning on Shinnecock." 12 **heralding**: emendation of *herding* in accord with 1916.
- "A Hero of San Juan." 9 **feeble**: emendation of *feeble's.* 30 **form**: emendation of *from.*
- "Regret." Published in *The Voice of the Negro* in 1905. A slightly different version appeared in *Driftwood* (1914). 9 **mine;**: revised to *mine!* in 1914. 11 **Tears of**: revised to *Ah! deep* in 1914.
- "Heart-Throbs." 34 **'Twere**: emendation of *"Twere.*

Mrs. Minot Carter

- "Raindrops." 10 **you**: emendation of *your.*
- "Fancies." 10 **again"?**: emendation of *again?"* 13 **sunset's**: emendation of *sunsets.* 14 **true"?**: emendation of *true?"*

Stella LeFlore Carter

- "Inauguration Day." The name listed after the poem is Stella LaFlore Carter, presumably a typo for Stella LeFlore Carter.

Arsenius Chaleco

- "The Indian Requiem." 25 **comma**: emendation of period.

Chaw, Wawa. See Wa Wa Chaw

Laura M. Cornelius

- "A Tribute to the Future of My Race." The text comes from *The Red Man and Helper*, which says that it is reprinted from the *Riverside Daily Press*, without providing a date. I have not seen the *Riverside Daily Press* version. The punctuation at the ends of lines is unclear and occasionally includes commas that look like periods. To determine the end-line punctuation, I have occasionally relied on my judgment regarding the sense of the lines. 2 **Aegean**: emendation of *Aegian.* 22 **wind**: emendation of *Wind.* Longfellow's *The Song of Hiawatha*, the source for this passage, reads *wind.* 37 **green lanes**: emendation of *greenlands.* Longfellow's *The Song of Hiawatha*, the source for this passage, reads *green lanes.*

J. C. Duncan

- "The Red Man's Burden." **10 The**: emendation of *the.* **14 "Christians"**: emendation of *"Christians.* **42 The**: emendation of *the.* **47 though**: emendation of *thuough.*

Eleazar

- "In obitum Viri verè Reverendi D. Thomae Thacheri. . . ." **5 palma**: emendation of *palmo.* **9 Gentique**: emendation of *Gentiquae.* **21 Caelos**: emendation of *Caeles.*
- "On the death of that truly venerable man D. Thomas Thacher. . . ." For another translation, see Wolfgang Hochbruck and Beatrix Dudensing-Reichel. For commentary on the Latin text, see Leo M. Kaiser ("Thirteen"). Earlier translations from 1748 (Muses), 1825 (Anonymous, "The Aborigines"), and 1855 (Robinson) make no effort to provide more than a remote summary of what the poem says. **25 κόνις**: emendation of *κονίν.*

Israel Folsom

- "Lo! The Poor Indian's Hope." The text relies on transcripts in the American Native Press Archive at the University of Arkansas at Little Rock. **10 forests**: emendation of *forest.*

Alfred C. Gillis

- "The Bird with the Wounded Wing." **16 comma**: emendation of period. **21 its**: emendation of *it's.*
- "To the Wenem Mame River." **26 Wintoons'**: emendation of *Wintoons.* **28 Yea**: emendation of *Ye.* **44 Vigil**: emendation of *Virgil.*
- "The Sacramento River." **2 comma**: emendation of period.

James Roane Gregory

- "The Promised Seal." **4**: apostrophes added by emendation. **10 Will**: emendation of *will.* **13**: apostrophe and period added by emendation. **15 dash**: emendation of hyphen.
- "Otheen, Okiyetos." **3, 15, 30, 31**: apostrophe added by emendation.
- "Rain." **12 remain**: emendation of *remaim.* **13**: apostrophe added by emendation.
- "Storm Lights." **21 the**: emendation of *tha.* **37**: apostrophe added by emendation.
- "Nineteenth Century Finality." **12 Science**: emendation of *Sscience.*

Gust-ah-yah-she

- "The Indian's Plea." **31 passed**: emendation of *passes.*

Mary Cornelia Hartshorn

- "The Poet." **14 closed quotation mark**: added by emendation. **15 seemed**: emendation of *seemd.*
- "Three Poems of Christmas Eve, Tonight." **12 all.)**: emendation of *all).*

Hen-toh

- "Pontiac." **85 pitiable**: emendation of *pitabe.*
- "The Seasons." As the typographer seems to have had difficulty arranging this poem, it has been slightly emended to regularize the indenting of lines.

- "Smokin." 5 **thinkin'**: apostrophe added by emendation.
- "A Borrowed Tale." 29 **closed quotation mark**: added by emendation.
- "Triplets." 23 **period**: added by emendation.
- "August." 16 **'aint**: emendation of *'Aint.*
- "Weengk." 1 **closed quotation mark**: added by emendation.
- "Agency Police I." 18 **'notha'**: emendation of *'notha'.* 19 **'roun'**: emendation of *'roun'.*
- "Agency Police III." 18 **closed quotation mark**: added by emendation. **Note:** closed quotation mark after *yet* added by emendation. Period after *on* added by emendation.

William D. Hodjkiss
- "Song of the Storm-Swept Plain." 12 **lullabies**: emendation of *lullabys.*

An Indian (Jesse Bushyhead?)
- "The Indian's Farewell." 5 **oft**: emendation of *of't.*

Kingfisher
- "After the Curtis Bill Passes." 15 **Jamaica**: emendation of *Jamaca.* 42 **comma**: emendation of period.

Joseph M. La Hay
- "Consolation" 17 **your**: emendation of *you.*

Ben D. Locke
- "Hobachi (Echo)." 8–9: stanza break by emendation.

Joseph Lynch Martin
- "Stanzas by Uncle Joe." 1 **nieces**: emendation of *neices.*

D'Arcy McNickle
- "The Mountains." 33 **But when . . .** : A page break falls before this line, making it uncertain whether a stanza break belongs there.

Melinda Metoxen
- "Iceland." 2, 41 **Arctic**: emendation of *Artic.*

Carlos Montezuma
- "Civilization." The typography in this poem crowds the lines together, making the stanza breaks hard to distinguish, except for the last two, which are printed in a less crowded column and stand out more clearly. The columns divide between lines 47 and 48, so the decision to render a stanza break there depends on editorial judgment but seems consistent with the ongoing pattern.

Ruth Margaret Muskrat
- "Songs of the Spavinaw." Because the poem's typography has a large initial letter ("I") that crowds lines 2–3, an editor is left to guess at the correct indentation of those lines.
- "Sentenced." 9 **conquered**: emendation of *conquerd.*
- "The Hunter's Wooing." 12 **Senecas**: emendation of *Seneca's.*
- "The Warriors' Dance." 4 **weird**: emendation of *wierd.*

N.

- ["Farewell."] **Title:** The poem appears under the headline "Poetry," but that seems not to be its title. The present editor has supplied the title "Farewell."

Our Contributor

- "The Ne'er Digressing Quartette." **1 Ever:** emendation of "*Ever.* **9 digressed:** emendation of *disgressed.* **12 Chippewa:** emendation of *Chippews.* **19:** an indentation at the beginning of this line, presumably a typesetting error, is removed by emendation.

John Palmer

- ["I Remember You."] **1 always:** emendation of *allways.* **2 everything:** emendation of *every thing.* **60 songs:** emendation of *song.* **66 sister, I:** emendation of *sister I.*

Arthur Caswell Parker

- "My Race Shall Live." **4 prove:** emendation of *proove.*

Alexander Posey

- "Wildcat Bill." **2 me be:** emendation of *be be.* **10 Kin:** emendation of *Kin'.*
- ["In UNCLE SAM'S dominion."] **7 comma:** emendation of period. **8 mote:** emendation of *moat.*
- "Callie." **3 period:** added by emendation. **10 Offer:** emendation for *offer.*
- "When Love Is Dead." **Note:** This version of the poem, following Sivils, reproduces the text of Posey's surviving manuscript, which matches the version published during his lifetime. In the version published by Minnie H. Posey, which she might have revised, the poem has no stanza breaks; each pair of lines in the present text is one line; and *night* (line 8) is *height.*
- "On the Capture and Imprisonment of Crazy Snake, January, 1901." **Title, 1901:** emendation of *1900.* Minnie H. Posey, who may have provided all or part of the title, probably introduced the erroneous date.
- "Saturday." **14, 20, 44 period:** added by emendation. **20 'roun':** emendation of *'round.*
- "A Freedman Rhyme." **6 period:** added by emendation.

John Rollin Ridge

- "An Indian's Grave." **8 threw:** emendation of *thew.*
- "The Dark One to His Love." **7 buoyant:** emendation of *bouyant.* **22 spirit's:** emendation of *spirits.* **34 thee:** emendation of *the.*
- "Mount Shasta." **64 children:** emendation of *childen.*
- "The Atlantic Cable." **19–20:** Stanza break by emendation. A page break comes between these lines, making it impossible to tell whether a stanza break comes there or not.
- "Humboldt River." **47 comma:** emendation of period.
- "To a Star Seen at Twilight." The 1849 version differs from the 1868 version reprinted here in its punctuation, by indenting every second line, and in other ways as observed in the notes below. **11 soul's:** *clear* [1849]. **19 feel:** *wish* [1849]. **20 grow bright:** *could be* [1849]. **28–29:** stanza break [1849]. **29 look:** *gaze* [1849]. **33 world:** *earth* [1849]. **40–41:** stanza break [1849]. **46 burning worlds which:** *wandering worlds, that* [1849]. **50:** italicized [1849].

- "October Hills." The 1867 version has minor differences in punctuation, including one obvious mistake (*their's* at line 10). **18 exclamation point:** because the 1868 version lacks needed punctuation at the end of this line, the present text takes the exclamation point from the 1867 version. **21 unseen:** *serene* [1867], apparently a typo, given that it rhymes with the same word in line 23.
- "Erinna." The 1848 version has minor differences of punctuation, italics, and stanza division as well as the differences listed below. **11 Aegean** [1848]: *Aegena* [1868]. **15 golden:** *silken* [1848]. **20 sweetly rounded:** *full-developed* [1848]. **21 Twin spheres of love and Pleasure's burning:** *Those heaving breasts, like Pleasure's very* [1848]. **25 That:** *Which* [1848]. **33 the:** *a* [1848]. **37 form its bloom and:** *very form its* [1848]. **43 semicolon:** because the 1868 version lacks needed punctuation at the end of this line, the present text takes the semicolon from the 1848 version. **44 hath:** *has* [1848]. **46 that:** *who* [1848]. **48–49:** not in the 1848 version. **57 that charms the listening:** *and feel it in our* [1848].
- "Lines on a Humming Bird Seen at a Lady's Window." **28 upborne:** emendation of *upborn.*
- "Poem." ("All hail, the fairest, greatest, best of days!"). **24 unveiled:** emendation of *unvailed.*
- "A Scene Along the Rio de las Plumas." **19–20:** Stanza break by emendation. A page break comes between these lines, making it impossible to tell whether a stanza break comes there or not.
- "The Still Small Voice" ("Alas, how every thing will borrow"). The 1848 version has minor differences of punctuation, as well as the differences listed below. **31 the die:** *the fearful die* [1848]. **34 of toil:** *and toil* [1848]. **38–39 While birds make music on the air? / No:** *When none with me my grief can share? / Alas, no* [1848]. **47 fiat of:** *fiat in* [1848].

Joshua Ross

- "My Ruling Star." **14, 21, 26:** apostrophes added by emendation.
- "The Wanderer." **9 hills:** emendation of *bills.*

Wanda Short

- "On Straight to Freedom." **13 fathers':** emendation of *father's.* **43 period:** added by emendation.

Samuel Sixkiller

- "To Class '95." **4 Americans:** emendation of *American.* **17:** question mark at end of line removed by emendation.
- ["My First Winter Out of School."] **23, 77 it's:** emendation of *its.*

Thomas Dewey Slinker

- "Our Side of It." **24:** indented by emendation.

Leta V. Meyers Smart

- "A Young Man's Adventure with Opportunity." **30 someone:** emendation of *some one.* **33 And:** emendation of *Vnd.* **59 fastened:** emendation of *fasteded.* **80 stifled:** emendation of *stiffled.*

Molly Spotted Elk

- ["Down in the land of roses."] **12 myriads of stars:** emendation of *myriads stars.*

- ["I never knew of such a place."] 14 **banana:** emendation of *bannana.*
- "We're in the Chorus Now." 23 **Audrey:** emendation of *Audery.* 29 **chameleon:** emendation of *chamelon.* 72 **Than:** emendation of *Then.*

Sunhair

- "A Song of Hope." 2 **Wakonda:** emendation of *Wakonda'.* 5 **invoke:** emendation of *envoke.* 10 **nigh:** emendation of *neigh.*

Te-con-ees-kee

- "Suggested by the report, in the Advocate, of the laying of the corner stone of the Pocahontas Female Seminary—Cherokee Nation." 1 **heart's:** emendation of *hearts.* 4 **on:** emendation of *ou.* 8 **comma:** added by emendation. 19 **wings:** emendation of *wing.* 42 **Tahlequah:** emendation of *Talequah.*

Zoe A. Tilghman

- "Squaw-lls." 17 **kidnapping:** emendation of *kidnaping.* **20:** indented by emendation.

Too-qua-stee / DeWitt Clinton Duncan

- "The White Man's Burden." The end-line punctuation is not always clear and may include an occasional error by the poet or printer, but the sense is generally clear, making it possible for the editor to determine the punctuation without concern about editorial distortion. Beneath the poem appear the following place and date: "Vinita, I. T. [Indian Territory], March 10, 1899." 32 **censer's** [1928]: *censor's* [1899]. 54 **sulphurous:** emendation of *suphurous.* 95 **venal:** the 27 March 1899 printing has *venial,* but the 30 March 1899 reprinting has *venal,* which seems to make more sense, suggesting that *venial* was a mistake by Too-qua-stee or the printer. **97–98:** stanza break added by emendation, in accord with the second printing (March 30, 1899).
- "The Dead Nation." 5 **on:** emendation of *ont.* 6 **feet:** emendation of *fee.*
- "A Vision of the End." 35 **as:** emendation of *ns.* **49–56:** These lines are arranged differently from the others, in one eight-line stanza with no indented lines. That may be a printer's error. Their left margin also appears a little farther to the left than the left margin of the other stanzas, but—on the assumption that the different margin is indeed a printer's error—the left margin of these lines has been emended to match the left margin of the rest of the poem.
- "Cherokee Memories." 38 **personnel:** emendation of *personel.* **96–97:** A seemingly accidental stanza break between these lines has been removed by emendation. 104 **demon's yelp:** emendation. The print is obscured in the copy seen by the editor, so that the letters between *m* and *l* cannot be read.
- "Truth Is Mortal." 29 **laughs:** emendation of *laugh's.*
- "Sequoyah." 3 **arctic:** emendation of *artic.*
- "Dignity."The end-line punctuation is not always clear and may include an occasional error by the poet or printer, but the sense is generally clear, making it possible for the editor to determine the punctuation without concern about editorial distortion.
- "Thanksgiving." The end-line punctuation is not always clear and may include an occasional error by the poet or printer, but the sense is generally clear, making it

possible for the editor to determine the punctuation without concern about editorial distortion.

Tsoo-le-oh-woh

- "A Red Man's Thoughts." Several irregularities in the indentation of lines in the last four stanzas have been regularized. 10 **sell**: emendation of *shell.*
- "What an Indian Thought When He Saw the Comet." 1-2 **comma**: removed by emendation at end of lines. 9 **shoreless**: emendation of *shore less.* 11 **phrenzied**: emendation of *phrezried.* 15 **wrathful**: emendation of *wrath full.* 15 **damnation**: emendation of *dam nation.* 16 **direful**: emendation of *dire full.* 17 **off**: emendation of *of.* 30 **Wide-spread eyeball**: emendation of *Wide—spread eye ball.* 31 **Direful regions**: *Dire full regious.* 33 **didn't**: emendation of *did'nt.*

Francis L. Verigan

- "The Martyrdom of Funny Face." **downstairs**: emendation of *downstair's.* 20 **closed quotation mark**: added by emendation. 31 **won't**: emendation of *wont.* 42 **period**: added by emendation.

James E. Waters (Wild Pigeon)

- "Montauk." 14 **life**: emendation of *like.* 23 **cliffs**: emendation of *cliff.*
- "King Philip (Pometacom)." 14 **whisp'ring**: emendation of *whis'pring.* 19 **Massasoit**: emendation of *Massaoit.*
- "The First American Alliance." **1636, he**: the reprint used as the source for this edition has a bracketed emendation that the present editor has not followed: *1636, [when] he.* 5 **freely**: emendation of *feely.* 7 **underbrush**: emendation of *under-brush*, in light of lines 2 and 17.

Wa Wa Chaw

- "The Trial of the Mission Indian." 9 **Therefore**: emendation of *There for.*
- "The Indian Game." 5 **Chieftains**: emendation of *Chieftians.* 20 **Buffalo**: emendation of *Buffallo.*
- "Gone Are the Days." 15 **Ya-wil-chi-ne, Mariano**: comma added by emendation. 23 **closed quotation mark**: added by emendation.
- "The Present Indian Slave." The manuscript of this poem, found among *The Papers of Carlos Montezuma* (reel 9), is written on Wa Wa Chaw's personal stationery, with the words "Wa Wa Chaw my *work*" written on the side of one page. The transcription preserves the manuscript's idiosyncrasies as much as is practical. Underlined words, here represented in the conventional way by italics, are sometimes underlined with two and sometimes with three lines. That distinction, likely a casual one, is lost in the use of italics. The irregular indentation has been slightly regularized. Such adaptations of italics and indentation represent what Wa Wa Chaw would likely expect from an editor, though the punctuation and spelling have been left as they appear in the manuscript. 28 **Grave**: emendation of *Gave.*

Wenonah

- "Thanksgiving." 9 **perished**: emendation of *per- / perished.*

Emma Lowrey Williams

- "Life." 2 **We**: emendation of *What.*

Works Cited

Abel, Annie Heloise. "History of Indian Consolidation West of the Mississippi." *Annual Report of the American Historical Association for the Year 1906*. Vol. 1. Washington: U.S. GPO, 1908. 233–450.

"Adams Essay Contest." *Southern Workman* 49, 4 (April 1920): 186.

"Adams Prize Debate." *Southern Workman* 49, 3 (March 1920): 140.

"Ainslie 'Princess' Repudiates Title." *New York Times*, 11 November 1924: 25.

Anderson, James H., ed. *Life and Letters of Judge Thomas J. Anderson and Wife*. Columbus, Ohio: F. J. Heer, 1904.

Annual Report of the Commissioner of Indian Affairs. 1894. Washington, D.C.: U.S. GPO, 1895.

Anonymous. "The aborigines of this country. . . ." *Boston Monthly Magazine* 1, 5 (October 1825): 244–47.

Apess, William. *On Our Own Ground: The Complete Writings of William Apess, a Pequot*. Ed. Barry O'Connell. Amherst: University of Massachusetts Press, 1992.

"Athletic Notes." *Southern Workman* 49, 12 (December 1920): 574–75.

Baird, W. David. *Peter Pitchlynn: Chief of the Choctaws*. Norman: University of Oklahoma Press, 1972.

Beck, David R. M. *The Struggle for Self-Determination: History of Menominee Indians since 1854*. Lincoln: University of Nebraska Press, 2005.

Bennett, Paula Bernat, ed. *Nineteenth Century American Women Poets: An Anthology*. Oxford: Blackwell, 1998.

———. *Poets in the Public Sphere: The Emancipatory Project of American Women's Poetry*. Princeton, N.J.: Princeton University Press, 2003.

Bhabha, Homi K. "Of Mimicry and Man: The Ambivalence of Colonial Discourse." In Bhabha, *The Location of Culture*. London: Routledge, 1994. 85–92.

Blue, Bennis Marie. "Reclaiming a Multiracial Heritage: Race, Identity, and Culture in the Life and Literary Works of Olivia Ward Bush-Banks." Ph.D. dissertation, Ohio State University, 2000.

Blue Feather, Princess, Aztec of Mexico. *Indian Mother's Lullaby*. Philadelphia, 1934.

Braunlich, Phyllis Cole. *Haunted by Home: The Life and Letters of Lynn Riggs*. Norman: University of Oklahoma Press, 1988.

Brewer, Phil D. "A Biographical Sketch with Excerpts from His Diary." *Chronicles of Oklahoma* 4, 1 (March 1926): 55–60.

Brown, David J. "Kee-too-wah." *The Telephone* 3, 10, 26 July 1889.

Brudvig, Jon L., ed. and comp. "First Person Accounts as Written by American Indian Students at Hampton Institute, 1878–1923." 1996. http://www.twofrog.com/hamptonstories2.html.

Bryant, William Cullen. *The Poetical Works of William Cullen Bryant.* Ed. Parke Godwin. 2 vols. New York: Appleton, 1883.

"California Indians in Yuma County, California, 1928: The Costanoan-Ohlone Indian Canyon Resource." http://www.indiancanyon.org/pics/census1928names/yuma1.html. Accessed 11 October 2008.

"Capt. Ben Locke, Noted Indian Soldier-Writer, Passes Away." *American Indian* 2, 4 (January 1928): 6.

"Chief Wild Pigeon Dead on Long Island: Head of Montauk and Narragansett Tribes Also Known as James B. Waters." *New York Times*, 4 September 1927: B5.

"Children of Robert Ivey Jr. & Elizabeth West." http://www.genfiles.com/ivey/ivey-robert2children.htm. Accessed 7 January 2010.

Chute, Janet E. *The Legacy of Shingwaukonse: A Century of Native Leadership.* Toronto: University of Toronto Press, 1998.

———. "Shingwaukonse: A Nineteenth-Century Innovative Ojibwa Leader." *Ethnohistory* 45, 1 (Winter 1998): 65–101.

Connelley, William Elsey. *The Life of Preston B. Plumb, 1837–1891.* Chicago: Browne & Howell, 1913.

———. *The Provisional Government of Nebraska Territory and the Journals of William Walker Provisional Governor of Nebraska Territory.* Lincoln: State Journal, 1899.

Cornsilk, David. "The Lucy Allen Story." African-Native American Genealogy Forum, 15 February 2007. http://www.afrigeneas.com/forume/index.cgi?noframes;read=14098. Accessed 28 January 2008.

Cox, Barbara. "Re: Noah G. Gregory." 8 July 2002. http://genforum.com/gregory/messages/4568.html.

DeMallie, Raymond J. Email to Robert Parker. 19 July 2009.

Doane, George S. "Report of Quapaw Agency." *Report of the Commissioner of Indian Affairs.* Washington, D.C.: U.S. GPO, 1897. 133–36.

"Dr. Anna Lewis, Choctaw Historian." http://www.usao.edu/lewis/fp03.htm.

Dunbar, Paul Laurence. *The Complete Poems of Paul Laurence Dunbar.* New York: Dodd, Mead, 1913.

Eells, Myron. *Ten Years of Missionary Work Among the Indians at Skokomish, Washington Territory, 1874–1884.* Boston: Congregational Sunday-School and Publishing Society, 1886.

Everett, Homer. *History of Sandusky County, Ohio.* Cleveland, Ohio: H. Z. Williams, 1882.

Finley, J. B. Letter. *Baltimore Patriot* 28, 33, 11 August 1828.

Fitzgerald, Stephanie. "Intimate Geographies: Representing Citizenship and Community in *The Autobiography of Delfina Cuero* and Benita Nuñez's *Diaries.*" *American Indian Culture and Research Journal* 30, 1 (2006): 109–30.

"Five Strung Up. The Infamous Buck Gang Expiate Their Crimes on the Gallows." *Cherokee Advocate*, 11 July 1896: 1.

"Foreign Mission School." *The Religious Intelligencer . . . Containing the Principle [sic] Transactions of the Various Bible and Missionary Societies with Particular Accounts of Revivals of Religion* 7, 4, 22 June 1822: 64.

Foreman, Caroline Thomas. "The Foreign Mission School at Cornwall, Connecticut." *Chronicles of Oklahoma* 7, 3 (September 1929): 242–59.

———. "Notes on DeWitt Clinton Duncan and a Recently Discovered History of the Cherokees." *Chronicles of Oklahoma* 47, 8 (Autumn 1969): 305–9.

Foreman, Caroline Thomas, and M. H. W. [Muriel H. Wright]. "S. Alice Callahan: Author of Wynema: A Child of the Forest." *Chronicles of Oklahoma* 33 (1955): 306–15.

Foreman, Grant. *Indian Removal: The Emigration of the Five Civilized Tribes of Indians.* Norman: University of Oklahoma Press, 1972.

Geller, Adam. "Past and Future Collide in Fight over Cherokee Identity." *USA Today* (Associated Press), 10 February 2007. http://www.usatoday.com/news/nation/2007-02-10-cherokeefight_x.htm. Accessed 28 January 2008.

Gravitt, Winnie Lewis. "Anna Lewis: A Great Woman of Oklahoma." *Chronicles of Oklahoma* 40, 4 (1962): 326–29.

"Gregory, James Roane Interview." Transcribed by Barbara Thompson Cox. http://okgenweb.org/pioneer/ohs/gregory-james.htm.

Gridley, Marion E. "William J. Kershaw." *Indians of Today.* Chicago: Indian Council Fire, 1936. 70.

Guillaume, Bernice F. "The Life and Work of Olivia Ward Bush (Banks), 1869–1944." Ph.D. dissertation, Tulane University, 1983.

Hardy, Thomas. *Thomas Hardy: The Complete Poems.* London: Macmillan, 2001.

Harman, S. W. *Hell on the Border; He Hanged Eighty-Eight Men.* Fort Smith, Ark.: Phoenix, 1898.

Hartshorne, Mary. "Hollywood's Movie Stars and Shops Attract Visitors." *American Indian* 3, 5 (February 1929): 2.

———. "The 'Talkie Movies.'" *American Indian* 3, 5 (February 1929): 2–3.

Harvey, Gretchen V. "Cherokee and American: Ruth Muskrat Bronson, 1897–1982." Ph.D. dissertation, Arizona State University, 1996.

Hauptman, Laurence M. "Designing Woman: Minnie Kellogg." In *Indian Lives: Essays on Nineteenth- and Twentieth-Century Indian Leaders*, ed. L. G. Moses and Raymond Wilson. Albuquerque: University of New Mexico Press, 1985. 159–88.

Hoig, Stanley W. *The Cherokees and Their Chiefs: In the Wake of Empire.* Fayetteville: University of Arkansas Press, 1998.

Hochbruck, Wolfgang, and Beatrix Dudensing-Reichel. "'Honoratissimi Benefactores': Native American Students and Two Seventeenth-Century Texts in the University Tradition." *Studies in American Indian Literature* 4, 2/3 (Summer/Fall 1992): 35–47. Reprint in *Early Native American Writing: New Critical Essays*, ed. Helen Jaskoski. Cambridge: Cambridge University Press, 1996. 1–14.

Howe, Henry. *Historical collections of Ohio: containing a collection of the most interesting facts, traditions, biographical sketches, anecdotes, etc.* Cincinnati: Derby, Bradley, 1847.

Indian Helper 12, 48 (19 September 1897).

Indian Helper 14, 23 (31 March 1899).

"Indian Maid Sings to Aid Native Arts." *Washington Post*, 1 August 1933: 9.

Indian Territory: Descriptive Biographical and Genealogical Including the Landed Estates, County Seats Etc. Etc. with a General History of the Territory. New York: Lewis, 1901.

"In the Indian Country." *Galveston Daily News*, 30 November 1891: 7.

"Introducing Elsie [Elise] and Elisebeth Seaton." *American Indian* 4, 12 (September–October 1930): 5.

"Introducing Miss Hartshorne." *American Indian* 2, 10 (July 1928): 11.
Iverson, Peter. *Carlos Montezuma and the Changing World of American Indians.* Albuquerque: University of New Mexico Press, 1982.
Jackson, Andrew. *The Papers of Andrew Jackson.* Vol. 7, *1829.* Ed. Daniel Feller et al. Knoxville: University of Tennessee Press.
Jantz, Harold S. *The First Century of New England Verse.* Worcester, Mass: American Antiquarian Society, 1944.
Johannsen, Robert W. "The Lecompton Constitutional Convention: An Analysis of Its Membership." *Kansas Historical Quarterly* 23, 3 (Autumn 1957): 225–43.
Justice, Daniel Heath. *Our Fire Survives the Storm: A Cherokee Literary History.* Minneapolis: University of Minnesota Press, 2006.
Kaiser, Leo M., ed. *Early American Latin Verse, 1625–1825: An Anthology.* Wauconda, Ill.: Bolchazy-Carducci, 1984.
———, ed. "Thirteen Early American Latin Elegies: A Critical Edition." *Humanistica Lovaniensa: Journal of Neo-Latin Studies* 23 (1974): 346–81.
Katanski, Amelia V. *Learning to Write "Indian": The Boarding-School Experience and American Indian Literature.* Norman: University of Oklahoma Press, 2005.
Kilcup, Karen, ed. *Native American Women's Writing: An Anthology c. 1800–1924.* Oxford: Blackwell, 2000.
Kipling, Rudyard. "The White Man's Burden." In Kipling, *Complete Verse: Definitive Edition.* New York: Doubleday, 1940. 321–23.
Klopfenstein, Carl G. "The Removal of the Wyandots from Ohio." *Ohio Historical Quarterly* 66, 2 (April 1957): 119–36.
Lindsey, Donal F. *Indians at Hampton Institute, 1877–1923.* Urbana: University of Illinois Press, 1995.
Littlefield, Daniel F., Jr. *Alex Posey: Creek Poet, Journalist, and Humorist.* Lincoln: University of Nebraska Press, 1992.
Littlefield, Daniel F., Jr., and James W. Parins. *A Biobibliography of Native American Writers, 1772–1924.* Metuchen, N.J.: Scarecrow Press, 1981.
———. *A Biobibliography of Native American Writers, 1772–1924: A Supplement.* Metuchen, N.J.: Scarecrow Press, 1985.
———. "Introduction." Bertrand N. O. Walker (Hen-toh), *Tales of the Bark Lodges.* Jackson: University of Mississippi Press, 1995. vii–xvi.
———, eds. *Native American Writing in the Southeast: An Anthology, 1875–1935.* Oxford: University Press of Mississippi, 1995.
Longfellow, Henry Wadsworth. *Evangeline.* 1847. *Poems and Other Writings.* Ed. J. D. McClatchy. New York: Library of America, 2000. 57–115, 829–30.
———. *The Song of Hiawatha.* 1855. *Poems and Other Writings.* Ed. J. D. McClatchy. New York: Library of America, 2000. 141–279, 831–38.
Manypenny, George W. *Our Indian Wards.* Cincinnati: Robert Clarke, 1880.
Mason, Philip P., ed. *Schoolcraft: The Literary Voyager or Muzzeniegun.* East Lansing: Michigan State University Press, 1962.
Mather, Cotton. *Magnalia Christi Americana: or, The ecclesiastical history of New-England.* Book 3. London: Thomas Parkhurst, 1702.
———. *Selected Letters of Cotton Mather.* Ed. Kenneth Silverman. Baton Rouge: Louisiana State University Press, 1971.

Maxwell, Amos. "The Sequoyah Conventon, Part II." *Chronicles of Oklahoma* 28, 3 (1950): 299–340.
McBride, Bunny. *Molly Spotted Elk: A Penobscot in Paris.* Norman: University of Oklahoma Press, 1995.
McCutcheon[, John T.] "Injun Summer." *Chicago Tribune*, 30 September 1907: 1.
McDonogh, John. *The Last Will and Testament of John McDonogh.* New Orleans: Daily Delta, 1851.
"Members of Indian Board Visit Harris." *California Indian Herald* 2, 6 (June 1924): 15.
Meserve, John Bartlett. "Chief Dennis Wolfe Bushyhead." *Chronicles of Oklahoma* 14, 3 (September 1936): 349–59.
———. "Governor William Malcolm Guy." *Chronicles of Oklahoma* 19, 1 (March 1941): 10–13.
Meserve, Walter T. "English Works of Seventeenth-Century Indians." *American Quarterly* 8, 3 (Autumn 1956): 264–76.
"Mewuk Indian Tribe Burns 'Old Man Digger' in Effigy at Ione Festival." *California Indian Herald* 2, 4 (25 April 1924): 5–6.
Meyers, Leta V. Letter to Carlos Montezuma. 10 December 1920. In Montezuma, *Supplement to the Papers of Carlos Montezuma, M.D.*, ed. John W. Larner, Jr. Microfilm. Wilmington, Del.: Scholarly Resources, 2001. Reel 4.
Miller, Guion. *Roll of Eastern Cherokees entitled to participate in the fund arising from the judgment of the Court of Claims of May 28, 1906.* Washington, D.C.: Press of Bryon S. Adams. 1909–1910.
Morris, Genoa. "Oklahoma." *Harlow's Weekly* 30, 16 (16 April 1927): 9.
Montezuma, Carlos. *The Papers of Carlos Montezuma, M.D.* Ed. John William Larner, Jr. Microfilm. Wilmington, Del.: Scholarly Resources, 1983.
Morrison, W. B. "Fort Arbuckle." *Chronicles of Oklahoma* 6, 1 (March 1928): 26–34.
Morse, Jedidiah. *A Report to the Secretary of War of the United States, on Indian Affairs, Comprising a Narrative of a Tour Performed in the Summer of 1820, under a Commission from the President of the United States, for the Purpose of Ascertaining, for the Use of the Government, the Actual State of the Indian Tribes in Our Country.* New Haven, Conn.: S. Converse, 1822.
"Mr. Collett's Reply to Helen Dare." *California Indian Herald* 1, 1 (January 1923): 3–4.
Muses, Philo. "While weeping friends. . . ." *American Magazine and Historical Chronicle* 1 (December 1743): 166.
Neri, Camillo. *Testimonianze e Frammenti.* Eikasmos Studi 9. Bologna: Pàtron Editore, 2003.
"News Notes About Members and Friends." *American Indian Magazine* 4, 2 (April–June 1916): 183–85.
Nichols, Deborah. "Richard C. Adams: 'Representing the Delaware Indians.'" In *Legends of the Delaware Indians and Picture Writing*, ed. Nichols. Syracuse, N.Y.: Syracuse University Press, 1997. xv–xlv.
Norris, L. David. "Fort Arbuckle." *Encyclopedia of Oklahoma History & Culture.* http://digital.library.okstate.edu/encyclopedia/entries/F/FO028.html
Nuñez, Benita Wa Wa Calachaw. *Spirit Woman: The Diaries and Paintings of Benita Wa Wa Calachaw Nuñez.* Ed. Stan Steiner. San Francisco: Harper & Row, 1980.
O'Beirne, H. F. *Leaders and Leading Men of the Indian Territory. With Interesting Biographical Sketches. I. Choctaws and Chickasaws: With a Brief History of Each Tribe:*

Its Laws, Customs, Superstitions and Religious Beliefs. Chicago: American Publishers' Association, 1891.

O'Beirne, H. F., and E. S. Beirne. *The Indian Territory: Its Chiefs, Legislators and Leading Men*. St. Louis: C. B. Woodward, 1892.

"Obit for James Roane Gregory." Rogers County, Oklahoma Archives. http://ftp.rootsweb.ancestry.com/pub/usgenweb/ok/rogers/obits/g6260005.txt.

"Obituary [Joseph L. Martin]." *Cherokee Advocate* [Tahlequah], 18 November 1891.

Oliphant, J. Orin. "The Report of the Wyandot Exploring Delegation, 1831." *Kansas Historical Quarterly* 14, 3 (August 1947): 248–62.

Parins, James W. *Elias Cornelius Boudinot: A Life on the Cherokee Border*. Lincoln: University of Nebraska Press, 2006.

———. *John Rollin Ridge: His Life & Works*. Lincoln: University of Nebraska Press, 1991.

Parker, Dorothy R. *Singing an Indian Song: A Biography of D'Arcy McNickle*. Lincoln: University of Nebraska Press, 1992.

Parker, Robert Dale. *How to Interpret Literature: Critical Theory for Literary and Cultural Studies*. New York: Oxford University Press, 2008.

———. *The Invention of Native American Literature*. Ithaca, N.Y.: Cornell University Press, 2003.

Peter, William, ed. *Specimens of the Poets and Poetry of Greece and Rome*. Philadelphia: Carey and Hart, 1847. 2nd ed., 1848.

Peyer, Bernd C. "Introduction." In *The Singing Spirit: Early Short Stories by North American Indians*, ed. Peyer. Tucson: University of Arizona Press, 1989. vii–xxi.

———. *The Tutor'd Mind: Indian Missionary-Writers in Antebellum America*. Amherst: University of Massachusetts Press, 1997.

Philp, Kenneth R. *Termination Revisited: American Indians on the Trail to Self-Determination, 1933–1953*. Lincoln: University of Nebraska Press, 1999.

Plato, Ann. *Essays; Including Biographies and Miscellaneous Pieces, in Prose and Poetry*. 1841. Reprint New York: Oxford University Press, 1988.

Pope, Alexander. *The Poems of Alexander Pope*. Ed. John Butt. New Haven, Conn.: Yale University Press, 1963.

Porter, Joy. *To Be Indian: The Life of Iroquois-Seneca Arthur Caswell Parker*. Norman: University of Oklahoma Press, 2001.

Posey, Alexander. *The Fus Fixico Letters*. Ed. Daniel F. Littlefield, Jr., and Carol A. Petty Hunter. Lincoln: University of Nebraska Press, 1993.

———. *The Poems of Alexander Lawrence Posey*. Ed. Minnie H. Posey. Topeka, Kan.: Crane, 1910.

———. *Song of the Oktahutche: Collected Poems*. Ed. Matthew Wynn Sivils. Lincoln: University of Nebraska Press, 2008.

Pratt, Mary Louise. *Imperial Eyes: Travel Writing and Transculturation*. London: Routledge, 1992.

"Prize-Speaking Contest." *Southern Workman* 49, 1 (January 1920): 46.

Proske, John George, and John Renatus Schmidt, "Extract from the Journal of the Mission at Spring-Place among the Cherokee Indians. From July 1821, to December 1822." *United Brethren Missionary Intelligencer, and Religious Missionary* 1, 10 (2nd Quarter 1824): 445.

Prucha, Francis Paul. *American Indian Treaties: The History of a Political Anomaly.* Berkeley: University of California Press, 1994.

R & A Petrilla, Booksellers. *Indian Mother's Lullaby.* http://www.petrillabooks.com/bookdetails.asp?book=BOOKS020151I

"Allottments of Lands in Severalty to Certain Indian Tribes. Committee on Indian Affairs." U.S. Senate, 5 March 1892. *Reports of Committees of the Senate of the United States for the First Session of the Fifty-Second Congress.* 1891–92. Washington: U.S. GPO, 1892.

Report of the Annual Meeting of the Montauk Tribe of Indians. Sag Harbor, L. I. August 29th, 1919. Reprint *The History & Archaeology of the Montauk*, ed. Gaynell Stone. Readings in Long Island Archaeology & Ethnohistory 3. 2nd ed. Stony Brook, N.Y.: Suffolk County Archaeological Association, Nassau County Archaeological Committee, [1993]. 473–87.

Ridge, John R. *Poems.* San Francisco: Henry Payot, 1868.

Robinson, Lucius F. Translation of "On the Death of that Truly Reverend Man, Thomas Thacher." In Cotton Mather, *Magnalia Christi Americana or, The ecclesiastical history of New-England.* Book 1. Hartford, Conn.: Silus Andrus, 1855. 496–97.

Roff, Joe T. "Reminiscences of Early Days in the Chickasaw Nation." *Chronicles of Oklahoma* 13, 2 (June 1935): 169–90.

Rogers, Robert. *A Concise Account of North America.* London: J. Millan, 1765.

Rosenwald, Lawrence. "*Voces Clamantium in Deserto*: Latin Verse of the Puritans." In *Puritan Poets and Poetics: Seventeenth-Century American Poetry in Theory and Practice*, ed. Peter White. University Park: Pennsylvania State University Press, 1985. 303–17.

Rough, E. C. "Henry Frieland Buckner." *Chronicles of Oklahoma* 14, 4 (December 1936): 456–66.

Ruoff, A. LaVonne Brown. "Editor's Introduction." S. Alice Callahan, *Wynema: A Child of the Forest.* Ed. Ruoff. 1891. Reprint Lincoln: University of Nebraska Press, 1997. xiii–xlviii.

Schoolcraft, Henry Rowe. "Notes intended to be used in drawing up a biographical notice, or memoir of Mrs. Henry Rowe Schoolcraft." Ms. published as "Notes for Memoir of Mrs. Henry Rowe Schoolcraft by Henry Rowe Schoolcraft." Ed. J. Sharpless Fox. *Michigan Pioneer and Historical Collections* (title listed in multiple ways) 36 (1908): 95–100.

———. "Weeng." *Algic Researches.* Vol. 2. New York: Harper and Brothers, 1839. 226–28.

Schoolcraft, Jane Johnston. *The Sound the Stars Make Rushing Through the Sky: The Writings of Jane Johnston Schoolcraft.* Ed. Robert Dale Parker. Philadelphia: University of Pennsylvania Press, 2007.

Shakespeare, William. *The Riverside Shakespeare.* Ed. G. Blakemore Evans. 2nd ed. Boston: Houghton Mifflin, 1997.

Sharp, Debbie, Richard Chadwick, and C. Roland Earsome. *Murray County Oklahoma.* Charleston, S.C.: Arcadia, 2000.

Shirley, Glenn. *Thirteen Days of Terror: The Rufus Buck Gang in Indian Territory.* Stillwater, Okla.: Barbed Wire Press, 1996.

Sibley, John Langdon. *Biographical Sketches of Graduates of Harvard University, in Cambridge, Massachusetts.* Vol. 2, *1659–1677.* Cambridge: Charles William Sever, University Bookstore, 1881.

Sivils, Matthew Wynn, ed. *Song of the Oktahutche: Collected Poems.* Lincoln: University of Nebraska Press, 2008.

Snyder, Jane McIntosh. *The Woman and the Lyre: Women Writers in Classical Greece and Rome.* Carbondale: Southern Illinois University Press, 1989.

"Some Chickasaw Indian Lore and Characteristics." *Daily Ardmorite*, 18 August 1907.

Spotted Elk, Molly. *Katahdin: Wigwam's Tales of the Abnaki Tribe and A Dictionary of Penobscot and Passamaquoddy Words.* Orono: Maine Folklife Center, 2003.

Starr, Emmet. *History of the Cherokee Indians and Their Legends and Folk Lore.* Oklahoma City: Warden, 1921.

Strong, John A. *The Montaukett Indians of Eastern Long Island.* Syracuse, N.Y.: Syracuse University Press, 2001.

Szasz, Margaret Connell. *Indian Education in the American Colonies, 1607–1783.* Albuquerque: University of New Mexico Press, 1988.

Taylor, Ann. "My Mother." *Original Poems for Infant Minds. By Several Young Persons.* 1804. New York: Garland, 1976. 76–78.

Thoburn, Joseph B. *A Standard History of Oklahoma.* Vol. 4. Chicago: American Historical Society, 1916.

Tilghman, Zoe A. "Squaw'ills." *Harlow's Weekly* 30, 14 (2 April 1927): 3.

United States Census, 1920. National Archives and Records Administration microfilm. Series T625, Roll 1935:101.

United States Commission to the Five Civilized Tribes. *The Final Rolls of Citizens and Freedmen of the Five Civilized Tribes in Indian Territory.* Washington, D.C.: U.S. GPO, 1907.

Usher, Ellis Baker. *Wisconsin: Its Story and Biography, 1848–1913.* Chicago: Lewis, 1914.

Walker, B. N. O. "Sketch of B. N. O. Walker." *Chronicles of Oklahoma* 6, 1 (March 1928): 89– 93.

Wallis, Michael. *Oil Man: The Story of Frank Phillips and the Story of Phillips Petroleum.* Garden City, N.Y.: Doubleday, 1988.

"Washbourne Family." http://www.paulridenour.com/washbourne.htm. Accessed June 25, 2008.

White, Lonnie J. *Panthers to Arrowheads: The 36th (Texas-Oklahoma) Division in World War I.* Austin: Presidial Press, 1984. http://www.texasmilitaryforcesmuseum.org/36division/white.htm.

Womack, Craig S. *Red on Red: Native American Literary Separatism.* Minneapolis: University of Minnesota Press, 1999.

Wright, Muriel C. "A Report to the General Council of the Indian Territory Meeting at Okmulgee in 1873." *Chronicles of Oklahoma* 34, 1 (Spring 1956): 7–16.

Young, Tyler. "The Indian of Tomorrow." *Missions* 13, 1 (January 1922): 35–36.

Index

Acknowledgments

One day, as we walked down the hall of the English Building at the University of Illinois, Carol Thomas Neely, the feminist literary historian and Shakespeare critic, said that in the long run, good editing of valuable but little known or unknown literary writing would make more difference to readers than almost any literary criticism, no matter how good the criticism. Carol got me wondering. Could I think of something out there waiting to be edited that readers would find more valuable than the best literary criticism I might aspire to write? Could I enjoy editorial work as much as critical work? How could editorial work also be critical work? Could I combine editing and literary criticism? Those questions led to this book and to the other book that spun off from the work on this one: *The Sound the Stars Make Rushing Through the Sky: The Writings of Jane Johnston Schoolcraft*. I will always be grateful to Carol Neely for laying down the challenge.

Many people have helped with this book, and I am enormously grateful to them. First and most, it is an honor to name Daniel F. Littlefield, Jr., and James W. Parins, whose monumental bibliographical and archival work have proved invaluable. Their *Biobibliography of Native American Writers* is a treasure trove, as are their Native American Press Archives at the Sequoyah Research Center at the University of Arkansas at Little Rock, where Dan Littlefield was a helpful and gracious host. I see this book partly as a challenge to other scholars to make more use of the cornucopia of resources that these two indefatigable and welcoming scholars have built over many years of imaginative and dogged work.

Jodi Byrd, D. Anthony Clark, Jill Doerfler, Tol Foster, and Matthew Sakiestewa Gilbert provided keen and helpful readings of part of the manuscript. LeAnne Howe has been a paragon of support and encouragement. Brenda Farnell, Frederick E. Hoxie, and Debbie Reese helped in many ways to set the atmosphere that made this research possible. The support of all these colleagues offers testimony to the superb Program in American Indian Studies they have helped build as faculty and visiting scholars at the University of Illinois. Robert Warrior, recently arrived to lead our program, helped in both practical and abstract ways to foster the completion of this project. In the Department of English at Illinois, William J. Maxwell and Michael Rothberg provided astute readings of part of the manuscript, and Nina Baym and Cary Nelson provided much-appreciated encouragement as well as inspiring models in their own scholarship. Early in the research, Isabel Quintana-Wulf and Cristina Stanciu helped figure out many of the tasks that daunted me, and near the end, Ann Hubert provided terrific help with Eleazar's Latin and Greek.

Carter Revard read part of the manuscript and offered valuable encouragement and insight. Siobhan Senier pointed me to the papers of Molly Spotted Elk and helped make them available and transcribe them. I eagerly await her anthology of American Indian writing from New England. John D. Nichols and Margaret Noori helped with Ojibwe language topics and provided inspiration and encouragement. Ron Wilburn offered stimulating discussions of Ann Plato. Gretchen Harvey helped with the research on Ruth Muskrat. Rosemary McCombs Maxey cheerfully translated James Roane Gregory's title "Otheen, Okiyetos." Raymond J. DeMallie helped with a language question. Mark Wasserman unraveled some historical knots. And Marlie P. Wasserman was a constant source of cheerful support.

Librarians are my heroes and (more often) heroines—and many more librarians and library workers have helped with this book than I can name. In most cases I do not even know their names. But some of those who stand out include Jo Kibbey, Kathleen Kluegel, and Mary Stuart at the University of Illinois, who each helped in many ways. I am indescribably grateful for the tireless work of Kathryn Danner and Nick Rudd and their colleagues in the Interlibrary Loan office at the University of Illinois Library. I am also grateful to librarians at the American Antiquarian Society, the Amistad Research Center at Tulane University, the Arkansas History Commission, the Harris Collection at Brown University, the University of Kansas Library, the Maine Folklife Center, the Newberry Library, the Nash Library at the University of Oklahoma, the University of Tulsa Library, and the Wisconsin Historical Society, among many others, along with the many additional librarians and archivists thanked in *The Sound the Stars Make Rushing Through the Sky.*

For most of the poems in this book, the copyright has long since expired. "Filled with You" and "Symbols" by Olivia Ward Bush-Banks are transcribed from papers in the Amistad Research Center, Tulane University, with permission from Bernice Elizabet Forrest. The poems of Alexander Posey that first appeared in *Song of the Oktahutche*, ed. Matthew Wynn Sivils (Lincoln: University of Nebraska Press, 2008) are reprinted by permission of the University of Nebraska Press. The poems of Lynn Riggs are reprinted by permission of Random House from Lynn Riggs, *The Iron Dish* (Garden City, N.Y.: Doubleday, Doran, 1930). The poems of Molly Spotted Elk are published by permission from the Maine Folklife Center, University of Maine, Orono, Maine. Northeast Archives #2573 box 5 f6. "Prologue," "In Memory of My Homosexual Friend," "My Secret World," "My Psyche and Wassaja" from *Spirit Woman: The Diaries and Paintings of Bonita Wawa Calachaw Nuñez*, ed. Stan Steiner, copyright © 1980 Stan Steiner. Reprinted by Permission of HarperCollins Publishers.

Financial support from the University of Illinois, mostly through the advocacy of Richard P. Wheeler, then Head of the Department of English, made it possible even to conceive of doing the research for this book.

Rarely do I hear of scholars who have the good fortune to work with so superb an editor as Jerome E. Singerman, my editor at the University of Pennsylvania Press. Jerry's suggestions and encouragement made this a much better book, and they also helped make finishing the book a pleasure. I am also deeply grateful to Alison A. Anderson and her colleagues for their excellent work in copyediting a challenging manuscript and to the superb designers who transformed the idea into a visual object.

This book is dedicated to the forgotten writers and readers of Indian America. I hope that it can encourage others to join the process of reading and recovering an invaluable heritage. And as always, this book is dedicated to Janice N. Harrington.

CPSIA information can be obtained
at www.ICGtesting.com
Printed in the USA
JSHW021240100921
18614JS00004B/6

9 780812 222180